Russian Energy Policy and Military Power

This book examines the interplay between energy policy and security policy under Vladimir Putin and his drive to re-establish Russia's 'greatness'.

Assessing conflicts and divergences between these policies, this book argues that Russia's desire to strengthen its role of 'energy security' provider is undermined by its inability to secure growth in production of oil and gas and by the desire to maximize political dividends from energy exports. The pressing demand to channel more resources into the military–industrial complex clashes with the growing need to invest in the energy complex, and the attempts to apply energy and military instruments for boosting Russia's prestige undermine its international credibility.

In conclusion, the author anticipates how these contradictions could be resolved and suggests three short scenarios for Russia's continuing transition in the next decade.

This book will be of interest to students of Russian politics, European politics, and international security.

Pavel K. Baev is a Research Professor at the International Peace Research Institute, Oslo (PRIO).

Contemporary security studies

NATO's Secret Armies
Operation Gladio and terrorism in Western
Europe
Daniele Ganser

**The US, NATO and Military Burden-
Sharing**
*Peter Kent Forster and
Stephen J. Cimbala*

**Russian Governance in the Twenty-First
Century**
Geo-strategy, geopolitics and new
governance
Irina Isakova

**The Foreign Office and Finland
1938–1940**
Diplomatic sideshow
Craig Gerrard

Rethinking the Nature of War
*Edited by Isabelle Duyvesteyn and
Jan Angstrom*

**Perception and Reality in the Modern
Yugoslav Conflict**
Myth, falsehood and deceit 1991–1995
Brendan O'Shea

**The Political Economy of Peacebuilding
in Post-Dayton Bosnia**
Tim Donais

The Distracted Eagle
The rift between America and old Europe
Peter H. Merkl

The Iraq War
European perspectives on politics,
strategy, and operations
*Edited by Jan Hallenberg and
Håkan Karlsson*

Strategic Contest
Weapons proliferation and war in the
greater Middle East
Richard L. Russell

Propaganda, the Press and Conflict
The Gulf War and Kosovo
David R. Willcox

Missile Defence
International, regional and national
implications
Edited by Bertel Heurlin and Sten Rynning

Globalising Justice for Mass Atrocities
A revolution in accountability
Chandra Lekha Sriram

Ethnic Conflict and Terrorism
The origins and dynamics of civil wars
Joseph L. Soeters

**Globalisation and the Future of
Terrorism: Patterns and Predictions**
Brynjar Lia

Nuclear Weapons and Strategy
The evolution of American nuclear policy
Stephen J. Cimbala

**Nasser and the Missile Age in the
Middle East**
Owen L. Sirrs

War as Risk Management
Strategy and conflict in an age of
globalised risks
Yee-Kuang Heng

Military Nanotechnology
Potential applications and preventive arms
control
Jurgen Altmann

NATO and Weapons of Mass Destruction
Regional alliance, global threats
Eric R. Terzuolo

Europeanisation of National Security Identity
The EU and the changing security
identities of the Nordic states
Pernille Rieker

International Conflict Prevention and Peace-building
Sustaining the peace in post conflict
societies
*Edited by T. David Mason and
James D. Meernik*

Controlling the Weapons of War
Politics, persuasion, and the prohibition of
inhumanity
Brian Rappert

Changing Transatlantic Security Relations
Do the US, the EU and Russia form a new
strategic triangle?
*Edited by Jan Hallenberg and
Håkan Karlsson*

Theoretical Roots of US Foreign Policy
Machiavelli and American unilateralism
Thomas M. Kane

Corporate Soldiers and International Security
The rise of private military companies
Christopher Kinsey

Transforming European Militaries
Coalition operations and the technology
gap
Gordon Adams and Guy Ben-Ari

Globalization and Conflict
National security in a 'new' strategic era
Edited by Robert G. Patman

Military Forces in 21st Century Peace Operations
No job for a soldier?
James V. Arbuckle

The Political Road to War with Iraq
Bush, 9/11 and the drive to overthrow
Saddam
Nick Ritchie and Paul Rogers

Bosnian Security after Dayton
New perspectives
Edited by Michael A. Innes

Britain, America and the Dynamics of Alliance, 1962–68
Kennedy, Johnson and NATO
Andrew Priest

Small Arms and Security
New emerging international norms
Denise Garcia

The United States and Europe
Beyond the neo-conservative divide?
Edited by John Baylis and Jon Roper

Russia, NATO and Cooperative Security
Bridging the gap
Lionel Ponsard

International Law and International Relations
Bridging theory and practice
*Edited by Tom Bierstecker, Peter Spiro,
Chandra Lekha Sriram and
Veronica Raffo*

Deterring International Terrorism and Rogue States
US national security policy after 9/11
James H. Lebovic

Vietnam in Iraq
Tactics, lessons, legacies and ghosts
Edited by John Dumbrell and David Ryan

Understanding Victory and Defeat in Contemporary War
Edited by Jan Angstrom and Isabelle Duyvesteyn

Propaganda and Information Warfare in the Twenty-first Century
Altered images and deception operations
Scot Macdonald

Governance in Post-Conflict Societies
Rebuilding fragile states
Edited by Derick W. Brinkerhoff

European Security in the Twenty-First Century
The challenge of multipolarity
Adrian Hyde-Price

Ethics, Technology and the American Way of War
Cruise missiles and US security policy
Reuben E. Brigety II

International Law and the Use of Armed Force
The UN charter and the major powers
Joel H. Westra

Disease and Security
Natural plagues and biological weapons in East Asia
Christian Enermark

Explaining War and Peace
Case studies and necessary condition counterfactuals
Jack Levy and Gary Goertz

War, Image and Legitimacy
Viewing contemporary conflict
James Gow and Milena Michalski

Information Strategy and Warfare
A guide to theory and practice
John Arquilla and Douglas A. Borer

Countering the Proliferation of Weapons of Mass Destruction
NATO and EU options in the Mediterranean and the Middle East
Thanos P. Dokos

Security and the War on Terror
Edited by Alex J. Bellamy, Roland Bleiker, Sara E. Davies and Richard Devetak

The European Union and Strategy
An emerging actor
Edited by Jan Hallenberg and Kjell Engelbrekt

Causes and Consequences of International Conflict
Data, methods and theory
Edited by Glenn Palmer

Russian Energy Policy and Military Power
Putin's quest for greatness
Pavel K. Baev

Russian Energy Policy and Military Power

Putin's quest for greatness

Pavel K. Baev

LONDON AND NEW YORK

First published 2008
by Routledge
2 Park Square, Milton Park, Abingdon, Oxon, OX14 4RN

Simultaneously published in the USA and Canada
by Routledge
270 Madison Ave, New York NY 10016

Routledge is an imprint of the Taylor & Francis Group, an informa business

Transferred to Digital Printing 2009

© 2008 Pavel K. Baev

Typeset in Times by Wearset Ltd, Boldon, Tyne and Wear

All rights reserved. No part of this book may be reprinted or reproduced or
utilized in any form or by any electronic, mechanical, or other means, now
known or hereafter invented, including photocopying and recording, or in
any information storage or retrieval system, without permission in writing
from the publishers.

British Library Cataloguing in Publication Data
A catalogue record for this book is available from the British Library

Library of Congress Cataloging in Publication Data
A catalog record for this book has been requested

ISBN10: 0-415-45058-6 (hbk)
ISBN10: 0-415-55877-8 (pbk)
ISBN10: 0-203-93260-9 (ebk)

ISBN13: 978-0-415-45058-4 (hbk)
ISBN13: 978-0-415-55877-8 (pbk)
ISBN13: 978-0-203-93260-5 (ebk)

Contents

Preface	ix
List of abbreviations	xi
Introduction	1

PART I
Three backgrounds — 5

1	The military reform that never happened	7
2	The oil-and-gas dividend that was too low – and has become too high	18
3	The dream of a new 'greatness' that has come truly false	32

PART II
Deadlocked energy-security dilemmas — 43

4	The trickle of the oil money for the military	45
5	Counter-terrorism and the Caspian oil games	56
6	Alliance-building with virtual commitments and energy power	68

PART III
Military muscle as the ultimate proof of 'greatness' — 79

7	Virtually extended deterrence of the 'Great Power'	81
8	The Army and power-projection in the new 'Empire'	93

viii *Contents*

9 Internal order and security in the 'Civilization' 105

PART IV
Energy power and the quest for 'greatness' 117

10 Applying the gas lever for qualifying as a 'Great Power' 119

11 Reconstituting the 'Empire' as an oil-and-gas cartel 130

12 Hydrocarbon foundation for the imagined 'Civilization' 142

Conclusion 155

Notes 163
References 195
Index 228

Preface

This book was a self-imposed quest undertaken without a compelling reason and stubbornly brought to completion against the author's better judgment. If the academic wisdom 'Everything you have to say can be said in any amount of time' holds true for written texts, a reader pressed by time (and aren't we all?) can get a good enough impression of the 90,000 words narrative by downloading any of my weekly 1,000 words columns in *Eurasia Daily Monitor* (http://jamestown.org/edm/). The urge to make the case of Putin's Russia political trajectory even more complicated than it comes out in current analysis and to argue it at great length was therefore not entirely rational – and the acknowledgement of the debts amassed along the way to the friends who encouraged the author and the sponsors who kept him going cannot rationalize it in any convincing way.

The first word of gratitude should go to the International Peace Research Institute, Oslo (PRIO), a dynamic and open-minded think-trailer (certainly not 'tank') that back in October 1992 invited on a short-term contract a Russian researcher, still shell-shocked by the collapse of the Soviet Union, and has not found a way to get rid of him since. PRIO Director Stein Tønnesson has been supportive and tolerant way beyond any conventional definition of a 'good boss'; my colleagues have provided so many examples of sheer dedication and unpretentious brilliance that I could not think about disappointing them by abandoning this quest halfway. My association with the Centre for the Study of Civil War (CSCW) at PRIO has opened for me new perspectives in examining 'frozen' and smoldering conflicts in Russia's southern 'underbelly', the war in Chechnya being the one that continues to demand particular and emphatic attention.

Life at PRIO is so vibrant because its driving force is our endless search and struggle for funding, and this book project would not be possible without generous support of two key sponsors. The first one is the Norwegian Defense Ministry that has supported my research into various aspects of Russia's defense posture for more than ten years, thus granting me a great – and greatly appreciated – opportunity to build an expertise in the area that has perhaps gone out of strategic fashion but remains of importance for Russia's future. The second key sponsor has a collective nature, but the key actor behind grants provided by the

x *Preface*

Norwegian Research Council and the Ministry for Oil and Energy has invariably been *Statoil*; a few experts and managers in this company have back in 2000 seen some merit in my rather far-fetched ideas that Russia was transforming itself from a military super-power into an energy powerhouse – and their interest has stimulated my research in the Caspian area and in the currently overcrowded field of 'energy security'. It has been a pleasure to do my research business with these sponsors – and I hope to keep doing it even if there will hardly be a new book in the making for some time.

An important source of inspiration for my work has been the network of American and Russian scholars known under the acronym PONARS, the exact meaning of which is long forgotten but the ties of friendship that bind us together keep growing stronger with every passing year that typically ends with a get-together December conference in Washington, DC (check www.csis.org/ruseura/ponars/).

The lonely struggle with words would have been unbearable without the endless interruptions coming from and the unbelievable tolerance shown by my family. I know I would not impress my teenager with this dull volume, but maybe it would give my father a moment of joy that could help him in his brave fight. Olga, thanks for bearing with me, and now we can find new fun in life after this book.

Pavel K. Baev

Abbreviations

ABM	the Anti-Ballistic Missile Treaty (1972, cancelled by United States in 2002)
bcm	billion cubic meters
BTC	the Baku–Tbilisi–Ceyhan oil pipeline (launched in 2005)
CEO	chief executive officer
CES	the Common Economic Space (2003)
CFE	the Conventional Forces in Europe Treaty (1990, modified in 1999)
CIS	the Commonwealth of Independent States (1991)
CPC	the Caspian Pipeline Consortium (2001)
CSTO	the Collective Security Treaty Organization (from 1992 to 2002, Collective Security Organization – CSO)
EEC	the Eurasian Economic Community (2000)
EU	the European Union
FSB	the Federal Security Service (*Federalnaya Sluzhba Bezopasnosti*)
GDP	gross domestic product
GKO	short-term state bonds (*Gosydarstvennye kratkosrochnye obyazatelstva*)
GLONASS	the Global navigation satellite system
GROU	operational command group (*Gruppa operativnogo upravleniya*)
GRU	Main Intelligence Directorate of the General Staff (*Glavnoe Razvedyvatelnoe Upravlenie*)
G8	the Group of Eight (in 1997, the Group of Six or G6, from 1976 to 1997, the Group of Seven or G7)
IAEA	the International Atomic Energy Agency
IPO	initial public offering
ICBM	intercontinental ballistic missile
IMF	the International Monetary Fund
INF	the Intermediate Nuclear Forces Treaty (1987)
KGB	the State Security Committee (*Komitet Gosudarstvennoi Bezopasnosti*)
MAD	mutual assured destruction
NAC	the National Anti-Terrorist Committee (2006)

xii *Abbreviations*

NATO	the North Atlantic Treaty Organization (1949)
OMON	special purpose police detachment (*otryad militsii osobogo naznacheniya*)
OPEC	the Organization of Petroleum Exporting Countries (1960)
OSCE	the Organization for Security and Cooperation in Europe (in 1973–1995, Conference on Security and Cooperation in Europe, CSCE)
PR	public relations
RAO UES	the Unified Energy System Company
SCO	the Shanghai Cooperation Organization (from 1996 to 2001, the Shanghai Five)
SOBR	rapid response police unit (*spetsialnyi otryad bystrogo reagirovaniya*)
SPS	the Union of Rightist Forces (*Soyuz Pravyh Sil*)
START II	the Strategic Arms Reduction Treaty (1993), a follow-up to START I (1991)
USSR	the Union of Soviet Socialist Republics (1922–1991)
VDV	the Airborne Troops (*Vozdushno-Desantnye Voiska*)
VPK	the military-industrial complex (*voenno-promyshlennyi kompleks*)
WMD	weapons of mass destruction

Introduction

This book involves one problematic assumption about Russia's immediate future: spring 2008 will see President Putin stepping down and a new leader moving into the Kremlin executive office. This prospect has constituted the central theme of debates in Russian political salons and kitchens since the start of Putin's second term, and this author has no urge to add a fresh argument or a penetrating insight. The first words in the manuscript were written in early November 2005, a few weeks after the armed uprising in Nalchik, the capital of Kabardino-Balkaria, that was swiftly suppressed by Russian security forces. Putin's ambivalent response to that crisis left a distinct impression that he did not know about the explosive potential in the smouldering North Caucasus; so, all efforts of Dmitri Kozak, his plenipotentiary envoy to that region, to develop an agenda for action had been apparently in vain. In the middle of this work, in September 2006, Putin listened attentively to a report from Defence Minister Sergei Ivanov on the successful launch of a strategic missile by a submarine that reached the North Pole under the Arctic ice. The report did not mention a failed test of the highly advertised new generation strategic missile *Bulava* the day before or the fire in a nuclear submarine three days prior – and left the impression that the Commander-in-Chief, who had seen too many military disasters starting from the *Kursk* tragedy in August 2000, did not really want to know about the problems in the Navy. For a leader who has consistently demonstrated obsession with hands-on control, this attitude of not knowing and not wanting to know what was going on in the vital areas and key structures was perhaps the most telling sign of longing for a resignation. Hardly any interest in solving problems could be detected in the omnipotent leader who preferred to pour money – plentifully available due to exorbitant oil-and-gas revenues – over them in order to buy himself just enough time for departure in style. By the time of my last sprint to the deadline in May 2007, the Russian political elite had acknowledged for fact the forthcoming change of leadership assuming, as one astute columnist put it, that 'the Kremlin brigade has finally accepted Putin's resignation' (Piontkovsky, 2007).

A reader would have the advantage of knowing whether this '2008' hypothesis is indeed validated, but the author has made sure that his assumption, significant as it is, is by no means central to the organization of this analysis.

2 *Introduction*

Putin's two constitutional terms are united by a set of themes that have followed a particular pattern in their interconnected development towards a logical closure; it appears possible to argue that the July 2006 Strelna G8 summit was staged as the grand finale after which his 'era' would slowly draw to the last culmination of naming a successor. A third term, still entirely possible at the moment of this writing, has been advocated by many over-zealous lackeys as 'more-of-the-same', but it would inevitably signify a break of this pattern and forging of a new one that necessarily follows a different political logic (Baev, 2007a).

Never a strategist and even less a conceptualist, Putin has nevertheless shown a remarkable consistency in pursuing the broadly defined aims to which he has committed himself from the very first weeks after Yeltsin's astonishing choice. Far from being a natural leader, he was also uniquely unprepared for the colossal responsibility – but had a few firm convictions about the essence of the job. His central idea was that of control, and it underpinned most other goals and features of his leadership, from the over-centralization of political power to the suppression of free media and from the expansion of state control over economy to the spectacular growth of corruption.[1] The time for a comprehensive evaluation of the impact of Putin's control on Russia's overall trajectory would probably come in a few years time, and it will certainly require a far broader expertise and greater capacity for integrating diverse topics than this author possesses. The focus of analysis here is significantly narrower, and the goal is less ambitious.

Two themes have had a prominent profile in Putin's policy throughout his reign setting the most significant watersheds and determining the evolution of many other issues. The first theme is the military security, and its pivotal role was established by the Second Chechen War that served as a launching pad for Putin's presidency. The second theme is the energy security, and its top priority was underpinned by the unprecedented dominance of the oil-and-gas sector in the Russian economy. Both themes have complex internal structures and are driven by their own particular logic; there is, however, a common direction – they constitute two key elements of Russia's power that is typically conceptualized as 'greatness'. The proudly declared intention and the really existing urge to re-establish and re-constitute Russia's 'greatness' shape the third key theme of Putin's policy that in some ways contradicts his devotion to political 'pragmatism', which in fact is often reduced to a mix of cynicism, commercialism, and vulgar materialism. Nevertheless, the desire to manipulate Russia's strategic nuclear assets for asserting its 'Great Power' status appears as genuine as the longing for politicizing the energy exports in order to turn Russia into an 'energy super-power'. These three themes are, therefore, closely interconnected and shape the essential contours of Putin's 'era'.

This book aims at identifying the key issues in the dynamic interplay between the three themes – restoring the military power, instrumentalizing the energy potential, and rebuilding the foundation of 'greatness' – and getting a measure of these interplays, as far as the results can be summed up a year before the 2008 deadline. This three-dimensional aim determines the structure of the narrative,

Introduction 3

which starts with three separate assessments, or backgrounds, focused respectively on the posture of the Armed Forces, the development of the energy sector, and the substance of the intentions to restore Russia's 'greatness' during the seven years of Putin's presidency. Then, the three interplays are taken one by one, examining how the huge increase in state income secured by the energy sector facilitates but also limits the military build-up, how the real and perceived military strength impacts upon Russia's status and integrity, and how the disproportional strengthening of the oil-and-gas industry transforms Russia's international profile and self-perception.

There is no particular significance in the order of analysing one interplay after another, and some issues are inevitably re-emerging in these examinations, while an attentive reader would easily discover shallowness of attention to other issues, for instance the Russian–Chinese energy-security relations, which Putin currently portrays as one of his major achievements. The book brings together the fruits and, inevitably, the shortcomings of several research projects conducted by the author over the course of fast-running years of this decade; the references to own work might appear irritatingly numerous, but the honest intention has been to avoid even more irritating self-repetition.

Many pieces of evidence amassed in this narrative are certain to be overtaken by events, perhaps even before the book will find its first reader, and many risky propositions will become perfectly trivial if not dead wrong, but the book might still be useful in addressing the question that will be hanging in the stuffy Kremlin air by the end of this decade. It will hardly be similar to the one famously asked at the start of it: 'Who is Mr. Putin?' Recycled in hundreds of smart headlines and scientific analyses, it was dropped without finding a convincing answer; but the new one will quite probably be of the 'How happened?' character as the scale of wasted resources gradually becomes evident. Shunning ideology and refusing to put his name on a doctrine, Putin nevertheless advanced a vision of Russia that combined such features as 'strong' and 'modern', 'dynamic' and 'prosperous'.[2] As his presidency enters into the autumnal year, he invokes this vision – as in the 'historic' Munich speech – only as a matter of public relations (PR) exercises or verbal attacks against the 'hostile' West that seeks to enforce upon Russia its 'alien' rules and values (Lukyanov, 2007a).

Russia under his leadership has relapsed into the familiar pattern of self-deception and political passivity resembling the 'golden age' of Brezhnev's slow stagnation or *zastoi*. In real terms, it has become less modern than it was a decade ago – and this de-modernization has consumed no less resources than a comprehensive reform project would have required. Whatever the name of the next hand-picked 'great leader', experts would be hard pressed to explain how Putin's failure happened and why it was not duly discovered – and the ambition of the book is to supply the beginning of an answer.

Part I

Three backgrounds

> Balaganov looked at the triangle with respect. Panikovsky's arguments did not appear convincing to him but there was such a truthful inevitability in the triangle that Balaganov wavered.
>
> Ilf and Petrov (2006)

The three background chapters that form this first part of the book address massive and hugely complex 'pillars' of the present day 'Russia House', each of which could have easily made a subject for a book-length research project. The intention here has never been to supply a solid mass of figures on the composition of the Armed Forces or diagrams on oil-and-gas reserves and production, or indeed maps on particular 'hot spots' and pipeline projects. These maps and graphs are easily available in the virtual universe a click away, but the problem with the figures is not only that they are always too old and could never reflect the latest break of trends but more that they are so unreliable and often deliberately distorted that the statistical reality exists quite separately from the facts of Russia's life. The real intention in these chapters is to extract the analysis of the real capabilities of the Russian Armed Forces and of the real strength of the Russian energy complex out of the realm of the esoteric expert discussions and emphasize the main conflicts that form the drivers in the interplays examined further in the book. As for the aspirations to reassert Russia's 'greatness', their examination is also aimed at escaping from the eternal debates between 'Slavophiles' and 'Westernizers' and identifying the politically relevant content in the on-going construction of Russia's post-Soviet identity. It is the three distinctly different logics of organization and operation, neither of which is strictly Aristotelian, that are under investigation in the pages below.

1 The military reform that never happened

The task of reorganizing and upgrading the badly deteriorated military structures loomed large as one of the hardest challenges for such an inexperienced and accidental leader as Vladimir Putin at the time when he was chosen as the successor by somewhat less than clear-minded Boris Yeltsin in autumn 1999. Indeed, not ten years prior, the discredited and bankrupted Soviet Union had collapsed under the burden of its own massively redundant military efforts. The tanks in the streets of Moscow in August 1991 proved that politics would not shy away from using such high-impact instruments, while Yeltsin's monumental failures in both employing and modernizing them created a situation where the Army, in the opinion of this author, 'has become a major source of insecurity for the state it was supposed to protect' (Baev, 2004d, p. 43). The risks of doing nothing appeared grave, while the opportunities were difficult to grasp but still imperative not to miss in order to prevent a looming disaster of nuclear proportions.

Putin, however, constructed a different balance of risks and opportunities, where upholding the military organization that had emerged by default rather than by design was the key guideline. The policy of moving ahead by incremental changes and postponing indefinitely most already overdue fundamental reforms appeared incompatible with the high political demand for usable military means and impractical for deterring real and specific security challenges. Yet, wrapping up his second presidential term, Putin had every reason to believe that his choice for such a policy was correct, since it had brought exactly the desired results, first of all, in terms of securing effective control over the military machine. Many key issues in this policy, such as financing the military–industrial complex (Chapter 4), downsizing the nuclear forces (Chapter 7), and building a deployable, if not exactly 'rapid deployment', conventional force (Chapter 8), are examined further in this book. This chapter, besides providing a general background, deals with such key issues as the command structure, the draft system, and the general approach to modernizing the Armed Forces.

The struggle for survival in the 1990s

By the start of the 1980s, the Soviet Union had achieved, according to many Western assessments, a clear military superiority over any combination of

8   *Three backgrounds*

potential adversaries on every theatre of operations around its borders.[1] Just a decade later, Russia entered into possession of many disjointed fragments of a colossal military machine that had lost its strategic purpose and organizing idea. The new state leadership was uniquely unprepared for managing an institutional catastrophe of such scale and nature, which had a profound impact not only on Russia's own political trajectory but also on the uncertain transitions of all newly born post-Soviet states.[2] The failure of Yeltsin's constantly reshuffled team to develop any coherent plan for reorganizing the inherited military assets and liabilities was justly criticized and even condemned, including by this author, but in retrospect, the radical demilitarization of the state achieved during the 1990s can be acknowledged for avoiding most breakdowns and blunders that could have greatly surpassed Chechnya.

The illusions about preserving a unified command over the tightly centralized Soviet Armed Forces were abandoned in a matter of few months in 1992 as the suddenly independent states engaged in 'nationalizing' and 'privatizing' the units and infrastructure that happened to be on their territories. That left Yeltsin with the urgent need to organize two hugely complicated processes: 1) the withdrawal to the Russian territory of those military assets that came under Moscow's control while being located in the so-called 'near abroad', from the tens of thousands of troops in Azerbaijan and the Baltic states to the hundreds of nuclear weapons in Belarus, Kazakhstan, and Ukraine; and 2) the reduction of the inherited military structures to a level that would be economically sustainable in the period of devastating depression.

It was possible at that moment to undertake a radical reorganization of the High Command, and the task of building from scratch a new system of civilian and political control over the traditionally self-governed institution was probably feasible. Yeltsin, however, opted for adopting the old Soviet Defence Ministry and the General Staff avoiding even the most necessary streamlining of these over-staffed and functionally overlapping bureaucratic super-structures. That choice was driven primarily by the desire to secure loyalty of the 'top brass' that was seen by Yeltsin, with his natural political gut feeling, as the crucial factor in winning the brewing political struggle for power.[3] Tanks did arrive to secure his victory over the mutinous parliament on 4 October 1993, but the preservation of the quasi-Soviet system of control without accountability essentially blocked the prospects for reforming the military and, perhaps more importantly, marked a major turn in Russia's political trajectory determining many further setbacks in the transition to democracy.[4]

The two initial tasks – reducing the total strength of the military by half to about 1.5 million and relocating about 500,000 troops inside Russia – were basically resolved by mid-1994. That was also the year when Yeltsin, being confident that he would not need any big guns against his political opponents in the future, sanctioned deep cuts in military expenditures. That could have pushed a wiser military leadership to launch reforms, but in the Russian case, that draught in financing directly undercut any prospects for reforms. Seeking to regain the eroded political influence, the High Command tried to play up its successes in

The military reform that never happened 9

'peace' operations, improvised rather than organized in 1992–1993. That inadvertently contributed to a blunder, which, as Georgi Derluguian (2003) noted, appeared 'terribly overdetermined' but at the same time 'consistent with Yeltsin's period of megalomania'. The December 1994 invasion into the quasi-independent and completely failed Chechnya was a mistake on every count, but for the military it was a near-catastrophic defeat.[5] It revealed the depth of deterioration of the military structures caused by the re-deployments, reductions, and under-financing – and the depth of incompetence in the High Command. There was a short-term mobilizing effect as the Army was forced to concentrate all its efforts and gather all its combat-capable units in that tiny theatre; however, the demoralizing effect caused by the disapproval of the war by the public opinion, which strongly condemned its own army, was far greater.

Remarkably, neither the unfolding disaster of the Chechen War nor the urgent need in reforming the fighting army was a major issue in the 1996 presidential election. Yeltsin's hard and unscrupulously earned victory, nevertheless, made it possible to end the war by accepting defeat – and also to sack Aleksandr Lebed who had the courage to put his name under the Khasavyurt peace accord. While the society was content with cutting Chechnya out and forgetting about the responsibility for the war, the military had to deal with the consequences of humiliating defeat.[6] Political leadership and targeted funding were necessary for translating the lessons of the lost war into guidelines for reforms, but neither was provided. When Defence Minister Igor Rodionov became too insistent with demands to address the crisis in the Army, he was duly replaced with more complacent Igor Sergeev; the debates among civilian experts led by Yuri Baturin and Andrei Kokoshin abated as both disappeared from the political arena.[7]

The limited resources that were allocated for addressing the most immediate problems were wiped away by the financial meltdown of August 1998, which left Sergeev with the mandate to keep the military problems away from the political battles in the new election cycle, the cheapest possible way. As the former commander of the Strategic Missile Forces, he found an entirely feasible way to implement this mandate by concentrating the meagre funding on modernizing the strategic triad seeking to unite it under one command (Yakovlev, 1999). The inevitable aggravation of war-inflicted traumas in the neglected conventional forces created a dynamics, which Stephen Blank (1998, p. v) described as 'fast approaching a point of no return'.

The pre-emptive elimination of the 'military opposition'

Arriving at the Kremlin on the 'war ticket', Putin was in no position to advance any reform project or even indicate an intention to contemplate it after the victory, confidently promised but in fact quite uncertain. He was put in a risky position of assuming responsibility for the war not of his making where the only way to proceed was to give the angry generals a *carte blanche* for conducting the operations as they saw fit. The Army was at a record low combat-readiness level, but the mobilizing effect was far stronger than in the first war, since this

10 *Three backgrounds*

time the society, shocked by the terrorist attacks, was firmly behind the intervention expressing no reservations whatsoever against the massive use of firepower on any kind of civilian targets. The high-stakes gambit that Putin was forced to play paid off nicely in securing his grasp on political power, but the military problems did not go away under the loud drums of 'patriotic' rhetoric.[8]

It was the scandalous public clash between Defence Minister Igor Sergeev and Chief of the General Staff Anatoly Kvashnin in summer 2000 that alerted the abecedarian Commander-in-Chief about the brewing discontent among the 'top brass' (Golts and Pinsker, 2000b). Always attentive to hidden agendas, Putin recognized in that 'debate' not a straight clash of personalities and not a traditional inter-service rivalry but the first sign of a mutiny of the 'Chechen generals', who had successfully covered the defeat with a victory, perhaps not entirely convincing, and began to demand their rewards, first of all in terms of political influence. Kvashnin acted as a leader of that emerging 'military opposition' and Putin, while demonstrating his particular sympathy to the army and showing unwavering commitment to bring the deadlocked war to the real end, inferred that combat experience and camaraderie were extremely dangerous political qualities.[9] Instead of confronting head-on the seasoned veterans who were cherishing new political ambitions, he granted them a hollow victory by sending Sergeev to retirement but appointed his most trusted lieutenant Sergei Ivanov as the new Defence Minister.[10]

On that cross-roads, it was possible to address systematically the problem of composition, organization, and functions of the High Command, which constituted a natural starting point for any reform project. The key was in Ivanov's hands since the Ministry of Defence needed to be transformed into civilian institution dealing specifically with the budget and more generally with setting priorities in the military policy. That, however, would have left the General Staff as the top headquarters in the military chain of command – and Putin was clearly not prepared to take such a risk.[11] Ivanov's mandate in fact involved a gradual undermining of Kvashnin's leadership, while Putin one by one transferred the 'Chechen generals' into political positions of secondary importance, like a regional governor (Vladimir Shamanov, Georgy Shpak) or presidential envoy in the Far East (Konstantin Pulikovsky) or presidential adviser (Gennady Troshev).[12] Typically, their performance in political roles has been far from successful, which helped in compromising the whole cohort.

Only in late 2003, Ivanov launched a well-prepared offensive against isolated Kvashnin by shifting some of the key functions from the General Staff to the Ministry of Defence; protestations were duly dismissed, and in July 2004, Kvashnin received the long-expected sack together with the appointment as the presidential envoy to the Siberian federal district (Baev, 2004j). His successor Yury Baluyevsky, being a good professional with no connections to Chechnya, managed to secure the return of the 'lost' authority to the General Staff and that helped in restoring the structural coherence of the High Command. However, this politically uncontroversial compromise still preserved so many redundant

The military reform that never happened 11

branches and functional overlaps that the over-staffed top echelon of the Armed Forces remained an essentially self-serving super-structure.

In December 2005, Baluyevsky proposed a plan for scrapping the system of military districts and separate commands for every branch of the Armed Forces, creating instead three regional commands ('West', 'South', and 'East') and strengthening the role of the General Staff (Babakin, 2005c). The plan was breathtakingly radical for the conservative military establishment and immediately ran into stiff resistance, which took no account of the objective reality of irrelevance of the Soviet command structure for the Armed Forces that had not only shrunk to the level of 1,000,000 personnel but also had to deal with new and fast-evolving security challenges. Lacking political clout, Baluyevsky and his small team of *genshtabists* were unable to count even on support from Defence Minister Ivanov, who did not want these 'technicalities' to compromise his larger ambitions. The plan was quickly reduced to an 'experiment' that was tested in Urals/Siberian exercises conducted in August–September 2006 that revealed serious difficulties in organizing efficient command over joint forces.[13] As one comment pointed out, 'it makes no sense to scrap the system of military districts created by Miliutin in 1861 if there is no XXI century army' (Myasnikov and Grigoryev, 2006).

What happened instead in early 2007 was the predictable but still sudden promotion of Sergei Ivanov to the position of First Deputy Prime Minister and the appointment of Anatoly Serdyukov as the new defence minister. The High Command was shocked with this reshuffling as Serdyukov clearly possessed no qualifications whatsoever for the job except loyalty to the CinC – and was only partly mollified by the further strengthening of the role of the General Staff (Myasnikov, 2007a; Baev, 2007e). Putin's choice, however, while quite possibly a last-minute one, was more logical than it first seemed. Money was the key to keeping the top brass in check during the delicate transfer of power, and Serdyukov with his experience in leading the Federal Tax Service was perfectly capable to take control over complicated military finances – if not to form a 'strategic' opinion on priorities for reforms.

It has always been clear that the success of any meaningful reform project requires a determined drive from a team of reformers – and it was by no means impossible to organize such a team in the military establishment, conservative as it always is. Putin, however, sought primarily, and perhaps even exclusively, to secure passivity (if not loyalty) and controllability of the High Command, from which 'Chechen warriors' were carefully expelled. He wasted his first term eliminating the shadow of a 'military opposition' and saw no need to do anything about the dysfunctional but harmless command system, except for trimming it a bit as a way to maintain discipline.[14] The belated initiatives announced in 2006 were only supposed to provide foundation for decisions to be taken in 2008 – presumably by a new Commander-in-Chief.

12   *Three backgrounds*

The non-decision on abandoning the draft system

The issue of moving away from the old Soviet system of 'universal' conscription into the Armed Forces (as well as several other 'power structures', including the Interior Troops) and adopting a model of an all-volunteer army has attracted so much heated debate since before the collapse of the USSR that its resolution has inescapably become the central point in any reform project. It was convincingly argued by many experts that a comprehensive military reform has to address a great number of interconnected problems (Arbatov, 2005), but for the general public, the meaning of the term 'military reform' has become synonymous with 'contracts-instead-of-draft'. Already in the autumnal decade of the USSR, the conscription was broadly perceived – mostly because of the war in Afghanistan – as punishment, avoidable if a young man in question was able to qualify for high education. With the start of the First Chechen War, draft-dodging became an entirely acceptable social norm; so President Yeltsin, struggling on the 1996 campaign trail, had to promise that the conscription system would be cancelled by the year 2000, i.e. inside his second presidential term.[15]

Putin had to weasel out of that promise during the first year of his presidency, but he could not fail to see that even the wave of 'patriotic' enthusiasm raised by the start of the Second Chechen War did not change the societal attitude towards the draft system in any significant way.[16] Attentive as he always was to the public opinion, Putin had no intention of alienating the 'top brass' by enforcing a radical breakthrough that pertained not only to the manning of military structures but also to the very core of military culture. This culture traditionally had a pronounced bureaucratic character but was evolving due to the growth of various 'warrior' traits, so that even the 'parquet' generals had to acknowledge that a 'mercenary' army would answer better to the real-life requirements and that a shift to contract-based recruiting was necessitated by the experiences gained in combat operations, first of all in Chechnya. With his background in the huge bureaucracy of the Committee for State Security (KGB), Putin was very sympathetic towards the bureaucratic culture in the Army – and he was strongly suspicious about the influence of the 'Chechen generals' who embodied the alternative 'warrior' culture.[17]

The Kremlin was therefore content to leave the issue for minor political actors to exploit and observed with satisfaction the uphill battle fought by the Union of Rightist Forces (SPS) that made the transition to an all-volunteer army a key point in its party-political platform. The proposed plan was perhaps not entirely realistic, but energetic politicians like Boris Nemtsov made great effort at popularizing it, and the public opinion registered a further shift in the anti-draft direction.[18] The military establishment reluctantly agreed to stage some 'experiments' with units manned exclusively by soldiers serving on contract (so-called '*kontraktniki*'), while Defence Minister Ivanov instructed his subordinates: 'It is impossible to underestimate the negative influence of certain political forces trying to undermine the prestige of the military service'.[19] That alleged influence went sharply down as the SPS failed to gather enough votes in

The military reform that never happened 13

the December 2003 parliamentary elections and was unable to form a faction in the State Duma; it tried to organize a referendum on the question of discontinuing the draft system, but the initiative was effectively suppressed by the Kremlin.

The issue, however, did not go away as the draft cohort continued to shrink due to demographic reasons; draft-dodging remained high, while the widespread bulling in the barracks (so-called '*dedovshchina*') made it increasingly difficult to hide the alarming statistics of violent crime, suicide, and desertion.[20] Putin (2004a) skipped over these problems in his 2004 address to the parliament mentioning in the most general terms the need for 'increasing the prestige and attractiveness of military service'; he did not mention it at all in the next year address. It was only at the large press conference at the end of 2004 (Putin, 2004b) that a presidential opinion on resolving the problem was expressed: 'I should say, and this is no secret, that we are not seeking to have a completely professional army. However, combat ready units must be professional'.

Ministry of Defence translated this rather vague guideline into a plan that included two key elements: 1) the reduction of duration of the compulsory service to 18 months in 2007 and to one year from 2008; and 2) the immediate cancellation of most of the loopholes in the draft legislation, so that a far greater share of the young generation would become eligible (Plugatarev and Tsiganok, 2005; Baev, 2005m). A massive propaganda offensive around this plan overwhelmed the resistance which the SPS tried to reinvigorate in cooperation with the Committee of Soldiers' Mothers, so that in 2005, opinion polls for the first time registered an increase of support for the draft system.[21] Sergei Ivanov pushed through the parliament various pieces of necessary legislation, while the military departments in many civilian colleges that provided for the students an opportunity to avoid the draft were closed down.

The campaign appeared unstoppable in early 2006 when a particularly brutal case of *dedovshchina* related to near-lethal torture of Private Andrei Sychev received an unusually wide coverage in the mainstream media. Many commentators saw a political context in the spinning of that case and interpreted it as a twist in the intrigues around Putin's choice of successor aimed at compromising Ivanov (Leibin, 2006). Investigations organized by the office of the Prosecutor General revealed a dismal picture of crumbling discipline in the Army, with 13 per cent increase in the crime rate in the first half of 2006 (Plugatarev, 2006c).

Putin deliberately downplayed the problem in his 2006 address to the parliament and emphasized that 'We need to realise that the armed forces are part of ourselves, part of our society, and that service in their ranks is of immense importance for the country and for the entire Russian people' (Putin, 2006b). He then abruptly removed Vladimir Ustinov, who appeared to advance his own presidential bid by attacking Sergei Ivanov, from the position of prosecutor general and made him instead the minister of justice (Baev, 2006f). That took the heat off the Ministry of Defence but achieved nothing in improving the atmosphere in the barracks.[22]

There could hardly be any doubt in Putin's mind that the draft problem has

14 *Three backgrounds*

become the focal point of deepening antagonism between the Armed Forces and the society, but he is apparently confident that the pressure from both sides would remain manageable until the political watershed of 2008. He probably knows that the funds allocated towards expanding the contract system are not sufficient for converting the 'high-readiness' divisions and brigades into 'all-professional' units (Golts, 2006e). He is certainly aware that the reduction of duration of the compulsory service will create massive problems with manning the unreformed structures since 2009 – but the positive PR could be maintained in 2007 and cover the appalling statistics of suicides in the Armed Forces (Plugatarev, 2007b). The society remains too divided and disheartened by the lack of political alternatives for any determined protest or civil disobedience, and the 'top brass' is content with the procrastination expecting that a new Commander-in-Chief would duly acknowledge their insistence on preserving the 'sacred' tradition of conscription.

The doctrine of quasi-modernization

At the formal meeting of the High Command and the political leadership on 2 October 2003, Defence Minister Sergei Ivanov asserted that the period of numerical cuts and reforms was over and that the Armed Forces would no longer struggle for survival but continue with normal full-fledged military build-up.[23] Putin (2004a) confirmed his consent and in the 2004 address to the parliament emphasized: 'Undoubtedly, modernization of the army is a task of national importance'. For many military experts, that change of rhetoric, allegedly of 'doctrinal significance', was disconcertingly odd since no proper military reform had been launched in earnest at any moment of post-Soviet transition. It appeared possible, however, to interpret the rejection of the term 'military reform', which was seriously compromised among the 'top brass', as the beginning of a new effort at reforming the dilapidated military structures under the slogan of 'modernization' (Tsimbal, 2004).[24]

Such an effort was indeed more feasible than at the start of Putin's first term since several major obstacles had disappeared, while the political control over the military, about which Putin reminded in his 2004 address to the parliament (meaning, quite clearly, the Kremlin's 'civilian' control over the High Command), was significantly strengthened.[25] The war in Chechnya was by no means finished, but its burden for the army greatly diminished as only a small number of mobile units and *Spetsnaz* detachments were engaged in active operations, while the bulk of the patrolling and policing duties were carried out by the forces subordinated to the Interior Ministry (Mukhin, 2004b). Despite the dominant counter-terrorist discourse, there were in real terms not that many new tasks for the Armed Forces related to the struggle against terrorism, so they could concentrate on accumulated internal problems.

The opportunity for addressing these problems was uniquely favourable in the sense that the amount of money available for the Ministry of Defence registered a significant increase. Military expenditures were growing since the start of

The military reform that never happened 15

Putin's reign, but in 2000–2002, all the extra funds were directed towards sustaining the operations in Chechnya and delivering some urgently needed raises in officers' salaries. Sergei Ivanov was unable to secure any meaningful expansion of the 2003 military budget and missed again on the distribution of additional resources earmarked for the war against terrorism in mid-2003.[26] Since 2004, however, funding of the defence requirements has been strongly and steadily growing ahead of many other parts of the expanding state budget.

This redistribution of rising oil-and-gas revenues made it possible to break the vicious circle that had bedevilled all military reform projects since Gorbachev's desperate tackling of the enormous Soviet military machine: reforms were necessary in order to make the Armed Forces 'affordable' to the state, but they required extra investments beyond the limit of 'affordability'. Now the flow of 'new money' was channelled directly to the aim of modernization that has shaped up as the key proposition of the broad political consensus around the military policy. As Alexei Arbatov (2006) pointed out,

> one has to grant that on the level of strategic missions and concept formulations, Russian military policy is entirely comparable with the official postures of United States, other NATO countries and Japan – and in some instances considerably more clear and logical.

The political elite has embraced wholeheartedly this clarity agreeing to ignore the fundamental contradiction between the aim of modernization and the two underlying propositions: 1) the Armed Forces should be maintained on the level above one million; and 2) the military expenditures should not exceed 2.6–2.8 per cent of the GDP or 15–16 per cent of the state budget. As a result, 'modernization' is interpreted in very narrow terms as acquisition of modern weapons and equipment. This even causes some discontent in the underpaid officer corps; for instance, in 2004, their salaries fell behind the run of inflation (Plugatarev, 2004); so Putin (2007d) in his last address to the parliament promised new increases. There is, indeed, a great need in this kind of 'modernization' since long years of dramatic under-funding have left the military armed with enormous arsenals of Soviet-made weapons degraded by lack of proper maintenance and often past the expiration date. The somewhat paradox result of this priority funding for military acquisition is that the real delivery of new armaments to the troops has not increased in any significant measure.

The data on the structure and real implementation of military budgets is extremely limited, but it is still possible to establish with reasonable certainty that the funding for research and development (R&D) and acquisitions doubled from 2003 to 2006 (from 115 to 240 billion roubles, comparing with some 50 billion in 2001). At the same time, the delivery of the key types of weapons remained basically on the same level: 14 main battle tanks T-90C were purchased in 1993, 31 in 1994, 17 in 1995, and 31 in 2006; the figures for armoured personnel carriers for these years are in the range of 100–120, and four to seven Su-27 fighters were annually modernized to the Su-27CM

16 *Three backgrounds*

modification (Myasnikov, 2005a). One part of the explanation for this low level of physical acquisitions is the relatively high level of funding for the R&D (up to 40 per cent) organized in dozens of over-staffed and non-competitive institutions. Another reason is the high share of the low-return programmes related to the strategic forces, particularly to the new generation of nuclear submarines. Inflation also needs to be factored in, but more important is the steep rise of prices on military production driven by the reorientation of the defence industry towards the export markets.[27] This phenomenon is examined in more detail in Chapter 4, but it is beyond doubt that for major enterprises in naval shipbuilding, air defence systems, combat aircraft and tank production, customers in China or Venezuela are by far more important than the meagre orders from the Russian Armed Forces.[28]

It appears quite certain that by the end of Putin's second term the Armed Forces would have next to nothing to show for the 'modernization' efforts as the deliveries of new equipment cannot even compensate for accidental losses, first of all in the Air Force. The acquisition of 'battalion sets' of new tanks also falls far short of a breakthrough that Ivanov had tried to wish into existence before leaving the politically unpromising post of Defence Minister.[29] While there are useful designs for weapon systems of new generations, the Russian Army remains unable to make use of them not due to the lack of funds but primarily because such systems require a higher level of military organization. Modern communication and intelligence equipment, computers, and integrated control systems are the elements strikingly missing in the military structures from the top level to the battlefield, but 'shopping' for such equipment and technology makes little practical sense. This kind of modernization would require a different quality of manpower, from thoroughly trained and motivated soldiers to well-educated and computer-literate officers to dynamic and innovatively thinking generals. The debates about a new military doctrine in early 2007 showed that the top brass was keen to advance new demands for more of everything playing on the hypothetic US and NATO threats (Felgengauer, 2007). The Russian Army appears stuck in the old Soviet ways – and Putin's 'modernization' has been essentially aimed at preserving this outdated and basically unsustainable pattern for only a few more years, with hardly any considerations given to mid-term prospects.

Conclusions

Many military analysts have pointed out that the core structures of the Russian Armed Forces are fundamentally unreformable; so it would be easier to build a new army than to transform the existing one according to the requirements of the era of revolution in the military affairs (Sharavin, 2005; Solovyev, 2002; Trenin 2004b). The reference point in such conjectures is the breakthrough achieved at the start of the eighteenth century by Peter the Great, who scraped the old-fashioned forces and built from scratch the 'new type' regiments that secured him the victory over mighty Swedes.[30] Putin, while often expressing his admiration for Peter I, has never indicated any intention of following such a

The military reform that never happened 17

'revolutionary' course. Nevertheless, some of his plans for modernizing the military, for instance, expanding the 'experiment' with the 76th Airborne Division into building a few dozen of all-professional units of 'permanent readiness', resemble an attempt to create a small combat-capable army within the old military structures. The resemblance, however, remains quite superficial as the rot in the larger conscript army inevitably spreads to the contract service and the semi-reformed units remain parts of the same profoundly decayed institution.[31]

It has become clear during Putin's second presidential term that the lack of resources is not the main obstacle on the way of reforms, as plentiful new funds have been pumped into the old structures in order to preserve their integrity. The overall military posture has been stabilized but on a level of very low functionality. With hindsight, it is possible to establish that targeted channelling of these financial flows towards clearly defined reform goals could have produced tangible results within 2–3 years, so that by 2008 a crucial watershed in reorganizing and modernizing the Armed Forces would have been passed. Instead, all the hard decisions have been postponed until after that supposedly fateful moment of transfer of the supreme political power, while incremental steps in addressing urgent crises only increase the sum total of misbalances and incompatibilities. The key issue in the military reform is inevitably the quality of armed people in uniform, from the High Command that needs to be streamlined and focused on preparing the Armed Forces for the challenges of the new era, to the officer corps that needs a new system of education, to the professional corps of non-commissioned officers and sergeants that is yet to be created, to the soldiers who have to be motivated to perfect their skills. Astonishingly little is being done for improving the lives of these people, except for palliative solutions aimed at keeping the generals loyal, the officers hopeful about their salaries and housing conditions, and the soldiers locked up in their barracks.[32]

This kind of political non-leadership rests on the conviction that the Armed Forces would not really be needed in the near future for repelling any real-terms security threats and that the PR-spin put on their still-impressive total strength and colossal Soviet arsenals would suffice for deterring most indirect security challenges. That conviction lies behind Putin's (2006b) rather confusing guideline spelled in the 2006 address to the parliament: 'We need armed forces able to simultaneously fight in global, regional and – if necessary – also in several local conflicts'. In essence, this means, as Dmitri Trenin (2004c) pointed out, that 'our army is today by 85 per cent aimed at waging the third world war, which we had prepared to fight for decades, until 1991'. Maintaining the structures that consume significant resources for performing an entirely fictitious function might appear going beyond the outer limits of political common sense, but in fact it fits into Putin's notion of 'pragmatism'. The quasi-Soviet Armed Forces answer perfectly to the pseudo-democratic state model that has taken a rather rigid shape during Putin's second term when a colossal godsend increase of oil rent has fuelled the over-growth of bureaucratic super-structures. This profoundly un-modern state can afford a useless top-heavy and rotten-to-the-core military machine but cannot take a risk of building a professional and efficient army.

2 The oil-and-gas dividend that was too low – and has become too high

It was only during Putin's presidency that Russia has become a *bona fide* 'petro-state' – and not only in terms of the share of the energy sector in the gross domestic product (GDP) or the composition of export, but also in self-perception. Being a major producer and exporter of oil and natural gas for several decades, the country used to imagine itself as an advanced industrialized power (leaving aside the ideological clichés); it was only by the middle of the first decade in the new century – some 120 years after the Nobel brothers established their Villa Petrolea in Baku – that Russia's image changed distinctly in the Organization of Petroleum Exporting Countries (OPEC) direction. The stagnation of traditional industries, the decline of fundamental science, the belated and slow penetration of information-era technologies all contributed to that shift, but the main factor was the mind-boggling rise of oil prices. Not only corporate experts but the whole political class and even restless pensioners now recognize the pivotal role of hydrocarbons for the country's well-being and watch with hope and fear the fluctuations in the world markets. The main concern, informed by the financial meltdown of 1998, is about a sudden drop in oil prices, while in fact the hugely increased inflow of petro-roubles has gradually turned into a challenge that threatens to undermine the integrity of state structures and institutions.

The Soviet bankruptcy

In the period of accelerated industrialization, the Soviet leadership saw nothing special in oil or gas, prioritizing other resources: it was the electrification during the first and second five-year plans; the production of iron and steel in the pre-war industrial spurt and post-war reconstruction; and the nuclear energy plus new hydro-power projects in the 1950s and 1960s. Despite deep involvement in the Middle Eastern affairs, the tripling of the world oil prices in 1973 was a complete surprise – and in many ways an eye-opener.[1] It coincided with the discovery of vast new oil-and-gas fields in Western Siberia that were recognized as major strategic assets for a new surge in industrial modernization as well as for foreign policy.

The assessments of proven and potential reserves still remain buried in the

The oil-and-gas dividend 19

mountains of discarded GOSPLAN secret files, and the data on investments is not very meaningful since orders and planning directives had far more weight than roubles.[2] The only reasonably reliable statistics is on production and export of oil and natural gas, and it shows export of oil nearly doubled during the 1970s and the export of gas increased from 3.3 bcm to 54.2 bcm, so that the share of energy in the total value of Soviet export increased from 15.6 per cent in 1970 to 46.9 per cent in 1980 (*Sotsialisticheskie strany*, 1987). That period is known as Brezhnev *zastoi* (slack), since the reform plans developed at the start of the decade were abandoned as unnecessary. The windfall of hard currency provided for steady growth of quality of life and a significant trickle of consumer import, so this time is still nostalgically remembered as 'developed socialism'. The main part of the 'oil dividend' was certainly invested into expanding the military–industrial complex, but there appeared to be no need to choose between 'guns' and 'butter'.

With the start of the 1980s, that optimistic perspective began to fade as the demand for resources was growing faster than the supply, particularly since the détente's breakdown necessitated massive new efforts at building up the military might. Despite a new doubling of the oil prices in 1979–1980, the expenditures on subsidizing the imploding economies of the 'brotherly socialist states' (particularly Poland, shocked by the *Solidarity* strikes) and sustaining the war in Afghanistan pushed the budget into the red (Shmelev and Popov, 1989; Sinelnikov, 1995). Expectations in the geriatric *Politburo* that Western Europe being dependent on the enormous 'gas deal' sealed in 1980 would be reluctant to engage in a new round of confrontation amidst economic recession proved to be wishful thinking.[3]

Mikhail Gorbachev arrived at the Kremlin in March 1985 with a strong feeling that something was seriously wrong with the Soviet economy, since it was lagging behind the 'stagnating' West, and also with a conclusion that simple administrative stimuli applied by his mentor Yuri Andropov would not suffice.[4] He saw the need to reduce the military burden and dared to break the escalatory trend in the strategic arms race. The instant success of the first initiatives prepared in a rather experimental manner for the October 1986 summit with Ronald Reagan in Reykjavik was a great inspiration for Gorbachev; he moved full speed towards the horizons opened by the 'new political thinking' – and was flabbergasted that the 'peace dividend' never materialized.

The spontaneous self-destruction of the USSR – 'the major geopolitical catastrophe of the XX century', in the opinion of Vladimir Putin – could be interpreted from any analytical angle, but it is the energy factor of the economic collapse that is relevant here.[5] Gorbachev had rotten luck with oil prices, which dropped sharply in 1986 and again in 1988, so that the budget deficits increased to about 10 per cent of the GDP, while the external debt snowballed.[6] The first setback was considered a temporary aberration, so the easy way out was taken – to compensate the diminishing value with the increasing volume of the oil export. The shortage of resources for investment in developing new oilfields was compensated by the more intensive exploitation of the most valuable assets and

20 *Three backgrounds*

not by introducing more advanced technology but mostly by increasing pressure in the productive 'horizons' by pumping water. Investments for rehabilitation of these over-exploited oilfields were not forthcoming because the 'bad times' in the export markets continued, so the decline in production was inevitable.[7]

Prime Minister Valentin Pavlov complained in spring 1991 that the oil production had declined by 53 million tons in the previous two years: 'What economy could hold such a strike?' (Doklad, 1991). Desperate attempts to stabilize the consumer market by printing money while keeping the basic prices fixed resulted in ugly distortions and shortages. Åslund (2002, p. 68) observed that 'Soviet wholesale price of crude oil fell to less than half a per cent of the world market price in 1991, calculated at the free exchange rate'. Financial bankruptcy was so complete that the top state officials who launched a coup against Gorbachev in August 1991 could not convince anybody that they would be able to reinvigorate the defunct state.

Yeltsin's privatization – and a new bankruptcy

Boris Yeltsin's decision to disband the Soviet Union in order to assume power in the Russian Federation was astonishing in its boldness. Being a natural political animal, he knew that he could get away with it only if the newly born country would instantly get going – and also that it was too late to be afraid of radical solutions. The background of a Soviet regional party boss gave him no clue about the scale of necessary economic reforms but he felt instinctively that the risks were deadly. That gut feeling informed his decision to entrust the government not to a band of cronies and loyalists but to a team of young economists led by Yegor Gaidar and Anatoly Chubais, perhaps with a premonition that they could be sacrificed within a year. With the first decree to abolish state control over most consumer prices, the 'shock therapists' entered into the race against time, but it was not only their rush that caused mistakes – the complexity of the post-Soviet economic disaster was clearly beyond their academic expertise.[8]

Monetary measures, often described as the main content of Gaidar's 'shock therapy', helped to unblock the key economic processes, but the new government was convinced that market economy would take root in Russia only if the institute of private property was firmly established. President Yeltsin could have doubts in the virtues of capitalism, but he saw the urgent need in preventing a Communist backlash and so advanced the privatization of major economic assets; a new class of owners was expected to emerge and deter the restorative momentum. The rapid implementation of vast privatization programme with vouchers (checks for stock shares) issued to every Russian citizen could have secured public support for the new regime – but turned out to be the source of non-abating resentment and anger (Goldman, 2003).

The energy sector had plentiful assets useful and attractive for privatization, but for various reasons, its key parts such as the nuclear, electricity, and natural gas industries were excluded from the privatization programme. The rationale

The oil-and-gas dividend 21

for preserving the state monopoly over production and distribution of gas was not exactly rock solid, but Viktor Chernomyrdin, Soviet minister of Gas Industry since 1985, was able to assert the decisive influence in this area. Sensing the storm, he reorganized his ministry already in August 1989 into a joint-stock company GAZPROM that was owned entirely by the state. Amidst the excitement of sweeping reforms, he resisted the pressure for splitting his domain citing the need to maintain steady supply to industries and households at fixed low prices. In December 1992, Yeltsin yielded to the pressure from the parliament and replaced Gaidar with Chernomyrdin as the Prime Minister. GAZPROM was not left unattended: Chernomyrdin's trusted Deputy Rem Vyakhirev became its CEO and Chairman of the Board; this effectively terminated all projects aimed at dividing this behemoth of a company into smaller functional units that could be privatized.[9]

The situation in the oil industry was significantly different as privatization changed its basic organization beyond recognition. Vagit Alekperov was appointed acting minister of Fuel and Energy only in August 1991 and had far less authority than Chernomyrdin, so he opted for the 'every-oilman-for-himself' strategy that promised him a reasonable chance of success. In most units and enterprises in the industry, there was strong drive for 'self-determination', and Alekperov, instead of resisting this pressure, lumped together several promising assets that could form a basis for a manageable company. That was fine with Gaidar who had in mind a dozen or so vertically integrated companies that would be competitive on internal and international markets. Alekperov's *Lukoil*, however, did not become a model since in most other cases directors struck deals with trade unions in order to privatize their enterprises without any external interference.[10]

This rather chaotic development resulted in the survival of several medium-sized companies, for instance, *Surgutneftegaz* (whose CEO Vladimir Bogdanov tried to implement a populist model of 'people's company'), a number of smaller regional companies (for instance, *Tatneft* in Tatarstan under the patronage of President Shaimiev), and great many independent 'minors'.[11] Essential production ties were often severed, investment capital evaporated nearly entirely, and production went into spiral decline. Domestic demand, however, shrunk even greater, so the volume of export remained stable – but the government had serious difficulties in taxing this profitable business. Internal prices on gasoline remained fixed and this eliminated any possibility for the newly independent enterprises to earn money on the domestic market. Centrifugal trends therefore quickly gave way to centripetal as the 'majors' began to swallow unviable but potentially useful bits and pieces, thus acquiring more of a vertically integrated profile.

This process accelerated as the privatization entered into a new phase in 1995–1996, when political expediency dictated very questionable concessions to the new captains of business. At the start of 1996, Yeltsin had approval ratings in single digits and entrusted to Chubais the management of his 'must-win' re-election campaign. The miracle victory in July was generously sponsored by

22   *Three backgrounds*

several outrageously if not quite legitimately rich entrepreneurs, who in return were granted unprecedented opportunities to expand their fiefdoms at the expense of the state.[12] While Chernomyrdin, Vyakhirev, Alekperov, and Bogdanov wisely kept low political profile at that time, Roman Abramovich and Boris Berezovsky who together owned *Sibneft*, Mikhail Khodorkovsky who in 1996 took control over *Yukos*, and Vladimir Potanin who had a major share in *Sidanco* were among the self-proclaimed 'oligarchs'.

In a sharp contrast with the first phase of privatization, which in essence was not about money (since the monetary reform wiped off private savings), from the start of Yeltsin's second term, money became everything. Gathering vast business empires, the 'oligarchs' acquired also considerable stakes in the state itself and so, in principle, could have seen a point in paying taxes. The reality, however, defied classical scheme of relations between big business and state, and a new extraordinary deep fall in world oil prices was a major factor in distorting that reality. The dramatic shrinking of income forced the government to resort to short-term borrowing, and these GKO bonds (short-term state bonds) offered returns so high that it made very little sense to invest in anything else. The enterprises just stopped mutual payments, so their outstanding credits snowballed to 85 per cent of the GDP in 1998 (Gaidar, 2005, p. 397). This 'virtual economy' was clearly unsustainable, but the government had no alternative to continue building this financial 'pyramid' – and was indeed very close to escaping from the hole with the massive IMF credit secured in July 1998.[13] A bit of luck with the oil prices might have provided a lifeline – but it was not to be, and the partial default on the GKO exploded into a colossal economic and political disaster, so that August 1998 marked a watershed nearly as steep as that of August 1991.

Out of the doldrums with Mr Putin

The recovery from that catastrophe was at first hesitant but gained momentum with the perfectly organized transition of power from Yeltsin to his hand-picked successor, a pure-bred 'dark-horse' who had little if any experience in public politics and appeared quite uncomfortable in the position of power. Only a couple of 'oligarchs' – Berezovsky and Abramovich – really had a hand in his meteoric rise, while others preferred a non-aligned stance. Arriving at the Kremlin, Vladimir Putin asserted that this distancing suited him just fine and when Berezovsky tried to claim a privileged access, he was forced into exile, which only earned the new president extra credit of respect from the big business.[14]

The steady rise of oil prices was certainly a valuable bonus for reconstituting the basic links inside Russia's energy sector, but even more important was the re-discovery of a reasonable value of money, including a meaningful exchange rate as the rouble became about four times cheaper against the US dollar. This eliminated the centrality of banks in the vertically integrated companies and shifted the centre of gravity to the productive units. The owners began to see the

The oil-and-gas dividend 23

direct benefit of paying good salaries to their workers and engineers and what is more, they found good reasons to expect immediate profitability of investments in upgrading and rehabilitating their worn and much-abused assets. For the technically bankrupt 'minors', such calculations were entirely hypothetical, but the 'majors' moved on with acquisitions on the cheap and targeted investments in the quick-return equipment. This was enough to break the decade-long trend of falling production, and with small increases in the volume of pumped oil and far greater increase in its value, the gloom of protracted economic depression turned into hopes of unstoppable growth.[15]

Radical consolidation in the oil industry left only a handful of key players in the market: Alekperov with *Lukoil*, Khodorkovsky with *Yukos*, Bogdanov with *Surgutneftegaz*, Abramovich with *Sibneft*, and Arkady Vekselberg with *Tymen* (TNK). They jointly owned several semi-detached 'minors'; there were also a couple of regional companies (*Tatneft* and *Bashneft*) and one state-owned company *Rosneft*. It was due to be privatized in mid-1998 but was 'saved' by the August meltdown and waited in the shadows for a chance to crash back to the central stage. Dominant as the super-'majors' were, they accepted very reasonable rules of the game established by the state. The first of these rules was about paying taxes – and the swiftly implemented tax reform with the flax income tax of only 13 per cent and much-reduced corporate profit tax convinced the captains of the business that it was in their best interests to normalize their fiscal relations with the state. The second rule was about firm state control over the export secured by the monopoly ownership on oil pipelines granted to the state-owned *Transneft*. The government demonstrated that it was ready to shoulder the responsibility related to this control and invested sufficient efforts in expanding the export capacity, first of all with the Baltic Pipeline System, while the Tengiz–Novorossiisk pipeline became the only exception where international and private ownership in the Caspian Pipeline Consortium (CPC) was accepted. The third rule was about inviting international investors and treating them as valuable partners. By the end of the 1990s, most Western 'pioneers' had pulled out of Russian energy sector with no small losses, but in 2001, the BP resolved its conflict with *Tymen* over 10 per cent stake in *Sidanco*, which signalled positive changes in the climate.[16] Later that year, *ExxonMobil* announced its commitment to invest US\$4 billion in 'Sakhalin-1' project, and in a major breakthrough in early 2003, the BP merged its Russian assets with TNK forming a jointly owned company TNK–BP, which was, according to its website 'among the top ten privately-owned oil companies in the world in terms of crude oil production' and aimed at developing a large-scale Kovykta natural gas project in Southern Siberia (see www.tnk-bp.com/company/).

It was not the fear of punishment that forced the owners of the oil 'majors' to accept these rules, it was much more their own desire to clean the records and become acceptable players on the international arena. Mikhail Khodorkovsky became a true champion of this cause deciding in earnest to reinvent himself from a sleazy banker with a *Komsomol* past to a respectable and trustworthy industrialist. That required more than just a generous public relations (PR)

24 *Three backgrounds*

budget and a few charitable donations, but he was ready to make every necessary effort starting with making *Yukos* the first Russian company that introduced international standards of accounting and transparency.[17] The rise of *Yukos* from a troubled and indebted failure-of-a-company in 1996 to the largest and best-managed Russian oil 'major' in 2002 with shining international prospects is, probably, the best story of that period when Russia appeared on track to full recovery.[18]

There was, however, a different story from the same period that attracted less attention but had greater impact on further evolution of the energy sector: the restoration of state control over GAZPROM. Formally speaking, the control remained the same since the distribution of shares did not change much, while strictly speaking, it was not state but rather the presidential administration that needed to reassert its control. The fact of the matter was that during the second half of the 1990s, GAZPROM became pretty much a personal domain of Chernomyrdin and Vyakhirev who made all strategic decisions while transferring profitable assets to murky semi-detached subsidiaries, like *Itera*, not forgetting their family members. Putin knew that he would never have real authority over the country if he would not take on a short leash the company that accounted for 7 per cent of its GDP, but he waited for more than a year before replacing Vyakhirev with Alexei Miller as the CEO in May 2001.[19] This young manager from St Petersburg at first seemed no match for the tightly knit team of old-timers, but he mobilized effective support not only from the Kremlin but also from the Federal Security Service (FSB) and the prosecution to put pressure on the 'dissidents', wrestle with 'separatists', and reclaim lost assets.[20] The government still entertained ideas about terminating GAZPROM's 'unhealthy' monopoly, but in Putin's narrow circle the conclusion on redundancy of further reforms had ripened by spring 2003.[21]

There was much uncertainty about these success stories, and the fears about a possible new drop in oil prices were quite visible behind the self-congratulatory annual reports. Gradually, nevertheless, new confidence was emerging among the 'majors' who accumulated sufficient reserves underground and in the bank accounts to weather a possible next storm. This confidence was reflected in the 'Energy Strategy' developed by the government that envisaged the increase in oil production from 379 million tons in 2002 to 445–490 in 2010 and 450–520 in 2020, and in natural gas production from 595 bcm in 2002 to 635–665 bcm in 2010 and 680–730 bcm in 2020.[22] The significant margins in these plans were linked to possible fluctuations in prices, but when this strategy was approved in late August 2003, the storm for the whole Russian energy sector was already gathering – but not in the world markets.

The persecution of Khodorkovsky and the expropriation of *Yukos*

The high-voltage atmosphere in Moscow in Summer 2003 was charged with rumours swirling among chattering political classes that the Kremlin was seri-

The oil-and-gas dividend 25

ously unhappy about the pattern of its relations with big business. The report 'The state and the oligarchy' (2003) prepared by the little-known Council on National Strategy made a splash with the mind-boggling proposition about a constitutional coup planned by a group of oligarchs who allegedly were investing their fortunes in the forthcoming parliamentary elections.[23] The counter-strike delivered by the Kremlin PR guru Gleb Pavlovsky (2003), who published in electronic *Russkii zhurnal* his memo 'On the negative consequences of the "summer offensive" of the minority group opposed to the course of the President', revealed an equally incredible conspiracy inside the Kremlin.[24] The arrest of Platon Lebedev, one of the top managers of *Yukos*, in July appeared to be just a warning signal from the Kremlin that a demonstration of loyalty was due (Yasin, 2003). Khodorkovsky, however, refused to oblige and launched a public campaign in defence of his business, defying even 'friendly advices' to leave the country. On October 25 he was arrested – and that day became a watershed in the transformation of Russia's energy sector and perhaps in its general trajectory as well.

The legal proceedings and political intrigues around the trial were examined from every possible angle in hundreds of publications, so only several points pertaining to the fallout from this cataclysm have to be made here.[25] The first one is that the conspirators in Putin's team definitely underestimated Khodorkovsky but measured other 'oligarchs' about right. Securing consent from the president who cherished a personal grudge against the hyper-successful and arrogant entrepreneur, this cabal aimed merely at cutting the upstart down to size and did not plan for a protracted all-or-nothing struggle. Khodorkovsky assuming that his enemies did not have a case called their bluff – but the Kremlin could not afford to lose this one and so went ahead with a 'show trial' that badly damaged its international reputation but delivered the desired verdict. He probably expected a stronger show of solidarity from the big business 'colleagues' counting on their collective self-preservation instinct, but Putin hit more directly on this very instinct demanding 'to stop the hysterics', and the 'oligarchs' as well as the officials in Kasyanov's government immediately saw how much wiser it would be to shut up.[26]

Another point is that Khodorkovsky's defiant stance made it far more difficult to dismember and 'renationalize' *Yukos* than the schemers in the Kremlin had expected. The tax-avoidance case against the company was prosecuted in parallel with the trial of Khodorkovsky and Lebedev – and was full of such blatant manipulations that the court-ordered auction for the most valuable asset of the company, *Yuganskneftegaz*, in December 2004 turned into an awkward scandal.[27] The state-owned *Rosneft* that used questionable funds and phoney front companies in order to acquire this 'tainted jewel' faced a number of international lawsuits that complicated its fund-raising, including the IPO at the London Stock Exchange in mid-2006 ('Thou shalt not steal', 2006). This borrowing was necessary for reorganizing the newly acquired assets, but the problem of profitability had no easy solution since the quality of management in

26 Three backgrounds

the *Rosneft* that prioritized connections to the Kremlin was not exactly superb (Novikova, 2006).

That mismanagement was directly linked to yet another relevant point about the *Yukos*/Khodorkovsky saga: the far greater economic resonance of this carefully isolated case then had been envisaged by the 'experts' with background in special services in Putin's 'narrow circle'. The political part of their plan worked perfectly, and the December 2003 parliamentary elections under the 'anti-oligarchic' slogans sealed the triumph of the pro-Kremlin quasi-party 'United Russia'. As for the economy, however, both shocked international investors and scared domestic entrepreneurs saw a need to take a pause in their activities. The growth in oil production that exceeded 10 per cent in 2002 dropped to zero in 2005 and even the incredible run in the oil prices did not persuade the 'majors' to invest in exploration and long-term projects.[28] The massive growth of export revenues camouflaged that stagnation, so that only a couple of percentage points were shaved from Russia's strong economic growth; the experts, however, started to question the quality of that expansion.[29]

The slackening growth undermined Putin's officially proclaimed goal of 'doubling the GDP', but what was far more important for him was the serious reputation damage on the international arena. His economic adviser Andrei Illarionov called the dismemberment of *Yukos* 'the swindle of the year', but Putin had no chance to distance himself from it and had to confirm that he personally knew the 'experienced professionals' who had placed the winning bet at that staged auction.[30]

Finally, the divisive and corruptive influence of the *Yukos* 'affair' on the Putin's team should be mentioned. It was clear that the government, which had to deal with the economic consequences of that protracted abuse of power, was forced to swallow its reservations (spelled most clearly by German Gref, as noted in Baev, 2004c), and the abrupt replacement of Prime Minister Kasyanov with Mikhail Fradkov generated little enthusiasm. More importantly, the presidential administration, even after Voloshin's departure, remained split over the *Yukos* issue, and the bitterness of this squabbling only increased when the time for dividing the loot came in late 2004. The tightly knit and low-profile group led by Igor Sechin very skilfully exploited Putin's personal animosity to Khodorkovsky, but at some stage the president apparently developed suspicions that his trusted aides were in fact manipulating him.[31] The bickering were in no small part driven by plain greed, so the whole campaign portrayed as punishment of corrupt 'oligarchs' brought an entirely predictable explosive growth of administrative corruption. Many observers point to the February 2003 meeting when Khodorkovsky presented to Putin documents proving that members of his team were involved in sleazy deals with *Rosneft* as the true beginning of his relentless persecution.[32] The abuse of power and disregard of law were so blatant that on every level of the overgrown 'vertical' of executive power, Putin's loyal servants received a signal that the time was right to 'expropriate' whatever profitable business their mini-'oligarchs' had managed to build.

Post-*Yukos* re-Sovietization

The *Yukos* 'affair' was announced to be one of a kind, a special case that would not signify any revision of the overall results of privatization. The demonstration effect, however, was so strong, and the chain of direct consequences went so far that a break of the overall trajectory of Russia's economic development was inevitable. Andrei Illarionov (2005b) defined 2004 as 'The Year of a great breakthrough' comparing it with Stalin's rejection of relatively liberal guidelines of the 'New economic policy' and the adoption of methods of forceful mobilization in 1929.

It was in the oil industry that the impact was the most immediate and easily measurable. *Yukos*, hit by tax bills far in excess of its US$3.0–3.5 billion annual profits, had to reduce drastically its investments in 2003 and stopped them entirely in 2004; *Sibneft*, involved in a complicated merger with *Yukos*, also discontinued its investment programme. These two companies delivered up to 30 per cent of Russia's oil production in 2003, and *Yukos* alone accounted for 5 per cent of the federal budget's income even with its 'underpaid' taxes. The brutal attack on the best-performing company convinced the other 'majors' that strategic investment was not a good idea in the circumstances; they covered only the most basic needs, and even *Lukoil* – always attuned to the signals from the Kremlin – preferred to build its assets abroad, from Kazakhstan to the United States.[33] Veteran oilmen argued that the fast increase of Russia's output in 2000–2003 was only a recovery growth secured by the investments of about US$8 billion a year mostly in wells repair and logistics; massive new drilling was necessary to achieve sustainable growth – and that required at least US$15 billion a year through the rest of this decade and 20–30 billion a year in the next one.[34] This double and treble increase, prescribed also by the 2003 Energy Strategy, failed to materialize – and the oil production stalled with no prospects for another surge five years ahead.[35]

It was possible to compensate for the decline in domestic investment by attracting vast amount of foreign capital, since the negative impression caused by the *Yukos* destruction did not discourage those investors who counted on their networking in the Kremlin and were deaf to advice from Garry Kasparov (2007):

> Anyone trying to make a fast buck investing in Russian President Vladimir Putin's police state should first practice our traditional triple kiss. That's one for kissing off moral principles, another for Mr. Putin's backside, and the last to kiss their money goodbye when a fresh government comes in and starts looking into all these dirty deals.

However, even such investors were allowed to buy only minority stakes in, for instance, *Lukoil*, but the proposition that international 'majors' could own Russia's oil treasures has become increasingly unacceptable, as illustrated by the hostile takeover of the 'Sakhalin-2' project from a consortium led by *Shell*

28　*Three backgrounds*

(Kramer, 2006). The only exception was the TNK-BP, which experienced endless tax 'complications', and neither the personal visits of Lord Browne to the Kremlin nor the 'patriotic' exhibitions of the priceless Faberge eggs purchased by Arkady Vekselberg helped in resolving these (Ostrovsky and Gorst, 2005).[36] The most sensitive 'pressure point' for the company is the Kovykta oil/gas field in Southern Siberia where TNK-BP had the controlling stake but was unable to proceed with development since its plans to build an export pipeline to China were effectively blocked. The company wanted to start the development with a small project aimed at supplying gas to the Irkutsk oblast, but GAZPROM convinced the governor that it would be much wiser to rely on its deliveries from several minor gasfields.[37]

GAZPROM was also affected by the *Yukos* 'affair' albeit in a very different way. After re-establishing control over semi-privatized subsidiaries, Miller announced the intention to expand into the oil business. Technologically and structurally it makes perfect sense, since in many gasfields, natural gas condensate and oil are also available for production, and the flexibility of the oil market could complement more rigid long-term gas contracts. The easiest way to proceed appeared to be the 'friendly takeover' of the state-owned *Rosneft*, but its CEO Sergei Bogdanchikov had a very different vision. He made the company instrumental for dismembering *Yukos* and with few doubts purchased *Yuganskneftegaz* calculating that the discount at the staged auction would more than compensate for the negative balance of the bankrupted producer and would suffice to cover the loans he had to make for the purchase. Building close alliance with Igor Sechin, he managed to outmanoeuvre Miller in the Kremlin corridors, forcing him first to forget about *Rosneft* and then to settle for acquiring *Sibneft* (Bremmer, 2005/2006; Baev, 2005n). There was no discount in the latter deal, and GAZPROM had to pay more than US$13 billion for the company that had exhausted the potential for growth 'on-the-cheap' and needed infusion of capital of about the same scale in order to maintain its 10 per cent share in Russian output.[38] Characteristically, the accumulation of a single 50 per cent package of GAZPROM's shares as the end result of these questionable deals was celebrated as the necessary consolidation of state ownership with only pro forma acknowledgement of the long-promised 'liberalization' of market circulation of these shares that was nevertheless crucially important for boosting the market capitalization of the company to some US$250 billion (as of mid-2007).[39]

All that political intrigue inevitably derailed and eventually seriously depleted GAZPROM's investment programme that each year (until 2007) was approved by the government with long delays and then revised back and forth.[40] As a result, the development of even more available fields, like Yuzhno-Russkoe, was delayed, while the massive work on huge but hard-to-get new fields on Yamal (like Bovanenkovskoe) has been postponed towards the middle or end of the next decade. The surprise decision to develop the giant off-shore Shtokman gasfield without a consortium with foreign partners has led many experts to the conclusion that this project would also experience significant

The oil-and-gas dividend 29

delays (Moe, 2006). The only way for GAZPROM to compensate for the falling production on its exhausted fields has been to acquire (often under duress) the independent producers who as a group showed spectacular results in increasing output to the level of 105 bcm (about 20 per cent of GAZPROM's plateau) in 2006 (Milov, 2007a). The key issue for GAZPROM, however, was the increase of domestic price on natural gas that in 2006 did not reach even 20 per cent of the export price to Western Europe. Despite aggressive lobbying in the Kremlin in autumn 2006, Putin's final decision limited the domestic price increase to only 15 per cent in 2007, while more significant increases that should narrow the gap between domestic and export prices to some 50 per cent by 2010 are essentially a problem for a new president to resolve (Milov, 2007b).

The expansion of state control and accompanying decline of dynamism in the oil-and-gas sectors have significantly affected other branches of Russia's energy complex. The ambitious reform of the electricity production that has been pushed through monumental bureaucratic obstacles by Anatoly Chubais, the CEO of state-controlled RAO Unified Energy System (UES), ties together the privatization of gas and coal plants and greatly expanded construction of new stations that should get on-line 34,000 MW by 2012 and up to 160,000 MW by 2020 with estimated investments in the range of US$420–540 billion (Aliyev, 2007). This privatization makes economic sense only if the domestic prices on electricity are allowed to increase to the level of profitability, and this remains a highly sensitive political issue; at the same time, GAZPROM's aggressive expansion into this emerging market threatens to replace one monopoly with another.[41]

The coal industry is under strong political pressure to increase production so that by 2020 its share in the electricity production would increase from current 23 per cent to 31–38 per cent in order to make more volumes of natural gas available for export. The explosion on the *Ulyanovskaya* coal mine in Kemerovo oblast in March 2007, which claimed 110 lives, was the worst disaster of this kind on record in Russia and was a reminder that strong demand could push this industry to over-exploiting its assets at the expense of safety (Vorontsov and Shirokov, 2007). The nuclear industry has since 2005 experienced a 'dynamic Renaissance', in the words of Sergei Kiriyenko, the CEO of *Rosatom*, that translates into plans to launch construction of two new reactors every year starting in 2007, while only two reactors were put into operation since the start of the decade; this is expected to secure the increase of the share of nuclear industry in the electricity production from 16 per cent to 25 per cent (Gorelov, 2007b).

The common problem for all these industries is that the implementation of their impressive but uncoordinated plans requires an unprecedented expansion of the heavy machine-building industry that used to be the backbone of Soviet economic might but spiralled into deep depression in the 1990s and now shows only tentative signs of revival. The state, while seeking to restore its control over the energy sector, has not added much value by setting priorities or providing targeted investments, and the endless bureaucratic infighting led by GAZPROM, which pursues its parochial interests, undermines any coherence in revising the

30   *Three backgrounds*

2003 Energy Strategy. As a result, the shortage of energy has become a serious impediment to Russia's economic growth; the mild winter of 2006/2007 did not see any dramatic breakdowns of electricity grids, but the increasingly obvious impossibility to balance the growing domestic demand and the stagnant production and the deliveries on export contracts could culminate in the remaining years of this decade in a full-blown energy crisis.

Conclusions

The assertive expansion of state control over the energy sector since mid-2003 has not been guided by a coherent ideology; instead, this forceful policy has been justified in a peculiar discourse that mixes the mantras of market economy, the maxims of quasi-Soviet dirigisme, and the expressive slang of 'shadow economy'. Making a perfect mockery of this eclectic 'doctrine', Vladislav Surkov, a deputy head of the presidential administration and the chief 'ideologist' in the Kremlin, even proposed to enrich the concept of 'economics of sovereign democracy' with the revolutionary guidelines of Che Guevara.[42]

What is, nevertheless, taken for granted in the confused but affirmative official thinking on energy interests is that state-owned vertically integrated companies that are created to dominate important segments of this business are the optimal organizational form for converting the energy flows into political power. This axiom, however, finds little empirical evidence in the operations of GAZPROM, *Rosneft*, *Rosatom*, and other 'champions' who have found great advantages in increasing their market capitalization but have demonstrably failed in shooting up production, advancing technological innovation, or achieving greater efficiency. The significant decline in profitability experienced by the Russian oil companies in 2006 on the background of absurdly high prices was a direct result of the progressively stifling state control (Shokhina, 2007).

One significant and probably not envisaged side effect of this control is the weakness of classical symptoms of the so-called 'Dutch disease' in the Russian economy, since the energy sector despite generating greatly increased volumes of profit does not undermine the growth in other sectors, first of all in construction and trade, while the appreciation of the rouble remains moderate. These profits are effectively expropriated by the state, so the malignant impact of the 'easy money' is transferred from the source of origin in the oil-and-gas industry to the state machinery. In the academic debates on this phenomenon, peculiarities of the Russian variation of the 'resource curse' have been put under scrutiny (Åslund, 2005, 2006; Gaddy and Ickes, 2005); the most complicated diagnosis was given by Andrei Illarionov (2006) who discovered a combination of the 'Dutch', 'Argentinean', 'Venezuelan', 'Saudi', and 'Zimbabwean' diseases.[43]

Such a verdict might appear opinionated rather than scientific, and the carefully selected evidence still cannot disprove the fact that the Russian economy, at least as of mid-2007, does not show predilection to slipping into recession. The long growth, nevertheless, has accumulated many unhealthy distortions so that even without the much feared sudden drop of the oil prices, a minor

The oil-and-gas dividend 31

disturbance in the often-panicking banking sector or in the overheated housing market could resonate with devastating force. The unbalanced combination of over-regulated control mechanisms in some economic spheres and uncontrollable 'invisible hands' of market in other would hardly be able to generate a coherent and timely response in a crisis situation. High vulnerability to external shocks is an irreducible economic weakness, but the character of state control that has been expanded and enforced during Putin's second presidential term could seriously aggravate it. This control provides no advantages of strategic planning or setting rational priorities but exposes the key economic sectors, and first of all the energy complex, to the demands of political expediency and vicissitude of palace intrigues so that the '2008 problem' becomes not only a political puzzle but also a macro-economic problem.

3 The dream of a new 'greatness' that has come truly false

Pragmatism was the political philosophy that Vladimir Putin embraced from the very start of his presidency, perhaps interpreting it in a rather unsophisticated manner but insisting upon connecting feasible goals with available means. The advantage of this 'just-do-it' type of decision-making was in eliminating any need in a coherent ideology that would guide and justify the efforts aimed at strengthening the state machinery. There was, nevertheless, a lingering perception that a Russian 'national idea', which Boris Yeltsin had failed to discover during his turbulent 'epoch', still had to be formulated – and the combination of pragmatic slogans like 'modernization', 'competitiveness', and even 'doubling the GDP' was not convincing enough; hence Putin's (2007d) sour joke in his last address to the parliament about the search for 'national idea' as a 'favourite pastime' in Russia.

It was only in the middle of Putin's second presidential term that conceptual experiments and public relations (PR) marketing led by Vladislav Surkov, the chief Kremlin 'ideologist', focused on the combination of two ideas: the 'sovereign democracy' and the 'energy super-power'. The former appeared vague and contradictory, as Dmitry Medvedev, First Deputy Prime Minister and a hopeful in the presidential succession, pointed out.[1] The latter, to the contrary, appeared so simplistic that commentators made a sport of ridiculing it, and Surkov himself was perhaps guilty in 'selling' it in a rather primitive manner: 'If you have strong legs, you should go into long-jump and not to play chess.'[2] There was, however, more to it than just grasping the lucky opportunity created by the market: 'When oil prices are 20 dollars per barrel, we are a raw material appendage, when they are 60 – we are "energy super-power".'[3] It was Sergei Ivanov (2006), then defence minister and another presidential hopeful, who suggested that the 'sovereign democracy' together with strong economy and military power form a 'new triad of national values'.

This conceptual exercise in putting together several PR clichés so that a semblance of a coherent ideology would emerge showed that in the views of Putin's 'class', the perceptions of Russia's power (based on its unique natural richness) blended with the far-stretched notion of 'sovereignty'. Ivanov was perhaps too blunt, but his elementary scheme resonated distinctly with the deep-rooted belief that Russia was entitled to 'greatness' of some kind that had been lost due to bad

The dream of new 'greatness' 33

leadership or hijacked by hostile competitors and should be restored. Some similarity could be found between this inflated self-perception and the French Gaullist idea of *grandeur*, but it constitutes a complex social phenomenon that cannot be dismissed ironically.[4]

The Great Power, the Empire, the Civilization

Patriotic pride has various intensity and dissimilar manifestations in different countries, and for many Europeans the pervasive display of 'stars-and-stripes' in the US appears as odd as the ever-present portraits of Mustafa Kemal Atatürk in Turkey. The Russian longing for 'greatness' shapes the patriotism of a very particular kind that has few visible symbols but many political implications. It is rooted in Russia's insurmountable geography and 'unpredictable' history and is typically blended with self-reproducing myths about the Western irreducible hostility towards Russia, its own unique global mission, or the natural moral superiority and 'spirituality' of the Russian national character.[5] A thorough deconstruction of this phenomenon is a task far beyond the qualifications of this author, but for the purpose of this study, it appears possible to identify three distinct traits in the politically constructed idea of 'greatness'.

The first dimension is the easiest for political analysis as it is centred on the well-established notion of 'Great Power'. The basic assumption here is that Russia has developed and possesses inalienably certain material components of state power so that by the sum total of their combination it qualifies for a small group of extra-powerful states that essentially determines the pattern of international affairs.[6] Among these components, the sheer size of the territory is perceived as an undeniable asset, perhaps even more significant than the size of population; the military might is believed to be an indispensable instrument; and the colossal nuclear arsenal is seen as the final proof of 'greatness'. One additional element of state power that is often invoked is the space programme that started with the first *Sputnik* in 1957 and Yuri Gagarin's flight in 1966, which provided the most celebrated achievement of the Soviet era.[7] In this context, the capacity to supply the world with much-needed energy is seen both as a key element of state power and as a means to rebuild the eroded and neglected military might.

The second flow of thinking about Russia's inherent 'greatness' is more turbulent and meandering as it goes towards the notion of 'Empire' loaded with much controversy. Richard Pipes can be recognized as the founding father of the school of political analysis that maintains that expansionism is an essential and irreducible feature of the Russian state that has forever sought to subdue and incorporate its neighbours.[8] While many other Western scholars are cultivating more balanced views on the historical patterns and contemporary manifestations of Russian imperialism, Pipes' diagnosis finds much corroborating evidence in the ratiocinations of such pro-Kremlin 'neo-imperialists' as Aleksandr Dugin and Mikhail Leontyev.[9] They express the widely held view that Russia could 'organically' exist only in the form of empire, and this implies asserting

34 *Three backgrounds*

effective control over political development of neighbouring states and accepting responsibility for their security. Energy is now perceived as a crucial bond holding this post-Soviet empire together and securing Russia's dominance, while also providing it with surplus income that could be converted into muscle and influence.[10]

The third trait of the desired 'greatness' is even vaguer and boils down to the indefinable notion of 'Civilization'. Typically, the incoherent but quite widely shared ideas that Russia has its own unique 'way' or 'civilizational mission' incorporate perceptions of three different kinds: ethno-nationalist (greater-Russian more than pan-Slavic), religious (Orthodox Christian but with demonstrated 'respect' to Islam), and statist (authoritarian paternalism as the 'natural' Russian political model). They broadly correspond to the traditionalist formula '*samoderzhavie–pravoslavie–narodnost*' (autocracy–Orthodoxy–national character) invented by Count Sergei Uvarov back in the 1830s,[11] which opens to a wide variety of political prescriptions. Opinions differ on whether Russia is straddling a crucial fault-line in the 'clash of civilizations', which remains a remarkably popular political model, or can pull itself away from the frontal clash between the West and Islam.[12] The general thrust of this longing for 'greatness' is that Russia should reject Western models of and prescriptions for democratization, while an extreme version advocates the advantages of self-isolation in the 'Fortress Russia'.[13]

While not entirely compatible, these three traits of 'greatness' – Great Power, Empire, and Civilization – are blended together in the mainstream political thinking that proceeds from the assumption of the pivotal importance of the state (*gosudarstvennost*) to the centrality of the broadly understood 'sovereignty' (*suverennost*) and towards the ideal of a proud and powerful country (*derzhavnost*). The ingredients have been mixed in different proportions, but it appears possible to identify three stages with distinct blends in the evolving ideology of Putin's presidency.

Qualifying as a 'Great Power' by exploiting counter-terrorism

Restoring Russia's 'greatness' was a key electoral slogan of the rather improbable presidential candidate, the newly appointed Prime Minister Vladimir Putin, who spelled out his views, rather atypically, in an essay published on his website.[14] It was the second war in Chechnya, launched with brutal determination, that signified a breakthrough in convincing the society that *derzhavnost* would make a comeback and in rebuilding confidence in the political elite, but that war did not help at all in improving Russia's international profile and establishing the new leader's credentials.

It is essential to remember that Putin had started from a very low point on the international arena as the negative resonance of the state default in August 1998 was further aggravated by the fallout from the Kosovo crisis in spring 1999. With hindsight, it is apparent that the North Atlantic Treaty Organization

The dream of new 'greatness' 35

(NATO) attack on Yugoslavia erected a major watershed in the evolution of Russia's philosophy of relations with the West and in its self-perception as well; the shock of the financial meltdown in August 1998 has been alleviated by the nine years of strong economic growth – but the shock of witnessing a perfect impunity of sustained bombing campaign has transformed into mistrust and estrangement. All three parts of Russia's perceived 'greatness' were suddenly deflated. Its firm opposition to an intervention was dismissed – and that constituted a violation of the 'Great Power' status, despite Yeltsin's ill-conceived 'reminders' about the nuclear deterrence.[15] The ability to project power towards the Balkans – a region with rich history of Russia's 'imperial' exploits – was tested in the improvised 'march on Pristina' and found lacking.[16] The imaginary 'civilizational' ties with Serbia turned out to be of no security significance or political relevance.

The depth of that perceived humiliation was such that the newly elected accidental leader felt heavy pressure of public expectations to deliver a miracle that would reconstitute Russia's status. His dubious reputation in the West did not help much, and it was only the June 2001 Ljubljana summit with President George W. Bush, still fresh in the job, that created for Putin an opening as he passed the 'look-in-the-eye' test.[17] It is highly questionable whether Putin would have succeeded in pulling through that narrow opening the far-fetched proposition that Russia was the 'bulwark' of Western civilization in the global confrontation with Islamic extremism, but a miracle indeed happened – and of a truly cataclysmic nature. Not only was Putin quick to call Bush with expressions of sympathy and outrage a few hours after the attack often described by simple numerals '9/11', but he was also quick to see that the configuration of international relations suddenly became subject to major changes so the relative 'weights' of actors would be measured anew. Against the opinions of his lieutenants, Putin promptly anchored Russia to the newly formed US-led anti-terrorist coalition and this helped instantly in getting it back into the short list of 'Great Powers'.[18]

It was this dimension of 'greatness' that Putin concentrated his attention on in the next couple of years, quickly developing a taste for rubbing shoulders with the Western counter-parts and exploiting their disagreements for maximizing Russia's influence. He was successful beyond expectations, particularly in cultivating personal relations with German Chancellor Gerhard Schröder. What underpinned his 'charm offensive' was Russia's strong economic recovery led by the oil-and-gas sector where large-scale export-oriented projects, including the Baltic pipeline system (BPS), the *Blue stream*, and the Tengiz–Novorossiisk pipelines, were implemented. The 'energy dialogue' with the US was launched with much promise (as described in Chapter 10), and Mikhail Khodorkovsky, the CEO of the oil giant *Yukos*, became its most enthusiastic advocate.[19]

By the start of 2003, however, the main direction in Putin's pursuit of Russia's 'greatness' had started to shift. The decision to expand NATO with seven new members, adopted at the November 2002 Prague summit, was not that significant in this regard, and neither was President Bush's decision to

36 *Three backgrounds*

withdraw from the Anti-Ballistic Missile (ABM) Treaty. The most significant impact on Putin's manoeuvring, beyond doubt, was made by the US drive towards the war in Iraq, as determined as it was blind to the consequences. Moscow saw in that unilateralist exercise of overwhelming power a perfect opportunity to increase its own 'balancing power' and engaged in 'pragmatic' bargaining. For a couple of months, this game of indecisiveness made it into one of the crucially important capitals in the world, but the moment of truth came at the trilateral meeting in Paris on 10 February 2003 when Putin, Chirac, and Schröder announced that there would be no UN Security Council approval for a US intervention. Instead of consolidating Russia's profile as a *bona fide* 'Great Power', this choice set in motion its estrangement and alienation from the West that culminated in the quite unsuccessful G8 chairmanship in 2006.

That did not mean that the quest for 'great-powerness' was abandoned; it has merely changed direction since spring 2003, but that re-orientation was of major significance. Instead of expanding its contribution to the anti-terrorist coalition, the Kremlin has placed its bet on the US defeat in Iraq and the inevitable collapse of that coalition. Even the shocking terrorist attack in Beslan in September 2004 did not bring any deviation from that course as Russia's pursuit of the 'Great Power' status was at that point tightly intertwined with the desire to reconstitute its 'Empire'.

Rebuilding the 'Empire' by leading counter-revolutions

The dominant opinion among security experts in Moscow was that the war in Iraq would be protracted, costly, and eventually disastrous and that the trans-Atlantic alliance would be massively damaged by the US unilateralist blunder.[20] It proved about right on the first assumption (although hopes for a quick defeat were frustrated) but quite wrong on the second one, since the imagined 'tectonic rift' was narrowed to a usual disagreement between allies. Despite the initial intention in Washington to 'punish France, ignore Germany, and forgive Russia', in reality, Bush's re-election in early November 2004 convinced the European allies to close their ranks, while Russia drifted further apart with its attempts to play on the narrowing differences.[21] This drift was accelerated by a series of rushed actions based on the assumption that burdensome engagement in Iraq would limit the US attention to other regions, while Russia could begin converting its regained strength into dominance over the immediate neighbourhood.

The first tentative attempt to put pressure on the disrespectful neighbours was made in September 2002, when Putin issued an ultimatum to Georgia threatening to take military measures towards exterminating terrorists in the Pankisi Gorge. The US objections rendered that attempt unsuccessful, but by autumn 2003 Moscow had become convinced that in the world system deformed by the war in Iraq, it would face only minor obstacles on the road to its restored post-Soviet 'Empire'. In order to shape a nucleus for this neo-imperial project, the so-called 'Common Economic Space' was established between Russia, Belarus, Kazakhstan, and Ukraine.[22]

The dream of new 'greatness' 37

There was plenty of platitudes about Russia acting as a 'locomotive' for grateful neighbours, about its 'gravitation pull' that generated 'centripetal forces', but the real urgency in these alliance-building efforts was related to the spectacular public uprising in Georgia in late 2003 that swept away the corrupt government of Eduard Shevardnadze. Every post-Soviet regime suddenly felt threatened, and Moscow was eager to assume the role of guarantor of their longevity advancing an assertive claim that the states in question form Russia's 'natural' zone of national interests. One part of the problem with this course was its low cost-efficiency, since the shrewd leaders, from Aleksandr Lukashenko in Belarus to Askar Akaev in Kyrgyzstan and Emomali Rakhmonov in Tajikistan, expected material support for acknowledging Russia's leadership. As Dmitri Trenin (2004a) argued, 'Imperialism of any kind – conservative or liberal – is impractical for Russia. It is extremely expensive and involves risks of confrontation with the West. Obsession with geopolitical games disorients and in the final analysis weakens Russia'.

Warnings of this kind were falling on the deaf ears of Putin's courtiers inspired with the neo-imperial vision of 'greatness', but the problem with the 'Authoritarians of the CIS, unite!' course had another part: high risk of failure. The first signal came from Ajaria where Aslan Abashidze, despite strong support from Moscow, was deposed in May 2004 by a combination of pressure from Tbilisi and public discontent in Batumi. A few months later, Abkhazia sent another signal as the Moscow-backed candidate failed to win presidential elections; the clumsily imposed economic sanctions did not win Russia many new supporters in this breakaway quasi-state.[23] The lack of usable instruments for projecting 'imperial' influence was becoming apparent; as Fedor Lukyanov (2004) pointed out,

> Now that Russia has reconciled itself with the role of a regional and not global power and the relations with the CIS countries are finally declared the top priority, it is not clear at all how to implement this priority.

The central focus of this neo/post-imperial policy was on Ukraine since it was plain impossible to construct any kind of plausible 'Empire' without incorporating this most important neighbour and since Russia's 'greatness' of this kind cannot be established without securing its benevolent 'soft' control over the land that constituted a part of its historic 'core'. It was, therefore, inevitable that Moscow would seek to assert its ability to dominate Ukraine in the presidential elections of November 2004.[24] This interference was clearly counter-productive and aggravated further by the PR miscalculations and clumsy tactical mistakes resulting from the quality of policy-making in the Kremlin.[25] The stakes for the 'Empire' project were raised even higher when Putin made the victory of the 'pro-Russian' candidate a matter of personal prestige. While the split of Ukraine into the Russia-oriented East and South and the EU-oriented West and Centre was perceived by the Putin's court as a probable and basically acceptable option, the possibility that sustained and peaceful mass protests would be a decisive force was simply inconceivable.[26]

38   *Three backgrounds*

The shock of the defeat in Moscow was devastating. The claims of the humiliated 'political technologists' that Victor Yushchenko had prevailed due to massive support from the West were perhaps in tune with Putin's predilection to deny own mistakes and suspect 'enemy' intrigues behind every setback,[27] but a direct consequence was that Russia's positions as a 'Great Power' were deeply undermined. As the next 'coloured revolution' hit Kyrgyzstan in March 2005, the project centred on reconstituting an 'Empire' was radically revised so that energy ties acquired prime importance, and mercantilism became the key principle of 'non-brotherly' relations inside the Commonwealth of Independent States (CIS). At that stage, the Kremlin's efforts aimed at reaffirming Russia's 'greatness' were reformatted again with the increased emphasis on the idea of 'Civilization'.

Camouflaging the retreat from democracy as guarding Russia's 'Civilization'

Disappointed in the treacherous ways of post-Soviet regimes and alarmed by the frontal political collision with the West during the Ukrainian calamity, Putin's team concluded that Russia's 'greatness' could only be asserted by adding an emphasis on the concept of 'Civilization'. Gleb Pavlovsky (2005a), one of the architects of the political fiasco in Ukraine, formulated the idea: 'Russia defines itself as a European state which at the same time is also a civilization – a carrier of its own variation of the absolute values'.[28] What made the shift possible was the turn of the tide of 'coloured revolutions' after the May 2005 massacre in Andijan, Uzbekistan, which Moscow approved unequivocally as a legitimate response to a 'terrorist attack'.[29] What made it necessary, however, was the conclusion that Russia could be made safe from the threat of revolutionary regime change only by applying systematically tough preventive measures aimed at decapitating and suppressing every network of political opposition. This directive was to be implemented on the regional level as well because the October 2005 uprising in Nalchik, Kabardino-Balkaria, in many ways resembled the Andijan drama (Derluguian, 2005a).

The 'civilization' guidelines have never been drawn with much precision, but the passion has clearly increased in the aftermath of the 'orange' triumph in Kiev when the risk of 'import of revolution' was assessed as alarmingly high.[30] In the oddly shaped construct of counter-revolutionary 'Civilization', the ethno-nationalist 'pillar' (corresponding to Uvarov's *narodnost*) was the least prominent with only occasional observations from the Kremlin that 'the Russians for 500 years have been the state-forming nation'.[31] Putin's courtiers saw the potential value of fanning 'patriotism' with ethnic trumpets but were aware of the risks and so preferred to leave the field to the quasi-opposition parties like *Rodina* (Motherland) or misnamed 'liberal-democrats' led by Vladimir Zhirinovsky, who eagerly appropriated slogans like 'We are for the poor, we are for the Russians.'

Such cautious 'experimentation' stopped well short of provoking major

The dream of new 'greatness' 39

ethno-political conflicts, for instance, with Tatarstan or even Kalmykia, but brought a steady rise of xenophobia and small-scale ethnic violence across Russia. Human rights NGOs tried to raise awareness of these tendencies, but the Kremlin was not inclined to listen to warnings from such quarters. The official response to the rise of racial gang attacks targeting migrants from Central Asia or students from Africa had remained low-key until the anti-Chechen *pogrom* in Kondopoga, Karelia, in September 2006. Putin's instruction to protect the interests of 'indigenous' population shows that ethnically driven violence is perceived as a lesser evil than social protests and even a useful diversion of the accumulating anger in the society that offers little help or hope to vast impoverished groups.[32] This non-policy bears some striking resemblance to the official benevolent neglect of the *pogroms* of the 'black hundreds' some 100 years ago; the marching of nationalist groups in Moscow on the newly established holiday, the National Unity Day, illuminated that historic parallel (Baev, 2005b, 2006j).

Another pillar of the newly constructed Russian 'Civilization' has been shaped by the strengthened union between the state and the Orthodox church. Putin has always shown religious piety, but since early 2005 this personal devotion has acquired the character of a semi-official union; seeking to consolidate it, the Kremlin encouraged the reconciliation with the 'émigré' church outside of Russia (Makarkin, 2007b). As one keen observer pointed out, in the friendly parties, 'it has become quite dangerous to joke or just speak lightly on such topics as the Orthodoxy, its rituals, traditions and politics' (Kolesnikov, 2006a). Turning the church into a de facto part of the state apparatus, Putin has taken care to emphasize a particular respect towards Islam, on one occasion even calling Russia 'the most reliable, trustworthy, and consistent protector of the interests of the Islamic world'.[33] The Russian leadership strongly condemned the publication of 'blasphemous' cartoons in a Danish magazine and then in European newspapers in early 2006.

With all the friendly gestures towards Islam, it is the Orthodox church that has been entrusted with performing a key role in identifying the specific features of the Russian 'Civilization'. The content of this role and the character of these features became clear at the World Council of the Russian People that gathered in Moscow in early April 2006 and adopted the Declaration on Human Rights and Dignity. The thrust of that document was spelled out by Metropolitan Kirill (Smolensk and Kaliningrad) who condemned such features of Western lifestyle as abortion, euthanasia, and homosexualism and asserted that the Western concept of human rights was unsuitable for Russia.[34] Among the 'higher values' that were more in tune with the Russian national character, the faith, morality, sacred symbols, and the concept of Motherland were listed, to the considered approval of the more conservative commentators (Privalov, 2006a).[35] The emerging quasi-religious ideology is rather amorphous, but as Yulia Latynina (2006a) argued, 'the regime does not need an ideology as a collection of rules for action. It needs only PR that would certify that all its actions are right'.

While *narodnost* and Orthodoxy have indeed played mostly auxiliary and

40   *Three backgrounds*

ornamental roles in the 'civilizational' construct, state-centrism or *gosudarstven-nost* has certainly emerged as its main pillar. The absolute value of strengthening the state has been elevated to the status of a quasi-religious dogma often illustrated by the comparisons with the 'anarchy' and 'chaos' of the 1990s. The threats to the present-day stability are portrayed, accordingly, as results of incessant efforts of external 'enemies' who want to reduce Russia to a disorganized state controlled by the 'oligarchs' and maybe even to replay the break-up of the USSR that was, according to Putin (2005e), 'a major geopolitical disaster of the century'.[36] Malcontents who seek to disturb the hard-won 'normalcy' become, by perfectly logical extension, the 'fifth column' and the 'enemies of the state', a status significantly different from merely the opposition to the regime.[37] This recasting of political struggle into an eschatological battle between 'good' and 'evil' transforms the system of power into an absolutely rigid structure that can be altered only through a cataclysmic crisis – and so Putin's scheduled departure in 2008 has acquired the shape of a catastrophe foretold. Paradoxically, the achievement of maximum regime stability has made a revolution necessary for overcoming the political *zastoi* (stagnation and passivity) and generating a new modernization impulse; as Lilia Shevtsova (2006a) argues, 'the way out of this type of regime cannot be found without its defeat, but its continuation inevitably leads to a crisis'. At the same time, the rise of 'patriotism' leads to a situation where, as an editorial in *Kommersant* speculated, 'a national-populist political project in Russia appears to have far better prospects than any "orange revolution" with social-democratic slogans' ('From Koptsev to Kondopoga', 2006).

The logic of the over-centralized system of power 'liberated' from any institutional checks and balances has determined not only the identification of the state with its leader (reinventing the *L'etat c'est moi* motto) but also the escalation of ambitions from *gosudarstvennost* to *derzhavnost*. The key notion here is the *suverennost* that is understood not in the narrow sense of 'sovereignty' but in a more grandiose way as the ability of a state to determine its own destiny. The particular PR-spin in semi-official commentary is placed on Russia's ability to defend its 'civilizational uniqueness' against the pressure to adapt Western models, as implied by Surkov's (2006a) definition: 'Sovereignty is a political synonym of competitiveness'. Russian political system was accordingly defined as 'sovereign democracy', which in essence means rejection of such 'alien' prescriptions as limiting the executive power through empowering other branches or guarding the freedom of press. Reconstituting a Russian 'Civilization' in the final analysis turns out to be just adding legitimacy and a bit of *grandeur* to what Dmitri Furman (2004) described as Putin's 'bashful authoritarianism'.

Conclusions

The gradual evolution from the 'Great Power' to the 'Empire' and to the 'Civilization' in the pursuit of Russia's 'greatness', as described above, does not imply that one aim or slogan is abandoned with the adoption of the next. In fact, as Putin's second term is approaching the scheduled finish, all three ideas are in

The dream of new 'greatness' 41

use, while the added emphasis on 'Civilization' becomes more pronounced. Russia's chairmanship at the July 2006 G8 Strelna summit was supposed to deliver the final proof of its 'Great Power' status, and the emphasis on upholding the CIS in Putin's May 2006 address to the parliament confirmed that 'Empire-building' was still a main political task. In the much-debated Munich speech, Putin (2007a) lashed against US unilateralism and demanded for Russia a place in the concert of 'great powers' since 'Russia is a country with a history that spans more than a thousand years and has practically always used the privilege to carry out an independent foreign policy.' Just a month later, however, he saluted the EU (Putin, 2007c) and invoked the authority of Dostoevsky: 'The great writer sensed perfectly that Europe would never be itself in the world without Russia and, at the same time, that Russia would never cease its "longing for Europe"'. This manoeuvring could not undo the fact that the shift towards reconstituting Russia's own 'Civilization' was counter-productive for achieving 'greatness' in other ways. That clash of guidelines was targeted by US Vice-President Cheney (2006) who emphasized that 'Russia has a choice to make', expressing hope for a 'return to democratic reform' but adding a warning: 'None of us believes that Russia is fated to become an enemy.'[38]

Following chapters of the book examine in much detail the interplay between the desire to restore Russia's 'greatness' and its military and energy policies; one proposition, however, belongs at the end of this 'background' chapter, which suggests that different traits of 'greatness' are connected with different elements of military and energy power. Thus, the claims for 'Great Power' status are underpinned by the nuclear arsenal, while the attempts to rebuild 'Empire' requite usable power-projection capabilities. Similarly, energy dialogues with the EU and US are key parts of 'Great Power' politics, while energy exports to post-Soviet states are closely linked to the policy of 'Empire'-building. Securing effective Kremlin control over the oil-and-gas sectors and enforcing stability in the turbulent North Caucasus are necessary for giving credibility to the imagined 'Civilization'. It remains to be seen what combination of these poorly compatible elements would constitute Putin's ideological heritage and whether he would be able to orchestrate the transfer of power without falling into the trap of 'Fortress Russia'.

Part II

Deadlocked energy-security dilemmas

> Nobody in this country understands the global energy security issues better than Putin.
>
> Shuvalov (2006), Putin's aid and G8 'sherpa'

The proposition that the energy business and, more specifically, the export of hydrocarbons pertain directly to the security agenda is in fact quite new in the Russian political thinking, despite the direct causal link between the drop in oil prices in the late 1980s and the collapse of the USSR. The sharp spasm of financial and political crisis in August 1998 confirmed that shrinking of export revenues continued to be a massive security challenge, but it was only the spectacular climb of oil prices in 2004–2005 that prompted a shift to a proactive application of the energy instruments. The net amount of energy that Russia exported did not increase in any meaningful quantity, but the value of this export became such that it was indeed possible to conceptualize the use of 'energy weapon'.

In this 'securitization' of energy, even the quite traditional interplay between the energy sector and the military–industrial complex has acquired new intensity as the seriously strengthened oil-and-gas lobby demands money for investing in the former but shows little interest in 'feeding' the latter. One area where energy and security have been tightly intertwined since mid-1990s is the Caspian, but here also the spike in oil prices has sharply raised the stakes in the geopolitical 'games' and so necessitated a re-evaluation of Russia's security interests. The Russian leadership has discovered another difficult dilemma in this interplay: the desire to strengthen the system of security alliances in the post-Soviet space has come into conflict with the intention to sell gas at maximum possible prices. The new energy 'mercantilism', while an entirely pragmatic approach, is not really compatible with the burdensome but still appealing role of security 'guarantor', and the Kremlin has agonized over the choice.

4 The trickle of the oil money for the military

The nostalgia for Soviet times typical for the second half of Putin's 'era' includes, besides many sentimental second thoughts, one clear proposition: the revenues from exporting energy should not be 'eaten' through consumer spending but must be invested in building military muscle. Only dim reflections remain on the entirely irrational scale of transfer of resources towards maintaining the colossal and, at the end of the day, useless military machine. There are, nevertheless, widely shared perceptions that in the first post-Soviet decade, the Armed Forces were neglected and allowed to deteriorate to a dangerous degree, while Russia's status, ability to withstand external threats, and even territorial integrity would ultimately depend upon possessing usable military power.

The economic demilitarization achieved during the 1990s was swift and profound, but the 'therapeutic' effect of that 'shock' was by no means evident. The High Command was instructed to submit the absolutely minimal requests for funding that was mercilessly cut down and 'sequestrated' despite the heavy burden of the First Chechen War and the pains of the post-war healing. The mammoth military industry abruptly lost its vast 'market', since the Armed Forces stopped most acquisition programmes, and had to find other customers for whatever goods it was outpouring.[1] In the public eyes, that military–industrial catastrophe was exacerbated by the greedy 'oligarchs' who captured the most profitable energy assets and denied the state not only its due income but even taxes.

President Putin was expected to reverse all three of these disastrous trends – and he indeed committed himself to rebuilding the military might that would 'guarantee Russia's security and territorial integrity no matter what the scenario', as he emphasized in the 2006 address to the parliament (Putin, 2006b). This chapter will first examine the results of the much-expanded financing of the military made possible by the huge increase of the oil-and-gas revenues. It will then take a look at the defence industry attempting to assess to what degree the new funding has contributed to reconnecting it to the Armed Forces that are supposed to modernize and generate strong new demand. Finally, it will address one aspect of the complicated issue of expanding state ownership in the energy sector seeking to establish whether and to what degree have the remaining and newly appointed 'oligarchs' become more 'patriotic' and inclined to finance security-related projects.

46 *Deadlocked energy-security dilemmas*

The 'black hole' of the military budget

Embarking on the course of accelerated reforms in the first weeks of 1992, Yegor Gaidar and his team of 'young reformers' harboured few illusions that they would be able to convince the 'top brass' to rationalize their demand for resources so that the Armed Forces would become affordable for the dramatically reduced state budget. They also accepted for a fact of life that it was impossible to gather and empower a team of military reformers since President Yeltsin kept the cadre policy under his personal control pursuing a hidden agenda that came into play in October 1993, when tanks decided his victory over the mutinous parliament. Gaidar had to proceed on the basis of the proposition that the pain of irreversibly reduced supply of resources would force the military to adapt their rigid structures to the new realities.[2] Characteristically, another team of 'young reformers' organized by Yeltsin in early 1998 around Prime Minister Sergei Kiriyenko acted on much the same proposition for the short time it had until the August financial meltdown.[3]

The military, however, opted for a different survival strategy based on preserving every shrunk- and hollowed-out structure that was able to withstand the severe under-funding instead of selecting a few that would have been worth keeping at full strength. The High Command pursued that self-destructive course through the 1990s and placed all its expectations on the new president as the defence expenditures fell to their lowest level of 2.34 per cent of the gross domestic product (GDP) in 1999. Putin felt the pressure of these expectations all the more immediately as his presidency was hanging in balance: the new war in Chechnya was in progress – and only the military were able to deliver the victory of whatever sorts. The war was not that expensive per se, since next to nothing was spent on rebuilding the thoroughly devastated 'subject' of the Russian Federation.[4] Unlike in 1995, the invasion made it possible to increase spending on defence because the society – swept by 'patriotic' propaganda – was for once prepared to grant a larger share of resources to the army. Putin was careful not to overtax the uncertain mobilization and prioritized the immediate need in raising officers' salaries making sure that the accumulated arrears were fully covered. At the same time, he postponed the investments in 'hardware' and answered to the demands of the 'Chechen generals' by reducing the spending on strategic forces without any corresponding increase in procurement of conventional weapons.[5]

The gradual increase of the state budget's income related directly to the 'healthy' growth of the world oil prices helped Putin to deliver tangible rewards to the military without squeezing other sensitive programmes. Nevertheless, he felt obliged to stress at the Security Council meeting in early 2003: 'Our defence outlays must not fall on the people as a burden, obstruct economic growth and the resolution of social problems'.[6] In the course of that year, however, a significant shift in economic–security perceptions occurred under the impact of factors as dissimilar as the triumphant US invasion in Iraq and the cruel prosecution of *Yukos* and its owner Mikhail Khodorkovsky. By the end of that year, the

The trickle of the oil money for the military   47

cautious assumptions that the state budget would stabilize had given way to much bolder expectations that the rise of the oil prices was not a spike but a firm trend and so the distributive power of the state would continue to grow accordingly. Putin's court was not seriously worried about the 'technicalities' of re-election – but it suddenly discovered opportunities to set ambitious goals for the second term and provide the necessary resources for their implementation.

Some experts at that time developed detailed proposals for a meaningful military reform that could have been swiftly advanced with only moderate increases of defence expenditures to the long-earmarked 3 per cent level of the GDP (Arbatov and Romashkin, 2003; Arbatov, 2004). Putin, however, had a different idea; so – as described in Chapter 1 – in late 2003, he approved the thesis that the period of reforms in the army was over and in the 2004 address to the parliament, he established that modernization of the Armed Forces was one of the key state priorities. In essence, this change of guidelines amounted to the decision to buy some usable military capabilities by investing new money into the old structures. Putin was certainly aware that the result could not mature overnight but had high expectations regarding the near prospects, since sustained 25–30 per cent increases in funding accompanied by minor reductions in personnel strength and significantly reduced burden from Chechnya should have guaranteed impressive results.

Defence Minister Sergei Ivanov who previously had to negotiate down the demands of the 'top brass' and convince the officer corps that their predicament was taken into account, now was expected to guide the new momentum. His immediate attention was focused on the generously financed combat training, but the pompously staged exercises were marred by embarrassing accidents, from the collision of two Mi-24 helicopters in August 2003 to the failure to launch ballistic missiles from two nuclear submarines in February 2004. As the new 30 per cent increase in military spending was announced for 2005, experts issued strong warnings that the money would be mostly wasted, while the Account Chamber discovered large-scale misappropriations.[7] These signals were ignored, and the 2007 state budget envisaged the 24.5 per cent growth of the defence expenditures, which was high by any standard but still below average as compared with the total expansion of state expenditures by 26.5 per cent.[8] The increase in military acquisitions was planned to reach nearly 30 per cent and that, in financial terms, would signify the largest 'defence order' ever.

A big part of the problem was the closed character of the military budget that was presented to and approved by the State Duma as a sum total of a dozen or so of the most basic parameters, while only a few more 'confidential' details were presented to the members of the Committee on Defence who had the necessary security clearance (Solovyev and Tsimbal, 2007). That shroud of secrecy answered perfectly the Kremlin's demands for keeping the decision-making processes absolutely closed, but it also secured for the High Command a position of minimal accountability. The experts were strongly discouraged from looking into details by a series of Federal Security Service (FSB) investigations against scientists who allegedly revealed some 'state secrets'; the journalists

48 *Deadlocked energy-security dilemmas*

were only able to point out that 'the budget is not militaristic; it is made for thieves' (Latynina, 2002).[9]

Another part of the problem was the inability to determine priorities in modernization coupled with the pronounced desire to purchase as many new weapon systems as possible. It was the acquisition budget that increased the most in absolute figures (from 50 billion roubles in 2000 to 240 billions in 2006 and 300 billions in 2007) with annual increases up to 40 per cent that, in principle, could have sufficed for starting a massive rearmament. The resources, however, were spread among hundreds of projects that were reconfigured and rescaled every year depending upon the skill of their lobbyists; so the total deliveries announced annually by the Defence Minister remained truly pitiful.[10] The Kremlin rediscovered the value of nuclear deterrence; so, the funding for the programmes on new strategic missiles and submarines that had taken a dip in the first half of the decade expanded again – but the returns were disappointingly low (as described in Chapter 7). In the conventional forces, the system of acquisition was in permanent reorganization so that only the projects that generated nice profits for insiders, such as repairs and upgrades by affiliated workshops, were safe (Tsyganok, 2005b).

Yet another key part of the problem, often hidden by 'muscular' rhetoric and impressive figures of total increases in funding, was the fact that Putin remained reluctant to preside over a real-terms reallocation of resources from the energy sector to the military build-up. Arriving to the conclusion that the inflow of 'petro-roubles' would not dry up anytime soon, he sought to channel only so much of it towards the defence needs that neither the interests of oil-and-gas producers would be seriously squeezed nor numerous other demands on the 'oil rent' would be completely neglected. Attuned to the shifts in public opinion, his court correctly identified that the society was not ready for any kind of sacrifices for the Armed Forces, whatever the post-Beslan demands for a victory in the war against terror. Responding to escalating expectations, Putin in late 2005 announced an initiative for generous new funding for 'national projects' in the most socially sensitive areas, like health care, education, and housing, but not a single additional rouble was promised to the military. In the 2006 address to the parliament (Putin, 2006b), giving an extensive positive evaluation of the Armed Forces' posture, he nevertheless asserted: 'We must not resolve our defence issues at the expense of economic and social development. This is a dead end road that ultimately leaves a country's reserves exhausted. There is no future in it'. In the budget guidelines for 2008–2010, the key emphasis was on reducing the direct redistribution of the oil-and-gas revenues through the state budget (Butrin and Netreba, 2007). And in the 2007 address to the parliament, despite taking a confrontational stance against North Atlantic Treaty Organization (NATO), he again insisted on keeping defence efforts 'commensurate with our economic possibilities' (Putin, 2007d).

A careful examination of the fruits of the three years of expanded financing of the military structures could have provided data for re-focusing further efforts; there was however hardly any intention to conduct such an investigation in February 2007, when Sergei Ivanov reassured the State Duma in steady improvement of the Armed Forces capabilities, as it turned out just a week before being promoted to the post of First Deputy Prime Minister (Plugatarev, 2007a). The Kremlin did not need any hard evidence that would support the conclusion that funding on such a level could have brought a serious improvement in combat capabilities if it was combined with a far-reaching military reform. Without meaningful reforms, a far greater allocation of resources, perhaps indeed to the scale of 3.5 per cent of the GDP, was necessary in order to achieve moderately significant results. Putin, however, was content to continue with propping up dysfunctional structures and staging public relations (PR) campaigns around hollow military exercises (Tsyganok, 2006). The State Armaments Programme for 2007–2015 approved in 2006 at the grand scale of 4.9 trillion roubles is trumpeted as a plan for a far-reaching military modernization, but the failure of the still on-going programme for 2001–2010 is carefully camouflaged. The incontrovertible proof of this failure is the fact that only 20 per cent of arms in the current inventory could be defined as 'modern', and this share could increase by the end of this decade only if the definition of 'modern' is conveniently stretched to cover the Soviet designs of the 1980s (Rastopshin, 2007).

Reassembling the military–industrial complex

The steadily expanding 'defence order' is supposed to constitute the essential link between the Armed Forces and hundreds of industrial enterprises that are listed as elements of the 'military–industrial complex' (VPK in the Russian abbreviation). Vladimir Putin presented his vision of the VPK prospects a week before the 2000 presidential elections in a remarkable speech in Nizhny Novgorod, one of the bastions of defence industry (Putin, 2000). He acknowledged the accumulated problems but asserted that the available capacity 'is quite sufficient for both maintaining the deployed weapon systems and for equipping the Russian army with modern arms that have no analogues in the world'. It came quite clear in that address that the future president saw the VPK not as a major cause of the collapse of the USSR but as the backbone of Russian industry.

That vision was seriously detached from the reality since the VPK had not just 'suffered losses in the transitional period' but had practically ceased to exist in any integrated form. As the Armed Forces stopped to order new armaments back in the early 1990s and began building bad debts, the multiple Soviet-era connections between the military and the defence industry were irreparably broken.[11] At the same time, the cooperative ties between dozens of enterprises involved in production of complex weapon systems lost economic rationale, while in some cases former partners became separated by new state borders. Putin quickly approved some far-reaching plans, like the Armaments Programme for 2001–2010 and a package of documents on reforming the VPK, but could put only very limited money behind them; so, the producers remained unmoved. As one insightful expert observed, 'the VPK is dominated by ideological vacuum and institutional chaos'.[12] For most enterprises, the main

50 *Deadlocked energy-security dilemmas*

rationale for being listed as 'defence unit' was protection from bankruptcy and the opportunity to engage in profitable sell-off of the 'mobilization reserves' they had maintained since the Soviet times, while additional profits came from renting out some of their floor space or filling out false employment lists that granted to young men protection from the draft (Shlykov, 2004).

There was, however, a group of successful companies that managed to survive the collapse of the VPK system by re-orienting towards exports and establishing own reputation among picky foreign customers. Putin was quick to see the potential value of this market, but, unlike Yeltsin, he sought to re-establish control over these profitable enterprises. One part of his policy, elaborated during a visit to the NPO *Mashinostroenie*, a major producer of missiles, in late 2002, was to encourage these companies to incorporate independent sub-contractors transforming themselves into integrated 'holdings' (Sokut, 2002c). It was much easier for the Defence Ministry to assert effective control over such 'holdings', particularly since the hostile takeovers that accompanied their expansion generated protracted conflicts, often with political ramifications.[13] Another part of Putin's plan was to consolidate the role of the state in regulating the export of arms, so that the profits would go not to the companies but to a special department of the Defence Ministry that would distribute orders and funds. To that end, Andrei Belyaninov, former director of *Rosoboronexport*, was in April 2004 appointed the director of the Federal Agency for Defence Order, which was to secure better balance between export deliveries and responses to the needs of the Armed Forces.[14] Sergei Chemezov, the new head of *Rosoboronexport*, had, however, his own ideas about this balance – and also his own direct channel into Putin's inner circle (Myasnikov, 2007b).

The consolidation policy was moderately successful in 2003–2004, particularly in terms of achieving a steady growth of arms export, and was expected to move from strength to strength in 2005–2007 as financing of the 'defence order' was further increasing. This, however, did not happen, much to Putin's irritation, even if hidden behind statements that 'this year saw the start of mass defence equipment procurement for the Defence Ministry's needs' (Putin, 2006b). The deliveries, contrary to that self-deceiving assertion, remained on the same very low level (as described in Chapter 1), and a key reason behind that was the firm set orientation of the key producers on external markets, as the arms export in 2005 reached the record level of US$6.1 billion and increased further to 6.5 billion in 2006.[15] The steady strengthening of the rouble caused by the inflow of 'petro-dollars' resulted in fast increases of prices on weapon systems and spare parts; estimates of the 'internal' inflation in the VPK technological cycles reached 25–30 per cent, which effectively nullified the increases in defence expenditures.[16]

The export-oriented companies remained unresponsive to the needs of the Russian Armed Forces as their orders were insignificant; many other companies listed as the VPK 'members' were stuck in dire economic straits.[17] That cast a shadow over the ambitious Armaments Programme for 2007–2015 approved in mid-2006, particularly since the mechanism of its implementation was not suffi-

The trickle of the oil money for the military 51

ciently developed.[18] For instance, assessing the guidelines for the shipbuilding industry, experts concluded that the programme 'does not provide for keeping the Navy on the level of minimal sufficiency' (Puchnin, 2006). Basically, a significantly greater transfer of resources from the energy sector to the VPK is necessary in order to re-connect its parts and re-establish the functional interdependence between the military and the industry that is supposed to deliver on their requirements. As Vitaly Shlykov (2005) argued:

> The raw materials complex has created a parallel economy where there is no place for the VPK. The expectations of the Russian leadership that the impoverished defence industry would be able not only to survive by exporting arms but also to finance the rearmament of the Russian army with weapons of a new generation are truly odd.

Putin indeed remained reluctant to exploit the oil-and-gas industries for the benefit of the VPK, which in principle would have been entirely compatible with his 'modernization' rhetoric. The critical issue of obsolesce of up to 75 per cent of the equipment and technology in the 'strategic' enterprises was never taken up, but the question that did receive much attention was the further consolidation and centralization of the key elements of the VPK. The main focus was on uniting all companies involved in aircraft production, including *Sukhoi, Ilyushin,* and MiG, into one huge corporation that could be competitive on the world market. Despite Putin's personal involvement, this aggrandizement proceeded painstakingly slow as smaller companies were concerned that *Sukhoi* (with its 50 per cent share in the holding) would twist the cartel-type arrangement to its own favour.[19] The next step along this way was to unite the key industrial assets in shipbuilding with its traditional predominant orientation on naval orders, in one corporation (Gnusarev, 2007).

The central point in the plan for reviving the VPK without overtaxing the energy sector or cutting down on social programmes, however, was the streamlining of the system of defence order that, as Putin proposed back in his 2000 Nizhny Novgorod speech, should be controlled from one office. After experimenting with several committees and personalities, in late 2005 Putin decided to grant the authority to Defence Minister Sergei Ivanov who was promoted to Deputy Prime Minister.[20] This authority was formalized in March 2006, when a permanent Military-Industrial Commission was formed under Ivanov's chairmanship very nearly resembling a 'parallel government' (Ivanov, 2006b; Netreba, 2006). Putin (2006b) assured the parliament: 'I very much hope that this will also have a positive impact on overcoming corruption in the armed forces', but in fact none of his administrative reforms has produced such an impact. Ivanov's role was further strengthened in February 2007 when he was appointed First Deputy Prime Minister with the mandate to give a new impetus to the 'innovative' industrial policy with the particular emphasis on modernizing the VPK (Baev, 2007e). It is by no means certain that Ivanov would be able to make a difference, since his administrative talents are somewhat less than

52 Deadlocked energy-security dilemmas

hugely impressive and his influence is mostly based on the reputation of 'loyal friend' to the president, which is hardly good enough for managing the VPK.

Cadre decide everything, or so it seems

The Ivanov's case exemplifies two major features of Putin's system of power – its extremely narrow political base and the water-tight character of decision-making. While Putin presides over a colossal bureaucratic pyramid and enjoys broad public support, his ability to initiate and carry through meaningful reforms has been in fact quite limited, as the resistance to change in the system increases proportionally to the amount of resources that are available for distribution. One of the key limitations to effective functioning of the government has been Putin's pronounced reluctance to delegate executive authority to ministers and minions, who have only limited amount of his trust, and the obsession with amassing control over all politically significant activity in the presidential office. While the formal system of checks and balances has been reduced to purely decorative functions, the need to have a presidential approval for every step checks the progress of even the most necessary initiatives. The system rewards passivity and punishes dissent.[21]

Arriving to the summit of power through a rather haphazard process, Putin was firm set on eliminating all independent centres of power – and this aim necessarily involved both securing the loyalty of the army and establishing control over the wealth generated by the energy export. These two tasks were interdependent, as the loyalty could not be won by cheap gestures like arriving to Grozny in a fighter jet but had to be bought, and the money in sufficient quantity could only be found through 'nationalizing' a significant part of the profits earned by the oil-and-gas companies. The public opinion was massively against the 'oligarchs', seen as 'parasites' plundering the natural resources for personal enrichment, but Putin – who was delivered to the Kremlin by some of these individuals – knew first-hand that their fortunes could buy too much of political clout. This source of risk to his leadership had to be reduced to the minimum, and the seemingly neutral slogan of keeping the 'oligarchs' at 'equal distance' in real terms meant the intention to take them on a short leash.[22]

The campaign was opened by the swift persecution of media-magnate Vladimir Gusinsky and continued through the expulsion from political arena of the quintessential 'oligarch' Boris Berezovsky, who had seriously overplayed his hand while orchestrating Yeltsin's departure.[23] The main battle, however, was given for the control of GAZPROM, which had remained 'neutral' during the political melee of succession – which certainly was not good enough. In parallel with this protracted battle (as described in Chapter 2), several 'special operations' targeting other energy companies were conducted, for instance the mysterious kidnapping of a top *Lukoil* executive Sergei Kukura in September 2002 (Tavernise, 2002).[24] Putin's primacy was upheld but still remained uncertain; the only way to secure it was found in 'taming' *Yukos* – the company that

The trickle of the oil money for the military   53

demonstrated that it was possible to achieve spectacular success while refusing to play by the Kremlin's new rules.

Strong pressure was applied on its owner Mikhail Khodorkovsky, but he demonstratively refused to bend forcing Putin to escalate the conflict and then to stage a 'show trial'. That ruthlessness made a strong impression on 'dissidents' among the big business but also involved heavy reputation damage and made it necessary for Putin to fire several malcontents, including the head of presidential administration Aleksandr Voloshin, Prime Minister Mikhail Kasyanov, and later presidential advisor Andrei Illarionov. Quite probably, Putin did not plan for such a major coup but insisted on achieving a decisive victory, and even 'overkill' as envy and irritation gave way to personal vengeance. While feeling betrayed by those who opposed the destruction of *Yukos*, he also had reasons to suspect that he was set up by those who pushed for 're-nationalization' of the 'stolen' assets. Such suspicions could have increased as Putin had to cover with his authority the faults of his minions who were eagerly dismembering the oil giant and scrambling for the spoils. The only response available to him was to play one group of 'loyalists' against another, which resulted in a protracted squabble where GAZPROM was outmanoeuvred by smaller but utterly unscrupulous *Rosneft* (Baev, 2005n). That game, however, was played on him as well, as the emboldened courtiers became adept at manipulating the boss by pushing the buttons of vanity and obsession with control. Thus, in a matter of three weeks in June 2006, one intrigue brought a downfall of Prosecutor General Vladimir Ustinov, who had allegedly cherished too high political ambitions, but another intrigue convinced Putin to appoint him the justice minister in order to preserve the Kremlin balance (Radzikhovsky, 2006c).

In retrospect, those cut-throat quarrels are far less exciting than they seemed to observers, but they did make a profound impact on the dynamics of the energy sector. It might have appeared to Putin that taming Yeltsin's era 'oligarchs' and replacing the incorrigible ones with his own appointees with impeccable FSB pedigrees would guarantee state interests and provide for channelling the resources towards the goals of modernization, including the Armed Forces (Baev, 2007c). What really happened was a series of bitter squabbles among his lieutenants, who sought to 'regulate' the financial flows, and progressive demoralization of the 'oilmen', who were helpless to check the greedy *chekists* that had invaded their habitat. The state indeed claimed a far greater share of the oil-and-gas wealth, but the over-taxed companies became reluctant to invest in their basic assets, while the emphasis on increasing the state ownership of the oil sector resulted in a further decrease of its efficiency and stagnation of production.[25]

In principle, the vastly increased confiscation of profits in the energy sector allows the state to pump money into the army and the VPK, but the strength of intimately close relations between the Kremlin and GAZPROM, as well as *Rosnfet*, determines quite different priorities in resource allocation. The FSB, being a party to these relations through its multiple networks, is able to advance its parochial interests and convincingly 'recommend' the very receptive private

54 *Deadlocked energy-security dilemmas*

oil companies to make contributions to such 'good causes' as the struggle against terrorism and to donate to particular 'charities'.[26] Defence Minister and then First Deputy Prime Minister Sergei Ivanov, despite being Putin's close friend, has no place in the Kremlin–GAZPROM and *Rosneft*–FSB alliances, and the military cadres, unlike the *chekists*, have not been welcome in the sprouting networks. The Armed Forces, thus, have been effectively cut out of the revenue management and have few opportunities to advance their claims. The VPK has few effective lobbyists in the presidential administration, while *Rosoboronexport* under Sergei Chemezov has its own political agenda and so is quite stingy about sharing the profits from arms export with the producers. Staying away from the clashes of the key Kremlin clans, Ivanov could have fancied his chances as an 'outsider' in the competition for winning Putin's blessing as a successor, but the lack of access to the incalculable and unaccounted extra-budgetary financial flows is certainly a major handicap.

Conclusions

At the start of his second presidential term, Putin made a claim that the Armed Forces had emerged from the era of decay and 'reforms' and entered into the period of stable development; by the closure of the term, he was able to present some supporting evidence. Indeed, the total increase of the defence budget to 820 billion roubles in 2007 from 140 billions in 2000 appears hugely impressive, particularly since the nominal value of the rouble in US dollars remained unchanged. On a closer look, however, the claim transforms into a mix of half-truths, PR-spin and self-deception.

Discovering the depth of crisis in the army at the start of the Second Chechen War, Putin had a choice of launching far-reaching reforms or reproducing the Soviet model; the first option would have required an increase of military expenditures to approximately 3 per cent of the GDP; the second would have been perhaps twice more expensive. Putin postponed the choice and faced it again in 2004 when the 'oil money' began to pour into Russia's coffers, while the war in Chechnya began to 'normalize', at least as far as the military were concerned. Fancying neither of the two options, Putin had charted a middle course that amounted to piling money over the deep-rooted problems and building virtual might useful primarily for politicized military exercises and demonstrations. Behind the polished façade, the rot continued occasionally breaking to the surface in news about suicide or fratricide in the barracks or accidents involving nuclear systems.[27]

Putin's key word for the Armed Forces has been 'modernization', which meant essentially the reconstitution of Soviet-type ties between the military and the defence industry, albeit on a reduced scale as the total strength of the Armed Forces has remained at about 20 per cent of the USSR level in the 1980s. However, the basic guidelines for maintaining the Armed Forces at slightly above 1,000,000 personnel and for keeping the military expenditures in the range of 2.6–2.8 per cent of the GDP were proven to be incompatible with the

The trickle of the oil money for the military   55

aim of upgrading the combat capabilities (Arbatov, 2006a). Moreover, it has turned out that the VPK cannot function on such a level as hundreds of enterprises have become empty shells protected from bankruptcy, while a few successful 'holdings' have clearly prioritized external markets. In 2005 and 2006, the nominal value of the 'defence order' was 30 per cent more than the value of arms export, but the number of major weapon systems delivered and scheduled for delivering to the Russian Armed Forces was and is certain to remain lower by the order of magnitude than those exported to such key customers as Algeria, China, India, Iran, and Venezuela.

As the breathtaking run of world oil prices continued and started to be perceived not as a stroke of luck but as a long-term trend, Putin's political priorities have increasingly shifted towards the energy sector. It would have been a bad idea indeed to overtax it and pump the resources into militarization, reproducing the pattern that brought the USSR to bankruptcy just 15 years ago. Refusing to mark that anniversary, Putin has been quite aware of the risk; his own policy, however, involves a quite similar level of over-taxation but the appropriated revenues are channelled not towards the build-up of military might but to supporting a colossal and still-expanding bureaucratic pyramid that looms large as the transmogrified 'vertical' of executive power. The Armed Forces, in the meanwhile, are entirely dependent on the financial life support system that has to deliver more and more resources in order to keep the military in the same dismal state. This pattern is not any more sustainable than the Soviet hypermilitarization, but at least Putin has made sure that in any future crisis the Army would hardly be a useful instrument.

5 Counter-terrorism and the Caspian oil games

The shift of Russian energy interests towards the Caspian area has started already in the mid-1990s, but in the first few years, the discord between corporate strategies and uncoordinated activities of federal bureaucracies prevented the emergence of a coherent state policy. By the end of that decade, two features of the shifting political and security landscape of that non-region, situated between several conflict zones, had clearly manifested themselves. The first one was the diffuse nature of interactions that did not resemble at all the 'Great Game' model but involved great many small games and petty intrigues played by state, sub-state, and non-state actors. The second feature was the reasonably safe environment for investment with significantly lower level of risk of violent interstate as well as intra-state conflicts than predicted.[1]

Vladimir Putin, assuming unexpected leadership in late 1999, was not entirely comfortable with the first feature and not at all convinced that the second one would last, with the new war in Chechnya gearing up. He took energy interests very seriously and saw perhaps not the need in protecting them but rather a range of possibilities for their advancement by employing Russia's traditional source of strength, the military. Translating these possibilities into new guidelines for the Caspian policy was the agenda for the special meeting of Russian Security Council on 21 April 2000.[2] Pragmatism moderated ambitions in these guidelines, so the 'energy–military' nexus would have probably remained limited if not the massive alteration of the security situation since mid-September 2001. The main epicentre was hard-to-reach Afghanistan, so as Cornell (2006, p. 29) argued, 'With strategic access crucial to the prosecution of the war, the republics of Central Asia took centre stage in the most important conflict to confront the United States in decades'. While by no means a 'Caspian war', this engagement had a massive resonance; one pre-Iraq RAND analysis concluded: 'The likelihood of Army deployment to Central Asia with a mission that is internal to the region has increased greatly in the post-September 11 security environment, at least for the near term'.[3]

Counter-terrorism has become the prime strategic rational for the swift 'securitization' of the energy agenda in the Caspian area, from which both Russia and the United States expected to benefit. It appears possible to suggest, nearly six years into the campaign, that on balance Russia has been able to collect more

Counter-terrorism and the Caspian oil games 57

dividends as the United States struggled with keeping the engagement in Afghanistan on track while concentrating efforts and resources on the multi-faceted war in Iraq.[4] The overall size of that dividend, however, has proven to be moderate, since the usefulness of military instruments in the Caspian has turned out to be quite limited and the drive to 'securitization' has gradually exhausted its power. This chapter first examines Russia's continuing military build-up in the context of persistent Caspian security tensions; it then attempts to identify Moscow's aims in orchestrating the interplay between counter-terrorism and counter-revolution; finally, it looks into the special case of Dagestan, which has more relevance to the Caspian security than is commonly assumed.

Gunboat diplomacy and the Caspian boundaries

One of the key international controversies in the region that Putin inherited from the 1990s was the protracted dispute about dividing the Caspian seabed and waters into national sectors.[5] Seeking to achieve a quick breakthrough, he appointed experienced Viktor Kaliyzhny (former minister for fuel and energy) as a special envoy with the mandate to hammer out a compromise paying particular respect to the Iranian claims. In order to add some muscle to this 'shuttle diplomacy', naval exercises were staged as a background for Putin's visit to Baku in January 2001.[6] These diplomatic efforts and displays of the 'small stick' were upset in July 2001, when Iran sent a couple of patrol crafts (inevitably labelled as 'gunboats') and a jet fighter to chase a BP-owned exploration vessel out of the disputed waters that Azerbaijan claimed as its 'indisputable' possession.[7] That exercise in 'gunboat diplomacy' (which was not repeated once in the next six years) not only created an uproar in the Western media but convinced Moscow that a targeted application of a small force could make a big difference, since that promising sea area was completely closed for development.

Putin kept pushing for a summit meeting of the Caspian five, despite Kaliyzhny's reports about irreconcilable differences and deadlocked arguments. After several postponements, the summit took place in Ashgabat, Turkmenistan, on 24 April 2002 – and did not produce any last-minute compromises as the political will was predictably absent (Romanova, 2002). That discord was portrayed as a failure of Russian policy and Putin himself expressed deep disappointment about the 'irrational claims' of his counterparts. With hindsight, however, it is possible to suggest that he achieved exactly the result he wanted. Indeed, an agreement, however imperfect, would have paved the way for removing a major security problem from the agenda and, perhaps, to demilitarization of the 'five owners' sea. The lack of agreement, to the contrary, preserved the security challenge and made it possible for Moscow to put into play its main trump card – the Caspian Flotilla.

It was to the base of this naval grouping in Astrakhan that Putin headed from Ashgabat and ordered Admiral Kuroedov, the commander-in-chief of the navy, to organize in just three months time large-scale exercises 'maximum close to

58 Deadlocked energy-security dilemmas

real combat'.[8] The unprecedented exercises (the name was never revealed) took place in the first two weeks of August and involved 10,500 troops and 60 combat and auxiliary ships. Besides 'politically correct' aims such as search and rescue, fire drill, and hot pursuit of caviar poachers, the exercises also included the landing of a marine battalion for exterminating a designated 'terrorist band' blocked in a coastal area by army units.[9] There were no aims directly related to hydrocarbon production or border disputes, but Defence Minister Sergei Ivanov observed the naval manoeuvring from an oil platform owned by *Lukoil*. As I argued at that time, 'it is not the oil as such that is the target for the military might. What Russia aspires to is the role of security guarantor/provider for the inherently unstable region' (Baev, 2002d).

The resonance from these war games was perhaps not quite what Moscow expected as Kazakhstan and Iran expressed in no uncertain terms their disapproval of such threatening activities. The exercises of this scale and duration have not been repeated since, but Putin has made sure that his order to increase Russia's military presence in the Caspian was implemented.[10] In 2003, the Caspian Flotilla received a new flagship, missile frigate *Tatarstan*; the 77th Marine brigade based in Kaspiisk received new landing crafts and artillery and was gradually relieved from combat duties in Chechnya; a new series of gunboats was launched in the St. Petersburg shipyard, with the first ship *Astrakhan* arriving to the Caspian in 2006 and two other, *Kaspiisk* and *Makhachkala*, scheduled for 2007 and 2008.[11] Seeking to emphasize this superior force, Putin met with the representatives of the Caspian states at a security conference in July 2005 on board of the *Tatarstan* (Blagov, 2005a).

While building its military muscle, Moscow took care to resolve its border problems with Azerbaijan and Kazakhstan through bilateral agreements, so that nothing would stand in the way of developing the oil-and-gas fields in the northern part of the sea. At the same time, despite emphasizing the value of maintaining the multilateral formats of networking, Putin has proposed no fresh initiatives aimed at reaching a comprehensive solution, so the tensions between Azerbaijan, Iran, and Turkmenistan persist and the exploration of the southern part of the sea remains stalled.

Russia has shown eagerness in developing bilateral military ties with each of the four Caspian neighbours but does everything possible to discourage Azerbaijan's and Kazakhstan's cooperative engagements with United States and North Atlantic Treaty Organization (NATO). As seen from the Kremlin, such generous gestures as, for instance, the delivery of three rapid patrol boats from the United States to Kazakhstan's Border Service is certainly not aid but 'unwanted interference'.[12] It appeared entirely possible to neutralize these encroachments by, for instance, staging joint exercises 'Caspian-2006' and 'Frontier-2006' involving Russian and Kazakh border guard and marine units but primarily the Caspian Flotilla (McDermott, 2006b; Plugatarev, 2006). Seeking to make it double on every US military 'gift' to Kazakhstan, Putin could not do the same with Azerbaijan which did not stop him from expressing his disapproval of US 'forward deployment' in no uncertain terms, particularly when the issue of stationing in

Counter-terrorism and the Caspian oil games 59

the Caucasus the radars of US anti-missile system was raised in early 2007 (Stepanov, 2007). Moscow would grumble about the US-sponsored *Caspian Guard* programme, limited as it is, but it goes positively ballistic when the issue of establishing a US base in Azerbaijan comes up.[13] Its main argument, however, is not the risk of an arms race in the Caspian but the much more direct risk of triggering a nervous over-reaction in Iran, and the looming US–Iran confrontation is certainly one conflict that Baku would absolutely prefer to stay clear of (Ismailzade, 2007).

Whatever small capabilities Azerbaijan and Kazakhstan acquire and Iran gradually builds, Russia's military dominance in the Caspian is firmly established and in the near future might even increase. Moscow could stage some more demonstrations of its might, but overall, it has not been able to gain that much political leverage from this position of power. The oil deals have been struck or broken without much regard to the potential combat capabilities, and Kazakhstan is currently contemplating the options for delivering its oil to Azerbaijan paying very little attention to the guns of the Caspian Flotilla (Gabuev, 2007). It is even possible to argue that it is exactly the Russian unquestionable naval superiority that has ensured relative stability in the hydrocarbon-rich zone that has many seats of conflict around it.[14] At the same time, the practical usefulness of military instruments for advancing energy-related interests has proven to be far smaller than most geopolitically minded strategists in Moscow hoped for.

Transforming counter-terrorism into counter-revolution

Putin was quick to see the strategic importance of energy interests in the Caspian area, but from the very start, the key leitmotif of his policy certainly was counter-terrorism. It appeared only natural to try to establish a nexus between the two, but the Kremlin soon discovered that counter-terrorism was a topic on which a superficial consensus was easy to reach, but substantial cooperation was hard to promote. While every state designated its own 'enemy of choice' in the universal struggle against terrorism, none of the Caspian neighbours was prepared to compromise on the energy agenda. To a large degree, that was the result of Putin's own clearly communicated desire to keep Chechnya out of any international discussions, even inside the Commonwealth of Independent States (CIS). The Caspian states had no problem with treating the issue as Russia's 'internal affairs', but then there appeared to be very little substance in the counter-terrorist theme.[15]

The US decision to undertake a military intervention in Afghanistan in response to the terrorist attack of 9/11 changed completely the profile and the content of this theme. Putin might have found some satisfaction in that validation of his trademark concern, but he could not fail to see that his decision to join the US-led coalition, against the advice of his lieutenants, reduced Russia's role to that of a supporting partner. The August 2002 Caspian naval exercises were portrayed as 'counter-terrorist', but even that unprecedented demonstration

60 *Deadlocked energy-security dilemmas*

of military might did not in any significant way challenge the US ability to determine the course of the newly launched 'war against terror'.

The majority view in Moscow was that counter-terrorist cooperation could not 'soften' the competition for the Caspian hydrocarbons and that the United States, using its new role as security provider, was seeking to gain advantage in access to these resources.[16] This view reflected, often in a distorted way, geopolitical analysis abundant in Washington at that time, which meshed together the strategic significance of Central Asia in the war against terror with US Caspian energy interests.[17] Trying to outplay the United States in this competition, Moscow encountered a problem that was often missed in simplistic geopolitical schemes, while it does not really take a microscope to discover it: the energy and counter-terrorism policies have different geographic foci. Indeed, in US and European strategic thinking, the counter-terrorism map is centred on Kabul and the Caspian energy map – on Baku; the distance between these two focal points (which are both outside post-Soviet Central Asia) is no less than 1,600 km. Russian military-security thinking is centred on Dushanbe and Bishkek, where its troops are based, while the energy-related assessments are concentrated about 1,000 km to the West at the Caspian shores of Kazakhstan and Turkmenistan, where major oil-and-gas projects are being implemented. The main consequence of this huge gap was that for Azerbaijan, Kazakhstan, and Turkmenistan, the theme of counter-terrorism did not appear that urgently relevant; despite its persistent exploitation by Moscow (as well as by Washington), Baku, Astana, and Ashgabat saw not a threat but an opportunity to gain freedom of manoeuvre between the two competitors (McDermott *et al.*, 2002).

US invasion into Iraq in March 2003 made the gap even more apparent as Washington's attention to Central Asia sharply declined. As Peter Rutland (2003, p. 47) noted, it 'alarmed Caspian Basin leaders, who were already pursuing a "weather vane" foreign policy, finely tuned to the ebb and flow of US interests in the region'. Russia, however, found few new opportunities to advance its positions as the Caspian states saw little need in accepting its 'patronage' (Galeotti, 2002). What changed that attitude was the spectre of 'coloured revolution' that had acquired frightening proportions by early 2005. Iran has remained immune to that scare, but each of the post-Soviet Caspian states had its particular exposure to the risk of a spontaneous explosion of public protest – and Moscow was keen to exploit the fears of the ruling regimes.

Testing ground for the creative merger of the counter-terrorism and counter-revolution strategies was found in Turkmenistan, and it was there that the first success was registered even before the dynamics of the 'coloured revolutions' acquired full power in 2004. Paying a visit to Ashgabat in April 2002 in order to renew for another ten years the Friendship and Cooperation Treaty (1992), Putin found President Sapurmurat Niyazov not particularly receptive either to his anti-terrorist proposals or to gas-focused advances. Terrorism had never been a matter of concern for Niyazov who managed to strike an informal deal with the Taliban in the late 1990s and then established an 'understanding' with the post-Taliban regional authorities in Herat and Mazar-e-Sharif.[18] Feeling reasonably

Counter-terrorism and the Caspian oil games 61

safe against the threat of Islamic radicalism, Niyazov saw no need in committing himself to fixed contracts for exporting natural gas and abruptly cancelled in 2001 the project for Transcaspian pipeline much favoured by the United States.[19]

Putin appeared to be the only leader in the world who considered the self-appointed 'Father-of-Turkmens' (or Turkmenbashi) as a man he could do business with and in just half a year after his visit to Turkmenistan that assessment was proven correct. The turning point was the arrest in Ashgabat of Boris Shikhmuradov, the leader of the opposition, after which severe repressions were unleashed on all opposition groups accused of having collectively organized an assassination attempt on the president.[20] It is entirely possible that the 'conspiracy' was a crude fabrication of Nyiazov's special services, but Putin appeared ready to buy it as a genuine 'terrorist attack' that justified the swiftly executed 'counter-measures'. The reward was the deal, finalized during Niyazov'a visit to Moscow in April 2003, granting Russia for the next 25 years the exclusive right to buy all Turkmen gas that was not covered by previous arrangements.

That framework deal was certainly not the end of the story; Niyazov was a capricious customer indeed, and his mood swings were far less predictable than the movement of his grandiose statue in Ashgabat that was engineered to follow the sun. Moscow nevertheless remained confident that Turkmenistan would deliver on its part of the bargain even when the gas tap was suddenly turned off in early 2005.[21] The main source of that assessment was political insight: Niyazov in the last years of his reign was as scared by the spectre of revolution as any other post-Soviet ruler. He could have summoned this 'evil spirit' himself in late 2002, but the 'sudden death' of Akaev's regime in Kyrgyzstan in February 2005 turned the fake 'enemy' into a frighteningly real challenge.

The period from mid-2004 to mid-2005 was indeed the *annus horribilis* for Central Asian presidents for life who saw how easily their power bases and structures of governance could collapse. Moscow, while also quite nervous about domestic instabilities, was able to exploit their anxiety for consolidating its influence and advancing its energy interests. Its proactive strategy was based on two propositions which the panic-stricken despots found convincing and easy to subscribe to. The first one was that the revolutions of whatever colour were not spontaneous eruptions of public protest but subversive special operations carefully planned by Washington where the Bush administration became obsessed with the spread of 'democratization'. The second proposition established that such operations could be derailed and defeated by determined application of force and that it was only the lack of political will to crush the externally guided 'revolutionaries' that had resulted in the spectacular events in Tbilisi, Kiev, and Bishkek.[22]

The imaginative transformation of the counter-terrorist strategy provided a usable political discourse for this second proposition. It was rather difficult to portray the 'tulip revolution' in Kyrgyzstan as an operation of Islamic extremists particularly as the new leadership quickly turned to Russia in order to maintain its shaky grasp on power.[23] It was the uprising in Andijan, Uzbekistan, in May 2005, brutally suppressed by troops acting on direct orders from President Islam

62 *Deadlocked energy-security dilemmas*

Karimov, that provided a perfect case for applying the retooled strategy of 'counter-terrorism/revolution'. Moscow with few doubts asserted that the uprising was in fact a terrorist attack and effectively shielded Karimov from international pressure.[24] That unambiguous stance made an impression on the concerned neighbours, while the US condemnation of the indiscriminate use of force against civilian population strengthened their suspicions that Washington was aiming at consecutive 'regime changes' by the means of orchestrating radical 'street' actions of sponsored opposition groups.[25]

While the focus of that particular political intrigue was on Uzbekistan, Moscow was definitely aiming at a larger audience with its strategy of integrating counter-revolutionary aims and counter-terrorist means. Kazakhstan was the central target, and the Kremlin calibrated its aim with utmost precision. President Nursultan Nazarbaev had never been impressed by Putin's counter-terrorist rhetoric and not particularly worried about domestic Islamic radicalism, merely indicating to Russia that its troops were expected to 'hold the line' in Tajikistan in order to prevent a spillover of destabilization. The revolutionary threat, however, was an entirely different matter: Nazarbaev felt vulnerable since presidential elections were approaching; it was possible to postpone them by a year but he inferred that time was hardly on his side. Leaving nothing to chance, Nazarbaev put effective pressure on the opposition and made sure that all the necessary repressive instruments were oiled and sharpened.[26] Moscow reassured him in its unwavering support – but it was provided at a price.

Kazakhstan had to agree on a joint development (with no Western participation) of a colossal Kurmangazy oilfield (as described in more detail in Chapter 11). Uzbekistan, finding itself on the receiving end of demarches and even sanctions orchestrated by the United States and the EU, reached 'cordial' agreements with *Lukoil* on developing the Khandym–Khauzak–Shady gas fields in the south of the country and with GAZPROM on developing gas fields on the Ustiyrt plateau and on modernizing the transit and local pipelines that should have guaranteed exporting additional volumes of gas to Russia.[27] Turkmenistan also agreed to expand energy cooperation, and President Niyazov visiting Moscow in January 2006 showed his best behaviour in terms of prices and every readiness to back the Russian position in the gas confrontation with Ukraine (Blagov, 2006b). Russia's counter-revolutionary leadership covered by counter-terrorist rhetoric appeared to generate tangible energy dividends.

By the start of 2007, however, that momentum had visibly slackened. Kazakhstan was again exploring 'multiple vectors', while Turkmenistan dared to confront Russia head on demanding a sharp prices increase on the gas which GAZPROM needed to buy as cheap as possible in order to keep in black its complicated balance of payments between domestic market and export contracts.[28] Uzbekistan also presented serious new demands for energy investments to Prime Minister Fradkov who visited Tashkent in March 2007 (Blagov, 2007a). Partly that new decline of Russia's influence was a consequence of the visible reduction of the revolutionary threat: presidential elections in Kazakhstan in December 2005 went according to Nazarbaev's plan with no excesses; in

Counter-terrorism and the Caspian oil games   63

Uzbekistan, social protest was effectively subdued and Karimov regained authority despite Western ostracism. Partly it was a response to the revised political message from Washington which emphasized that the support for democracy did not imply planning any revolutions and that the Nazarbaev regime was perfectly acceptable; Vice President Cheney personally delivered these reassurances visiting Astana in May 2005.[29] To a no small degree, however, this roll-back of Russia's dominance was caused by a more sober assessment of its intentions and capabilities by its Caspian allies. Their leaders had to recognize the perhaps disheartening fact that the Kremlin never planned for sending expeditionary forces in order to suppress a revolution threatening an ally; it merely promised assistance and political coverage to the friendly regimes that had stomach to defend themselves with force in an emergency situation.

Granting Russia privileged access to energy resources appears to be price too high for this limited security guarantee, but the spectre of revolution has not disappeared for good and might perform a spectacular comeback. Uzbekistan remains fundamentally unstable, but of all Caspian states, it is certainly Turkmenistan that has the most pronounced predisposition to a sudden failure. Turkmenbashi presided over a hyper-centralized despotic regime and sought to eliminate the threat of a 'palace coup' by the endless reshuffling in the leadership of the army and law enforcement structures as well as in the government. His sudden death in the last days of 2006 caught the key political clans unprepared and triggered a squabble for the vacant throne in which constitutional arrangements for succession were unceremoniously thrown away (Dolgin, 2006).

Moscow should have been aware that the lifetime of Turkmenbashi's exotic regime would quite probably run out sooner rather than later but preferred to focus its attention on this capricious customer.[30]

Indeed, Turkmenbashi had always seen the point to stop short of alienating Russia which was the only ally with a vested interest in his survival; his successors, however, might entertain different ideas and give more serious consideration to China's and Iran's advances or even to the US signals for reviving the Transcaspian project.[31] Even if a new leader would pacify the clan feud, he could never be sure that the long suppressed public discontent would not explode and that troops, demoralized by too many purges, would follow 'shoot-to-kill' orders should an Andijan-type emergency occur. Russia has high stakes in this rapidly evolving political 'thaw', but the Kremlin has to acknowledge that it has few options for securing the implementation of its privileged energy contracts and few instruments for managing an entirely possible violent crisis. This acknowledgement, however, might be overruled if the Kremlin concludes in the wake of Putin's visit to Ashgabat in May 2007 that only a direct application of force might prevent interventions from other interested parties, much the same way as the gerontocratic *Politburo* concluded in late 1979 that only massive invasion could stop Afghanistan from falling under hostile dominance.

64 *Deadlocked energy-security dilemmas*

Dagestan in the Caspian

Most analyses of the energy-security interplays in the Caspian area include into their 'natural' scope countries such as Kyrgyzstan, Tajikistan, and even Afghanistan despite the geographically obvious fact that they are no closer to the sea in question than, for instance Syria. At the same time, the impact on the 'littoral' security situation from the protracted crisis in Dagestan, a uniquely troubled 'subject' of the Russian Federation, is commonly left out, despite the easily observable length of its Caspian shore, not much shorter than that of Azerbaijan. In most cases, Dagestan is analysed in the context of political processes in the North Caucasus where it administratively belongs; however, it is separated from the rest of this sub-region by the Chechen war zone and so faces many particular challenges that resonate across the Caspian area.

It was not by chance or miscalculation that the famous Chechen terrorist Shamil Basaev and his Arab deputy known as Khattab attempted to establish a new independent base in the mountain areas of Dagestan by invading it in summer 1999 with the troop of some 300–500 *mujahideen*. Their immediate goal was to take control over several villages in the Botlikh district that had decided to administer their life in accordance with the Sharia law, but the larger strategic goal was to unite Chechnya and parts of Dagestan in one Islamic state that would have access to the Caspian Sea and thus acquire a prominent international profile.[32] The armed incursion met a strongly negative response in Dagestan where Basaev and Khattab were perceived as adventurers who sought to break the traditional balance of power between ethno-political clans; this response translated into determined armed resistance that helped the Russian troops to repel the attack in the course of three weeks of heavy but rather ineffectual fighting.[33]

That local victory on the eve of the Second Chechen War made it possible for Moscow to execute its strategic plan for isolating Chechnya and re-routing all major communications in the wider Caucasian region around that 'black hole'. Of particular importance in this respect were the rail link to Azerbaijan through Dagestan and the new bypass oil pipeline connecting Baku with Novorossiisk without crossing the Chechen territory. With that infrastructure in place, Russian troops were given orders to destroy the refineries and pipelines in Chechnya (and even the Oil Institute in Grozny) beyond repair, while in the first war they had been spared to the degree possible.[34]

The new transport 'corridor', however, did not increase to a significant degree the strategic importance of Dagestan. The main rear bases for military operations in Chechnya were in North Ossetia (Mozdok, Vladikavkaz) and further north in Rostov-on-Don and Volgograd. The main naval base on the Caspian and the headquarters of the Caspian Flotilla were in Astrakhan, while the strengthened 77th Naval Infantry Brigade based in Kaspiisk, Dagestan, was engaged in combat operations in Chechnya. In the geo-economic perspective, the expanding drilling projects that explored the hydrocarbon fields in the Russian sector of the Caspian Sea were also based in Astrakhan, which had the

Counter-terrorism and the Caspian oil games 65

advantage of river communications and a tanker terminal, so Dagestan did not feature in the plans for developing the energy sector. In essence, it was pretty much left alone by Moscow to boil in its own political juices and that brought in the matter of a few years a near-catastrophic deterioration of the internal security situation in the republic.[35]

The Russian leadership continued to ignore the disturbing tendency that during 2004 and first months of 2005, there were more ambushes and explosions in Dagestan than in Chechnya until Dmitri Kozak raised the alarm.[36] His memo to the Kremlin identified a 'critical level' in accumulation of socioeconomic and political problems and suggested that 'a clear territorial concentration of ethno-political problems could prompt the extremist forces to create de-facto several quasi-state structures in the North, South and in the central part of Dagestan, which would amount to a break-up of the republic'.[37] Putin responded with a brief visit to the Federal Security Service (FSB) centre outside Makhachkala and the border post near Derbent on 15 July 2005; he emphasized the government's awareness of the situation in Dagestan but took no action on Kozak's proposal for introducing a direct administrative control from Moscow or, at least, for removing the scandalously corrupt Magometali Magomedov from the position of leadership. Ignoring Kozak's warning about the risks of 'pushing the problems deeper inside' by applying forceful methods, Putin promised more troops insisting that the southern borders of Dagestan should by sealed off in order to prevent the penetration of rebels towards the resorts of the Krasnodar kray, where 'millions of Russians are making their holidays'.[38] That self-deceiving 'net assessment' of risks as coming from outside was strikingly inadequate to the real structure of the crisis in Dagestan that was driven by the angry public protest against the degenerating predatory system of power.

An explosion of mass unrest was expected by those experts who dared to have an independent view, but it actually happened not in Makhachkala but in Nalchik, Kabardino-Balkaria, in October 2005.[39] While the 'victory' came easy for the troops that outnumbered the desperate rebels 20:1, the Kremlin was alarmed by the continuation of the chain of 'coloured revolutions' and finally launched the long-overdue cadre reshuffling, starting with the 'irreplaceable' Magomedov. It was the spread of Islamic networks, revealed by Nalchik, that forced Moscow to revise its 'have-no-worry' threat assessment, and on a closer look, it discovered that many villages in central Dagestan, for instance Gimry, had turned to self-governance according to strict Sharia law, much the same way as Karamakhi did back in early 1999.[40]

That placed Dagestan in a very different geopolitical picture: instead of being an insignificant corner in the Caspian area, it emerged as a crucial gateway of global radicalized Islam that had blazed important inroads across the North Caucasus and even towards the Muslim communities in Moscow numbered in hundreds of thousands.[41] The Kremlin could have paid little attention to the repeated explosions on the 'non-strategic' oil-and-gas

66 *Deadlocked energy-security dilemmas*

pipelines in Dagestan, but all of a sudden, Putin, making an express-visit to Grozny in December 2005, gave his full attention to the need to rectify the 'distorted interpretations of the Koran' propagated by 'those on the other side'.[42]

These words would have hardly made much of an impression by themselves, but combined with the removal of the most notoriously corrupt politicians, more restraint use of brutal force, and new funding, they did contribute to a decrease of tensions noticed by many observers in the second half of 2006 (Izmailov, 2006). In late October, for that matter, the questions Putin received from Kaspi-isk during the annual television Q-&-A show were no different from those asked in nine other pre-selected locations.[43] A sustained de-escalation of the deeply rooted conflict, however, could be achieved only by gaining a new dynamism of economic development through a far greater engagement of Dagestan into the energy-related projects in the Caspian area (Isaev, 2006). These projects are increasingly prioritized by Moscow, which has remained reluctant to subject them to the security risks emanating from Dagestan. This reasonable caution left only limited opportunities for reducing these risks and in fact narrowed the scope of interstate cooperation in the Caspian.

Conclusions

From the start of Putin's second presidential term, Russia has embarked on a pro-active course in the Caspian area seeking to roll back the tide of 'coloured revolutions' and advance its energy interests on the strength of its posture as 'security provider'. Counter-terrorism was the key strategy for maintaining the relevance and applicability of military instruments that guaranteed for Moscow a position of unquestionable superiority. The build-up of the Caspian Flotilla's strike capabilities and every naval/air force/special services exercise in the area, from the large-scale show of force in mid-2002 to the joint Collective Security Treaty Organization (CSTO) exercises in August 2006, were centred on deterring and the preparations for repelling terrorist attacks. The much-valued 'position of strength', however, was proven to be essentially unusable.

Aliev's regime in Azerbaijan managed to organize the dynastic father-to-son transfer of power without Russia's assistance and effectively suppressed the 'revolutionary' opposition with the silent approval of the United States, which acquired only very limited security access to this pivotal corner of the Caspian. Turkmenistan did grant Russia an exclusive deal on exporting its gas but refused it any direct involvement in the production cycle; without exploitable military-security ties, Moscow had to rely on mercurial Niyazov's word – and now can only watch how the energy contracts are dealt with in the messy wrangle for power. Kazakhstan accepted a tighter alliance with Russia when the threat of 'coloured revolution' was at its peak but then has found a way to disentangle itself from a too tight embrace and has begun to cultivate oil con-nections with Azerbaijan. The place where military power and counter-terrorist

Counter-terrorism and the Caspian oil games 67

strategy were most immediately relevant was Dagestan, but Moscow until late 2005 had remained in denial of the need to address this crisis and later has shown reluctance to grant this troubled republic a place in the Caspian security system.

6 Alliance-building with virtual commitments and energy power

Claiming a leading role in providing global energy security, Moscow cannot fail to see that the validity of this claim depends upon its ability to organize and regulate complex relations between the post-Soviet states, with the obvious exception of the Baltic trio. The character of these relations varies from the frozen confrontation between Armenia and Azerbaijan to the stalled merger between Belarus and Russia, while the common Soviet past is a factor with diminishing import for the transition of the 12 not-so-newly independent states to uncertain but inevitably quite dissimilar futures. With hindsight, it appears predetermined that in the political realm, the simultaneously launched state-building projects could have only established their viability by increasing the distance from one another. In the economic relations, to the contrary, a well-organized co-ordinating mechanism could have helped in transforming the ties directed by central planning into a new market-driven cooperation. It was the devastating economic crisis of the early 1990s that pushed each country to sever most of these ties, putting own survival first, and the financial meltdown in Moscow in August 1998 cut into pieces the newly weaved fabric of economic exchanges.[1]

Inheriting the position of informal leadership in the interstate system that was high on symbolism and low on substance, Vladimir Putin initially sought to streamline it with a pragmatic approach that was centred on Russia's interests defined in 'costs-benefits' terms. By the end of his first presidency, however, this pragmatism had given way to 'great-regional-power' ambitions, while the pronounced desire to increase profits from exporting energy was mixed with the interest in maximizing political dividends from manipulating prices. The shocking effect of the 'orange revolution' in Ukraine in late 2004 has caused radical but incoherent changes in Russia's agenda of alliance-building.[2] This chapter will examine Moscow's shifting aims and plans for the Commonwealth of Independent States (CIS), the Collective Security Treaty Organization (CSTO), and the Shanghai Cooperation Organization (SCO).

The dysfunctional CIS lingers on

By the time of Putin's arrival at the Kremlin in late 1999, the CIS – being the oldest and the most representative of post-Soviet organizations – had already

Alliance building   69

disappointed every expectation that could have been linked to it. The amount of accumulated paperwork was immeasurable, but the only real function that the misnamed 'Commonwealth' was able to perform was top-level networking that preserved the peculiar camaraderie of Soviet *nomenklatura* among the ageing presidents and often younger prime ministers and 'socialized' up-and-coming deputy prime ministers who always had a few horses to trade.[3]

Putin, being himself a graduate of a very different school, saw little value in such networking, and Sergei Ivanov, his trusted lieutenant, dropped a heavy hint at the international conference in Munich in early 2001 that the CIS could not be a vehicle for real integration and could be disbanded (Kasaev 2001). Within two years, however, the prevailing view in the Kremlin shifted towards making the CIS a priority in Russia's policy since it secured a commanding position in the very centre of multiple networks, while other participants had only thin ties between one another. The Chisinau summit in October 2002 was quite possibly the turning point in shaping the new Moscow's course towards restoring its 'big-brotherly' leadership in the post-Soviet space. Not that the fellow presidents were that convincing with their presents on Putin's fiftieth birthday or pleas to retain chairmanship in the CIS; what made the difference was their collective readiness to follow Russia's lead in 'managing' or, rather, curtailing democratic reforms combined with expectations of economic subsidies and preferences.[4]

As long as Moscow was ready to supply its camp followers with gas, oil, and electricity at reduced prices, the course, aiming at a gradual rollback of the geopolitical retreats, particularly in Central Asia, appeared infallible and destined to succeed. However, just a year into implementation, the 'CIS project' experienced two major setbacks when Moldova suddenly rejected the plan for resolving the long-lasting conflict with Transdniestria that had been ironed out by Putin's aid Dmitry Kozak, while in Georgia a routinely falsified election triggered a forceful and victorious uprising against the Shevardnadze regime that marketed itself as the 'rose revolution'.[5] The Kremlin barely had time to reconfigure its course and reassert the nervous leaders-for-life in the reliability of its support when political clouds started to gather over Kiev.

There were no doubts whatsoever in Putin's team that the presidential elections in Ukraine constituted the ultimate test for Russia's ability to lead the motley crew of allies and dependents; so, the cautious 'wait-and-see' approach that was adopted towards Georgia in the first months of the 'rose regime' was simply a non-option. The result of that test was so astonishingly negative that the illusions about 'the integrative potential of the Commonwealth completely evaporated', as Mikhail Delyagin (2005b, p. 147) pointed out, and 'only representatives of Russian bureaucracy with their skills in resolutely ignoring the reality could continue to pretend' that the project was on track. The March 2005 'tulip revolution' in Kyrgyzstan (that flower was quickly discarded) made even these feeble pretences irrelevant;[6] so by the next CIS summit scheduled for August 2005 in Kazan, the Kremlin had to decide what to do with the clumsy organization.

Against expectations, nothing much happened at the summit itself, which was

70 *Deadlocked energy-security dilemmas*

distinguished only by pompous celebrations of Kazan's 1,000 years and, perhaps, by Turkmenistan's rather unexpected decision to reduce its membership status to the questionable 'association'.[7] The decision in the Kremlin, nevertheless, did mature and was conveyed to the concerned parties in remarkably clear terms. The sobering conclusion from the typically closed 'lessons learned' exercise was that economic privileges and incentives were entirely inefficient instruments for stimulating loyalty of 'newly independent' elites and anchoring the CIS states in Russia's sphere of influence. What followed logically was the decision to raise the prices on the energy exported to the CIS partners close to the level of current deals with the European Union (EU) member states. While seemingly pure 'mercantilist', the decision contained hidden political agenda that gradually crystallized in the course of the high-resonance 'gas war' with Ukraine during December 2005–January 2006.[8]

Moscow calculated that sharply jerked prices on electricity and gas would be more than just a due punishment for 'treacherous' Georgia, Moldova, and, first of all Ukraine; they could provoke a swift change of 'revolutionary' public mood in these states balancing on the brink of failure and thus lead to collapses of pro-Western elite coalitions. At the same time, it appeared possible to offer loyal friends, like Armenia or Tajikistan, economic aid packages that would minimize the pain from the high-energy bills without compromising the newly established 'market principles'. In any case, the Kremlin had every reason to assume that 'pariah' regimes in Belarus and Uzbekistan, as well as the post-revolutionary government in Kyrgyzstan, had nowhere else to go seeking protection against the threat of 'coloured revolutions' that had subsided by the start of 2006 but could have come back with the suddenness of tsunami.[9] The defeat of the 'orange coalition' in the parliamentary elections in Ukraine in March 2006 and the resurrection of Viktor Yanukovich as Prime Minister was seen in Moscow as a validation of its new strategy. However, the 'gas-and-oil war' with Belarus in January 2007 (as described in Chapter 12) demonstrated that the 'market' foundation could not provide for 'ever-closer' ties since, as Fedor Lukyanov (2007b) concluded, 'the states in this part of the planet are not ready for any integration, and Russia is the least ready of them all'.

The fact of the matter is that the habitual but unloved Commonwealth has become a completely unsuitable format for advancing or regrouping Russia's interests in the post-Soviet space. Moscow could see much rationale in strengthening institutional structures in Central Asia, but only unilateral contacts make sense in dealing with friends and foes in the Caucasus as well as with the two crucially important European neighbours. In early 2006, Georgia and Ukraine sent a series of 'trial balloons' about their intentions to leave the CIS, but Russia remained icily indifferent, showing readiness to scrap the inefficient umbrella framework, which suddenly started to seem more useful for the 'dissidents' than for the otherwise engaged 'hegemon'.[10] The disappearance of the economic agenda due to Russia's unilateral withdrawal of energy privileges, eagerly emulated by Kazakhstan and Turkmenistan, has left only top-level political networking beneath the heavy 'integrationist' symbolism of the CIS, but it still might

Alliance building 71

linger on unless Ukraine would gather strength for a breakthrough in the European direction.

Virtual strengthening of the non-existent collective security

Moscow has always sought to build a hard core in the incurably amorphous CIS that would have all the attributes of a real alliance with proper security commitments and military-to-military cooperation. The first attempt was undertaken already in May 1992 when Armenia, Kazakhstan, Kyrgyzstan, Russia, Tajikistan, and Uzbekistan established the Collective Security Organization (CSO, also known as the Tashkent Treaty). Azerbaijan, Belarus, and Georgia joined in 1993; but in 1999, when the agreement was up for renewal, Azerbaijan, Georgia and Uzbekistan effectively seceded (the name 'Tashkent Treaty' was therefore dropped). The main problem with this formally solid alliance was that Russia never wanted to take on binding security commitments and reduced its functions to organizing symbolic exercises, regulating small-scale arms trade and providing education for 'friendly' officers in Russian military academies. The allies, on their side, were reluctant to be drawn into Russia's quarrels with North Atlantic Treaty Organization (NATO) and insisted on setting their Partnership for Peace programmes independently.

The situation changed drastically in Autumn 2001 when Moscow discovered that the limited deployment of US troops in Central Asia brought a very significant reduction of its influence. The reinvigoration of security cooperation in the CSO was seen as a key means of counterbalancing the US encroachments; so in May 2002, the quasi-alliance was 'upgraded' to the Collective Security Treaty Organization (CSTO). Particular attention was given to the old issue of joint air defence system, which suddenly acquired a political edge as the 'loyal allies' like Kazakhstan and Kyrgyzstan bargained with NATO about military air traffic with no regard to the 'collectively' approved rules and procedures. Russia sought to reassert its overall control over the 'friendly' airspace by investing more resources in the infrastructure and joint exercises, but the chain of accidents and setbacks, from the crash of a Su-27 fighter that lost its way in Lithuanian airspace in October 2005 to the failure to detect the missile launches by North Korea in July 2006 and the Chinese anti-satellite test in January 2007, demonstrated that joint air defence existed only on a symbolic level.[11]

Far more important for the 'collective security' participants was the new emphasis on joint struggle against terrorism, which many of them were inclined to interpret as direct 'friendly' support in suppressing domestic opposition groups designated as terrorist networks. Moscow, while quite eager to play on the fears of its authoritarian allies accentuated by the rising challenge of 'coloured revolutions', was reluctant to provide any military security guarantees. For that matter, the CSTO counter-terrorist exercises scheduled for March 2005 in Kyrgyzstan were urgently moved to Tajikistan in order to avoid the impression of a possible intervention in the revolutionary chaos.[12] The joint Anti-Terrorist Centre created back in 2000 remained essentially a

72 *Deadlocked energy-security dilemmas*

public relations (PR) exercise without even a solid database (Plugatarev, 2005a).

Cultivating the system of virtual security commitments, Moscow extended a cordial invitation to Uzbekistan to rejoin the CSTO, demonstratively against the Western efforts to isolate Karimov's regime after the May 2005 Andijan massacre; this enlargement was finalized at the June 2006 summit (Socor 2006b). Russia also made insistent effort to present the CSTO as a 'natural' partner-organization for NATO, particularly in Central Asia.[13] The Atlantic Alliance, while quite dependent upon access to Manas, the key airbase in Kyrgyzstan, and other facilities in the region for sustaining its operations in Afghanistan, remained reluctant to legitimize the Russia-dominated organization with unclear aims and functions. Touring Central Asia in early 2007, Nikolai Bordyuzha, the CSTO secretary general, scorned this attitude and revealed that NATO sought 'to separate us one by one, but our unity prevents them from carrying out these plans' (McDermott 2007).

The issue about the CSTO's primary strategic aim came up with unexpected spat and squabble at the same June 2006 Minsk summit where Uzbekistan was embraced back. Prior to that high-profile gathering, informed experts in Moscow and CSTO officials had been advancing the proposition that the organization should prioritize the task of protecting oil-and-gas pipelines, drawing parallels with the special units that Azerbaijan, Georgia, and Turkey were training for patrolling along the Baku–Tbilisi–Ceyhan pipeline (Plugatarev, 2006a). It remained unclear, however, what kind of threats requiring military counter-measures were envisaged for the strategic pipelines going from Kazakhstan and through Russia. Aleksandr Lukashenko, the tough-talking president of Belarus, dismissed that abstract proposition and announced that the main task of the CSTO was 'to defend our Western borders like a sacred place. We are 120 per cent ready for that task!'[14] That idea, however, found little support among the members of the 'alliance'. Kazakhstan's President Nazarbaev objected that the CSTO had to concentrate on Central Asia and plan military responses to a possible aggression against any member state in that region, adding that Uzbekistan's return increased the urgency of that task (Kolesnikov, 2006c).

Unlike the scenario for defending the Brest fortress against invading NATO forces, the menu of possible violent conflicts in Central Asia was indeed very rich, and the demands of the concerned presidents were entirely rational. Russia, however, preferred to train its troops against the least probable 'aggressor' precisely because it did not want to find itself trapped in chaotic hostilities with no 'exit strategy' except for cutting the losses and abandoning its hopeless allies 'in need'. After many discussions about joint peacekeeping forces, the ten battalions (five of them Russian) that are formally earmarked for these operations are only nominally combat-capable at their bases, hundreds of miles from one another; so the task of assembling this 'rapid reaction corps' at the CSTO (in fact, Russian) airbase at Kant, Kyrgyzstan, would require many weeks of hard logistical work. What Russia really wants from this quasi-alliance is to exchange its virtual security guarantees for privileged access to energy resources in Kazakhstan and

Alliance building 73

Uzbekistan (Turkmenistan makes a special case), while granting only carefully measured subsidies to the energy-dependent Armenia, Belarus, Kyrgyzstan, and Tajikistan. Even in the surprisingly good-weather security conditions of 2006, this 'something-for-nothing' arrangement appeared barely satisfactory for all six. As for Lukashenko's strategic vision, the sharp deterioration of Russia–Belarus relations in January 2007 left some commentators wondering whether the next 'collective' exercises would envisage the deployment of Russian troops for securing the strategic pipelines rather than the joint counteroffensive against a Western assault (Golts, 2007a).

The hollow promise of the Shanghai cooperation

Besides the 'hard security'-oriented CSTO, Moscow has assumed during Putin's first presidency a central role in several organizations dealing with economic and 'soft security' challenges, starting from the narrowest Common Economic Space (CES) with Belarus, Kazakhstan, and Ukraine launched in 2003 and including the Eurasian Economic Community (EEC) created in 2000 on the basis of the feeble Custom Union, to the Central Asian Cooperation Organization (CACO), which Russia joined in 2004. Ukraine's post-revolution Westward drift left the CES in limbo, while the CACO in October 2005 was merged into the EEC, which connected Belarus to the four states in Central Asia (minus the non-cooperative Turkmenistan) and to Russia. The embarrassing functional overlaps were thus reduced, but the ability of the streamlined EEC to perform any practical function was not significantly improved.[15]

The organization that has been strongly profiled by Moscow and indeed gaining political importance is the SCO, created in 2001 by Russia, the four Central Asian states (minus Turkmenistan), and China.[16] Initially, the SCO focused its activities primarily on countering the non-traditional security challenges, and as Putin (2006d) wrote in a special essay, 'Now we already have effective ways to fight together against what our Chinese partners call the "three evils" – terrorism, separatism, extremism'. Achievements in the security area were in fact not that significant, and all member states expressed interest in expanding this narrow focus, first of all with regard to the economic agenda. Putin himself suggested at the 'jubilee' June 2006 meeting in Shanghai to create an 'energy club' that could discuss and design joint projects in the oil-and-gas sector. There are, however, serious problems for Russia stemming from the plain fact that it cannot effectively control the activities of the SCO.[17]

One group of problems is related to the ambiguities and hidden tensions in the bilateral relations between Russia and China. The phenomenal dynamics of China's unstoppable economic growth are assessed in Moscow with no less concern than in Washington, even if the scale of trade is approximately ten times smaller. In the 1990s, the doubts were mostly focused on the impact of Russian arms export on the modernization of Chinese armed forces, as Beijing insisted on acquiring the most advanced technologies and Moscow remained reluctant to lift restrictions on their transfer. By the middle of the current decade, according

74 Deadlocked energy-security dilemmas

to Russian experts, bilateral military–technical cooperation had 'passed the peak of full blossom'; the focal point of relations had shifted to China's access to Russia's raw materials and, first of all, energy.[18] Moscow understands perfectly well that it is the steady growth of demand in China that has brought the sharp increase in world oil prices, from which Russia has benefited so handsomely. At the same time, it is neither willing nor able to respond in kind to Chinese political advances featuring direct investments and long-term contracts on exporting 'strategic' quantities of oil through a new pipeline.

There is, perhaps, a psychological context in the protracted negotiations about building this pipeline; becoming a 'raw materials appendage' to China is far less attractive than playing the same role vis-à-vis Europe where Russian elites have most valuable connections and personal assets.[19] Public opinion, while still generally positive towards China, is also shifting in the direction of more pronounced worries, so that the share of Russians who saw China as a 'friendly state' declined from 67 per cent in 2001 to 48 per cent in 2006, while 41 per cent agreed with the opinion that China's strengthening could threaten Russian interests ('Hidden threat', 2006).

Putin opted for a resolute step forward in advancing the energy cooperation with China, making the agreement on gas export the central point of his visit in March 2006. Shifting the emphasis to gas, he was probably following his instincts more than any calculations; but as a result, both the Europeans, who knew precisely how much Russian gas they would need in the next ten years, and the Chinese, who had not counted on this source of energy before, found themselves in a delicate position of a suitor. Putin pencilled only a preliminary deal, but one parameter was firmly agreed upon: China was prepared to pay the European price for gas, abandoning its search for bargains. Two other parameters are reasonably clear and constitute a sharp contradiction: GAZPROM can build the US$10-billion pipeline from South Siberia to China by 2011, but it will not be able to increase its annual production by 30 bcm of gas to pump into that pipeline. The costs of construction had to be covered from the extra export profits; so the two competing consumers would be hard-pressed to bid one over another.[20]

One possible way to resolve this pre-planned shortage of supply is to increase Russia's purchase of gas in Turkmenistan, Kazakhstan, and Uzbekistan, which would require sustained investments in their production capacity. That prospect is directly related to the second group of problems in the SCO that stem from Moscow's concerns about, and the desire to check, China's penetration into Central Asia. From Beijing's point of view, this organization opens excellent opportunities for cultivating direct contacts with the states of the region and, for that matter, to negotiate long-term contracts on importing oil and gas without Russian self-interested intermediary regulation. The first significant success for China was the opening in late 2005 of the Atasau–Alashankou oil pipeline that brought the Caspian oil to Xingjian. Other energy-related contracts with Kazakhstan, Uzbekistan, and Turkmenistan are in the 'pipeline', which means, in the opinion of Russian analysts, that 'close friendship' between Russia and China

Alliance building 75

would only be a nice cover for the fact that 'our countries will remain competitors and this competition will be very tough'.[21]

Seeking to keep China away from Central Asia, Moscow plays on the concerns of the leaders of Kyrgyzstan, Kazakhstan, and other states about the inflow of Chinese goods and traders that could undermine their fragile industries and wipe away local entrepreneurs. More importantly, Russia maintains that China could have only indirect security role in the region with the lowest possible military profile. Much attention has been given to cultivating 'hard security' ties , but strictly on bilateral level, as for instance at the much-advertised Russian–Chinese military exercises 'Peace Mission' in August 2005.[22] Preparing the next exercises in the Chelyabinsk oblast in summer 2007, Russia was eager to engage Kazakhstan and other Central Asian states on the symbolic (company/platoon) level and even expressed interest in engaging India but remained resolutely against staging 'war games' with the Chinese in Central Asia.[23]

This bickering did not hamper Moscow's efforts at instrumentalizing the SCO for forging a common political front against the threat of 'coloured revolutions', and President Karimov's emergency visit to Beijing immediately after the brutally suppressed revolt in Andijan underscored the crucial role of China in this 'authoritarian International' (Zygar, 2005). The readiness to confront the external 'interference' that fostered revolutionary discontent quite logically led to practical measures aimed at minimizing Western influence and, very specifically, US presence in Central Asia. In the fluid pre-revolutionary situation, Roy Allison (2004c, p. 478) had every reason to argue:

> The US military presence in Central Asia since autumn 2001 may tempt Moscow and Beijing to try to instrumentalize the SCO as a *regional* balancing structure against Washington. But this goal will not be accepted by its Central Asian members, keen on exploiting the limits of their new bilateral security ties with the United States.

Since mid-2005, however, the regimes in question have turned much more keen on checking the corroding impact of these ties, and the 'polite' reminder about the expected withdrawal of US 'footprints' issued by the SCO reflected these second thoughts.[24] In this sense, US General Richard B. Myers got it wrong arguing that Russia and China 'were trying to bully some smaller countries' (as quoted in Tyson, 2005). There was hardly any need in bullying Tajikistan, since President Rakhmonov knew perfectly well that only Russian troops could guarantee his grasp on power, while the awkward bargaining of the new Kyrgyzstan government for more US rent payment for the Manas airbase merely provided some free entertainment for Moscow (Chadova, 2006).

It is remarkably easy for Moscow to establish solid common ground with Beijing on the issue of pressing for withdrawal of US military presence, but it has to consider the link to the ongoing operation in Afghanistan, which is an issue of great strategic importance for Washington and a more significant strategic complication from the Russian perspective than from the Chinese one. The

76 *Deadlocked energy-security dilemmas*

Kremlin is certainly loath to see a success in Western efforts at reconstructing the Afghan state; even the very uncertain advances with power-sharing and competitive elections had by 2006 made Afghanistan into the most democratic state in the region. For Tajikistan and Uzbekistan, that constitutes the most compelling reason for sealing off the border with the troublesome southern neighbour, very much against the prescriptions of the 'Greater Central Asia' project developed in a couple of conservative think-tanks in Washington.[25] Moscow is resolutely opposed to this project seeing it as aimed directly against its interests, but it also understands that a very probable failure of US and NATO state-building intervention in Afghanistan would generate a hugely destabilizing resonance across the region. Claiming the role of a security guarantor for Central Asia, Russia would never be able to master capabilities sufficient for meeting such a security challenge.[26] Trapped in a strategic choice between two unacceptable options, Moscow opts for procrastination assuming that NATO would have to figure out an 'escape strategy' from Afghanistan (Baev, 2006h); but it is still not able to offer any comprehensible guideline to the increasingly impatient allies.

What the Kremlin offers instead is the maximum possible spin on the SCO and its cooperative endeavours. China and India (while only an observer without a formal application for membership) were invited as guests of honour to the G8 Strelna Summit in July 2006, and a special trilateral session was held in order to emphasize, in Putin's words, that 'our approaches to international problems are very close or, as diplomats would say, they practically coincide'. Kazakhstan was also introduced for the first time to that elite club, but the key intrigue was woven around the question of inviting Iran to join the SCO as soon as the heat around its nuclear programme would go down by a few imperceptible degrees (Beehner, 2006). In a peculiar way, Moscow's heavy advertising of the SCO reinforces the message of some conservative analysts in Washington that the expanding Shanghai framework represents a sum of individual aspirations of its members and candidates (Iran being a key point of reference) to counterbalance the United States.[27] Leaving aside both the self-congratulatory and the 'enemy-in-the-making' rhetoric, it is possible to suggest that the SCO will hardly live up to expectations of any kind except for serving as a symbolic vehicle for content-free cooperation that could usefully cover mutual suspicions and tensions.

Conclusions

Alliance-building has become an exercise to which much political value and PR-profile has been added during Putin's second presidential term. It was seen as an important element in realizing the key theme in the 'energy security' concept: ensuring for Russia a controlling position in regulating major flows of energy through long-term contracts and formalized political commitments. In reality, however, the interplay between energy policy and alliance-building has been turbulent and incoherent. Moscow sought simultaneously to tie the allies by accentuating their energy dependency and to punish the malcontents, to arrange

Alliance building 77

for itself the exclusive rights on purchasing gas at low prices, and to maximize profits from selling this crucial commodity. These political zigzags and opportunistic moves have brought few benefits for the energy sector but have seriously damaged trust and integrative dynamics in the system of alliances. Pointing to the 'inability of Russian leadership to develop and implement a real integration project based on common decision-making', Thomas Gomart (2006, p. 70) argued that it is a consequence of 'the unwillingness to make long-term commitments based on mutual trust. In this sense, Moscow's policy remains quite immature'.[28]

The shift towards economization or, more specifically, 'gasification' of relations with the allies that started in mid-2005 and reached one culmination in the 'gas war' with Ukraine in the first days of 2006 and another in the 'gas-and-oil war' with Belarus at the start of 2007 has not made this policy noticeably more mature. Putin concentrated on 'selling' the concept of 'energy security' to the EU and China (assuming correctly that the United States would not subscribe) while keeping the pressure on the 'enemies' like Georgia and trying to shorten the leash on 'close friends' like Belarus and 'neutrals' like Turkmenistan. Had the internally divided EU consented to Russia's 'special role' as its priority supplier of energy, Moscow would have been able to take up this pressure to a new level. Had the Iraq-preoccupied United States accepted Russia's 'controlling stake' in Kazakhstan and 'legitimate concerns' in Georgia, Moscow would have aimed at a real breakthrough in asserting its dominance, perhaps leaving Ukraine for a while to stew in the post-revolutionary juices. Putin deployed his 'big guns' with confidence and even panache targeting the G8 Strelna summit; as Fedor Lukyanov (2006c) noticed, 'the elephant's grace, senseless in a china shop, is quite appropriate in an enclosure where over-sized beasts are romping'. That kind of grace did not secure the success of that deployment, however; the EU remained of the opinion that Russia was more a problem than a solution for its 'energy insecurity', and the United States refused to wash its hands over Georgia and made new advances towards Kazakhstan. Putin was left to keep pretending that the overlapping structures with their confusing abbreviations, from the moribund CIS to the pretentious SCO, make real political sense and serve Russia's energy interests as well.

Part III

Military muscle as the ultimate proof of 'greatness'

> I think that Russia as a Great Power is over. As a state exerting pressure on its neighbours it has no future and will not have one for quite a long time. Russia's space will shrink. You can stand up from the gambling table. It is all over.
>
> Brodsky (1996)

In Russian security thinking, the proposition that the military might is a crucial component of state power, a necessary precondition for claiming serious influence in the power-based system of international relations, and a key means of countering hostile external pressure is an axiom established by hundreds of years of state history. The dictum of Alexander III that Russia had but two true allies, the army and the navy, is accepted as the quintessential wisdom of statesmanship; the witty aphorism that 'a country that cannot feed its own army will feed a foreign one' easily qualifies as common political sense; and the words of Russian philosopher Ivan Ilyin that soldier 'represents the national unity of the people, the will of the Russian state, strength and honour' are invoked for justifying the draft system. President Putin in his May 2006 address to the parliament praised the United States for spending on defence budget 25 times more than Russia did: 'This is what in defence is referred to as "their home – their fortress". And good on them, I say. Well done!'[1] In the much-debated Munich speech (Putin, 2007a), he asserted: 'Russia is a country with a history that spans more than a thousand years and has practically always used the privilege to carry out an independent foreign policy'. The only problem with this worship of military power is that Russia has far too little of it for supporting its claim for 'greatness'.

7 Virtually extended deterrence of the 'Great Power'

The automatic connection between possessing, preferably 'legitimately', an arsenal of nuclear weapons and enjoying the status of 'Great Power' is deeply ingrained in Russian security thinking. It has persisted despite multiple evidence of political uselessness of nuclear instruments and their irrelevance in real crises. This resilience in the age of globalization with its new range of unconventional challenges can be partly explained by the proven impossibility to reform the UN Security Council where the five permanent members are still the only states who legally own nuclear weapons. A larger part of the explanation, however, stems from the undeniable fact that Russia in the 15 years of its post-Soviet history had few other available assets that could have supported the claim for 'great-powerness'.

Addressing the parliament in May 2006, President Putin (2006b) concluded his brief threat assessment with an affirmative if not entirely politically correct statement:

> Finally, we need to make very clear that the key responsibility for countering all of these threats and ensuring global security will lie with the world's leading powers, the countries that possess nuclear weapons and powerful levers of military and political influence.[1]

The commander-in-chief did not allow himself a shadow of doubt that Russia was indeed one among those 'leading powers' and justified the expanded financing of nuclear programmes as investment not only in the country's security but also in its international prestige. As this chapter shows, Putin was far less nuclear-minded at the start of his presidency but developed a penchant for the 'absolute force' as criticism in the West of his authoritarian inclinations gradually increased and the 'strategic partnership', as Dmitri Trenin (2006a) observed, became 'a chapter that was never opened'. This progressive 'politicization' of nuclear weapons has remained strikingly disconnected from the real posture of the strategic nuclear forces characterized by shrinking and deterioration. This chapter examines this discrepancy and looks into one particular issue where Russia's 'Great Power' claims and nuclear ambitions have underpinned the search for tactical gains in geopolitical manoeuvring: the protracted international crisis driven by the advancement of Iran's nuclear programme.

82 *Military muscle as the ultimate proof*

Putin makes a non-nuclear choice

Vladimir Putin was uniquely unprepared for the job he was given on the first day of the year 2000, but an experience he was lacking the most was the command over strategic nuclear forces. None of his trusted lieutenants and hand-picked aids from St Petersburg had gone through even a prep-class in the school of 'nuclear deterrence', and most of the seasoned intriguers that he inherited from Boris Yeltsin were useless in that department. The total lack of expertise did not humble the team of novices but underpinned their rather exaggerated perception of political usefulness (if not military usability) of the vast and varied arsenal of nuclear weapons (Golts and Pinsker, 2000a). That perception was slightly mitigated by the only first-hand experience that Putin had acquired a year prior to the inauguration.

He was appointed the secretary of Russia's Security Council in March 1999 as the sharp political crisis around Kosovo escalated into the North Atlantic Treaty Organization (NATO) air campaign. Moscow was vehemently against any military intervention, and was shocked profoundly, from President Yeltsin and Prime Minister Primakov to the diehard communists and liberal reformers in the parliament, by the fact that Russia's 'veto right' was circumvented and that its nuclear power counted for nothing. Putin organized the special meeting of the Security Council on 29 April devoted to urgent upgrading of nuclear instruments; in the following months, he quite probably developed the impression that those efforts were mostly futile.[2] What made at least some kind of difference in the course of the crisis was the famous march of a company of Russian peacekeepers from Bosnia to Pristina on 10 June, which nearly resulted in a clash with NATO forces.[3] Despite the risk and the sobering fact that Russia was unable to reinforce or even supply that 'bridgehead', Putin, who apparently played no part in the impromptu decision-making on that operation, was in a position to draw the conclusion that even a small grouping of combat-ready conventional forces could be of greater value in the actual confrontation than hundreds of nuclear warheads on intercontinental missiles.

It is hardly a useful analytic exercise to discern the 'lessons learned' from the Kosovo war in the texts of the National Security Concept and the Military Doctrine approved by Putin before his formal presidential inauguration in May 2000; in hindsight, the real political value of these ambitious documents (still formally in force) is quite miniscule.[4] The first serious decision on the build-up of nuclear forces that Putin actually had to make was of quite different character as in summer 2000 the smouldering conflict between Defence Minister Igor Sergeev and Chief of General Staff Anatoly Kvashnin burst into an open scandal.

The 'politics' of this clash is analyzed in Chapter 1, but its substance boiled down to Kvashnin's open mutiny against the priority in defence spending for strategic nuclear forces, first of all the land-based intercontinental ballistic missile (ICBM) *Topol*-M, as established by Sergeev.[5] Funding for the military at that time was quite tight, but Sergeev was able to present sound arguments that returns in the relatively compact strategic triad, which he wanted to gather under a single command, were far better than in the unreformed and strapped-for cash

Army. He also advanced a few propositions regarding the pivotal global importance of nuclear deterrence, but the timing was wrong, since Putin did not really fancy a trip down the mutual assured destruction (MAD) memory lane at that early stage of his presidency.[6] The security challenge that overshadowed all others at that time for the Kremlin was the Second Chechen war, and Putin could not afford alienating the generals who had received from him a *carte blanche* to bring it to a conclusive end, no matter what. Kvashnin, who planned the disastrous assault on Grozny back on the 1995 New Year's Eve, was the leader of these Chechen generals, and his strident demand for more money was not to be ignored.

At the Security Council meeting on 9 November 2000, Sergeev made the last desperate stand, but Putin had already made up his mind, and Kvashnin savoured his triumph in a couple of weeks when the commander-in-chief held a meeting with the top brass and criticized the cadre policy in the Ministry of Defence.[7] The departure of Sergeev's team in March 2001 signified the conclusion in the Kremlin that in the framework of 'minimal deterrence', nuclear instruments were of only limited political value.

Creeping re-nuclearization of security PR

In retrospect, it appears quite remarkable that in the first years of this decade, when Russia was still in dire economic straits and political doldrums, there was hardly any attempt to boost its international standing by leaning upon nuclear capabilities. Neither did the quite inexperienced leader show a discernible psychological need to pull the nuclear 'trump card' out of his sleeve when conducting the uneasy introductory talks with suspicious Western counter-parts. Putin responded with exemplary restraint on both the US unilateral withdrawal from the Anti-Ballistic Missile (ABM) Treaty in December 2001, merely calling it a 'mistake', and the approval of the Nuclear Posture Review in January 2002, which placed a high premium on flexibility in the options for using US strategic and non-strategic nuclear capabilities and opened the prospect of pre-emptive nuclear strikes (Sergeev, 2002). He found a way to overcome the pronounced reluctance in President Bush's administration to accept any legally binding limitations on strategic planning by arguing that codifying the unilateral reductions that both sides wanted to implement could not be a bad idea.[8] The Moscow Treaty (2002) was hardly a leap forward in arms control, particularly since the Kremlin announced that it would not implement the reductions required by the Strategic Arms Reduction Treaty (START II) (1993), but it provided for continuing the range of cooperative projects that Rose Gottemoeller (2002) characterized as 'quiet revolution'.

It is hard to pinpoint the moment when that revolution exhausted its drive and nuclear brinksmanship, mostly of virtual kind, began making a comeback. One of the key impacts, quite certainly, was the intense political manoeuvring around the start of the Iraq war in spring 2003 that altered some key variables in strategic risk assessments. The issue was not that the US justification for

84   *Military muscle as the ultimate proof*

launching the intervention was based on the premise of existence of a massive clandestine programme for developing weapons of mass destruction (WMD) but the rather convincing proposition that Saddam Hussein would have been safe against any external threat with only a few nuclear weapons at his disposal. The swift annihilation of his massive army by the US expeditionary corps also added some food for thought in the direction that only nuclear deterrence could guarantee Russia's security. These assessments were first reflected upon in Putin's May 2003 address to the parliament where he emphasized that 'work is also underway on creating new types of Russian weaponry, new generation weaponry. This includes what specialists have classified as strategic weapons. These weapons will ensure the defence capabilities of Russia and its allies in the long-term perspective' (Putin, 2003a).

That vague statement left experts guessing whether nuclear or advanced conventional weapons were prioritized (Gottemoeller, 2004); that guesswork received a new impetus from an anonymous report on the grave deterioration of Russia's nuclear deterrent that was spinned by Moscow tabloids.[9] The real shift of political attention towards the nuclear matters happened a few months later when the Ministry of Defence presented a new visionary document entitled 'Immediate Tasks of Development of the Armed Forces of the Russian Federation'.[10] The remarkably alarmist worldview presented in this 'White Paper' boiled down to the bottom line that only Russian armed forces could ensure global stability and prevent a destruction of the system of international relations based on common norms and law. The United States, while presented as a 'part of the solution', was also very clearly the addressee of the clarified definition of 'required damage' that would be 'subjectively unacceptable' to a potential adversary since it would outweigh any potential gains from attacking Russia. The president's concluding words that 'the main foundation of national security in Russia remains, and will remain for a long time to come, nuclear deterrence forces' (Putin, 2003b) marked the point from which Moscow has started to rely increasingly on nuclear means in its foreign policy manoeuvring.

The need in that nuclear discourse was not driven by any increase in the scale of external threats to Russia; quite to the contrary, as the US military began to encounter the expanding insurgency in Iraq, Moscow was becoming reassured that Washington would not be contemplating any hostile actions in the near future. On the European arena, the nuclear hints and reminders were not particularly helpful, since the British and French nuclear forces were never a subject to any political exchanges, while Germany was never comfortable with this topic.[11] Nevertheless, the ominous statements about new technologically advanced missiles that were allegedly capable to hit terrorist camps anywhere in the world with pinpoint accuracy and penetrate any multi-layered strategic defence system (which could hardly be associated with any terrorist organization) were issued by the Kremlin again and again.[12]

The real point in these repetitive statements was not in deterring any hypothetic military threats but in discouraging Western attempts at pulling Russia back to the track of democratization; any step along this track was perceived by

Virtually extended deterrence 85

the Kremlin as a walk along the plank leading inevitably to a situation where its firmly consolidated regime could be changed through a competitive political process. Open and direct support from the United States to 'regime change' first in Georgia (the 'rose revolution' in late 2003) and then in Ukraine (the 'orange revolution' in late 2004) through organized popular pressure spread panic in Putin's political class; so, by the start of 2005 it had become imperative to draw the line. Russia had to be marked as 'off-limits' for Western intrigues, and the proactive nuclear discourse was supposed to send a warning signal to the treacherous 'partners' that a 'coloured revolution' in a country with a huge arsenal of WMD is a dangerous and unpromising proposition. Relying on nuclear deterrence against unpredictable torrents of internal protest might seem a really bad plan, but it appears more logical if the point of Western sponsorship, management and guidance for revolutionary movements is accepted as the premise.

A perfect illustration was the Kremlin's reaction to the speech delivered by Vice President Cheney (2006) in Vilnius in May 2006, where he suggested that 'Russia has a choice to make' and emphasized that 'none of us believes that Russia is fated to become an enemy'. Mainstream commentators in Moscow raised hell about the 'ultimatum' of that 'new Fulton speech', but Putin's answer delivered in the address to the parliament was deliberately indirect and invoked yet again the ambitious plans for building up Russia's military might as the only security guarantee, since 'comrade wolf knows whom to eat'.[13] A more direct response was formulated in the 'historic' speech at the Munich security conference where Putin (2007a) bitterly complained about US unilateralism and singled out the plans for deploying elements of missile defence in Eastern Europe as particularly destabilizing.[14] Russian experts and officials rushed to promise all sorts of 'asymmetric responses', including even the withdrawal from the Intermediate Nuclear Forces (INF) Treaty (1988) and the revision of the 2000 Military Doctrine, but the appointment of Anatoly Serdyukov, a loyal bureaucrat with zero experience in military matters, to the post of Defence Minister just a week after the Munich speech showed that the Kremlin did not seriously mean any nuclear confrontation.[15]

It might appear mind-boggling that yet-to-be-tested missiles were given so much attention in the context of the yet-to-be-deployed US strategic defence system – and the real context was indeed different; material reality was all but irrelevant since the missiles in questions constituted merely an incantation that was supposed to exorcize the spectre of a 'coloured revolution'. Realist security thinking focused on assuring that thousands of nuclear warheads would remain fundamentally useless has given way to security public relations (PR) that has no reservations against putting a useful spin on nuclear instruments in order to score a point or two in the fight for the coveted status of 'Great Power'.

The perils of discounting the nuclear risks

The priority financing for the strategic forces, so painstakingly granted by Marshal Sergeev in 1998–1999, was justified by an irrefutable argument that the

86 *Military muscle as the ultimate proof*

available limited funds could buy a reasonable modernization of the nuclear triad – but would disappear without a trace if channelled towards the unreformable ground forces. Making his choice and giving Sergeev the sack, Putin did not bother to check whether the 'missile man' was right – but he had to do this homework when he discovered the need to rely more directly on the nuclear means. The 'White Paper' of November 2003 aimed at securing more resources for the key components of the deterrence potential, but by then some programmes had already been terminated and others had lost their momentum. In the complex cycles of research, development, testing and production, stability and sustainability matters more than sudden generosity. Defence Minister Sergei Ivanov had to learn that increased funding for new projects did not guarantee their quick fruition, while economizing on maintenance of the old Soviet weapons systems that had to be kept operational well beyond their expiration dates involved risks of failure that Western experts would consider far beyond the threshold of acceptance.

Problems have accumulated in every branch of the strategic deterrent, but it is in the Navy that they have manifested themselves with particular force. The *Kursk* catastrophe shocked the whole country in August 2000, and while that nuclear-powered submarine was not strategic, the dismal state of the fleet of some two dozen strategic submarines, most of which were slated for decommissioning within a decade, was revealed with undeniable clarity. All sorts of wild theories about US submarines colliding with or sinking the *Kursk* were advanced by admirals concerned about preserving 'honour' and denying responsibility, but Putin would have none of that and ordered a full investigation.[16] He kept his promise to raise the unfortunate submarine (in October 2001) but failed to deliver sustained attention to checking the deterioration of the Navy. A reminder struck in August 2005 when a mini-submarine *Priz* got stuck in the top secret but poorly maintained underwater antenna to the south of Petropavlovsk-Kamchatsky. Putin deserves full credit for calling for Western help against the advice of the 'patriotically-minded' admirals, and the British rescue team arrived just in time to save the sub not bothering much about the rusty 'sensitive' assets around it.[17]

In between these two underwater dramas, Putin took part in the strategic exercises of the Northern Fleet in February 2004 that should have demonstrated the undiminished capabilities of the naval leg of the strategic triad; instead, both planned missile launches from two strategic submarines failed.[18] Several successful launches in the next couple of years did not alter the net assessment that these strategic platforms were basically unreliable. Putin's hopes have been pinned on the new generation of strategic submarines, the first of which, *Yuri Dolgoruky* (or Project 955), was started with construction back in 1996 and launched out of Severodvinsk shipyard in early 2007. The delay was caused not only by poor financing but primarily by the controversial political decision in early 1998 to discontinue the *Bark* missile project, tailor-made for this sub, after four failed tests, and to reconfigure the launch tubes for a different solid-propellant missile, *Bulava* (or R-30), modelled after the land-based *Topol*-M.

Virtually extended deterrence 87

Two initial tests of this missile in September and December 2005 were success-ful, and Putin hastily proclaimed it to be ready for deployment with new manoeuvring warheads. However, three further tests in September, October, and December 2006 were unsuccessful, confirming that it is still a long way to go until the new submarine could become operational.[19] In the meanwhile, the Navy would have to rely on the ageing *Delta*-IV subs that have seen overhaul but also too much abuse – and would also be hard-pressed to demonstrate that it is fully deterrence-capable.

In the strategic aviation, the problems are generally less visible, perhaps because since the Soviet times it has been considered the least significant component of the deterrent triad. Since the early 1990s, the shortage of resources caused a drastic and sustained reduction of flying time, so that by the middle of this decade, a whole generation of pilots who had never had proper training or sufficient experience had become the backbone of this force. Poor maintenance of the planes, including the 14 relatively new Tu-160s (*Blackjack*), constituted another part of the problem, and the crash of one of these bombers during a test flight in September 2003 confirmed that it reached the point of crisis.[20] Additional funds have been provided for repairs and training, as well as for completing the project for developing a new type of cruise missile (Kh-101/102).

These improvements made it possible for President Putin to take a long ride on a Tu-160 in August 2005 and observe close-up the launch of long-range cruise missiles; he described that as 'a very useful experience to plunge not only into the problems of long-range aircraft, but the problems of the Armed Forces and the Air Force as a whole'.[21] Seeking to prove Putin's point that 'today our strategic aircraft are really up to standard', General Igor Khvorov, commander of the 37th Air Army, assured that in the course of exercises in April 2006, a group of Tu-160 penetrated into the radar zone near the Canadian shores without being detected.[22] In summer 2007, Putin ordered to resume regular flights of long-range bombers. However, the main assets of Russian strategic aviation are lagging so far behind the US forces in terms of technological innovation and combat readiness that it is quite problematic to impress Western audiences with this activity.

The land-based intercontinental ballistic missiles (ICBM) used to constitute the bulk of the Soviet deterrence potential; they were also in the centre of Sergeev's plans for modernizing the strategic forces – and it is exactly here that the shrinking of real capabilities is particularly striking. Where the USSR used to have about 1,400 deployed missiles, Russia in mid-2006 had 502, at least a half of which have to be decommissioned before the end of this decade (Podvig, 2007). One new missile system, the *Topol*-M (SS-27), has been entering service since 1997, but the annual rate of delivery has been set at 5–6 missiles, which is four times lower than the level of the economically efficient production at the Votkinsk plant. Everything possible has been done to extend the service lives of powerful SS-18 (ten warheads) and SS-19 (six warheads), and some 30 SS-19 were purchased from Ukraine, where they had been kept in 'dry storage'.[23]

88 *Military muscle as the ultimate proof*

So far, their test launches have been successful, and the development of a new manoeuvring warhead that would fit both *Topol*-M and *Bulava* has been nearly completed.[24] Putin never forgets to brag about these achievements but carefully avoids any mention of the fact that Kvashnin's proposal on reducing the number of ICBMs to about 150 (harshly criticized by experts back in 2000) is in fact being implemented.

The weakest element of the strategic deterrence forces is the system of intelligence gathering, early warning, and command and control, while its degradation attracts the least amount of political attention. With the break-up of the USSR, Russia has lost access to many fixed assets in this system located in other newly independent states. It has negotiated access or leasing arrangements with Belarus, Kazakhstan, and several other countries; however, poor maintenance has rendered the stations in Gabala (Azerbaijan) and Nurek (Tajikistan) barely operational; it appears entirely possible that Ukraine would press ahead with the closure of the stations in Sevastopol and Mukachevo.[25] Pavel Podvig (2006) argued that 'while the system is indeed past its prime, it has lost surprisingly little of its capability to do its job'; however, Lieber and Press (2006) can expect that their description of it as 'a mess' would be increasingly justified.

The situation appears particularly messy with the satellite assets of the system, since several reorganizations of the Space Forces command have undermined its strategic planning. Seeking to benefit from the expanding market for launching commercial satellites, Russian Space Forces command has often de-prioritized own needs, while many failures of the delivery vehicles resulted in the loss of crucial intelligence capabilities.[26] The development of a new generation of satellites with longer orbit life has been slow, and even the much-advertised global navigation system (GLONASS) that should replace the US-run GPS for Russian users still does not have enough satellites to provide guaranteed coverage.[27] Generally, isolated advanced projects based on modern information technologies in most cases underperform being ill compatible with the bulk of the system based on Soviet technologies of pre-computer era.

Overall, the level of investment in the strategic forces even on the high peaks of 2005–2006 has been insufficient to address many accumulated problems, while the political desire to harvest maximum dividend from demonstrating nuclear 'muscles' increases the risks of malfunctioning and accidents. The campaign for pressing nuclear arguments in political debates has gained considerable inertia; so, for instance, when Putin was preparing to discuss with President Bush a range of issues in US assistance to nuclear risk reduction at the February 2005 Bratislava summit, a series of alarmist comments in Russian media about US demands for full access to and even control of Russian nuclear facilities necessitated a change of focus in these discussions.[28] Putin thus discovered that it was quite difficult to ride on two 'strategic' horses, seeking simultaneously to develop nuclear cooperation with the United States and to exploit nuclear assets for demonstrating Russia's 'greatness'. Already at that moment, his freedom of choice was so limited that he had to almost hide cooperative initiatives in order not to compromise his ambitious rhetoric. Remarkably, it was not the heavy

Virtually extended deterrence 89

inheritance of the decades of confrontation materialized in thousands of warheads but the desire to give them a new lease of life that has determined this peculiar nuclear 'path dependency'. The ongoing re-nuclearization of security thinking and the downplaying of risks related to exploiting the ageing strategic assets have essentially shaped Moscow's political line in the main international nuclear controversy of the decade.

Russia learns to live with a nuclear Iran

The persistent even if incoherent international efforts aimed at convincing Iran to discontinue its programme of nuclear research and uranium enrichment has had so many zigzags, dramatic culminations, and false resolutions that a brief examination necessarily involves oversimplification. Many lines in the Gordian knot that was pulled so tightly by President Mahmoud Ahmadinejad, for instance the complicated heritage of the Islamic revolution of 1979 or the influence of the Israeli lobby on US policy-making on this problem, have to be left out of this analysis.[29] The question here is to what degree Moscow's ambitions in instrumentalizing the nuclear assets for asserting its 'Great Power' status have informed and influenced its policy towards nuclearizing Iran.[30]

Throughout the 1990s, Russia's policy towards Iran was shaped less by the particular interests in the Caspian area and more by the 'weight' of this issue in its relations with the US. Putin quickly discovered that the US obsession with isolating Iran could create some opportunities for Russia but needed more space for exploiting them, hence the decision to cancel the agreement on not exporting arms.[31] Warmly greeting Iranian President Mohammad Khatami in Moscow in March 2001, Putin was cautious not to step over the line beyond which his credentials could suffer – and was indeed able in only a few months to look in President Bush's eye with disarming sincerity. Russia strongly objected against including Iran in the ill-conceived 'axis of evil', but still Putin saw that paying the long-promised visit to Tehran would be inopportune and outlined his position while visiting Israel in April 2005.[32]

By that time, tensions around Iranian nuclear programme had already escalated to full-blown crisis, where Russia's position was of crucial importance indeed, which implicitly validated the claims for 'Great Power' status. The main line in manoeuvring during 2004–2005 was to position Russia close enough to the course of the European 'troika' (France, Germany, and the UK), while keeping open its own separate channels towards Tehran and Washington. That required squaring a tricky circle as Moscow sought to keep on track its flagship project for building the Bushehr nuclear power station without undermining the 'troika' bargaining power. The task was successfully resolved with the February 2005 agreement with Iran on returning the spent nuclear fuel to Russia and with the informal promise to the Western partners not to deliver the fuel to Bushehr until a framework agreement is reached.[33]

That success was tactical at best, since Moscow still had to agree to the transfer of the 'nuclear dossier' from the International Atomic Energy Agency

90 *Military muscle as the ultimate proof*

(IAEA) to the UN Security Council, and while it was much easier to draw its own line in the latter forum, the stakes became far greater. Russia sought to capture the central stage with two proposals that could have broken the deadlock: 1) to sell short-range air-defence missile systems *Tor*-M1 to Iran; and 2) to build on its own territory an international nuclear fuel 'service' centre, which Iran would be able to use for uranium enrichment. The first proposal was seen in the West as quite unhelpful, but the second was welcomed as a 'wedge', which, as Rose Gottemoeller (2006) put it, 'might turn a hopeless negotiation into a productive one'. Tehran was eager to bolster its air defence but recognized that the Russian centre, while probably making perfect economic sense, provided no answer to its security concerns; it showed some interest in the idea primarily as means of winning time and widening splits in the UN.

The embarrassing failure of its initiative left Moscow with a clear-cut choice on the UN Security Council Resolution drafted by the United States, UK, and France – and the crucial support was initially denied. The Kremlin was in no doubt that its agreement on imposing sanctions against defiant Iran was pretty much the only thing that Washington needed from Russia and was prepared to discuss.[34] Putin (2006b) tried to justify his ambivalent stance by emphasizing that 'we unambiguously support strengthening the non-proliferation regime, without any exceptions, on the basis of international law. We know that strong-arm methods rarely achieve the desired result and that their consequences can even be more terrible than the original threat'. The 'principled' position of being firmly against Iran obtaining nuclear weapons and equally firmly against sanctions or other forceful measures aimed at preventing such an undesirable development might appear logically inconsistent. In fact, however, it was perfectly logical and based on two coherent and compatible assessments.

The first one is focused on Iran and builds on the proposition that a programme of nuclear research and limited uranium enrichment under full control of the IAEA would involve less damage to Russian interests than economic sanctions that would block arms export and put the Bushehr project in limbo. The fundamental issue, however, is about a nuclear weapons programme, and while Moscow insists that there is no evidence of such a programme, it has to consider the scale of risk in the prospect of a nuclear-armed Iran. That prospect, while certainly non-optimal, is perceived by the Russian leadership quite differently from the US administration, as Iran is seen not as a 'rogue state' ruled by a fanatical regime seeking the destruction of Israel but as a rational state actor pursuing its legitimate interests, which would never permit providing usable nuclear devices to terrorist organizations or other non-state actors. In some ways, Russia, as a powerful nuclear state, might even find it easier to deal with Iran armed with only a few nuclear missiles; it would basically pose no greater risk to Russia's security than the nuclear Pakistan.[35]

The second assessment is focused on the United States and the coalition it seeks to build with the European 'troika' in the centre and a place reserved for Russia, much the same way as it was in the anti-terrorist coalition. In mid-2006, Iran was certainly not a 'bargaining chip' for Putin that could earn him a few

Virtually extended deterrence 91

favours with the Western partners; it was a test case that should have demonstrated that Russia had achieved a sufficient power to resist US pressure and insist on its chosen course of action in a major international crisis. That assessment required the intrigue to spin without tight 'moments of truth'; so Moscow found it expedient to grant its vote to the UN Resolution 1737 adopted unanimously on 23 December 2006 after making sure that its interests, including Bushehr, were not directly affected and after a special telephone conversation between Putin and Bush (Volodin and Iskenderov, 2006). In the assertive Munich speech, Putin gave much attention to Iran, defending Russian delivery of the *Tor*-M1 missiles, but he also made sure that Russia's stance on the next UN resolution 1747 (adopted by the Security Council on 24 March 2007) was seen by Washington as reasonably constructive, so that all his poignant philippics were swallowed with only mild riposte (Baev, 2007g).

Moscow certainly does not want to take yet another stubborn but futile stand against a possible US decision to use force, as it did in Kosovo in 1999 and Iraq in 2003. Only the ability to prevent an intervention would deliver a proof of Russia's 'greatness', and Putin is counting on the military overstretch of the world's 'hyper-power' that has got itself entangled in the unwinnable wars in Afghanistan and Iraq. The possibility of a unilateral US strike against Iran's nuclear facilities still cannot be discounted,[36] as Tehran firmly rejects the UN demands, but the Kremlin expects that a possible miscalculation would be compensated by a sharp jump in the oil prices. The scale of miscalculation, however, could turn out to be far greater as Russia finds itself not in a nice company of France and Germany, as in early 2003, but in a far more difficult corner with China.

Conclusions

Nuclear capabilities appear to be the most natural asset for Russia to lean upon in justifying its claim for a 'Great Power' status; yet Putin's persistent efforts to gain political capital from such leaning were unhelpful at best and, on balance, counterproductive. He probably shares the opinion of Gerbert Efremov (2006), general designer and director of a missile production centre, that 'strategic nuclear forces, created by the labours of several generations of our compatriots, are one of Russia's main treasures together with the talents of its people and natural resources'. This treasure, however, tends to turn into radioactive dust under his fingers.

One part of his problem is that he attempts to stretch the concept of 'deterrence' to cover the range of issues that are essentially incompatible with such instruments, since no amount of missiles and warheads could shield Russia from Western criticism of its retreat from democratic reforms or convince the political leaders in the United States and Western Europe that 'enlightened' authoritarianism à la Putin is their best bet. Extending the nuclear 'umbrella' over Belarus provides Moscow no leverage in dealing with the maverick Aleksandr Lukashenko, neither can it change the European attitude towards this defiantly

92 *Military muscle as the ultimate proof*

anti-democratic ruler. Russia's categorical objections against the US plan for deploying elements of strategic defence in Poland and the Czech Republic may be more rational than the heated rhetoric suggests, but the implicit linkage to the 'moratorium' on implementing the Conventional Forces in Europe (CFE) Treaty has left it in isolation.[37] A particular dent in Russia's nuclear status, not to mention Putin's personal reputation, was made by the poisoning of Aleksandr Litvinenko by the radioactive isotope Polonium-210, which prompted the US and British special services to reconsider their assessments of nuclear terrorism (Tendler and McGrory, 2006).

Another part of the problem, which now receives far less attention than in the mid-1990s, involves safety of Russia's nuclear arsenal. The Global Partnership Against Proliferation, established at the G8 summit in Kananaskis, Canada, has fallen far short of achieving its aims towards Russia, which now perhaps has sufficient funds of its own to invest in securing its nuclear assets but cannot find a way to use them as efficiently as was the case with the Nunn–Lugar Cooperative Threat Reduction programme.[38] Significantly, increased financing has done little in arresting the trend towards rapid shrinking of Russia's nuclear capabilities, but the political urge to demonstrate this 'super-muscle' has seriously increased risks of technical accidents and human errors.

The Iranian problem is a rare case where Russia's nuclear status indeed matters and its technological and industrial expertise could have been brought to bear in hammering out a solution. However, in the course of 2006, the year of Russia's feckless G8 chairmanship, the prevailing mode of asserting the 'Great Power' status became centred not on partnership but on rivalry with the United States. The consent to the UN Security Council resolutions 1737 and 1747, which imposed only symbolic sanctions, did little to reassure the baffled Western policy-makers that the Iranian defiance was seen in Russia, as Vladimir Milov (2006a) suggested, as a 'Che Gevarian struggle for freedom and independence', while the very clear prospect that 'nuclear warheads in Iran would be a threat to Russia' was dismissed. Moscow has lost much of the hard-won confidence and credibility in the West because of this stance; so, it is difficult to expect that Putin's suggestions for reviving the arms control agenda would find much positive response, despite their rational content.

8 The Army and power-projection in the new 'Empire'

Military power has traditionally been the prime instrument of building the Russian Empire, as indeed any other European empire, and the key mechanism of securing its integrity, whilst the others crumbled and fell apart. From the capture of Kazan in 1552 by Ivan the Terrible to the capture of Merv in 1884, the superior quality of arms helped the Russians to expand the eastern and southern borders of their state; suppressing Polish rebellions and 'pacifying' the Northern Caucasus in the first half of the nineteenth century and exterminating the *basmachi* rebels in Central Asia in the 1920s, Moscow showed unwavering readiness to apply brutal force for maintaining political control.[1]

With the collapse of the USSR, the newly born but centuries-old Russian state had to respond militarily to several urgent security challenges outside its unfamiliar and in many places uncomfortable borders. Conceptualization of these interventions remained quite underdeveloped with a peculiar mix of residual desires for imperial *revanche*, vague feelings of post-imperial responsibility, and imported ideas about 'muscular' peace-keeping.[2] The First Chechen War drastically reduced Russia's power-projecting ability, while the defeat accentuated the traumas of lost empire. Arriving at the Kremlin on the war ticket issued in the same Chechnya, Vladimir Putin was careful not to overplay the revanchist tune and not to commit himself to any neo-imperial enterprise. Praising the 'rebirth' of the Russian Army, he assumed pragmatically that in the near future it would not be ready for any sustained intervention since Chechnya would continue to demand a disproportional share of resources.

The arrival of US military to Central Asia, on which Putin reluctantly agreed in mid-September 2001, did somewhat alter the power balance in the region but made a greater impression on the prevailing perceptions in Moscow regarding the nature and intensity of geopolitical challenges to Russia. The desire to drive away the US bases went hand in hand with the ambition to restore the sphere of dominance that could be seen as an 'Empire' (as described in Chapter 3). Despite these aspirations, the actual use of military instruments has not increased at all during Putin's second term, which still could – in sharp contrast with the bellicose rhetoric – become the most peaceful period in Russia's new history. This chapter will address this apparent paradox, examining first the

94   *Military muscle as the ultimate proof*

development of usable capabilities and then their mostly virtual deployment in Central Asia and demonstrations aimed at Georgia.

What rapid-deployment forces?

As the old Soviet Defence Ministry was appropriated by Russia in May 1992 and instructed to design plans for a far-reaching military reform, the idea of Mobile Forces was the first one on the drawing table. The chain of violent conflicts in Russia's southern neighbourhood provided a clear strategic rational for this proposal, but it never came close to implementation in no small part due to the overambitious design. Defence Minister Pavel Grachev, a paratrooper to the bone, envisaged the Mobile Forces as a joint command that would include all the 'special' elements of the Armed Forces, from marine brigades to the *Spetsnaz* units, and supervise the deployment of newly trained peace-keeping divisions in the army.[3] Bureaucratic resistance and inter-service intrigue in the Armed Forces slowed down that radical reorganization, and the start of the First Chechen War effectively buried the plan since all available resources were channelled towards that hopeless enterprise. The end of the war provided an opportunity to rescue the rational content of the grand plan, but as described in Chapter 1, that opportunity was missed and the lessons of the defeat remained unlearned.

Sending the army back into the war, Putin initially refrained from advancing any plans for reforming the Armed Forces merely stating the ambitious and clearly unrealistic goals for their across-the-board strengthening in the new Military Doctrine. He understood the importance of keeping the 'top brass' happy in the early days of his presidency but, as a pragmatist, took stock of the requirements related to real security challenges. As the combat operations in Chechnya moved from urban centres in foothills to forests and mountains, it became clear that these requirements were centred on building mobile units capable of performing raids and ambushes with close air support. The heroic 'last stand' of an airborne company destroyed by superior rebel forces on 1 March 2000 became a personal matter for Putin who visited both the place of the battle and the 76th Pskov Airborne Division.[4]

In October 2001, these lessons from Chechnya were underscored by the swift and convincing success achieved by the US military in the 'post-modern' war in Afghanistan.[5] However, making the initial hard choices in setting priorities for the military build-up during 2001 and scaling down most of the ambitious designs for strategic nuclear forces, the Kremlin decided against any project for 'rapid deployment forces'. In late 2002, after the *Nord-Ost* hostage drama in Moscow, Putin demanded that military efforts should be concentrated on countering the threat of terrorism – but again opted against creating a new command in the traditional structure of the Armed Forces or building combat units and elements capable of performing a wide range of tasks in the broadly defined counter-terrorist operations.[6]

There was certainly more to that reluctance to build the clearly necessary

The Army and power-projection   95

forces than just the resistance of the General Staff that remained firm set on the traditional views on the character of wars and compositions of the battle order. The central element of any complex Mobile Forces could only be the Airborne Troops (VDV) – and since the early 1990s, there were persistent doubts about political loyalty of their command. The crucial role of the VDV in the fiasco of the August 1991 coup and their pronounced reluctance to support President Yeltsin in the October 1993 confrontation with the parliament made a strong impression on the Kremlin court, which could not ignore the plain fact of heavy concentration of the VDV units near Moscow. The traditionally strong esprit de corps in these forces was particularly suspicious due to high popularity of Aleksandr Lebed, a paratrooper par excellence turned politician, who was 'imported' into the Kremlin for securing Yeltsin's victory in the second round of presidential elections in July 1996 and then unceremoniously dumped after striking the necessary but unpopular Khasavyurt peace accord with Chechnya in September 1996.[7]

Putin had few reasons to worry about the loyalty of the airborne troops, particularly after Lebed's death in the helicopter crash in April 2002. Nevertheless, he was quite aware of the political risk related to setting a new joint command staffed with younger generals with plenty of combat experience and so preferred to keep the elite troops divided under various lines of command and, in particular, to keep the *Spetsnaz* units subordinated to the Main Intelligence Directorate (GRU).[8] Putin carefully reshuffled the command of the VDV, making General Georgy Shpak, popular in the ranks, the governor of Ryazan oblast.[9] The Airborne Troops suffered several numerical cuts, bringing their total strength down to 35,000; they also went through several 'experiments' aimed at combining draft with contract service but did not receive new weapons or gadgets for night-time operations, or modern communication equipment.[10] The only real improvement in the combat readiness of the VDV was related to the gradual reduction of their tours of combat duty in Chechnya during 2004–2006.

Despite the lack of efforts in upgrading and strengthening the mobile components of the Armed Forces, the Kremlin sought to demonstrate the ability to perform 'rapid deployment' operations in order to send a message to those neighbours who became overexcited about North Atlantic Treaty Organization (NATO) partnership. That was the central theme of the 'Mobility-2004' exercises in which some 800 troops (including a company from the 76th Airborne Division) were transported by air to the Far East, where they successfully attacked a position held by 'terrorists' (McDermott, 2004). The effect of that demonstration, however, was spoiled by the real rebel attack on Nazran, Ingushetia, when the Russian troops opted to stay in their fortified camps rather than risk night crossfire (Solovyev, 2004). It was also clear that Russian Military-Transport Aviation had only limited free capacity for strategic airlift (being engaged in many commercial activities), while the tactical mobility provided by helicopters was grossly inadequate and certain to decline further (Babakin, 2005b). Basically, the Airborne Troops have lost their key function of

96   *Military muscle as the ultimate proof*

being able to attack from the air and seize key strongholds in the 'enemy rear' – and became just a light infantry similar to those 'mountain brigades' that Putin promised to deploy in Dagestan for sealing off the border (as described in Chapter 2).

Instead of building capabilities for intervening militarily in potential violent conflicts to the south of Russia's borders, the Kremlin has shifted the emphasis on projecting power in a different way – by developing long-range strike capabilities. The official 'legend' for this emphasis was the proclaimed readiness to destroy terrorist camps beyond the borders of Russia, which appeared to have a degree of consistency with the expressed intention to 'punish' the Taliban back in 2000. In real terms, however, the rulers and governments of Caucasian and Central Asian states were the intended addressee of the message. In order to make the bragging about 'wonder missiles' more convincing, Putin himself took a ride on a strategic bomber in August 2005 and observed at a close range the launch of long-range cruise missiles, which obligingly hit their designated target.[11] The impression was spoiled, however, by the accident with a Russian Su-27 fighter that crashed in Lithuania on 15 September 2005 after losing its way in broad daylight and fair weather. More generally, it was rather hard to claim a 'surgical strike' capacity while not being able to deliver a single precise air attack on real terrorist camps in the North Caucasus.

Overall, despite the obvious strategic need in strengthening the power-projection capabilities, efforts and resources that were actually channelled in this direction by the Russian leadership since the start of the decade have been clearly insufficient. Nevertheless, the reduction of the burden from the regular tours of duty in Chechnya and a significant increase in normal training have resulted in a noticeable improvement of combat readiness of the VDV units, the marine brigades and battalions, and other forces that could be used for rapid deployment-type operations. All these units are designated as 'permanent readiness', which means that all their personnel are recruited on the contract basis, but this small 'elite army' shares many support structures with the larger conscript army (Arbatov, 2006a). The shortage of means for transporting troops, particularly by air, and supporting them in remote theatres of operations remains a key limiting factor. By the start of 2007, therefore, Moscow had partly restored the capacity for projecting power on the scale that could suffice for securing a desired outcome in violent conflicts of the character that was common across the former Soviet South in the first half of the 1990s. The questions about the aims of and rationale for possible interventions and, more generally, about the political will to take risks will probably remain open for the whole period of uneasy transition of power in the Kremlin.

Perpetual show of non-existent force in Central Asia

Of all the experiments with direct use of force that Russia attempted in the 1990s, it was in Central Asia that its military intervention was the most successful. The civil war in Tajikistan, probably the largest of post-Soviet violent con-

The Army and power-projection 97

flicts, was not only brought to a conclusive termination but also formally ended with a peace agreement. Moscow entered into that engagement without a clear assessment of its own interests but still was able to deploy sufficient force and sustain its commitment through years of low-intensity but high-stress hostilities.[12] By the time of Putin's arrival at the Kremlin, however, the convincing force of Russia's military presence in Tajikistan had been significantly eroded, while Yevgeni Primakov, the architect of the 1997 peace deal, was removed from any access to policy-making. Putin's team, in the meanwhile, had to deal with a new security challenge to Tajikistan and the whole Central Asia – the apparently unstoppable advance of the Taliban militia in Afghanistan.

Moscow had no doubt that the Taliban was a non-negotiable enemy and already in May 2000 issued a threat to deliver air strikes on the terrorist camps in case of direct attacks on its thinly stretched border troops.[13] The implementability of the threat was highly problematic, and Uzbekistan raised unexpected objections that Russia could trigger a regional conflict while avoiding any serious risk to itself (Mikhailov, Sokut, and Gornostaev, 2000). In late October, Russian Defence Minister Igor Sergeev met with Ahmad-Shah Masood, who had played a prominent role in defeating the Soviet forces in Afghanistan in the 1980s, and offered him generous logistical support.[14] Russian arms helped the Northern Alliance to hold its tiny corner of the Panjshir valley against the Taliban, but the outcome of civil war in Afghanistan appeared at that moment essentially predetermined. Moscow sought to play up its role as the 'shield' for Central Asia against the 'threat from the South' but did not offer any direct help to Uzbekistan and Kyrgyzstan when the Afghanistan-based Islamic Movement of Uzbekistan (IMU) organized a series of attacks in the Fergana valley in summer 2000 (Mamadshoyev, 2000).

That status quo policy was rendered thoroughly inadequate by the swift run of events following the landmark terrorist attack of 11 September 2001, when Moscow had to give its consent to the deployment of US forces in Central Asia. The request from Washington momentarily appeared as going way too far but the local regimes, including even the entirely Russia-dependent Emomali Rakhmonov in Tajikistan, were so eager to host American troops and provide basing services that Putin had no other choice than to gracefully accept the unavoidable setback. There was never a shadow of a doubt in the Kremlin and among the 'top brass', however, that the US and NATO military presence, limited as it was, constituted a challenge to Russian positions and so had to be counterbalanced and, whenever possible, compromised. The persistent 'clarifications' from Russian officials that US troops were stationed in Central Asia on a temporary basis were not very useful in that respect since it was clear in Dushanbe and Tashkent (though maybe less so in Washington and Brussels) that the coalition forces were set to continue combat operations in Afghanistan for years to come.

There was never a question in the General Staff about making a direct contribution to these operations, despite all the 'constructive exchanges' on counter-terrorist cooperation in the NATO–Russia Council.[15] The question was only

98 *Military muscle as the ultimate proof*

about how to restore the impression of Russia's ability to deter militarily major security challenges in Central Asia, including a not entirely improbable inter-state confrontation that could be triggered by cross-border rebel raids – or simply the temptation to grab some energy assets in the fragile Turkmenistan. The answer that was gradually formed during 2002 included three key elements: consolidating the military presence in Tajikistan, deploying some additional troops and assets to Kyrgyzstan, and turning Uzbekistan into a reasonably reliable ally.[16] In strategic terms, that answer was centred on the instabilities spreading from the Fergana valley and had little if any relevance for security posture in the Caspian area, as described in Chapter 5.

The option for Tajikistan was rather unproblematic – the only issue to resolve was the legal status of the 201st Motorized Rifle Division that had been for a decade covered by the temporary mandate of the Commonwealth of Independent States (CIS) peacekeeping forces but needed to acquire a permanent base. President Rakhmonov tried some hard bargaining but in October 2004 had to accept a package deal that included also writing off the debt to Russia amounting to some US$250 million and a long-term lease of the Nurek space communication centre. Visiting the newly established base, President Putin assured that it 'will provide a stability guarantee for the whole region', which in real fact these troops have never been able to do.[17] The 201st Division is now at least able to pay its bills, but it is so far detached from the bulk of the Russian Armed Forces and so dependent upon local supplies and recruits that it truly resembles a 'lost legion'.

It was also easy to arrange for a new deployment to Kyrgyzstan since President Askar Akayev expressed no reservations against establishing a new Russian air base at Kant, near Dushanbe. It proved rather difficult, however, to make this base work and to assemble a composite squadron of tactical aviation that could perform at least a minimum amount of combat tasks (Sokut, 2002b). Despite Moscow's best efforts at putting propaganda spin on this base as a joint asset for the Collective Security Treaty (CST), it was too obvious that none of its allies was able to contribute anything to its operations that remained quite abbreviated comparing with US and NATO operations from the Manas (Ganci) airbase nearby.[18]

Uzbekistan was the most difficult proposition and President Islam Karimov found much pleasure in irritating Russia in a variety of ways, including abandoning the CST and joining ranks with Georgia, Ukraine, Azerbaijan, and Moldova in GUAM.[19] This anti-Russian defiance earned him good credit with the US administration that was ready to close its eyes on the rather ugly features of his despotic regime. It was the May 2005 uprising in Andijan that abruptly ended that intrigue as Washington had to condemn the massacre while Moscow saw no problem whatsoever with that application of force against 'terrorists'. Karimov promptly struck a 'strategic alliance' with Putin – and ordered the United States to withdraw all its personnel from the Karshi-Khanabad (K2) airbase going even as far as closing Uzbekistan's airspace for transit flights.[20] Moscow saw that forced retreat of the United States as a hugely important

The Army and power-projection 99

victory that signified a crucial watershed, so that by the end of 2005, it had basically achieved its 'minimum-programme'.[21]

One security challenge for Central Asia that was not prioritized or even foreseen in Russia's initial strategy was drug trafficking that increased by an order of magnitude after the defeat of Taliban due to the huge growth of opium production in Afghanistan. Moscow recognized the scale of this challenge and gave it due political attention only after the inflow of heroin into Russia had reached unprecedented proportions.[22] In practical terms, however, the Russian authorities decided to do nothing about it, putting the blame squarely on NATO for failing to stop the poppy cultivation and refraining from entering into any real cooperation with the Eropean Union (EU) that expanded its programme for strengthening border controls in Tajikistan and Kyrgyzstan.[23] Abandoning its policy of 'holding the line', Moscow by the end of 2005 had withdrawn its border troops from Tajikistan harbouring few illusions about the capacity of the Tajik forces in drug-interdicting (Plugatarev, 2005c). The reasons for adopting such a 'do-nothing' policy may be quite similar to the reasons that prevent NATO from adopting a more aggressive policy against opium production in Afghanistan: this hugely profitable business has penetrated deeply into state structures in both Tajikistan and Kyrgyzstan, and Moscow has neither political will nor capacity for confronting the local elites.

In fact, putting high premium on symbolism of its military presence in eastern Central Asia, Russia has created very limited new capacity and gradually reduced much of the old capabilities, while politically it apparently prefers to avoid commitments. Most clearly, this reluctance to engage was demonstrated during the so-called 'Tulip revolution' in Kyrgyzstan in March 2005, which was accomplished by a crowd of only a few thousand 'rebels' entirely surprised by their victory.[24] Russian Defence Ministry even opted to move the scheduled anti-terrorist exercises from Kyrgyzstan to Tajikistan in order to avoid an impression of a possible interference. There were a number of reports that Russia planned to deploy ground troops in the Osh region of Kyrgyzstan or secure a permanent access to the former US K2 base in Uzbekistan, but none of those proved to be accurate (Ivanov and Plugatarev, 2005b; Socor, 2006c). An eruption of violent clashes on the Tajik–Kyrgyz border in May 2006 triggered no alerts either on the Kant airbase or among the Russian troops in Tajikistan.[25] Except for staging a series of small-scale joint exercises (for instance, 'Frontier-2007' involving about 500 troops in Tajikistan in April 2007), the headquarters of the Volga–Urals Military District, which was reformatted in 2001 for focusing its activities on Central Asia, has not shown any signs of preparing for engagement in this direction.

Moscow's desire to maintain only symbolic military presence in Central Asia and to harvest from it plentiful political dividends is quite understandable and has proven to work remarkably well from mid-2005 to mid-2006. However, the gradual increase of real-life security challenges, first of all the resurgence of terrorist networks and the spread of drug-trafficking channels, inevitably tests this virtual security arrangement (Rotar, 2006). The Kremlin ignores the fast-moving

100 *Military muscle as the ultimate proof*

state failure in Kyrgyzstan and Tajikistan's transmogrification into a drug-trafficking state; it expects a quick compromise in the clan struggle in Turkmenistan and apparently counts on the ability of the Tashkent regime to defend itself against instabilities driven by brewing public discontent dismissing the signals that 'Uzbekistan is well down the path of self-destruction' ('Uzbekistan: In for the long-haul', 2006). Moscow has focused on undermining the US ability to perform any stabilizing role in Central Asia and made a successful claim for the role of security guarantor, which it could plausibly perform only in a rare spell of good weather.

Keeping Georgia in the sights

Stepping into Yeltsin's shoes, Putin inherited intensely complicated relations with Georgia bedevilled by deadlocked security issues in Abkhazia and South Ossetia and barely improved by the reluctant promise to withdraw the military bases. The Chechen war did cast a long shadow, but it was still possible to make a new constructive start; instead, Putin adopted an unusually straightforward (even if never spelled out) approach: President Eduard Shevardnadze had to be replaced. His Soviet past and the propensity to exploit the 'Russian threat' in domestic manoeuvring were of little relevance, but the demonstrative pro-Western orientation and fairly positive reputation in the United States made him unacceptable for Putin who was yet to establish his own credentials.[26] Charting a master plan for overthrowing Shevardnadze required more expertise and imagination than Putin's team possessed and, in any case, the Georgian politics was perceived as too messy for any planning. Igor Giorgadze was kept in reserve for being inserted at an opportune moment (as Shevardnadze himself was in spring 1992), but the general assumption was that any new leader, with inevitably uncertain grasp on power and no international profile, would be better than the 'old fox'.[27]

Economic pressure was considered as the key means for bolstering opposition against Shevardnadze, and Georgia's energy dependence was identified as the key vulnerability. Winter 2000–2001 saw several cuts in supplies of Russian gas and electricity justified by Tbilisi's inability to meet demands for overdue payments; desperate appeals from Shevardnadze to Putin for re-scheduling payments and to Western leaders for emergency support helped to restore the supplies, but new cuts followed in a matter of weeks. Public discontent in Georgia was indeed growing, particularly since corruption in the state bureaucracy was outright scandalous.[28]

Putin was in no hurry to advance his ambitions and was inclined to give more time for the newly tightened visa regime with Georgia to make an impact, but the distant resonance of the 9/11 attack made a surprising amount of difference. Shevardnadze was as quick as Putin in declaring readiness to join the US-led international counter-terrorist coalition; Georgia obviously had very little to contribute to the first operation centred on Afghanistan; so it required a master-strike to secure a prominent place in the global war theatre. Declaring Georgia

The Army and power-projection 101

under immediate threat from international terrorism that had established a base in the Pankisi gorge, Shevardnadze performed a truly perfect manoeuvre during his October 2001 visit to the United States. Subtle hints that terrorists might threaten the the Baku–Tbilisi–Ceyhan (BTC) oil pipeline construction added more urgency to his plea for help and in February 2002 Washington established a small-scale 'train-and-equip' programme (GTEP) for the Georgian military that were in a truly pathetic state.[29]

The reaction in Moscow media was close to hysterical but Putin confidently asserted that 'It was not a tragedy', and the mainstream commentators duly calmed down.[30] A tragedy it was certainly not, but Putin appearently under-estimated the significance of the temporary deployment of just 200 US military trainers, which amounted to opening of a secondary-importance but clearly marked front in the global 'war on terror'. On 11 September 2002 (which hardly could have been a coincidence), he presented an ultimatum to Georgia demand-ing to take the Pankisi gorge under firm control or face Russia's unilateral mili-tary action.[31] Shevardnadze immediately appealed to international solidarity; President Bush reasoned with President Putin, who – after a disappointing review of available 'unspecified' measures – had to perform a rather humiliating back-pedalling.[32] Swallowing his own empty threats, he had to adjust the force-ful rhetoric to the hard strategic reality after the General Staff had reported that an airborne raid would be a near-certain disaster, and punishing air strikes were the only 'safe' option (Khodarenok, 2002b). Energy was used again to punish 'treacherous' Shevardnadze, but he survived another winter of discontent, as it turned out – his last one.

Undermining the Georgian leadership by every available means, Moscow never expected that a new team would gain a strong popular mandate – and could be consistently more pro-Western than Shevardnadze. The fast unfolding of the political crisis culminating in the storming of the parliament building by an angry mob on 22 November 2003 left the Russian leadership with no positive options, even if Foreign Minister Igor Ivanov helped to negotiate the terms of Shevardnadze's surrender of power. Putin's reaction was limited to expressing 'logical concern that the transfer of power in Georgia has taken place against a background of strong pressure of the use of force'.[33] His concerns were soon confirmed as Mikhail Saakashvili triumphantly swept the presidential elections and wasted no time moving forcefully against the long-uncontrollable but newly separatist Ajaria. Igor Ivanov had to negotiate another capitulation and airlifted the loyal Russian ally Aslan Abashidze to Moscow.[34]

Admitting mistakes and miscalculations was certainly out of the question, so the Kremlin appointed Saakashvili as 'arch-enemy' of the Russian state on the payroll of Washington. That very natural political response to an undesirable turn of events effectively blocked the only available avenue for building Russia's influence in Georgia – saving its economy. The country was starved of investment, and Saakashvili – appointing Kaha Bendukidze, a prominent Russian 'oligarch' of Georgia origin, as the minister of economy – confirmed his readiness, first expressed during his visit to Moscow in February 2004, to open

102 *Military muscle as the ultimate proof*

Georgia for Russian investment. An economic boom would have definitely consolidated his power basis and that was the last thing Putin wanted to see; so his very clear message to Russian entrepreneurs was 'No-go' (Tretyakov, 2004b). Only GAZPROM (with its semi-detached affiliate *Itera*) and the energy monopoly Unified Energy System Company (RAO UES) were encouraged to expand their assets in Georgia, but the aim certainly was not to modernize this sector but to increase the usability of energy dependency.

Economic levers were to be used in combination with direct military pressure, which was first applied in the escalation of tensions around South Ossetia in summer 2004. Saakashvili made the first move closing down the Ergneti market, which in fact was a 'free-trade zone' for smugglers, but then was forced to respond to a series of armed provocations featuring Ossetian militia backed by Russian 'peacekeepers'.[35] The escalation of the crisis was interrupted by the Beslan hostage tragedy, when Saakashvili gave his troops an order to back off. Diplomatic initiatives aimed at resolving the 15-year-old conflict were, however, far less convincing than the committed effort in Tbilisi to build the strength of its army to four brigades modernized and trained by NATO standards (Darchiashvili, 2005, p. 146). The new Military Doctrine approved in 2005 defined the goals for the Armed Forces in the context of restoring Georgia's territorial integrity – and Moscow was ready to help from its side in shifting the relations towards a military confrontation.[36] One issue that Georgia sought to exploit to the maximum effect in enlisting US support for its military build-up and advancing its plan for getting on a 'fast track' for joining NATO was the stalled withdrawal of Russian military bases. Eager as the Kremlin was to rub in that irritant, the strategic uselessness of the decrepit Soviet-era bases was quite obvious; so the idea to close this channel of Western involvement prevailed, and the agreement on evacuating all Russian troops by the end of 2008 was hammered out (Fuller, 2005); in the last days of 2006, they indeed quietly left Tbilisi.

That was by no means an indication of Moscow's adoption of a more balanced approach, and the explosions on the gas pipelines and energy grids supplying Georgia in January 2006 reminded Tbilisi of its vulnerability – and were used by Saakashvili for attracting Western attention to Georgia's precarious posture (Walsh, 2006). He was only partly successful in that as the attention waned when it was needed the most – at the Strelna G8 summit where Putin managed to stifle any discussion of conflict mismanagement in the Caucasus. Russian media was full of speculations that Tbilisi was preparing a provocation in order to spoil the summit, but after its closure, Moscow orchestrated a new escalation of tensions around South Ossetia that reached a dangerous peak in September (Anjaparidze, 2006). Defence Minister Sergei Ivanov set the tone for the PR offensive with the terse 'reminder' that 90 per cent of South Ossetia's residents were Russian citizens. He also clarified that the large-scale military exercises 'Caucasian frontier' in late July would imitate an operation in support of peacekeepers in South Ossetia.[37] The Russian leadership wanted to establish a new strategic reality based on the fact that with the end of major operations in

Chechnya, it had at its disposal far more powerful military instruments than those that failed to back the ultimatum of October 2002.

The demonstrated availability of such instruments is in itself a challenge for a policy whose key aim is to discredit and undermine the 'revolutionary' Georgian government. For one thing, it is certainly counter-productive, since external threats have invariably generated a boost of internal support for President Saakashvili, who is always eager to trumpet 'patriotic mobilization'. It remains entirely possible that Saakashvily could waste his popular mandate by promising too much, alienating business-oriented moderates and falling into the gap between the small pro-Western elite and disappointed population. Moscow, however, would hardly benefit from such a post-revolutionary elite crisis, since a wide political consensus has emerged in Georgia on the intensity of security challenge from Russia to its independence. The unanimous voting in the Georgian parliament on the issue of accession to NATO in March 2007 demonstrated the strength of this consensus.[38] Adopting a policy of economic sanctions and threats, the Kremlin has in fact abandoned all attempts to create a foundation for pro-Russian forces through cultivating the vast networks between the two societies.

Another and far more dangerous feature of this self-assertive and heavily armed policy is the absence of any institutional mechanism that could check a sudden rush into war. Putin is certainly not an impulsive risk-taker, but with so many overzealous 'warriors' in various uniforms around him and so few independent voices that could appeal to common sense, he could be incited to make a step too far after which hostilities could acquire their own dynamics.[39] Threat by threat, the show of force has become not a means to a political end but an exercise with its own rationale focused on maintaining the credibility of 'compellence' by adding a bit of a fresh twist to each new round. The risks of such self-serving virtual application of power are progressively increasing as more 'hard assets' need to be employed for making the same 'irrefutable' political point. Putin's entourage knows the value of a timely provocation – but has not learned any lessons from the failures in manipulating the secessionist conflicts. The policy of exploiting Georgia's energy dependency and discouraging it from engaging with NATO by demonstrating prevailing force may appear quite safe – but Russia has lost its ability to influence Georgia and to control the risks of escalation.

Conclusions

As Putin's second presidential term was entering the final year, the thinking in the Kremlin about the usability of force for advancing Russia's interests and strengthening its influence in the southern neighbourhood presented an incoherent and even illogical picture quite detached from the practical efforts at building such a force. In the crowd of courtiers, many of whom had background in special services, as well as in the narrow circle of trusted aids, the dominant perception was that only clear military superiority could provide a reliable basis for

104 *Military muscle as the ultimate proof*

consolidating Russia's 'sphere of influence' and thus restoring its 'greatness'. These vulgar *Realpolitik* views were increasingly coloured by the desire to roll-back the retreats of Yeltsin's era and setbacks of the first years of Putin's reign, for instance by 'moratorium' on implementing the Conventional Forces in Europe (CFE) Treaty. 'Revanche is a very positive and strong driver', – one prominent politician asserted – 'Such a revanche would mean that the authorities must give back to the people what was taken from them – a great power that fell apart.' As Fedor Lukyanov (2006d) pointedly commented, 'Cultivating revanchism is the way of the lowest resistance that as a rule turns out to be the most costly one for a nation'.

The loudly proclaimed ambitions are not translated into any consistent effort at expanding and upgrading military capabilities necessary for creating a credible political proposition for projecting force. It is the de-escalation of hostilities in Chechnya that has provided Moscow with some idle and reasonably combat-capable troops, first of all the 'all-professional' battalions of the VDV, that could be deployed to potential 'hot spots'. There is also some capacity for 'punishing' air strikes, though not of the scale or accuracy that Russian officials have grown fond of promising. These limited deployable military means are hardly sufficient for adequate responding to the most probable security threats, from mass unrest to terrorist attacks to narco-trafficking.

There is more than just the familiar gap between political ambitions and real capabilities beyond these inconsistencies and incompatibilities. Making a claim for a new 'Empire', Moscow is in fact quite reluctant to accept any responsibilities that such a role might entail. Russia certainly seeks to reduce and, if possible, eliminate the opportunities for the United States to maintain its 'strategic footprints' in Central Asia and the Caucasus, but it is not at all seeking for opportunities to expand its own military presence. In fact, making great fuss about the new airbase at Kant, Moscow has quietly withdrawn its border troops from Tajikistan and, perhaps reluctantly, moved on with implementing the agreement on closing down its bases in Georgia. Its forces in Transdniestria were reduced to a couple of lightly armed battalions that guarded the non-transportable ammunition depots and doubled as peacekeepers. Russia conducted quite a few military exercises in Central Asia and in the North Caucasus, but every time a crisis acquired a dangerous dynamics, it preferred to back down or assume a 'non-interference' stance. The available military capabilities are quite sufficient for this strategy of virtual power projection, but the real gap has opened between the *revanchist* rhetoric and the policy of holding the status quo but not taking any chances. The shocking defeat in the high-stakes political battle against the 'orange revolution' in Ukraine in late-2004 established for a fact that military force would not be applicable where it mattered, so the Russian leadership now see few reasons to risk an intervention that could boost its 'imperial' profile but involve possibly prohibiting costs. The rhetoric, however, could set an inescapable self-made trap.

9 Internal order and security in the 'Civilization'

Of all the disturbing features that the political system of the Russian state had at that fateful moment when Vladimir Putin suddenly found himself on the top of it, it was the lack of internal order that on the personal level was the most alien to him. Restoring the controllability of the state machinery most immediately and of the society at large by the state were the tasks that had precedence above everything else, since this control was perceived as a necessary precondition for regaining the lost momentum in the struggle for Russia's 'greatness'. It so happened that the place where the implementation of these tasks had to start was Chechnya, which was seen as the Archimedean fulcrum for the levers of control that would turn the country around. The violent character of that drive determined many essential features of Putin's gradually shaping Thermidorean political regime, so by the end of his first presidency, Russia had become so distinctly different from the West that it became not only possible but perhaps even necessary to describe it as a separate 'Civilization'. Yeltsin era's desperate and often flawed search for the ways to reconnect with Europe and to prove the compatibility with the globalized Western project was abandoned and the 1990s became the period, as Natalya Gevorkyan (2006) put it, 'about which we are now taught to speak with disgust and acceptable hatred'.

Putin's regime, as it has crystallized during his second presidency, is in fact not that different from what Marshall Poe (2003, p. 87) described as 'the Russian moment', which carried the state through the challenging period of modernity and included four key components: 'autocracy, control of the public sphere, command economics, and state-sponsored militarism'.[1] None of these components has re-emerged in the old shape, but it is in the last one that the difference is particularly striking. As it is shown in Chapter 4, the scale of transfer of resources into the military–industrial complex has remained far smaller than in the USSR, which had gone bankrupt before it collapsed. Putin's carefully verbalized regrets about this 'catastrophe' are not perfectly compatible with reassurances that he has learnt the lesson of over-investing in unusable 'assets', but he has definitely shown reservations against strengthening the army to such a degree that it could become a powerful political instrument on the domestic arena, and not necessarily in his hands.

The ideological proposition that the self-sustained Russian model of

106 *Military muscle as the ultimate proof*

'sovereign democracy' indeed constitutes a distinctive 'Civilization' has come to the political forefront since mid-2005, as described in Chapter 3, and that has added particular urgency to the question of achieving an internal order broadly accepted by the society and appealing for the neighbours. Indeed, for many Ukrainians, Putin's 'executive vertical' could appear a far more sensible arrangement than the post-revolutionary mess in Kiev, and for many Belarussians, the relative prosperity and openness of the Russian middle class could compare favourably with Lukashenko's rigid control. However, the intertwined issues of Chechnya and terrorism instantly undermined the attractiveness of the historically shared and culturally close 'Civilization'. The Kremlin had to demonstrate its ability to resolve internal conflicts without relying too heavily on the military means but also without accepting political compromises that could deform the model of strictly centralized state system. This chapter addresses the intertwined issues of the war in Chechnya, the struggle against terrorism, and the 'complex emergency' in the North Caucasus, seeking to assess their impact on Russia's political trajectory.

Chechnya: stabilizing the disaster area

The second war in Chechnya was rushed in September 1999 with utmost determination but without any plan for reintegrating this war zone into the sensitive south-western 'underbelly' of the Russian state. The immediate political function of that massive application of force – to create a launching pad for Putin's seemingly improbable presidential bid – was successfully performed during the first six months of hostilities; the victory, however, remained elusive. Putin was not able to say, as did Prince Aleksandr Baryatinsky, who brought the Caucasian War of the nineteenth century to the conclusive end: 'Everything that has happened during this disastrous war should be forgotten forever' (Aptekar, 2000).

Denied a victory, Putin had to transform the war into a controllable low-intensity and low-profile conflict, and in the course of that transformation, he had to resolve two interconnected but dissimilar tasks. The first one, conceptualized as a part of the global war against terror, was to contain and deter the challenge of terrorism, and it is examined later in this chapter, as well as in Chapter 5.[2] The second task was to establish a reasonably efficient control over the territory of Chechnya and restore order among its alienated and traumatized population. It was formally defined as an issue pertaining to securing the territorial integrity of the Russian Federation against the threat of secessionism, while in real terms there were hardly any doubts that Chechnya constituted a special case that had little relevance to the strength of ties between the federal centre and the vast periphery of the uniquely stretched state.[3] Characteristically, the Russian public opinion has never been supportive to this seemingly pre-eminent task; in January 2000, only 27 per cent insisted that Chechnya's secession should be prevented by any means, including military; by mid-2006, that number slipped to 20 per cent.[4] The majority of Russians were sure that the Chechens could be neither integrated nor reconciled with being forcefully kept within a state that

Internal order and security   107

had brutally suppressed them, hence a very low public support for funding aimed at post-war reconstruction.

Putin initially followed these prevailing attitudes in the society and emphasized primarily the role of the war in restoring the dignity and combat readiness of the Armed Forces, which earned new respect of the leadership and the population at large.[5] This military–patriotic rhetoric logically required a victory, which was duly announced in early 2001, after which the control over operations was transferred to the Federal Security Service (FSB). It appeared possible to proceed with a combination of administrative rule and relentless military pressure since the Russian public remained broadly supportive to 'punishing' Chechnya and did not expect any 'normalization', while the international criticism subsided to the level of irrelevance as the global 'war on terror' was launched by the United States in September 2001. However, the high level of combat casualties and the increase of spectacular attacks, like the explosion of the government building in the centre of Grozny in December 2002, convinced Moscow that a more efficient way of governing Chechnya was necessary.

The key figure in shaping the new policy was Akhmad-Khadzhi Kadyrov, who was appointed by Putin back in mid-2000 as the head of the republican administration but gradually managed to earn respect and trust in the Kremlin. The start of the policy of 'Chechenization' was given by the tightly controlled constitutional referendum in March 2003 that delivered the required overwhelming support for the proposition that Chechnya was an inseparable part of the Russian Federation, so that the separatist case was formally closed. In October 2003, Kadyrov was elected the president of Chechnya, but what really mattered for consolidating his grasp on power was the control over disbursement of the reconstruction funds provided by Moscow, which made it possible for him to form personal para-military forces from former rebels under the command of his son Ramzan.[6]

President Kadyrov's assassination in May 2004 marked a crucial watershed when Russia was close to losing control over Chechnya as rebels staged large-scale operations, such as the raid on Nazran, Ingushetia, in June, culminating in the September hostage-taking attack in Beslan, North Ossetia, that ended with a horrible massacre. Instead of resorting to massive punishing application of military force, Putin opted for expanding the 'Chechenization' policy and delegating key responsibility for maintaining order to local authorities. That choice might appear counter-intuitive, but it implicitly reflected the macro-political shift to constructing the image of a Russian 'Civilization' that was expected to demonstrate its vitality by proving the ability to pacify its own periphery, even if 'civilizationally' different, by the sheer strength of its 'gravitation pull'. Putin spelled this message paying a short visit to Grozny in December 2005 when he stressed, perhaps not entirely convincingly, Russia's multiculturalism and argued that 'those on the other side' who refused to lay down their arms were in fact undermining 'one of the pillars of Islamic world' (Baev, 2005c).

Words about benevolent control that respected local traditions would have hardly won many 'hearts and minds' after so much deliberately brutal abuse, but

108 *Military muscle as the ultimate proof*

the key element of 'Chechenization' was in fact an implicit 'amnesty-without-disarmament' deal with the moderate wing of separatist rebels.[7] The possibility to join the Kadyrov's 'guard' instead of undignified capitulation provided guarantees of personal security for the seasoned fighters; stable income was also a consideration for many, and there was always a chance to return to the 'mountains' if the terms of the deal were broken. The exodus of rebels from the non-extremist groups left their leader Aslan Maskhadov in isolation and that made it possible for the Russian special services to set a deadly trap for him in March 2005.[8] The small core of irreconcilable 'freedom fighters' sought to provide a new impetus to the struggle by recruiting new generation of militants through Islamic networks, but their cause suffered a heavy blow in July 2006 when Shamil Basaev, the arch-terrorist who evaded Russian manhunts for twelve years, found his death in an explosion, most probably accidental.[9]

With that much-celebrated triumph, Russia came close as never before to winning the war and anchoring Chechnya firmly to its North Caucasian frontier; the contours of the post-war order looked, however, too ugly to be sustainable. Empowering Ramzan Kadyrov, an ambitious warlord with few moral restraints, the Kremlin has become a hostage to his reckless power-plays. For many political clans in Chechnya, Kadyrov Jr, who shows little respect to the traditional culture of compromise, remains an unacceptable leader, but they could hardly garner any confidence in President Alu Alkhanov who received only symbolic support from Moscow and so had to resign in early 2007 (Makarkin, 2007a). Russian authorities are eager to delegate the most dirty and risky tasks in enforcing 'peace' to troops of former rebels subordinated to and paid by Kadyrov and so known as *kadyrovtsy*. That has brought a semblance of normalcy where some reconstruction projects could go forward, but law is basically absent and fear is the dominant political force. Such a short-term 'pacification' has only limited prospects for evolving into mid- and longer-term stabilization based on rehabilitation of the massive war traumas, but it has many built-in flaws that could easily trigger a new escalation of violent hostilities.

The concentration of an unconstrained power in Chechnya in the hands of maverick Kadyrov Jr constitutes a break with the local political traditions and a serious challenge to Russia's control over this alienated 'subject'. As Sergei Markedonov (2007) argued,

> There is an informal treaty between the Kremlin and the head of Chechnya. Kadyrov makes it possible for the Kremlin to maintain the image of a "pacified Chechnya" and receives in return a considerable freedom of action ... This treaty will have to be renegotiated in 2008.

Fundamentally, Moscow's ability to keep the *kadyrovtsy* in check to the degree possible and prevent an eruption of armed clan struggle depends entirely upon disbursement of progressively increasing 'reconstruction' funds.[10] This substitution of direct military oppression with bribes may look like an improvement, but

Internal order and security 109

it does not testify to the strength and influence of the imagined Russian 'Civilization'.

Counter-terrorism as a political instrument and as a way of life

The task of deterring and drastically diminishing the threat of terrorism was clearly connected but not necessarily fully compatible with the task of establishing effective control over Chechnya. During Putin's first presidential term, all terrorism in Russia (leaving aside conspiracy theories even if they are not entirely without ground) originated in Chechnya and that, in principle, called for far harsher repressions than those actually unleashed in the course of the 'counter-terrorist operation', as the invasion was officially designated. The discrepancy became particularly evident as deadly terrorist attacks in Moscow increased since the October 2002 *Nord-Ost* hostage drama, while the policy of 'Chechenization' involved a de-escalation of military activities in Chechnya. The inevitable even if somewhat paradoxical explanation is that Putin's counter-terrorism has always had other aims than just countering terrorism and has been instrumentalized for achieving political goals that shaped the character of Putin's regime and eventually – the outlook of the wished-into-being 'Civilization'.[11]

Vladimir Putin has arrived to the Kremlin with a conviction that Russia's existence was threatened by an unprecedented erosion of the very centre of the state system, and he was firm set on reversing that trend. He needed a lever to discipline the rotten bureaucracy – and the war against terrorism provided just that. Being himself a product of a breathtakingly successful public relations (PR) campaign, he knew exactly where to start – the main television channels were urgently taken under the Kremlin's direct control, and the media-oligarch Vladimir Gusinsky was briefly imprisoned and then thrown out of the country. Vital security interests related to waging the 'information war' against terrorists provided a rock-solid justification for that 're-nationalization', and they were invariably invoked with every squeeze on the free media, for instance, when Boris Jordan was fired from the already 'sanitized' NTV channel after the *Nord-Ost* tragedy or when Raf Shakirov was expelled as the editor of *Izvestia* after Beslan.[12] Tight control over the media provided the fulcrum for applying the lever of counter-terrorism on other elements of political system that was undergoing counter-*perestroika*.

A key dimension of this transformation was the concentration of political power in Moscow, since in Putin's opinion the diffusion of authority had reached the level where the integrity of the state was challenged. His vision of the Russian state re-centralized through firm administrative control was perhaps outdated, if compared with the modern concepts of regionalism and networking, but nevertheless appeared even 'progressive' on the background of post-Soviet neo-feudalism.[13] The Kremlin pressed forward with the plan for establishing a new layer of bureaucracy – seven administrative 'super-regions' over and above

110 *Military muscle as the ultimate proof*

the 89 constituent subjects of the Russian Federation – as a filter blocking the direct access to its corridors for the arrogant regional 'barons'. As it turned out, the implementation of the plan produced a clumsy and entirely redundant bureaucratic structure, but the republican presidents and governors were successfully tamed and put into the position of absolute dependency upon the federal centre.[14] This forceful reverse of seemingly 'natural' – in the state of such size and diversity – regionalism should be a subject for separate academic investigation, but what is relevant here is that one of the key means for pushing this swing of the pendulum was reasserting the central control over local law enforcement structures. Struggle against terrorism was one of the key drivers here, and the elite Interior Ministry units, such as Special purpose police detachment (OMON) and Rapid response police unit (SOBR), which the governors had grown to perceive as their 'praetorian guards', were firmly subordinated to Moscow and rotated through consecutive tours of combat duty in Chechnya. The most astounding exploitation of the counter-terrorist rationale was the presidential decision, announced two weeks after the Beslan tragedy, to cancel regional elections altogether, which essentially meant the 'elimination of the governors as an independent political class' (Petrov, 2004).

Progressive centralization of power in the Kremlin resulted in a colossal work overload in the presidential administration that assumed the functions of both the *Politburo* and GOSPLAN of the not-that-distant Soviet past.[15] For Putin, with his initially very narrow political base, it was only natural to look upon the special services as the main pool of cadre for his undertakings in reshuffling and reinvigorating the state machinery. He encouraged the 'import' of retired and active personnel from these 'power structures' into the state apparatus; the war against terrorism became a very useful tool for this policy: many state agencies were required to organize special departments for coordinating their efforts in countering terrorism. That proliferation of second- and third-level 'special' positions (deputy minister, head of department) in the ministries facilitated interdepartment networking between former colleagues and the appearance of several 'horizontal layers of influence' inside the presidential 'vertical of power'. Assuming that the steady quantitative growth of 'uniformed bureaucrats' inevitably leads to qualitative changes in the nature of the regime, sociologists and political commentators have popularized the slightly misleading term 'militocracy'.[16]

In reality, it was not the military but the Federal Security Service (FSB) that increased the most its profile as the lead counter-terrorist agency and influence as the natural centre of new networks. Unlike the Armed Forces (as described in Chapter 4), the FSB received tangible institutional benefits from massive new funding for the war against terror and advanced its long-cherished claim to restore direct control over several other special services, first of all the Federal Border Service and the Federal Agency for Government Communications and Information (FAPSI).[17] At the same time, and particularly after the *Nord-Ost* hostage drama in October 2002, it was very cautious not to assume the burden of main responsibility for combating terrorism. In mid-2003, the command over the operations in Chechnya was transferred to the Ministry of Interior; the so-called

Internal order and security 111

'operational command groups' (GROU), which were created in each of the North Caucasian republic after the Beslan attack, were also subordinated to that ministry.[18] It was only in early 2006, when the intensity of terrorist threat visibly diminished, that the FSB took charge of the newly created National Anti-Terrorist Committee (NAC) and thus received expanded authority to direct the efforts of all other 'power structures'.[19]

Counter-terrorism, therefore, provided a convenient and convincing justification for the progressive 'securitization' of the state. By the end of Putin's first presidency, the FSB had constructed such a system of all-penetrating networking that its outreach was not limited to the organization's parochial interests but reshaped a much broader strategic agenda, including the key guidelines for developing the energy sector.[20] Analysts in the Lubyanka headquarters have had good reasons since mid-2005 to assess the real political risks of terrorism as quite low; so, there was no need in any sustained mobilization of efforts and resources. What was conducted instead was only a mobilization of sorts that would suffice for preserving high public confidence in Putin, who portrayed the struggle against terrorism as his personal crusade, and for painting any opposition to his course as 'unpatriotic' and playing into the hands of 'internal enemies'. This 'pragmatic' course was put in disarray by the chain of attacks in mid-2004 culminating in the Beslan tragedy; so, Putin appeared to call for a real mobilization in a speech that struck tone quite similar to Stalin's famous 'brothers and sisters' in July 1941.[21] That emotional appeal, however, dissipated in a matter of a few weeks as it became clear that the public was ready to accept the blatant exploitation of the 'opportunity' by the Kremlin for advancing a package of political counter-reforms that had nothing to do with countering terrorism.[22]

Returning to the 'business-as-usual' pattern in the emphatically declared war against vaguely defined terrorist 'enemy', Putin's courtiers contemplated the proposition that having this mostly virtual war could have been more important than winning the physical one. Indeed, the public by and large internalized the reality that the probability of a sudden deadly attack would remain high and recognized the need for extraordinary efforts aimed at providing safety for the leadership.[23] Terrorism was becoming a feature of the normal way of life in the Russian 'Civilization'; so the sharp decline of attacks in Moscow since autumn 2004 did not even register on the background of such 'natural disasters' as the blackout in May 2005 or the collapse of the snow-laden roof of Basmanny market in February 2006. There were persistent concerns that the G8 summit in Strelna could be derailed by a particularly shocking act of terror, as the previous summit had been by the London bombings, but an explosion on 10 July destroyed instead the arch-terrorist Shamil Basaev (Gromov and Mamaev, 2006).

The unplanned victory in the politically useful war against terrorism came as a surprise, and the Kremlin was reluctant to wrap up the slogan 'Fatherland in danger!'[24] The National Anti-Terrorist Committee (NAC) sought to keep the 'enemy-at-the-gates' fears alive by announcing 'terrorist alerts', as for instance

112 *Military muscle as the ultimate proof*

in January 2007, but it has shown no interest in dealing with such new kinds of terrorism as the murder of a Chechen 'dissident' in downtown Moscow by an execution squad sent by Ramzan Kadyrov or, for that matter, the explosion on Cherkizovsky market in Moscow by a group of nationalist extremists.[25] Dismissing these new features of 'mature Putinism' and insisting that the Chechen problem is solved, the Kremlin paid little attention to the escalating instability in the North Caucasus that gradually became the main challenge to the very existence of the regime and the integrity of its 'Civilization' project.

The evolving complex emergency in the North Caucasus

One of the truly unique features of the Chechen wars is the surprisingly weak spill-over effect, despite their oscillating intensity and the availability of such agents as refugees and diasporas as well as links to other conflicts in the wider neighbourhood. The incursion of Basaev's '*mujahideens*' into Dagestan in summer 1999 only increased that feature as the remarkably strong defensive response in the Dagestani society (as described in Chapter 5) determined the interruption of most channels that could have transmitted the resonance from the Second Chechen war. That made it easier for Moscow to implement its strategy for isolating the war zone and cutting Chechnya out of all regional interactions so that it could be dealt with in a carefully maintained 'black hole'. Political stability in the republics of the North Caucasus, in the meanwhile, was enhanced through the steadily increasing subsidies and transfers from the federal budget, and that provided for minimizing the impact of occasional terrorist attacks and other 'disturbances' emanating out of Chechnya.[26]

While nothing resembling a coherent strategy for the North Caucasus was developed or, indeed, envisaged in Moscow, the central premise of Putin's approach was ensuring that political power in each of the republics remained in the hands of a clan demonstratively loyal to and significantly dependent upon the Kremlin. Following that approach, President Ruslan Aushev, who managed to keep his Ingushetia out of the harm's way during a turbulent decade, was forced out of office in late 2001, and a more controllable Murat Zyazikov was installed through a shamelessly rigged presidential election.[27] In Dagestan, Moscow became reluctant to accept the traditional way of balancing interests in the State Council, where political clans representing various ethnic groups engaged in delicate bargaining and put the stake on this Council's Chairman Magometali Magomedov, treating him as de-facto president. Both choices appeared entirely logical and rational, and both had disastrous consequences.

President Zyazikov proved unable to win support from key political clans and had to rely on heavy-handed policing, thus quickly alienated most of Ingushetia. Building internal tensions culminated in the night raid on Nazran in June 2004, when a troop of perhaps 150 rebels killed more than a 100 policemen and captured a large amount of arms.[28] In Dagestan, instead of a unified structure of leadership, a systemic crisis of governance was rapidly unfolding, with criminalized political clans engaging in violent competition for power. Moscow

Internal order and security 113

remained blind to the signals of escalating destabilization until its denial was broken by the Beslan tragedy in September 2004. That large-scale terrorist attack, while organized by the Chechen rebels, instantly undermined the structures of power in North Ossetia and threatened to reignite the smouldering Ingush–Ossetian conflict dating back to autumn 1992.[29] Recognizing the need to address the accumulated tensions, Putin appointed Dmitri Kozak, one of his most trusted lieutenants, as the envoy to the Southern District with expanded authority.

Just a month in the job, Kozak faced his first crisis when an angry crowd stormed the administrative building in Cherkessk, the capital of Karachaevo-Cherkessia, in October 2004. He managed to defuse the charged confrontation without resorting to force but discovered that the explosion of public discontent was driven by systematic gross abuse of power, which was typical for the whole region. Half a year later, he wrote in a report:

> Corporate clan associations have been formed in government structures which monopolize political and economic resources. The top positions in government and the main economic entities are surrounded by a network of family connections. Systems of checks and balances have become non-existent. The dominant clan-corporate associations are closed entities which are not interested in dialogue with ordinary people.[30]

For that matter, the unrest in Cherkessk was triggered by a 'business conflict' in which the son-in-law of President Mustafa Batdyev invited a key shareholder in a profit-making plant and his six associates to a meeting where they were murdered in an execution-style.[31]

The alarm raised by Kozak resonated in Moscow with the fears generated by the astonishing victory of the 'orange revolution' in Ukraine; so in early 2005, the prevention of mini-revolutions in the North Caucasus became a top priority strategic task. Decisive application of force was chosen as the main instrument of suppressing discontent; so the newly created operational command groups (GROU) conducted a series of 'special operations' where heavy arms, including tanks, were used for destroying suspected terrorist cells (Golts, 2005a). Reporting from the Ministry of Interior was quite upbeat, but in fact the situation continued to deteriorate as the 'loyal' political elites were eager to settle their scores under the cover of counter-terrorism portraying their competitors and political opponents as 'Islamic extremists' (Latynina, 2005e). The wave of brutal repressions only sharpened public indignation against the shamelessly corrupt leadership; the protest activities became increasingly channelled through the informal Islamic networks called *jamaats* that performed many self-help functions in the disgruntled communities but also accumulated the potential for militant resistance.[32]

Observing first-hand the 'sharp growth of radicalism and extremism', Kozak suggested and even pleaded in his report for curtailing military operations predicting 'the appearance of a macro-region of social, political and economic instability'. Forceful 'counter-terrorism' was indeed scaled down since summer

114 *Military muscle as the ultimate proof*

2005, but the compressed tensions still burst into the open in the 13 October violent uprising in Nalchik, Kabardino-Balkaria. In broad daylight, some 150 local residents, poorly trained and armed, attacked several police stations and bases of special services with no chance for success but determined to put an end to brutal persecution of Muslims.[33] Russian authorities, momentarily close to panic, pronounced the chaotic beating off the attack to be a 'decisive victory', but Kozak was given a strengthened mandate to replace those republican authorities who most clearly constituted a part of the problem. New figures with stronger ties to local business elites were promoted to the presidency of North Ossetia and Karachaevo-Cherkessia; then in February 2006, Magomedov was eased into retirement and widely respected Mukhu Aliev became Dagestan's first president.[34] The plan for getting rid of Hazret Sovmen, the president of Adygeya, by arranging a merger of this tiny republic with the Krasnodar kray was, however, cautiously postponed since public protests in Maikop threatened to get out of hand.[35] What was significant indeed, many key figures in law enforcement renowned for their abuse of office, such as the minister of Interior of Kabardino-Balkaria and the prosecutor general of Dagestan, were carefully removed.

These cadre reshufflings did help in defusing the most time-critical political mines; so since mid-2006, the situation across the North Caucasus has stabilized, albeit on a dangerous plateau.[36] The death of Shamil Basaev also produced a calming effect, since besides being a symbol of defiance, he performed crucial functions in connecting various *jamaats* with one another and with international Islamic networks. The fundamental causes of destabilization, nevertheless, remain barely addressed, and that determines a high probability of a new chain reaction of unrest across the region. Replacing the top figure, for that matter, can bring only a temporary reinvigoration in the political system as competition for opening positions stimulates 'useful' activity; in a matter of a few months, however, the new hierarchy settles and orients itself towards the most profitable function – distributing the financial resources provided by the federal centre. Kozak was alarmed by the corrupting effect of the inflow of money and proposed to limit the 'sovereign control' of the republics over the use of allocated resources so that 'the more a region is subsidized the less sovereignty local government will have'.[37]

That proposal, however, was resolutely blocked by regional lobbyists in the presidential administration. It came close to threatening the very nature of the neo-patrimonial regimes in the North Caucasian republics that build their power bases by channelling the grants and subsidies towards their extended 'families', clans, and other clients. The life cycle of such regimes is inevitably quite limited as the growing numbers and appetites of the 'dependents' demand more money, while the 'dispossessed' become increasingly discontent.[38] Moscow's palliative solutions, cheap generosity, and demonstrated readiness to apply indiscriminate force could bring some respites in the local fights for power and lulls in the storms of public anger; the general trend of destabilization, however, appears set to dominate the North Caucasus through the rest of this decade.

Conclusions

The constant threat of terrorist attacks and the arbitrary counter-terrorist measures, the never-ending low-intensity but high-brutality conflict in Chechnya, and the sporadic clashes across the North Caucasus have become the norm of political life in Russia. For that matter, public opinion was quite definite that the destruction of Shamil Basaev would not significantly change the pattern of the Chechen/Caucasian conflicts.[39] The Kremlin certainly recognized that these features reduce the attractiveness of the constructed 'Civilization' but saw them as quite useful for maintaining the tightly centralized system of political power that was the main pillar of that construct. Manipulating the risks and supplying requested 'victories', the authorities have been able to secure solid public support for President Putin as the commander-in-chief in the war against terrorism – but also to ensure that political apathy remained the prevailing attitude in the society.

The only major disturbance in that firmly controlled political environment was the escalating instability in the North Caucasus, so that as I argued in spring 2006, 'Chechnya no longer resembles a "black hole" that was created by the efforts aimed at isolating the war, but looks more like the eye of a storm engulfing the whole region' (Baev, 2006e). Despite the committed 'shuttle diplomacy' of Dmitri Kozak, who without doubt is one of the best administrators in Putin's team, the sustained manhunts for leaders of *jamaats* and the steady increase of funding, no break of trend in deteriorating security has been achieved. What made this deepening crisis particularly puzzling for Moscow is that the regimes in the North Caucasian republics are not any different in character from the structures of power that have come into existence in other 'subjects' of the Federation, but instead of 'normal' resignation and apathy, the population shows stubborn discontent. Seeking for simple explanations, the Kremlin is inclined to put the blame on the spread of Islamic extremism fuelled by external subversive strategies. The causal link between the incurable corruption of the 'loyal' regimes and the spontaneous growth of Islamic networks is indeed too disturbing to explore. It appears safer to remain in denial of the structural flaws in the 'vertical' design of the non-democratic political order that tries to camouflage its ephemeral nature by dressing up as a 'Civilization'.

Part IV

Energy power and the quest for 'greatness'

> But we have natural gas. That is first.
> And more natural gas ...
> And again natural gas ...
> So, in percentage points, you are behind by good hundred years.
>
> Galich (2003)
> *Klim Petrovich talks with tourists from West Germany (1970)*

The material business of managing energy flows and the passionate pursuit of Russia's 'greatness' might seem to be on entirely different political planes. Indeed, in the Cold War era, the Soviet leadership kept the complex decision-making on energy balances entirely separate from the planning of 'mortal struggle with imperialism'. The specific decisions on exporting and pricing oil and gas were certainly tied to the goals of keeping the satellites firmly under control and weakening the cohesion of the 'enemy camp', but in hindsight, the Soviet energy strategy was characterized by 'mercantilism' more than by insidious intentions for turning oil and gas into political 'weapons'.

Vladimir Putin has boldly overcome this separation and turned energy not only into an instrument for achieving 'greatness' but into a key substance of this elusive category. His concept of 'energy super-power' epitomizes this blending of energy business and power politics, where the aims of profit maximization and building positions of power are barely distinguishable; indeed, GAZPROM's market capitalization has become a key indicator of Russia's international status. Using three different traits of 'greatness' – the 'Great Power', the 'Empire', and the 'Civilization' – as proposed in Chapter 3, it is possible to evaluate the efficiency of exploiting various energy assets for advancing specific political projects. While the priority in Putin's 'grand strategy' has been shifting from the first one to the second and then to the third, this analysis is not strictly chronologic but has also regional and instrumental dimensions since each gradual shift involved a spatial reorientation and a particular choice of political means.

10 Applying the gas lever for qualifying as a 'Great Power'

The mental scheme of 'Great Power' is certainly the most habitual one, since the perception of Russia as an 'indispensable power' that is 'objectively destined to come out as an independent player, a separate centre of force not to be dissolved in any international amalgamations' is widely shared in the political elite (Nikonov, 2002). As the more traditional characteristics that justified Russia's claim for this status, like military might or cutting edge natural science, have been eroding, energy has become the default option that appeared infallible.

GAZPROM as house divided

Finding himself on the first day of 2000 on the summit of power carrying responsibility for a huge state-project, Vladimir Putin, who had never been in charge of anything in his bureaucratic career, did not immediately recognize the crucial significance of the energy sector. What he saw was the need to restore the controllability of GAZPROM, which had become the personal fiefdom of its CEO Rem Vyakhirev and, indirectly, former Prime Minister Viktor Chernomyrdin. In June 2000, Putin appointed Dmitri Medvedev, a young lawyer from St Petersburg who a year prior had been made a deputy head of the presidential administration, as a new Chair of GAZPROM's Board. It took Medvedev nearly a year to prepare Vyakhirev's deposing, but the choice of a new CEO betrayed the secondary priority of the task. Alexei Miller, while a man from St Petersburg, had never been a member of the circle of Putin's friends and 'comrades-in-arms' and had only limited experience in business management.[1]

During his first months in the office, Miller was reshuffling the management team by bringing in 'experts' with background in special services and trying to regain control over assets that had been transferred to semi-independent subsidiaries like *Sibur* or *Purgaz*. He was more successful in the first task than in the second, so in late October 2001, internal conflicts over the lost assets forced him to submit a letter of resignation.[2] The request was turned down, and Miller subsequently received heavy-handed support from the Federal Security Service (FSB), including arrests on criminal charges of *Sibur*'s top management, and that helped to resolve business disputes to GAZPROM's full satisfaction.[3] It also contributed to the crystallization of a new business culture in the company

120   *Energy power and the quest for 'greatness'*

centred on extracting political dividends from monopolistic control and reducing such 'values' as competitiveness, cost-efficiency, and even profitability to matters of secondary importance. Cadre decisions in the tightly closed top level of management have been executed with the swiftness and ruthlessness of 'special operations', a more recent one being the dismissal of Deputy CEO Aleksandr Ryazanov in November 2006 (Grivach, 2006b).

Pre-occupied with battles for control, Medvedev and Miller had few opportunities for contemplating ambitious expansion projects, focusing on completing the works on the Yamal–Europe pipeline and advancing the construction of the *Blue Stream* pipeline. The latter (as described in Chapter 11) was only of marginal interest for Putin's gearing-up 'Great-Power' campaign, but the former was of direct relevance. One of the first manifestations was the energy angle of the April 2001 Putin–Schröder summit in St Petersburg, where GAZPROM featured as an actor in its own right, and *Ruhrgas* expressed cautious interest in increasing its minority portfolio from 5 to 10 per cent providing that the trade in its shares was liberalized.[4] It was in that early period that GAZPROM's propensity for under-investing in its own production base and over-investing in export capacity grew strong (Milov, 2006c), and the inevitable consequence – the shortage of natural gas in the most abundantly endowed country in the world – was to complicate the attainment of the coveted 'Great Power' status in the autumnal period of Putin's 'era'.

Yukos dares too far and pays the price

The main energy intrigue at the start of the decade was developing between the Organization of Petroleum Exporting Countries (OPEC) and Western oil importers led by the United States; Moscow became involved in that tug-of-war without a clear understanding from which side it should pull. In late 2001, concerns about a possible drop in prices (which now might seem a mind-boggling proposition) prompted the OPEC Secretariat to begin active lobbying in Moscow for a voluntary reduction of export. Some Russian oil companies, led by *Lukoil*, which planned only moderate 3 per cent production growth for 2002, were in favour of striking a deal with the cartel. *Yukos*, aiming at a rapid expansion from 57.5 to 70 million tons of crude, argued against any self-imposed restrictions. Opinions in the government were split, but in the end, the worries about the budget that was crucially vulnerable to any volatility in the oil market prevailed, and the seasonal ceiling on export was introduced.[5] Nevertheless, the arguments advanced by Mikhail Khodorkovsky that the OPEC's ability to control the market was on the wane and that Russia's interests would be better served by building a profile of an alternative supplier created a strong resonance.[6]

Always suspicious of parochial corporate interests, Putin was not content to leave the issue of such importance to be decided by a brawl between *Lukoil* and *Yukos* and sought to establish his own channel of communication with the OPEC, meeting with Saudi Crown Prince Abdullah in September 2003. By far

Applying the gas lever 121

more important, however, was the November 2001 summit with President Bush in Crawford, where Putin got wind of an opportunity to add an energy dimension to the newly forged counter-terrorist alliance with the United States. Making Russia an answer to the US worries about the oil dependency from the Gulf would have greatly advanced his re-formatted claim for the 'Great Power' status. At the Moscow summit in May 2002, he pre-empted the critical voices that 'Mr. Bush must speak the truth about Russia's democratic backsliding' (McFaul, 2002) by suggesting to launch an 'energy dialogue'. The dialogue had a grand opening at the November 2002 US–Russia Commercial Energy Summit in Houston, and James A. Baker in the keynote address emphasized that, 'perhaps most important of all, the full development of Russia's immense potential by increasing diversity of international supply will reduce considerably the risk of instability at the world petroleum market that remains dominated by the volatile Middle East'.[7]

While some over-enthusiastic voices in Moscow promised to overtake Saudi Arabia as the top world exporter, the shrewdest experts suggested a less burdensome role of a balancer, since Russia 'is the only country that can play on the side of OPEC or against it, participating officially at conferences of both exporters of liquid fuel and consumers as well (G8), and playing the role of "petroleum referee"' (Nikonov, 2002). Such a high-prestige role as an arbiter would have suited Putin personally just fine and answered perfectly his ambitions regarding Russia's 'Great Power' status, if not one irritating nuance: Khodorkovsky was always two steps ahead of him. He was not only throwing powerpoint presentations to Western executives and organizing an 'experimental delivery' of Russian oil to the US market but also advancing breathtaking projects like the new pipeline to the new deep-water oil terminal in Murmansk.[8] He was making fast-growing *Yukos* respectable for its newly adopted transparency standards and preparing to acquire *Sibneft* while courting Western majors for possible partnerships. Given another half-year, this emerging international giant could have become a powerful independent player – but that would have left Putin with only symbolic supervisory functions and without any real control over decision-making.

The attack on *Yukos* was so vicious that it astonished even the most cynical Russia-watchers and spread panic among sensitive investors. The deep sources of Putin's personal vengeance have to be, and indeed are as the repressions continue to unfold,[9] a subject for another investigation, but what is essential here is the immediate and profound impact on the 'energy dialogue' with the United States. The second Commercial Energy Summit conveyed in St Petersburg in September 2003 turned out to be the 'high-water mark' in the cooperation as the 'man who symbolizes the development of a new, progressive and internationally-minded business class in Russia' was thrown in jail next month (Chow, 2003). Not only were the key investment projects derailed, but Russia's claim for the role of 'petroleum referee' was compromised beyond rescue, since Putin was made to understand that he would not be acceptable for the West as any kind of 'arbiter'.

122   *Energy power and the quest for 'greatness'*

GAZPROM conquers Europe

The Kremlin quite probably underestimated the resonance from the *Yukos* case in the United States, but its readiness to accept serious risks to its oil interests was based on the new assessments of prospects in the gas business. In early 2003, the focus of Moscow's 'Great Power' manoeuvring shifted to Europe as the long-anticipated war in Iraq materialized, and Putin was embraced by Chirac and Schröder as a key partner in the anti-US 'triumvirate'. Significantly, GAZPROM had overcome its internal squabbles by 2003 and so was ready to serve as a fully operational tool for this European intrigue. Miller had successfully consolidated control over the vast corporate assets and made a convincing case against any 'liberal reforms' that would have split the monopoly and limited the Kremlin's capacity for directing the flows of gas and cash.[10]

What hampered to a no small degree the efforts on the European direction during 2004 was the scramble for the *Yukos* spoils as GAZPROM sought to take over the state-owned *Rosneft*, which in turn aimed at grabbing *Yuganskneftegaz*, the juiciest bit of the loot. This complicated intrigue triggered an unusually bitter clash inside the Kremlin as one clan pushed for GAZPROM's aggressive expansion into the oil sector but another defended *Rosneft*'s 'independence', which essentially meant control by a different gang of Putin's 'loyalists'.[11] In the end, the merger fell apart, but the silver lining for GAZPROM was that it thus managed to stay clear of the dismemberment of *Yukos* that was succinctly qualified by Andrei Illarionov as 'the swindle of the year' (Baev, 2005d).

What did implicitly but significantly help the 'gasification' of Russia's quest for 'great-powerness' was the gradual change of energy policies in Europe. The Russia–EU 'energy dialogue' was launched as early as October 2000 but showed few practical results in the first three years primarily because Moscow remained reluctant to adjust its policy to the requirements of the Energy Charter (1994), in particular regarding the Transit Protocol and the opening of its domestic energy market for competition. Nevertheless, the completion of the Yamal–Europe pipeline provided for the increase of Russia's gas export to Europe from the plateau of 125–130 bcm during 1999–2002 to 156 bcm in 2005.[12]

This increase was not that significant in itself (Germany took the bulk of new gas), but it underpinned Moscow's successful lobbying against the so-called 'Acceleration Directive' ratified by the European Parliament in July 2003. Showing some flexibility on the issue of 'destination clauses', GAZPROM held firm on the issue of long-term contracts and scored an important victory with the Gas Security Directive passed by the European Union (EU) Council in April 2004, which established that 'the current level of long-term contracts is adequate' and emphasized their 'very important role'.[13] As Grant and Barysh (2003) argued, 'there is a growing mismatch between the EU's own efforts to liberalise its energy market and the supply of Russian gas through a monopolist, namely Gazprom'. In fact, as the oil prices started to climb beyond the 'comfort zone' of US$25–30 per barrel and the gas prices followed suit, the EU drive towards liberalization began to slacken; so, the 'mismatch' became less of an obstacle.

Applying the gas lever   123

Adopting 'economic nationalism' that would 'gladden the heart of Karl Marx', major European states began to support their respective 'national champions'. As *The Economist* ('The nationalist resurgence', 2006) pointed out, 'There are indeed some uncomfortable similarities between the European Union's mood just now and Russia's state-directed capitalism. The French government seems to favour a sort of Gallic Gazprom, that well-connected and politically influential behemoth.'

Moscow raised its 'gas diplomacy' to a new level with the EU expansion in 2004 building on its strong positions in the 'new Europe'. It did not quite manage to overcome the strong desire in Poland and the Czech Republic for diversifying the gas supplies but made important acquisitions in Bulgaria and engaged in intensive horse-trading in Hungary. The latter paid off in June 2006 when GAZPROM and MOL signed a deal on pipelines and gas storage facilities that could make Hungary a 'hub' for Russian gas in the South-Eastern Europe; somewhat ironically, the deal was finalized a few hours before President Bush arrived to Budapest to commemorate the fiftieth anniversary of the 1956 uprising (Dempsey, 2006).

Shedding minor reputation damage from the *Yukos* 'affair', Putin redoubled his efforts at lobbying GAZPROM's interests at every meeting with key European counter-parts exploiting every crack of opportunity, for instance making sure that his 'special friendship' with Italian Prime Minister Silvio Berlusconi would contribute to forging new links between GAZPROM and ENI.[14] The main focus of these networking activities, however, was Germany, where some suspicious contacts dating back to Putin's KGB work in Dresden in the late-1980s were tied to some unscrupulous characters that had surfaced in the era of 'wild privatization' and connected to intimate trust-based relations with highly respectable companies like *Kommerzbank*, *Dresdner Kleinwort Wasserstein*, or *Deutsche Bank*.[15] The moment of triumph for Putin's gas networking came on 8 September 2005 in Berlin, where he came to give a bit of support to Chancellor Schröder who badly needed good publicity in the final stage of a desperate parliamentary election campaign and also to finalize the long-discussed deal on the construction of a new North European pipeline from Vyborg to Greifswald across the Baltic Sea.[16] After narrowly losing the elections, Schröder accepted the position of the chair of the Shareholders Committee in the *Nord Stream* AG, joint venture company established by GAZPROM (51 per cent interest), BASF, and E.ON (24.5 per cent each) for constructing the pipeline, prompting *Washington Post* to comment: 'If nothing else, Mr. Schroeder deserves opprobrium for his bad taste' ('Gerhard Schroeder's sellout', 2005).

The economic fundamentals of this hugely expensive project remain questionable, particularly in terms of the significantly lower costs of such alternatives as the second trunk of the Yamal–Europe pipeline going across Belarus and Poland. What is more, its very rationale is far from rock-solid as Russia's production of natural gas is expected to stabilize in the near future and the amount of 'blue fuel' available for export is certain to decline (as examined in Chapter 1). It makes, nevertheless, perfect geopolitical sense as Russia is set to increase

124   *Energy power and the quest for 'greatness'*

the flexibility of its gas exports and thus acquire the ability to grant preferences to certain customers and award or withdraw transit benefits.[17] On the eve of 2006, pondering the immediate prospects for chairing the G8, Putin (2005a) was clearly excited about this perspective for maximizing the returns on his political investments and converting gas earnings into political dividends. For him, that was the essence of Russia's new status as a 'Great Energy Power', and he sought to convince the European partners that Russia would be a benevolent and reliable 'energy security' provider. Many Europeans, however, remained sceptical and wary – and the EU was spurred into action as Moscow made the first move in the direction where it expected to find only feeble resistance against its energy power.

The EU strikes back

The so-called 'gas war' with Ukraine in the first days of 2006 in retrospect appears such a monumental and entirely unnecessary blunder that it is hard to believe that the Russian leadership launched it consciously and deliberately. Yet, the special Security Council meeting on 22 December 2005 where Putin spelled the 'ambitious' task of achieving the position of 'the leader in the world energy market' and emphasized 'Russia's role in guaranteeing international energy security' proves beyond doubt that the course of actions was carefully planned.[18] Russia's right to increase the prices on gas exported to Ukraine was indeed entirely legitimate, but its desire to prove itself as 'energy super-power' could have been effectively achieved without destroying Putin's point that 'Russia values the reputation of a solid, reliable and responsible partner in the market for energy resources, a reputation it deserves.'

Three features of decision-making in the Kremlin interfered with the sound economic rationale and distorted the logic of 'energy security'. The first one was the pronounced urge to punish Ukraine for its European choice in the 'orange revolution', which for Putin was not just a major setback in asserting Russia's 'greatness' but also an acute personal humiliation. The intention to weaken the 'orange coalition' in the final stage of the parliamentary campaign could have also been a motivation but only of secondary importance.[19] The second feature was the strong preference in GAZPROM (and, accordingly, in the part of the presidential administration closely linked to its management) to preserve the well-established pattern of settling the gas disputes with Ukraine through 'friendly' deals involving non-transparent companies and undisclosed beneficiaries. Indeed, the swift termination of the 'gas war' followed that pattern, and the structure of ownership of the joint company *Rosukrenergo* that channelled nice profits to conspicuous mediators remained a mystery.[20] The third feature was the gross underestimation of the political costs of 'a-step-too-far' type of error, which was partly a consequence of the systematic distortion of information in the Kremlin court where every sycophant was all too eager to tell the 'tsar' exactly what he wanted to hear. For the most part, however, it was the result of the new arrogance of force stemming from the perception that Russia was in

Applying the gas lever 125

possession of resources so valuable that any kind of bad behaviour would be gladly forgiven.[21]

The decision, approved personally by Putin, to stop gas export to – but not through – Ukraine from 1 January 2006, even if legally impeccable, triggered a landslide reaction in Europe. The opponents of the North European pipeline (Sweden, Poland, and the Baltic trio) joined forces with those who argued against the overdependence upon GAZPROM (in the Czech Republic, the Netherlands, Italy) and the advocates of liberalization of the gas market (the UK) to press for a new EU policy. The contours of this policy were quickly outlined in the 'Green Paper' on the European Strategy for Sustainable, Competitive, and Secure Energy, that was discussed at the extraordinary Energy Council on 14 March 2006. While there were not that many new initiatives in this document, it re-established the priority and added momentum in the implementation of those 'de-monopolization' goals from the Energy Charter that GAZPROM had believed to be scrapped for good.[22]

Moscow responded to that counter-offensive by a stream of PR-exercises centred on Putin's (2006a) own essay where he criticized the 'energy egoism' allegedly displayed by the West. The main threat to global energy security was identified in 'the lack of stability in the hydrocarbon markets', while the common answer 'should be based on a long-term, reliable and environmentally sustainable energy supply at prices affordable to both the exporting countries and the consumers'. The practical translation of this philosophy, offered by Miller in several blunt statements, boiled down to demands to abandon plans for liberalizing the gas market in Europe and adopt instead the system of long-term contracts where guaranteed volumes would be linked to prices fixed on the current level characterized as 'fair'. GAZPROM also bitterly complained about 'double standards' that prevented it from acquiring downstream assets in the EU states, while its own shares were since 2006 traded without discrimination for foreign investors.[23] Straining to add convincing power to these complaints, Khristenko (2006) and Miller ventured threats that Russia would open alternative routes for its gas exports towards Asia.

These threats did not begin to look serious even when Putin put his signature on a declaration about a possible agreement on constructing a gas pipeline to China in order to begin deliveries in 2011, since the development of oil-and-gas fields in East Siberia required investments that GAZPROM was clearly not prepared to contemplate – and had no intention of inviting the Chinese companies to make. In fact, guarding its monopoly, it pulled every political string in order to prevent TNK-BP from developing the Kovykta field with the aim of exporting to China.[24] The bluff with flashing the unplayable 'China card' only increased the conviction in Europe that 'Gazprom's position is not entirely consistent, to put it mildly' ('Customer relations, Gazprom-style', 2006). Nevertheless, the EU remained wary to antagonize the irreplaceable supplier, particularly since a consensus on implementing the guideline for 'diversification' proved to be agonizingly difficult to reach.

GAZPROM had no intention to wait until this consensus would materialize

126 *Energy power and the quest for 'greatness'*

suspecting that time is not exactly on its side. Mobilizing every string in its German networks, it ironed out the agreement with BASF on assets swap, so that its share in *Wingas* increased from 35 to 50 per cent in exchange for 25 per cent ownership of *Severneftegazprom* that controls the huge Yuzhno-Russkoe gas field in West Siberia. Signed during Chancellor Merkel's visit to Tomsk in late April 2006, this agreement should have signified a major breakthrough, which was only slightly reduced by the delay of the complementary agreement with E.ON *Ruhrgas* that was to get another 25 per cent of GAZPROM's subsidiary in exchange for shares in its gas distribution systems.[25] Suspicions and reservations in the EU about GAZPROM's true aims in acquiring European energy assets, however, only increased after this half-deal, to which Merkel herself was less than fully committed, so that instead of a breakthrough, Moscow found itself sliding into an unprecedented crisis in energy relations.

The US administration made no secret from its position in this crisis warning the EU against increasing its dependency upon Russia and sending a stern signal to Moscow that 'No legitimate interest is served when oil and gas become tools of intimidation or blackmail, either by supply manipulation or attempts to monopolize transportation.'[26] The suggestion of Foreign Minister Lavrov that Vice President Cheney was 'misinformed' and the complaint by Minister of Energy Khristenko that Moscow is 'deeply puzzled by recent commentary in the West that distorts Russian energy policies' did nothing to defuse the tensions (Buckley, 2006). It became clear that the Russian script for the 'energy security' topic would be reduced to a hollow declaration at the G8 summit, since seven founding members of the club, despite their differences, were converging on the platform that would grant Moscow only a limited possibility for converting its hydrocarbon exports into political influence.

Putin launches the 'autumn offensive' – and retreats to a 'Gas OPEC'

It is entirely possible that Putin, pragmatic and sober as he fancies himself to be, fell victim to his own propaganda that trumpeted the Strelna summit as the 'best G8 event ever' and a 'triumph' of Russian foreign policy.[27] The approved 'Global Energy Security Action Plan' was appropriately full of wishful thinking and non-binding noble commitments, still leaving Moscow disappointed that the plan for making the 'energy security' topic into the battering ram that would break the walls of trans-Atlantic (as well as trans-Pacific) solidarity and deliver Russia to the position of privileged partnership beyond any 'unfriendly' criticism did not work.[28] There were also lingering suspicions that the lavish St Petersburg buffet did not entirely take away the aftertaste of the 'gas war' with Ukraine to which some drops of poison were added by agitated 'new Europeans' (Socor, 2006d).

Wasting little time pondering on this unfinished business, Putin launched a new 'gas offensive' on the European direction at the trilateral summit with Chirac and Merkel in Compiegne with the idea of revising the plan for develop-

Applying the gas lever 127

ing the Shtokman gas field from constructing an LNG plant aimed at the US market to a new pipeline towards Europe (Grib, 2006b). This idea was elaborated during Putin's 'sentimental' visit to Dresden in October when he suggested channelling great new volumes of gas from Yamal and Shtokman to Germany practically appointing it the European gateway for Russian gas. Merkel, however, was less than thrilled with the prospect of being Russia's privileged partner and turned down the generous offer, signing instead an agreement on energy partnership with France and confirming the adherence to the Energy Charter (Baev, 2006k).

Putin was stunned by that affront, but the message was rubbed deeper at the Russia–EU summit in Lahti, Finland, later that month where the member-states managed to adopt a common position based on the Energy Charter.[29] Moscow defied that unity and insisted on negotiating a new more balanced document that would take better account of its interests in 'security of demand'; its negotiating power, however, was further undermined by Poland that stubbornly insisted on settling the trade dispute about meat export before the talks on a new framework agreement could be started. Putin remained defiant and tried to shrug off the Polish intrigue, but he could not fail to see that the 'technical' disagreements about the protocols to the Energy Charter were just the tip of the deepening conflict in energy relations.

One part of the problem was the increasingly pronounced propensity in the EU and in Germany in particular to treat GAZPROM not as a powerful but essentially 'normal' company with legitimate commercial appetite but as a department of the presidential administration with an aggressive and barely hidden political agenda (Ostrovsky, 2006). Painstakingly advancing legislation on deepening the energy market, the EU Commission wanted to make sure that Russian energy-political 'mutant' would not take advantage of the newly liberalized business.[30] Whether Putin at that stage did cherish the ambition of becoming GAZPROM's CEO after stepping down from the 'throne' in spring 2008 or not, he took that 'unfair discrimination' very personally. Complaining bitterly that GAZPROM was denied investment opportunities in gas distribution networks, he was still unable to dispel the concerns among consumers that the Russian super-monopoly was not able to develop new gas fields, including Shtokman, but without the necessary increase in production, the 'penetration' into the downstream sector became a rather dubious proposition.

Another and perhaps greater part of the problem in energy relations was the broken link between Russia's gas export to Europe and its 'Great Power' status, which had been a key element in Putin's campaign plan. The Kremlin had calculated that the worries about 'energy security' in the EU would escalate to such an overriding obsession that Russia's offer to provide 'security guarantees' would grant it effective immunity from any political prosecution. That calculation was proven wrong, and besides the shortcomings in the content of the offer, it was also the arrogance with which Moscow slammed it on every negotiation table that convinced the Europeans to turn it down (Lukyanov, 2006e). The EU was ready to prioritize the energy matters but not to such a degree that it would

128 *Energy power and the quest for 'greatness'*

turn a blind eye on the murder of journalist Anna Politkovskaya, whom Putin sincerely believed to be a person of no importance.

Disappointment and irritation about the failure to convert the 'gas power' into political unassailability came through in Putin's 'anti-unipolar' Munich speech, in which energy issues were not emphasized (unlike in most presentations during 2006) but the claim for an 'independent' role in world affairs was made loud and clear. The translation of this claim into the language of gas deals came in a matter of a few days when Putin confirmed that the proposal of Iranian supreme leader Ali Khamenei to establish an organization of gas-exporting states similar to OPEC was 'an interesting idea'. A report of the North Atlantic Treaty Organization (NATO) economic experts on Russia's increasing politicization of energy export and the possibility of building a gas cartel was ridiculed by Moscow as having 'no substance at all' (Dombey, Buckley and Hoyos, 2006). Industry and Energy Minister, Viktor Khristenko, asserted that 'rumours about cartels and gas OPECs are figments of over-excited imagination' – but then was ordered by Putin to partake in the Doha conference, where such rumours came close to materialization (Tomberg, 2007). It was obvious for the experts that the gas-producing states were not going to establish a price-fixing mechanism that would disconnect natural gas from the oil market; so the fuss around the quasi-organizations amounted only to a political provocation.[31] Russia's readiness to take part in that provocation was, however, a clear evidence of its re-orientation to the use of more offensive gas weapons in the struggle for political position of power.

Conclusions

Moscow's policy of consolidating its 'Great Power' status by exploiting its position of 'energy strength' had a solid foundation in terms of resources and export capacity; yet it has turned out to be remarkably counter-productive. By 2007, it had become clear that its two main lines of political action, which could be labelled as 'mercantilism' and 'securitization', were ill compatible, while each of them was also internally incoherent.

In the first line, the attention was centred on the industrial and commercial aspects of the energy business, with the emphasis on Russia's readiness to play by the market rules and abide to the rigorous international standards of corporate ethics. That line was drawn quite convincingly by Khodorkovsky in 2002, but the destruction of *Yukos* directed by the Kremlin and looting of its assets wiped out most of the substance in the Russia–US 'energy dialogue'. Moscow's further manoeuvring on the oil market was sporadic, but its spectacular growth made it possible to shift the attention to the gas sector where mighty GAZPROM has emerged as a *bona fide* 'national champion'. The contradiction between the EU's aim of liberalizing the European energy market and GAZPROM's monopolistic character was in real terms a lesser obstacle that it might have seem to be, since many member-states appeared ready to sabotage that aim and preserve the system of non-competitive long-term contracts. GAZPROM, however, has

Applying the gas lever 129

remained unable to utilize many natural advantages of a monopoly, including control over domestic prices and, in particular, strategic planning of its own development. Its investment programmes remained driven by political intrigues and so, while showing great appetite for downstream assets in Europe, it now has to deal with the consequences of sustained and massive underinvestment in basic upstream infrastructure. Fundamentally, in both global oil market and European gas market, Russia's manoeuvring is constrained by lack of spare production capacity, and its influence is undermined by the structurally inevitable stagnation. Not being able to provide tangible answers either to emergency peaks in current demand (like in the unusually cold winter of 2005/2006) or to the expected growth in demand in mid-term perspective, Moscow cannot perform a role of 'energy security' provider.

The problems with the second line are even greater, since the 'securitization' of the energy business, where the issues of reliable energy supply are elevated into the realm of 'national security' matters, implies that the calculations of cost-efficiency and other commercial considerations are of only secondary importance. Emphasizing that decision-making on energy questions is shaped by the strategic logic of risk assessment and alliance-building, Russia then has to 'sell' itself as a reliable and 'safe' alternative to the volatile Middle East. With the United States, Moscow could not realistically aim at anything more than a modest contribution to the diversification of energy imports, but with the EU, the aim could have been far more ambitious; indeed, Russia by the end of this decade might be able to increase its share in the EU gas consumption to more than a third (from 25 per cent currently). From a 'national security' perspective, this sort of dependency could be acceptable only if the supplier is a trusted partner or, indeed, ally. Putin's Russia, in the real system of political coordinates, has been drifting away from Europe, and the four 'roadmaps' signed in mid-2005 that should have guided the emergence of four 'common spaces', including an economic one, have remained an atlas of wishful thinking. Putin's idea of a European 'Great Power' has been based on playing the trio of key partners (Germany, France, Italy) against the EU Commission, or Germany against Poland, or the main consumers of Russian gas against Ukraine. Energy is perceived as the main asset for this 'balancing', but that directly contradicts the proposition of making Russian into a supplier 'beyond reproach'; it is still possible to score some tactical points, but the strategic loss has become impossible to deny. In many ways, Ukraine being the most direct one, the failure to pull the rank of 'Great Energy Power' was caused by the parallel but conflicting efforts to use the energy instruments for advancing the political projects of the 'Empire' and the 'Civilization'.

11 Reconstituting the 'Empire' as an oil-and-gas cartel

In the poorly verbalized but deeply felt Russian aspirations for a true 'greatness', the achievement of this elusive goal is seen as possible through a combination of the 'Great Power' and 'Empire' projects. There is, indeed, a discernible logic in the proposition that the recognition by peers involves granting consent to a particular 'sovereign power' for assuming the responsibility for maintaining order and managing conflicts in certain areas outside its borders. As the key content of Russia's claim for the 'Great Power' status has been revised with a new emphasis on the capacity to deliver on the growing demand for energy, the main goals in rebuilding the 'Empire' have also been refocused on maximizing the control over energy resources and flows.

This shift towards exploiting the energy levers for expanding political influence that should in turn grant better access to the new as yet untapped sources of energy was first outlined by Anatoly Chubais in his 'Liberal Empire' concept. Despite the failure of his electoral platform in 2003, the resonance of this slogan attested that the imperial idea was politically powerful and practically usable.[1] The proposition that liberalism and empire-building were not necessarily incompatible political guidelines was dismissed offhand, but the argument that Russia's new economic dynamism could make a foundation for a profitable – rather than burdensome – engagement with post-Soviet allies was taken on board by the Kremlin team that was charting the course for Putin's second presidential term.

Chubais placed the emphasis narrowly on electric power generation and distribution, and he was ordered to continue with such politically loaded projects as the construction of two hydroelectric power plants in Tajikistan.[2] For Putin's courtiers, such projects, however, are only of marginal importance since their main preoccupation is natural gas and, to a lesser degree, oil – the commodities that have acquired unprecedented political profile and generate breathtaking profits. Their appetites have been steadily growing, and the assumptions of feasibility have been raised to include the aim of becoming a security guarantor for the authoritarian regimes in the former Soviet South and thus acquiring control over the development and transportation of the Caspian hydrocarbon treasures. The main efforts in building this 'illiberal energy empire' have been duly focused on the richly endowed Azerbaijan and Kazakhstan; this chapter will

Reconstituting the 'Empire' 131

examine them and include also Turkey, the traditional imperial competitor, which has become an important partner in this empire-reinventing.

Azerbaijan and the clash of pipelines

Making Azerbaijan the first priority in his yet-to-be-found Caucasian policy right after his arrival at the Kremlin, Putin surprised many Moscow experts whose advice was no longer required. His intentions at that stage were focused on gradually pulling Azerbaijan back towards Russia by offering 'friendly' alternatives to dependency upon Western support and investments. That inevitably involved downplaying ties with Armenia that was perceived by Moscow as a reliable ally with very limited freedom of manoeuvre; its loyalty was pretty much taken for granted, and few additional energy connections were planned. Putin's premonition of a possible breakthrough was based on two assumptions: that President Heydar Aliev was ready to turn to Russia and that the Azeri oil could be transported via Novorossiisk. Both assumptions were questionable – and indeed proven wrong – but they were not without ground.

It was not on Aliev's past that Putin was counting in his plans for winning his trust and re-launching the Russia–Azerbaijan relations from the top down, it was much more on the future of the matured quasi-monarchic regime in Baku. Struggling against odds with establishing his own credentials in the sceptical West, Putin was sure that for Aliev – whatever hydrocarbon riches could be found in Azerbaijan's sea shelf – the pressure from the US and other Western 'partners' for adopting more democratic methods of governance was more than just an irritant but probably an insurmountable obstacle for any sustainable Westernization. He thought that he had a trump ace in his hand for Aliev's approaching endgame, which aimed at transferring power to his son Ilham. Being himself a product of a miraculous political combination, Putin planned to reassure Aliev Sr that he would wholeheartedly support his plan, while the prospect of winning Western approval for this 'hereditary presidency' appeared rather slim. That was the message that he delivered personally paying an official visit to Baku in January 2001.[3]

In the meanwhile, serious efforts were invested in the second part of the plan – to open Novorossiisk for the Caspian oil business. In a matter of months, a bypass pipeline was constructed through Dagestan making it possible, and even imperative, for Baku to export some 'early oil' through Russia; the quantities were insignificant, but the option was proven workable. More importantly, immediately after the Russian Security Council energy meeting in April 2000,[4] all bureaucratic obstacles that had been blocking the construction of the 'private' Tengiz–Novorossiisk pipeline were resolutely removed, and the work moved ahead at record speed. The revised schedule prescribed completing all tests by mid-2001 and that could have appeared too late, since Azerbaijan, Georgia, and Turkey (with the United States acting as facilitator) signed an agreement on constructing their 'strategic' pipeline already in December 1999 [on the margins of the Organization for Security and Cooperation in Europe (OSCE) Istanbul

132   *Energy power and the quest for 'greatness'*

summit].[5] However, the economic rationale of this Baku–Tbilisi–Ceyhan (BTC) pipeline looked at that stage so shaky that Moscow had every reason to believe in its ability to derail this project without engaging in any political sabotage that could have had the undesired effect of confirming Washington's suspicions about Russia's intentions. The smoothly operating terminal with free capacity to serve dozens more tankers would have made a very convincing argument indeed, so Russian experts rather untraditionally advocated for 'fair competition' pointing to low costs of transporting via Novorossiisk (Aleksandrov, 2002). Indeed, as of early 2001, the probability of a new drop in oil prices appeared quite high, so the returns on the hundreds of millions of dollars that needed to be invested in the 1,750 km BTC pipeline looked problematic.[6]

Putin was certain that his embrace could not be turned down, but he was still a novice in the Caucasian politics, and the upset awaited him in the corner that he had considered 'safe' and not deserving presidential attention: Nagorno Karabakh. Armenia and Azerbaijan were both accepted to the Council of Europe in February 2001, and after the ceremony both presidents travelled to Paris on the invitation of French President Jacques Chirac who tested their readiness for compromise. Moscow interpreted that ice-breaking meeting as the usual diplomatic dance of no consequence and so was taken completely by surprise by President Bush's initiative culminating in the long and hermetically closed negotiations in Key West, Florida, in early April 2001. They did not produce a breakthrough, but according to reflections informed by the wisdom of hindsight, the two parties were close as never before (and never since) to hammering out a compromise.[7]

The failure of the US initiative did not get Putin's plan back on track. He held no grudge against President Bush and in a couple of months looked him in the eye with sincere respect at their first summit in Ljubljana, Slovenia. Armenian President Kocharyan was marked as a non-trustworthy character, and Putin has never tried to build a personal rapport with him. As for President Aliev, Putin had good reasons to believe that old *Partaigenosse* had made a dupe of him with little effort, in fact making no promises that could be listed as broken. He also suspected that Aliev secured not only a pledge from President Bush to discontinue the decade-old economic sanctions against Azerbaijan but, more importantly, an approval for his grand political scheme of dynastic succession.[8] These unverifiable suspicions were more important to Putin than any hard facts so he abandoned completely the policy of personalized rapprochement with Azerbaijan.

The oil policy was reversed accordingly: *Lukoil*'s Chief Executive Officer (CEO) Vagit Alekperov, who had accompanied Putin to Baku, was told to cancel the plans for entering into the BTC consortium and even to withdraw from joint projects for developing offshore oilfields in the Azeri sector.[9] It is possible to assume that there were some rational geoeconomic calculations, and not only hurt feelings, behind that turnaround. The Tengiz–Novorossiisk pipeline was indeed completed on schedule, and since July 2001 tankers with Kazakh oil (sprinkled with some 'sweet' Azeri oil) have begun to depart towards European terminals. Moscow was aware that most of new drilling in the south-

Reconstituting the 'Empire' 133

ern Caspian had been disappointing and so assumed that in order to fill the BTC pipeline, significant quantities of oil from Kazakhstan would be needed, which meant direct competition between the two 'strategic' pipelines with inevitable political interference.[10] There was enough oil for both 'corridors' in the northern part of the sea, including Russia's own sector, but experts in Moscow had reasons to worry that the arrival of Caspian crude in such vast quantities to the world market could push the oil prices down. Slowing down the construction of the BTC pipeline appeared, therefore, to be a good idea.[11]

The investors and engineers who worked on the BTC pipeline refused, however, to be slowed down. In summer 2000, adventurer-journalist Thomas Goltz with a few friends travelled the projected route of the pipeline, delivering on his motorcycle the first barrel of oil to Ceyhan.[12] In May 2005, the completion of the project was celebrated at a high-profile ceremony in Baku, but it took another year before the first tanker was loaded at the deep-water terminal.[13] By that time, worries about a possible drop in oil prices had largely evaporated, while analysts from BP and *Statoil* calculated that the reserves in Azeri oilfields would suffice to fill the BTC pipeline for at least five years, and that would generate nice returns on their massive investments.[14]

Russia remained unmoved and seemingly unimpressed with this geoeconomic and politico-psychological breakthrough but made sure that the crucial top-level channel remained open. Aleksandr Voloshin, the head of presidential administration, and Vladimir Rushailo, the secretary of the Security Council, visited Baku in the last weeks before the presidential elections on 15 October 2003 and confirmed that Moscow is firmly behind the presidential bid of Heidar Aliev's son Ilham.[15] Aliev Sr, however, was confident that the key questions about his succession had been resolved during his February 2003 visit to Washington and dismissed protestations from the OSCE about election irregularities as irrelevant.[16] It is interesting to note that the revolution in Georgia in November 2003 and the chain of quarrels between Moscow and Tbilisi did not have much of an impact on the pattern of Russian–Azerbaijani relations. The Kremlin has certainly expected the fear of revolutionary 'plague' to be a stronger 'driver', but Ilham Aliev is only slightly uncomfortable in the company of Georgian President Mikhail Saakashvily who eagerly exploits democratic rhetoric.

On the eve of the parliamentary elections in Azerbaijan in November 2005, Putin again sent several emissaries to Baku with the message of firm support, while the Commonwealth of Independent States (CIS) election monitors led by the same Rushailo issued the 'free-and-fair' conclusion with no reservations. In the run-up to the elections, Russian media eagerly speculated about the Western sponsorship of an allegedly brewing 'coloured revolution' in Azerbaijan, which should have registered with conspiracy-minded politicians in Baku (Kalabugin, 2005). Ilham Aliev, nevertheless, remained unmoved – and was duly rewarded by the invitation to the White House where the awkward questions about democratic reforms were removed from the agenda of the April 2006 talks.[17] Putin sought to neutralize the seductive power of the small talk in the Rose garden

134 *Energy power and the quest for 'greatness'*

with his own 'pre-emptive' visit to Baku in February 2006, but the vows in friendship did not get him very far, while the warning that Azerbaijan could find itself hard-pressed by the United States to join the anti-Iran coalition did not contain much of an incentive for rapprochement with Russia.[18]

That round of high-level exchanges has made it clear that Russia's withdrawal from the oil development and transportation projects in Azerbaijan was a mistake that has left it without important levers of influence. The attempt to manipulate prices on the gas and electricity exported to Azerbaijan backfired right in the face of Prime Minister Fradkov who was informed during the visit to Baku in December 2006 that Russian gas was no longer needed and that Azeri oil would no longer be exported via Novorossiisk (Kulikov and Panfilova, 2006).

In his counter-revolutionary angst, Putin has also overestimated the attractiveness of his political embrace and was disappointed when Aliev Jr visiting Moscow in November 2006 (on the way home from Brussels) politely refused to partake in energy pressure on Georgia (Butrin, 2006c). There is, however, still an option that may play strongly into Russia's hands. Opposition to the clan-based and spectacularly corrupt regime in Azerbaijan is not limited to marginalized politicians involved in horse trading with the authorities by the means of medium-size demonstrations. A sudden burst of uncontrollable protest energy is entirely possible, and the authorities would then have to resort to forceful means of suppression. Violence could acquire its own dynamics, but anything resembling the May 2005 massacre in Andijan, Uzbekistan, is certain to trigger a broad condemnation in the West. Moscow would waste no time in extending to Azerbaijan its 'brotherly support', and Ilham Aliev, being a much less self-confident and shrewd leader than his Committee for State Security (KGB)-trained and *Politburo*-seasoned father, might find himself in a position where he could not refuse Putin's offer.

Kazakhstan and the sum of 'multiple vectors'

From the perspective of an 'Empire' expanding towards adjacent hydrocarbon 'provinces', no country can stand next to Kazakhstan in potential value and significance for integrity of this 'thematic' neo-imperial project. Looking from Moscow, it is natural to see this big neighbour with its numerous Russian-speaking population and colossal reserves of oil and gas sitting right next to Russia's borders, not as a part of Central Asia, which borders Afghanistan and is affected by a unique mix of problems, from overpopulation to Islamic extremism, but as a separate entity – and the top-priority target for penetrating engagement. Setting the initial guidelines in 2000, Putin found himself at a disadvantage vis-à-vis an experienced and confident Nursultan Nazarbaev, president of Kazakhstan. Nazarbaev positioned himself as a consistent and even 'ideological' supporter of Eurasian cooperation, so Putin decided to play along seeking to build some leverage and correctly assuming that he could not take this 'strategic ally' for granted.[19]

Reconstituting the 'Empire' 135

There were few doubts in the Kremlin even in those early days that it was the Caspian oil that mattered, but already the first policy review by the Security Council confirmed that Russia had lost the initiative to transnational oil companies, led by *Chevron*, who had braved the risks of uncertainty and invested heavily in potentially high-return projects. Instead of instructing the Russian oil majors to challenge these competitors, Moscow opted for a more cautious strategy focused initially on securing 'benign' control over the transportation of the Kazakh oil to the world markets. The key to the success was the stalled project for constructing the pipeline from the Tengiz oilfield to the tanker terminal in Novorossiisk, and that key was immediately inserted into the strategic construct. Unlike all other Russian oil pipelines that are owned and operated by the state company *Transneft*, this one was a joint venture called the Caspian Pipeline Consortium (CPC) in which Russia had only 24 per cent of shares, while Kazakhstan had 19 per cent, Oman had 7 per cent, and the other 50 per cent were divided between several oil companies (*Chevron* had about 15 per cent). Putin's team had serious doubts about this arrangement but had to swallow them since completing the project was far more important at that time than securing firm control.[20] The oil started to flow through the pipe already in mid-2001, to the great relief of the international partners expressed by US Commerce Secretary Don Evans who attended the ceremony; the volume of the exported oil was steadily increasing to reach the peak of 31 million tons (or 660,000 barrels a day) in 2006.[21]

That breakthrough was highly significant but still left Moscow searching for new initiatives that could provide a more direct control over Kazakhstan's oil riches. As it was mentioned above (Chapter 5), Nazarbaev was completely unresponsive to ideas about cultivating cross-border ties engaging Russian communities in northern Kazakhstan; neither was he particularly taken by the proposals to expand the counter-terrorist cooperation. Putin, from his side, was far from enthusiastic about Nazarbaev's scheme of 'multiple vectors', which implied that Russia was only one of several important directions in Kazakhstan's external relations.[22] Seeking to put some substance into the shapeless Eurasian configurations, he proposed to upgrade the pattern of economic cooperation with Kazakhstan, together with Belarus and Ukraine, in the framework of the Common Economic Space, which was launched in September 2003.[23]

Quite possibly, this initiative would have fallen perfectly flat in a matter of a couple of years, but a nexus of several setbacks and challenges forced Nazarbaev to reconfigure his 'vectors'. The foremost among those challenges was the spectre of 'coloured revolution' that took a menacing shape in Kiev in late 2004 and then struck alarmingly close to home when Askar Akayev's regime in Kyrgyzstan collapsed with astonishing ease in February 2005. Nazarbaev probably understood that Russia could provide few guarantees against a sudden escalation of internal tensions, but he saw the growing criticism in Europe of his pre-emptive suppression of political opposition as very unhelpful while President Bush's refreshed commitment to promoting democracy appeared downright subversive. Schooled in the Soviet *nomenklatura*,

136 *Energy power and the quest for 'greatness'*

Nazarbaev was perfectly aware that words and deeds could be miles apart, but the apparent US readiness to extend practical support to 'revolutionaries' of different colours made him wary that a 'regime change' in his strategically important country could be an attractive proposition for some ideologically driven policy planners.[24]

In parallel with these political shifts, significant changes in the investment climate were occurring in Kazakhstan. By the end of 2003, Nazarbaev had concluded that *Chevron* and other transnational oil companies should return a more significant part of their profits to Kazakhstan, so Prime Minister Danial Akhmetov began pressing them to renegotiate the production-sharing agreements (PSAs) from mid-1990s and increase the cut of the state-owned *KazMunaiGaz* (Gavrichev, 2004). While the climbing global oil prices made the forced concessions less painful for the Western majors, they were worried that further demands could be raised and that other states, first of all Azerbaijan, could follow the 'bad' example. Their reluctance to invest in new projects led to delays with the development of the Kashagan offshore oilfield, the largest outside the Middle East, that was originally scheduled to come online in mid-2005 but now is not expected to deliver commercial volumes before the end of 2008.[25] It was not only the officially sanctioned squeeze on investors that was accentuating this reluctance but also legal investigations in the United States and some other states focused on the questionable corporate practices of the early- and mid-1990s.[26] Some of these investigations directly involve the Nazarbaev family and that merely illuminates the colossal spread of corruption in the state-controlled energy sector that has become a major impediment for doing business in Kazakhstan.[27]

Moscow was quick to recognize the opportunities opened by the withdrawal of Western investors, and Putin was eager to convert the counter-revolutionary momentum into tangible economic preferences. Russian oil companies, however, did not show much of an aggressive competitive edge. That passivity could only be explained by the echo of the 1993–1994 *Yukos* 'affair', which had no direct impact on bilateral relations since Nazarbaev wisely refrained from expressing any opinion whatsoever on such delicate internal matters; the indirect impact, however, has been greater than the Kremlin budgeted for. It is not just that the besieged *Yukos* had to cancel all its expansion plans in the Caspian area; other oil companies, including the traditionally proactive *Lukoil*, significantly reduced their investment activities as well.[28] Seeking a bit of extra security in cooperation, *Lukoil* opted for setting a joint venture with *KazMunaiGaz* for developing the Khvalynskoe oilfield in the Russian sector of the Caspian Sea, but both partners tacitly acknowledged that real work would start sometime by the end of the decade.[29]

The high point of Russia's energy offensive in Kazakhstan was reached in July 2005 when Putin and Nazarbaev signed the agreement on joint development of the Kurmangazy oilfield that was estimated to contain up to 980 million tons of extractable reserves and required some US$22–23 billion of direct investments (Glumskov and Shahnazaryan, 2006). It was the state-owned

Reconstituting the 'Empire' 137

Rosneft that became the operating company on the Russian side and that determined a very slow start of the project since the company until spring 2007 was much preoccupied with looting the *Yukos* assets. The successful initial public offering (IPO) in mid-2006 of some 20 per cent of its shares has helped in sorting out the accumulated debts, but a multi-billion investment activity still remains beyond its means.[30]

Nazarbaev was perfectly aware of these irreducible procrastinations, and apparently, he did not mind at all. He saw the tight economic union with Russia as inevitable but temporary – and was carefully working at restoring his freedom of manoeuvre. It was not at all difficult to strengthen the Chinese 'vector' – he merely gave a nod to the Chinese National Petroleum Corporation to acquire the controlling stake in *Petrokazakhstan* (for an impressive US$4.2 billion).[31] Full support was also granted to the US$800 million project for constructing the 1,000-km-long Atasu–Alashankou pipeline, so in December 2005 Nazarbaev proudly pushed the button at the pumping station sending the oil towards the refinery in the Xingjian region (Yermukanov, 2006). In fact, Beijing showed so much eagerness for investing in Kazakhstan's energy assets that Astana preferred to limit the scope of these cooperative engagements.

What Nazarbaev really wanted to achieve was to reconstitute the Western 'vector' of his external affairs. As the tightly controlled presidential elections in December 2005 secured him another seven-year term without any 'revolutionary' excesses, some demonstrative steps at democratizing the system of power at the local level were undertaken (Solovyev and Sidorenko, 2006a). That created the right atmosphere for the visit of US Vice President Cheney who arrived to Astana after delivering a strong speech in Vilnius advocating the advancement of democratic values but refrained from any criticism of the short supply of thereof in Kazakhstan.[32] Sparing no praise, Cheney also made it clear what was expected from Kazakhstan – and Nazarbaev was only glad to oblige, signing next month the agreement on exporting the Kazakh oil through the BTC pipeline which should secure its commercial viability beyond 2010.[33] Putin's riposte was timed to the G8 Strelna summit where Nazarbaev was invited in order to appear on Putin's side in the 'energy security' debates. The special occasion was appreciated, but Moscow's quiet sabotage of Astana's initiatives for reforming the CIS prompted Kazakhstan's president to re-assess the net results of his ten 'cordial' meetings with Putin in 2006.[34] Visiting Moscow in March 2007, Nazarbaev expressed his disappointment in the results of the energy partnership but implied that he had every reason to consider his September 2006 visit to Washington as a serious political success (Dubnov, 2007).

By the start of 2007, it had become obvious that Moscow all but missed its window of opportunity to tie Kazakhstan with binding arrangements that could have secured for the Russian energy companies dominant positions in developing vast hydrocarbon reserves in the north-eastern part of the Caspian Sea. Putin, however, performed an impressive counter-attack in the form of a long visit to Kazakhstan in May 2007 (combined with a trilateral summit in Turkmenistan) extracting from Nazarbaev a confirmation that he was 'absolutely committed to

138　*Energy power and the quest for 'greatness'*

transporting most if not all of Kazakhstan's hydrocarbons through Russian territory' (Baev, 2007h). In return, Putin had to promise to add a new pipe to the CPC (very much against *Transneft*'s preferences) and to cut Kazakhstan into the deal for constructing the bypass Burgas–Alexandroupolis pipeline. He also had to agree on a further increase of price on gas that would be exported to Europe by the *KazRosGaz* joint venture, thus setting an example for Turkmenistan and cutting short GAZPROM's hopes for 'saving' its gas balance by importing cheap gas from Central Asia. Nazarbaev left himself just enough space for oil-and-gas manoeuvring to make sure that the next Russian leader would be seriously dependent upon his goodwill. The 'Empire' had settled for this sub-optimal arrangement since it could offer too few political and security guarantees in exchange for its desperate need in keeping this energy relationship.

Turkey and the gas crossroads

In Russian imperial and post-imperial thinking, Turkey has always been a crucially important reference point representing a natural antagonist with whom only limited cooperation was possible. Through the 1990s, Russia's economic relations with Turkey were much closer than political dialogue, to a large degree due to the decentralized nature of the former, where shuttle trade and 'cheap-labour' construction projects were the dominant forms (Freedman, 2002). In the early Russian geopolitical drafts, Turkey was still designated as a major competitor in the Caucasus allegedly driven by an expansionist pan-Turkic ideology.[35] These perceptions reflected in a rather distorted way the vision of a new era of Turkish influence in Eurasia professed in the mid-1990s by President Turgut Ozal (Winrow, 1995). For Putin and his lieutenants, the imperative to neutralize this challenge was initially beyond doubt. The urgency of this task was further increased by the need to secure Turkey's 'neutrality' in the Second Chechen War, so that Ankara would refrain from providing and even expressing any support to the 'terrorists' for whom international legitimacy was crucially important.

The first messenger from Moscow was Prime Minister Kasyanov who visited Ankara in October 2000 and suggested that 'Russia and Turkey are not rivals but partners; from now on our government will proceed from this understanding' (Kuznetsova, 2000). The next signal continued the ice-breaking: Anatoly Kvashnin, the chief of the General Staff, paid a visit to Turkey in January 2002, the first ever direct contact on such a level, and signed an agreement on military cooperation. His advertising of arms for sale aroused only polite interest in Ankara, but, most importantly, a clear understanding was reached concerning outlawing and persecuting the terrorist organizations that could establish camps in one country and threaten another.[36]

These promising beginnings of a political dialogue possibly leading to setting a new balance of interests in the Caucasus were undercut by the escalation of controversies over transporting the Caspian oil, as the opening of the Tengiz–Novorossiisk pipeline in mid-2001 generated a sharp increase in

Reconstituting the 'Empire' 139

Russian tanker traffic through the Bosporus. Moscow's portrayal of the CPC as a cost-efficient alternative to the BTC pipeline, the latter perceived by Ankara as a major potential asset, added more fuel to this dispute. Ages-old imperial competition appeared to acquire an oil dimension; however, large-scale export of natural gas was identified by the Putin team as the key instrument for discharging the conflict. As Fiona Hill (2003, p. 63) argued, despite the divides over oil, 'agreements on gas served to bind Turkey and Russia together'. In hindsight, it is possible to see that the stake on the 'gas power' was based on the seriously inflated estimates of the potential demand in the Turkish market. GAZPROM engaged in acquisitions and infrastructure upgrades in Romania and Bulgaria, seeking to expand its capacity for supplying Istanbul. The main project, however, was for a new 1,400-km-long pipeline across the Black Sea called the *Blue Stream*. Italian ENI was chosen as the key partner in this ambitious undertaking, and despite serious difficulties in construction and inevitable overspending multiplied by corruption, the project was completed on schedule by the end of 2002.[37] That, however, was not the end of troubles for the pipeline: as it turned out, there was not enough demand for natural gas on the receiving end. The economic crisis of 2001 caused a serious shrinking of the Turkish market, so GAZPROM had to enter into protracted re-negotiations on cutting down volumes and prices.[38]

That unexpected stumble necessitated a significant reconfiguration of the means and ends in Russian policy. A hugely expensive project that had been expected to become a powerful lever for foreign policy turned out to be a liability – and the presidential policy had to be reoriented towards saving this 'white elephant'. A major watershed in the Russian–Turkish relations was crossed in December 2004 when Putin paid an official visit to Turkey and established political dialogue on a new level, far beyond the goals of geopolitical 'deterrence' that had been set at the start of his presidency.[39] Several difficult problems, particularly in the Caucasus, remained unresolved, but Prime Minister Erdogan's reciprocal visit to Moscow in January 2005 as well as his meeting with Putin in the retreat near Sochi in July 2005 demonstrated that the political commitment to building a 'mature partnership' remained strong. The claims for promoting stability in the Caucasus were perhaps not very convincing, and Putin's idea about breaking the 'economic isolation' of Northern Cyprus was of no immediate consequence, but as far as gas was concerned, the two partners definitely meant business (Politov, 2005). The Russian president lobbied vigorously every entry on GAZPROM's 'shopping list', including building underground storages and acquiring distribution companies.

Paying a new visit to Turkey in November 2005, Putin together with Italian Prime Minister Berlusconi 'opened' yet again the long-completed pipeline, thus establishing a new target for the *Blue Stream* – export of Russian gas through Turkey to southern Europe.[40] GAZPROM would then capture commanding positions on these markets ahead of the consortium led by BP and *Statoil* that developed the Shah Deniz gas field in Azerbaijan and constructed the South Caucasus pipeline (SCP), a sister project of the BTC pipeline going from Baku

140   *Energy power and the quest for 'greatness'*

to Erzerum in eastern Turkey. That solution to GAZPROM's problems on the Turkish market appeared to have the additional advantage of reducing Russia's dependency upon gas transit through Ukraine, but it was exactly here that Putin's plan hit the rocks. Russian–Ukrainian 'gas war' at the start of 2006 greatly alarmed the European Union (EU), and the prospect of receiving more gas from Russia via Turkey has become a challenge rather than an opportunity for Brussels. Instead, the EU leadership has placed the emphasis on the *Nabucco* project that aims at delivering Caspian gas to the Austrian 'hub' via Turkey by connecting with the SCP that was duly finished in late 2006.[41] Turkey is not particularly worried about GAZPROM's plans, but the *Nabucco* project is far more attractive as it offers Ankara some additional strength in the tortured negotiations on accession to the EU, so the second line of the *Blue Stream* has been put on ice (Katik, 2006).

Moscow has been careful not to put forward any political conditions for exporting its energy to and through Turkey; the evidence so far clearly points in the opposite direction – that Putin has been cultivating political ties for the purpose of advancing the gas-related agenda. Striking a deal with Turkmenistan on transporting its gas northwards in May 2007 and effectively killing the Transcaspian project, Putin was careful not to make any references to Turkey. As for the more controversial 'oil agenda', Moscow sought to reduce it to the minimum by striking the long-discussed deal with Bulgaria and Greece on constructing the Burgas–Alexandroupolis pipeline that would eliminate the Bosporus bottleneck for exporting from Novorossiisk.[42]

The implicit assumption in Russia's policy has been that Turkey's accession bid would be turned down by the EU or that Ankara would become so frustrated by the EU's demands and procrastinations that it turns away from Brussels. During 2006–2007, Moscow's political attention to Turkey visibly slackened as these expectations were disappointed; nevertheless, they still might come back as the trajectory of the uneasy EU enlargement remains unpredictable. It is rather unlikely, however, that Turkey might turn to Russia for striking a geopolitical bargain for a neo-imperial partnership in the Caucasus and Central Asia, whatever the intensity of the energy relations.

Conclusions

In the middle of the current decade, the revived Russian 'Empire' project has undergone a peculiar and historically unprecedented transformation as the energy ties have become its key content. Oil has been of only a secondary importance in this enterprise, primarily because for this commodity, the key rules are set by the market's 'invisible hand'. Natural gas, however, makes a different case, and here Moscow has become increasingly eager to dictate prices and political conditions, aiming at establishing maximum possible control over production, transportation, and distribution of this valuable source of energy.

In the West, these 'securitized' activities have often been interpreted as the building of a 'Gas OPEC', but in fact the Kremlin has never sought to construct

Reconstituting the 'Empire' 141

an interstate group resembling that quarrelsome and rather ineffectual organization.[43] Accepting Iran's initiative, it understood perfectly well that a new group would be 'trading air rather than gas' and sought primarily to send a warning signal to the EU (Strokan, 2007). Its master plan prescribed purchasing all the Central Asian gas available for export (as well as getting access, wherever possible, to its production and transportation) and thus acquiring an effective monopoly on supplying the EU, while also easing the pressure on its own domestic gas balance.

The plan was not without merit and rationale, but its key problem was how to secure the exclusive rights on trading the gas produced in Turkmenistan, Kazakhstan, Uzbekistan, and if possible, Azerbaijan. It was, in principle, possible to rely on multiple post-imperial ties and networks, from cultivating Russian as the common language to encouraging interactions between political elites, but Moscow showed little interest in all this tedious work and opted for exploiting the 'fear factor' related to the threat of 'coloured revolutions'. During 2004 and particularly 2005, this course indeed brought desired results as the nervous Central Asian leaders rushed under whatever protection Moscow offered, and even Azerbaijan appeared on the brink of reversing its pro-Western orientation. Turkey was shaping up as a key partner in this neo-imperial enterprise based on 'energy-regime security' interplay. In 2006, which accidentally was 'Russia's year' in Azerbaijan, these gains for Russia in reconstituting the 'Empire' on the energy basis were mostly lost – and it became the year of wasted opportunities.

It was not only the turn of the 'coloured' tide that brought this reverse of Moscow's fortune. The remarkable similarity between the post-Soviet regimes in the energy-rich fragments of the former Union of Soviet Socialistic Republics (USSR) does not in fact provide a basis for their rapprochement as each of them puts its own parochial interests first while 'solidarity' does not translate into readiness to come to the rescue of a leader-for-life in distress. Central Asian rulers concluded that Russia could not deliver any real help in a crisis situation and were also reassured that their style of leadership was quite acceptable for the West providing they avoid Andijan-type excesses. Moscow's politicized mercantilism in exploiting its monopoly on gas supply generated strong 'defensive' reaction in all neighbour-states, and the ensuing hard bargaining has revealed that Russia's claims for imperial dominance have a shrinking foundation. The sum total of authoritarian 'energy nationalisms' amounts neither to a stable hierarchy nor to pragmatic competition – but to a serious 'energy security' deficit.

12 Hydrocarbon foundation for the imagined 'Civilization'

The inherently vague ideas about Russia constituting a distinctively unique civilization have multiple roots in Russian 'statist' conservative political thinking that has experienced a rebirth in Putin's second presidency. As described in Chapter 3, the new demand for these ideas is driven by the logic of regime's evolution, which has to establish that its departure from the European model of state–society relations is not merely a deviation but a necessary separation leading to the reassertion of Russia's 'greatness'. In this incoherent project, the proposition that Russia's power is destined to grow since it is by far the world's largest producer of energy is one of the central tenets. While seemingly undisputable, it is also rather controversial because the desired 'greatness' is supposed to have a more sophisticated character than just being the largest 'petro-state'. The Kremlin ideologists have encountered various 'don't-ask-don't-tell' kind of problems in defining key features of this character; so, abundance of energy has become the national idea by default.[1]

The main interplay between building the energy power and constructing a complex societal structure that could qualify as civilization is certainly in domestic politics since the regime needs to justify its expanding control over the energy sector, as well as its muddled pattern of self-reproducing, by securing the flourishing of the country through a 'fair' distribution of the windfall rent. There is, however, also a crucial external dimension since Belarus and Ukraine are broadly perceived not as neighbour states but as parts of the same 'Civilization'; so the energy ties are supposed to secure not only the close economic interconnectedness but also the compatibility of political systems. This chapter will examine the role of oil and gas in Putin's regime-aggrandizement and then proceed to evaluating the energy connection in the policy of expanding Russia's 'Civilization' towards Ukraine and Belarus.

Securing 'sovereignty' by distributing the energy rent through 'national projects'

The need for designating Putin's 'vertical of power' as the main pillar of a uniquely Russian 'Civilization' appeared at the start of his second presidential term when the relatively open public debates of the year of elections were effect-

Hydrocarbon foundation 143

ively terminated. The surprising success of the newly created populist and quasi-opposition party *Rodina* (Motherland) at the December 2003 parliamentary elections confirmed that there was a strong demand on patriotic and nationalistic rhetoric in the politically active segments of the society, while the fiasco of two parties appealing to democratic electorate demonstrated the continuing fragmentation of this camp. The predictable disapproval in the West of Putin's triumph in the over-managed presidential elections pushed further the estrangement caused by the *Yukos* affair, while the enthusiastic support in the United States and Europe for the removal of a corrupt regime from power in Georgia by revolutionary means convinced the Kremlin that the strategic partnership had become a hollow shell.

What logically followed from that net assessment was the readiness to move proactively in shaping a more consolidated and monolithic domestic power base that would increase the ability to withstand external 'hostile' impacts. Dmitri Trenin (2006b) described that shift in Russia's political paradigm as its departure from an orbit, perhaps quite peripheral, in the US-centred world and an attempt to organize a small but independent 'solar system'.[2] Once embarked upon, this course has generated a particular self-propelling dynamics: every step in streamlining the structures of internal politics, for instance cancelling the elections of regional governors, involved mobilizing public opinion against external criticism and internal discontent, and this mobilization necessitated new steps against the political forces that opposed it, for instance adopting the law that tightly regulated the activities of NGOs. Asserting its 'sovereignty' to build a rigidly centralized quasi-democratic regime, Putin's 'team' discovered that the scale of challenges to the 'sovereigntly' defined interests, focused on regime preservation beyond 2008, increased proportionally to their readiness to advance them.

The Kremlin-controlled energy sector provided the major driving force for this self-reconstruction and conceptualization as a self-sufficient 'Civilization'. As the oil prices in the world markets continued their mind-boggling run, Western, and particularly European, resolve to confront Moscow over its retreat from democracy weakened to the point of irrelevance.[3] At the same time, domestic approval for Putin's policy remained high as strong economic growth continued, and the oil dividend trickled down securing a steady growth of real income. What the Kremlin essentially wanted to secure was not active support for its curtailing of democracy and collecting of energy assets but merely consent translated into political passivity. Whatever the expert warnings about the low efficiency of state management in the oil-and-gas industries, the public remained broadly in favour of re-nationalizing the assets that, according to wide-held views, had been stolen by the 'oligarchs' during the privatization frenzy.[4] It also showed readiness to grant Putin every extra authority he requested in order to preserve the political stability seen as the necessary condition for continuing the rare period of prosperity.

The authorities increasingly justified their predatory practices by the grand aim of making Russia one of the very few truly 'sovereign' states in the world system; the society by and large granted consent for postponing the difficult

144   *Energy power and the quest for 'greatness'*

reforms beyond the current 'good times' – and the end product of this hypocriti-cal 'social contract' was not a vibrant 'Civilization' painted by official propa-ganda but a rather stagnant 'petro-state'. The proverbial 'oil curse' that allegedly condemns the states that extract most of their income from exporting hydrocar-bons to retreating towards authoritarian and paternalistic governance works dif-ferently in each case, but as Michael Ross (2001, p. 356) emphasized in the path-breaking article, 'the harmful influence of oil is not restricted to the Middle East'. Thomas Friedman (2006, p. 31) popularized this thesis as 'The First Law of Petropolitics', which posits that 'the price of oil and the pace of freedom always move in opposite directions in oil-rich petrolist states'.[5] For Putin, the price has been moving in only one direction, but it was a price spike exactly at the start of his second term that pre-determined the retrogress towards a 'petro-state'. The key mechanism of this process was control over the media, first of all the national TV channels, and, as research of Russian economists demonstrated, the wealth generated by the energy sector played a key role in the decision to tighten this control because the stakes in the political competition had grown exponentially.[6]

On the surface of it, taking the media on a short leash worked perfectly well in establishing the axiom that there could be no alternative to the existing regime and thus perpetuating political apathy. The downside of this perfect spin was the suffocating shortage of information on the tiny top of the bureaucratic pyramid about the dissipation of 'supreme' orders inside it and indeed about the shifts of attitude in the society at large. Putin's unnaturally high approval ratings were watched minutely in the Kremlin, but their real meaning remained obscure except for the reminder that the transfer of authority to any chosen successor in 2008 would be not just difficult but outright dangerous.[7] Not blessed with sharp political instincts, Putin was still aware of the risk of falling victim to his own propaganda of the rising power of the reconstituted 'Civilization'. One pragmat-ically sober line of reasoning was that the exaggerated presentation of the energy power inevitably boosted expectations of material rewards, since in the Russian 'civilization' model the state that had expropriated key assets from the selfish 'oligarchs' was expected to take good care of its loyal subjects.[8]

Responding to these potentially insatiable expectations, Putin rather unex-pectedly announced in September 2005 the launch of four 'national projects' valued at US$ one billion each that had not been foreseen in the meticulously calculated state budget for 2006. The four target areas – education, health care, agriculture, and housing – were indeed seriously underfunded; so the order for 'focusing budgetary and administrative resources on improving Russian cit-izens' quality of life' (Putin, 2005d) appeared a sure winner, and Dmitri Medvedev who was entrusted its implementation was immediately identified as the designated successor. In just half a year, however, Medvedev complained that corruption and lack of administrative discipline had turned these projects into 'national shame'.[9] Despite the extraordinary propaganda efforts, including daily TV coverage, a special journal, and a website (http://rost.ru/), general public also remained sceptical.[10]

Hydrocarbon foundation 145

One part of the problem was that none of the four 'national projects' was shaped according to a basic definition of 'project' that implies a combination of feasible goals, estimated resources, schedules of advancement, and expected output; the state bureaucracy effectively sabotaged the attempt to introduce project-type planning (Privalov, 2006c). A far more serious part of the problem, however, was the drastic insufficiency of the 'national projects' to the scale of accumulated problems in each of the four areas where structural reforms were long overdue. Instead of creating a launching pad for reforms aimed at modernization, the presidential initiative essentially involved distributing resources towards the most apparent fault-lines in the crumpling structures. Such distribution, besides inviting administrative corruption, was not aimed at problem-solving but merely at postponing their critical escalation. The choice for 'optimization' against modernization, as Andrei Ryabov (2006) argued, is typical for 'petro-states' that are averse to any reforms that could erode the prevailing inertia by triggering social activity.

Shortcomings and design flaws in the 'national projects' were quite obvious, and their abundance was related to another typical feature of a 'petro-state' that aggravated the leaderships' ignorance about its real performance: low cost of mistakes. As the strikes of teachers and doctors in autumn 2005 and the 'revolt' of pensioners in early 2006 were pacified by disbursement of extra funds, the Kremlin stopped seeing any reason for doubt that 'oil would wash out everything', as Vladimir Todres (2006) pointed out. 'The problem with these mistakes and miscalculations', he added, 'is that they tend to accumulate and come into resonance going at a particular (but unpredictable) moment beyond the threshold of a critical mass'.

Low price of mistakes made it possible for the Kremlin courtiers to continue building the Potemkin skyscraper of Russian 'Civilization' plastering over the cracks in the pillars of 'national projects'. Their only nightmare was a sudden fall of oil prices, but in fact the real-life marathon run of these prices brought the shortage of the substance that was supposed to be the trademark of this 'Civilization' – energy. In the Russian economy, the efficiency of energy consumption remained appallingly low, and the sustained growth strained the supply–demand balance, as demonstrated by the 'blackout' in Moscow in May 2005.[11] The dilapidated gas distribution infrastructure and the lack of spare capacity in oil refining have been neglected so long that a snowballing of supply problems is guaranteed in the near future (Delyagin, 2005a).

This paradox of having truly abundant energy reserves and not being able to cover its own needs while claiming the status of stability guarantor in the world market points to a fundamental flaw in the design of the hydrocarbon 'Civilization' – Russia is just too big and complex to fit into the 'petro-state' model. Crudely approximate socio-economic measurements indicate that the total maximum size of the class of 'beneficiaries', who could claim a share of profits generated in the energy sector, could reach 50 million people – but that still leaves 90 million in the category of 'dispossessed' (Ryabov, 2006). It might be possible to control their frustration by redistributing financial flows at the

146 *Energy power and the quest for 'greatness'*

expense of 'beneficiaries', who so far have shown little readiness to share, but the dry economic rationale remains that large sectors and spheres, from academic science to space programme to subsidized agriculture, are redundant in a 'petro-state'.[12] The ambitious aim of reconstituting Russia as one of the 'sovereign' leaders of the world could only be achieved with a strategy of massive investment of resources produced in the energy sector into upgrading the human capital concentrated in the key industries and services that are the drivers of development in the new century (Fadeev, 2006).

By the end of 2006, Putin had recognized that the rather unsophisticated rentier-state model provided a poor foundation for the imagined 'Civilization', and so entering his last year in power, he suggested a more adequate course shifting emphasis back to 'modernization' as at the start of his 'era'. Sergei Ivanov was given the task to advance a new industrial policy centred on strengthening state control over key sectors and stimulating 'innovation' (Baev, 2007f). The efficiency of central control, however, remained appallingly low, and the positive effect of, for instance, forceful integration of key airspace companies, including *Sukhoi*, MiG, *Ilyushin*, and *Tupolev*, into one giant 'holding' was by no means certain, while the plain fact that 2006 was the worst year in the history of Russian aviation with 318 victims was undeniable.[13] The problem for the newly reinvigorated 'modernization' course was not that too little time was left for implementing the promises for providing Internet access to every village by 2015; the real problem was that the new public relations (PR) spin on 'innovations' only added to the public expectations that had been already pumped excessively high by the 'energy dividend' rhetoric. The society has become convinced that the incremental increase of disposable income is only the beginning of 'good times' of collecting rent, but the model of Kremlin-centric state control has only limited capacity for sustaining the economic boom. The 'Civilization' based on energy riches has thus entered into decline even before its ability to deliver prosperity was demonstratively exhausted.

Forging the never-union with Belarus

The gravity centre of the 'Civilization' project was certainly in the domestic politics, but the external environment shaped it in two important ways: first, it was necessary to establish that Russia was significantly different from Europe in its macro-political system, and this difference was set to increase in the course of cultivating the 'sovereignty'. Second, the viability of this model should be proven by demonstrating its attractiveness for the neighbours, so that the historically and culturally closest states would be pulled into value-based alliances by the gravitation field of this raising 'Civilization'. Belarus was certainly the prime case for this second proposition, but Moscow's increasing emphasis on energy relations has made this case far from convincing.

President Yeltsin embraced the idea of building an 'ever-closer' union with Belarus when it became clear that his December 1991 Belovezh initiative on dissolving the USSR was vastly unpopular. Seeking to deny his political opponents

Hydrocarbon foundation 147

the possibility to exploit the popular slogan of 'reunification' in the all-or-nothing presidential race, he signed with President Aleksandr Lukashenko an agreement on forming a Community (1996), which the following year was upgraded to a Union and in 1999 became a Union State. Yeltsin came to see this 'brotherly' alliance as an important part of his historic legacy, but Lukashenko, besides riding on strong pro-Russian sentiments in his country, cherished a not-improbable hope to become the successor to the ailing Russian 'Tsar Boris'.[14]

Arriving at the Kremlin, Putin explained in no uncertain terms that power-sharing in a hypothetic united state was out of the question fixing a rather bad chemistry of personal relations. Since the rapprochement remained a very popular process, Putin preserved the Union State framework but showed no interest in investing into its deepening, famously suggesting to treat 'flies separately, and meatballs separately'.[15] Lukashenko used the pause for cultivating Belarus' unique identity as an 'island of stability', emphasizing its difference not only from Europe, but from Russia as well, with its 'oligarchic capitalism', social tensions, and violent internal conflicts (Lukyanov, 2006b). Putin made a fresh attempt to advance the German model of reunification, so that six *oblast* of Belarus would become subjects of an enlarged Russian Federation, at a long meeting with Lukashenko in Sochi in September 2003, but predictably got nowhere (Trenin, 2005).

At that cross-roads, the disagreements about gas and transit prices escalated to the level of first-priority political problem eclipsing the much-advertised plan for introducing the Russian rouble as the single currency for the Union State, which was postponed indefinitely. Irritated GAZPROM went as far as switching off supply to Belarus in February 2004, but Lukashenko played hardball recalling his ambassador from Moscow and accusing Russia of 'terrorism at the highest level'.[16] The gas flow was restored in less than 24 hours; so GAZPROM's customers in Poland and Lithuania had no formal ground for complaints, but Lukashenko was counting not only on their pressure but also on the fact that by that time a mature union with Belarus had become invaluable for the Kremlin's ripening concept of Russian 'Civilization'. The re-elected Putin needed a solid reference point in his ideological stance against the raising threat of West-inspired revolutions, but he also counted on Lukashenko's departure at the end of his second term in September 2006.[17] His counter-part, however, had no plans for retirement and moved swiftly against objections from Moscow with the referendum on lifting the limit on presidential terms combined with the parliamentary elections in October 2004.[18]

By that time, the Kremlin's attention was totally focused on Ukraine – and the shock from the 'orange revolution' was so profound that Lukashenko was left alone in order not to sink the badly damaged 'Civilization' project. At the January 2006 summit, it was confirmed yet again that the reunification momentum was stalled completely; so, the opinions of 'political technologists' that the two leaders were fully committed but the bureaucracies were slowing down the process in order to secure their parochial interests appeared quite ridiculous.[19] Moscow asked Lukashenko in the spirit of mutual trust to show restraint in

148 *Energy power and the quest for 'greatness'*

dealing with the opposition in the March 2006 presidential elections, but the street protests in Minsk were suppressed with demonstrative brutality. That prompted Putin to resort to the instrument he perceived as infallible and irrefutable and in April GAZPROM announced its demand for a triple price increase in 2007 (Socor, 2006a).

The erupted dispute was portrayed by Moscow as purely commercial, but it was easy to see that there was more to that business ultimatum than just the desire to harvest extra profits, assert ownership on the *Beltransgas* pipelines, and grasp some other industrial assets. Recognizing Lukashenko as the main obstacle on the way to real integration, the Kremlin apparently decided to terminate his 'economic miracle' that was built entirely on the availability of cheap energy.[20] Putin apparently discovered a serious need for a positive breakthrough with the 'Civilization' project, which did not receive any boost from the noisy PR around the G8 Strelna summit; this need was intensified by the desire to organize a reserve option for the uncertain transition of power in 2008. His courtiers were sure that isolated Lukashenko was in a hopeless bargaining position but had to admit that in the course of building the Union State they had managed to lose all levers of influence on the closest ally and would have to overcome serious resistance in the tightly knit Belarussian elites.[21]

Lukashenko, however, had good reasons to see his position as pretty solid. He assumed that after the 'gas war' with Ukraine at the start of 2006, Moscow would not dare to cut the flow of gas through Belarus fearing the reaction of European consumers who would certainly not rush to his defence but had their own interests at stake. To Putin's great relief, Lukashenko agreed on the last-minute gas compromise, but the joy in the Kremlin turned sour when Minsk slammed custom fees on Russian oil transit forcing *Transneft* to stop deliveries and triggering an 'oil war'. Angry Putin (2007b) announced that the price of the 'gas deal' for Russia was US$3.3 billion of lost profit, which constituted a 'direct support to Belarusian colleagues'. Minsk made a step back but then advanced new demands including a US$1.5 billion zero-interest stabilization loan (Privalov, 2007).

Lukashenko was not just demonstrating stubbornness but playing directly on the contradiction between easily calculable economic interests and vague but acutely felt 'brotherhood' national interests in Russia's policy that made victory plain impossible.[22] He also knew that the plan of *Anschluss* was far more popular in Russia, where up to 70 per cent of population still wanted the rapprochement to advance, than in Belarus where the national identity based on juxtaposition with the 'big neighbour' had taken root ('Social-political situation in Russia in January–February 2007', 2007; Timmermann, 2006). Every forceful move from Moscow has gone against domestic public preferences and has inevitably produced a backlash in Belarus thus inflicting direct damage to the 'Civilization' project; hence Putin's re-affirmation of the commitment to the Union State in the 2007 address to the parliament. Lukashenko was also counting on the fast-approaching watershed of 2008, which essentially made it necessary for him to hold on only through the first half of year 2007; in that, however,

Agonizing over the Ukrainian dilemma

Ukraine constitutes a far more difficult but also significantly more important problem than Belarus for the evolving project of Russian 'Civilization'. The unstructured mix of ideas about common history, perceptions of cultural closeness, assessments of intensity of multiple ties, and worries about geopolitical risks has boiled down to a broad consensus in Moscow elites that Russia could only re-establish its 'Greatness' by making sure that Ukraine remains in its sphere of prevailing influence. Energy has always constituted a separate and conflict-rich dimension in these vague but ambitious aspirations. Unlike Belarus, Ukraine showed few reservations against accumulating debts for long-overdue bills and simply siphoning gas from transit pipelines, but Moscow, while periodically making scenes, was up to the end of Putin's first presidential term inclined to find a compromise. While some of these special deals struck with the help of sleazy mediators and through questionable off-shore joint ventures were probably quite profitable for the GAZPROM leadership, there have always been greater political considerations about 'brotherly ties' that underpinned the readiness to accommodate the capricious customer.[23]

Putin initially sought to shift the policy to a more pragmatic basis and insisted on sorting out the issue of Ukrainian gas debt and finding an arrangement for stable payments for the export and transit of the Russian gas. The high point of these efforts was the June 2002 trilateral Russia–Ukraine–Germany agreement for establishing an international consortium for managing transit gas pipelines, which however never came to implementation.[24]

By late 2003, Russian policy towards Ukraine had swung from pragmatism to ideological union-building where energy export was not a technical issue to iron out but a lever to drive the political project. Partly, this shift was caused by the assessments in Moscow of the political crossroads that Ukraine was facing, which Olexiy Haran (2002) described as 'either velvet revolution or Belarusification'. Mostly, however, the urge to interfere and determine the choice at that crossroads was driven by domestic developments in Russia, where Putin's 'sovereign democracy' was gearing up towards 'greatness' and Ukraine shaped up as a crucial test case. The key manifestation of that swing was the much-trumpeted agreement on Common Economic Space (CES) between Belarus, Kazakhstan, Russia, and Ukraine, reached in September 2003, where Ukraine was clearly the main subject of Russia's embrace.[25] CES was not without its practical advantages, making it possible, for instance, for the Russian companies to take part in large-scale privatization projects in Ukraine, but the ideology of 'reunification' and the strategy of making a common stance against Western 'encroachments' visibly dominated – and that condemned the initiative to a 'paper organization' (Moshes, 2004b).

Putin's new course was centred on ensuring that Ukraine's political system

150 *Energy power and the quest for 'greatness'*

was fully compatible with Russia's, and so, the presidential elections in Ukraine during October–November 2004 became a Stalingrad-type political battle where no price was too high for the 'winner-takes-all' victory. The massive explosion of public protest against election falsifications that the Kremlin 'task force' had failed to foresee was vividly described and thoroughly analysed from a variety of perspectives, besides producing its own mythology.[26] What appears important to reiterate here is that pragmatic political manoeuvring aimed at guaranteeing that whatever candidate comes first, Russia's economic, and first of all energy, interests would be given due respect, while seemingly the most rational course of action for Moscow had no place in Putin's strategy of asserting the power of Russian 'Civilization'. In fact, the energy interests were consciously sacrificed for gaining a minor political advantage when the agreement on selling Ukraine gas on fixed prices (US\$50 per $1,000\,m^3$) for the next five years was signed in early August 2004.[27]

The devastating and humiliatingly personal defeat delivered to Putin's 'grand strategy' by the cheerful crowds in the orange-coloured Kiev took a few months to digest; it was only in late August 2005 that an anonymous Kremlin official announced that the policy in the post-Soviet space would be radically changed so that the struggle that had been waged with no rules would be conducted in a 'civilized way'. While the intention was far-reaching, only one specific direction was outlined: Russia would stop subsidizing the economies of the CIS states through low energy prices since it only 'creates situations that lead to orange revolutions after which nothing changes for the people while the leaders, at least some of them, receive – directly or in a hidden form – salary from the Americans'.[28] Despite the pronounced anti-Western emphasis, the idea of commercializing the relations with post-Soviet neighbours, whether perceived as pro-Russian or not, appeared refreshingly rational, even if it was hard to believe that common political sense would gain ground after such a profound failure (Lukyanov, 2005b).

While the policy was presented as covering the whole Commonwealth of Independent States (CIS) area, it was no secret that the main target was set on Ukraine; so the GAZPROM's demand in December 2005 to increase the base price for imported gas came as no surprise. The negotiation position was so solid and the political backing so unwavering that the mainstream commentators felt triumphant 'like Brazilian football fans at the match with Iceland' (Privalov, 2005c). Showing zero flexibility in the hard bargaining, Moscow clearly overestimated its position of strength when the valve on the gas pipeline to Ukraine was demonstratively turned in the first day of 2006. The political resonance in Europe of that 'gas war' reached such intensity that in a matter of three days the compromise was hammered out, restoring the flow of gas. Both sides proclaimed 'victory', but it was quite obvious that GAZPROM had to make serious concessions both on prices and on the arrangement with jointly owned non-transparent trading companies.[29]

The Kremlin asserted that the agreement established 'market principles' that would guide further relations, but detailed analyses proved that the 'Russian

Hydrocarbon foundation 151

economy and GAZPROM in particular have gained practically nothing, the achievements are entirely political' (Rubanov and Sivakov, 2006). It was, however, equally possible to argue that Russia 'has suffered a fiasco in its attempt to speak with Ukraine in the language of ultimatums', in the words of Ukrainian Foreign Minister Boris Tarasyk.[30] Indeed, the politics of the 'gas war' remained even more muddled than its economics, and Putin's multiple denials of any political agenda were correct only in the sense that Moscow did not make any explicit linkages between prices and political concessions; so there was no blackmail in the strict sense of the term. However, GAZPROM's straight-forward pressure made very little economic sense and was certain to yield fewer rewards than firm but flexible demands for step-by-step increases – and was clearly politically driven (Leibin, 2005c).

It was hard to find any specific political aims related to the parliamentary elections in Ukraine in March 2006; indeed, the timing of the 'offensive' was even counter-productive, since as it was pointed out in Russian media, 'in Ukraine, the pro-Russian political forces (the anti-orange coalition) constitute first of all the party of low gas prices' ('Ukraine: A view through the gas pipe', 2006). It would have been perhaps too simple to reduce the political agenda to the demonstration of Russia's ability to hit where it hurts and take sweet revenge on treacherous Ukraine for turning its back on Russia.[31] Putin aimed at more than just punishment; in order to preserve any credibility of the damaged 'Civil-ization' project, it was necessary to push Ukraine to the brink of failure. Hence the massive and sustained anti-Ukrainian propaganda on the state-controlled TV channels that resulted in significant shifts in the public opinion where traditional sympathy towards Ukraine was gradually replaced with the image of 'hostile state'.[32] Hence also the joy about the protracted period of party quarrelling after the parliamentary elections and the collapse of the compromise in spring 2007, since this political 'chaos' was interpreted as a proof of failure of a democratic model 'imported' from the West.

Putin's team certainly understood that a profound state failure in Ukraine could not be achieved by one hit, however painful; so making a step back in the 'gas war', the Kremlin wanted to conduct a damage assessment before deliver-ing the next blow. Surprised by the heavy criticism of his 'strictly-business' approach in the West, Putin also recognized that his hands were tied until autumn 2006 by the G8 chairmanship, since the desire to have a smooth and prestige-boosting Strelna summit was overwhelming (Orlov and Fugfugosh, 2006). Taking a pause in the campaign against Ukraine, Moscow carefully examined the differences between the United States and the European Union (EU) that could be exploited further down the road. It probably gave Putin joy that President Bush was unable to pay a visit to Kiev in June 2006 (since there was no functional government), but the considered opinion among his courtiers was that Washington would encourage Yushchenko to assume a defiant stance by promising him to put Ukraine on the 'fast track' to the North Atlantic Treaty Organization (NATO) membership. As for the EU, the main conclusion was that the Union was not prepared to offer Ukraine a realistic mid-term prospect of

152   *Energy power and the quest for 'greatness'*

membership and would not be able to come to rescue when the energy-starved economy would enter into dire straights. That prompted Putin to present the issue very brusquely to the European counter-parts:

> Our western friends supported the 'orange events' in Ukraine in a very active way. We see perfectly well what is happening there the whole time. The country has been faced with a great deal of problems. But if you want to support what happens there in the future, then you will have to pay for it. Why should we pay for that?[33]

It appeared entirely possible to bankrupt Ukraine that had meagre financial reserves for alleviating the pain of unavoidable raise of gas price for its energy-wasteful heavy industry and communal sector. It also appeared easy to play on the deep political divisions over the issue of NATO membership in order to exacerbate Ukraine's ungovernability. Nevertheless, the plan for organizing a collapse of the former 'brotherly' state came to naught. It clearly underestimated the well-developed skills of Ukrainian elites to pursue their parochial interests through compromises within one clearly defined cooperative political space.[34] It overestimated by far the pro-Russian sentiments in the Eastern Ukraine, which in fact stopped far short from a desire to abandon one state project and join another, as well as the depth of the 'East–West' divide in Ukraine that did not by any measure reached the scale of a fault-line. Most significantly, such a plan had never had nearly enough political will or resources for its consistent implementation, since as Dmitri Furman (2006) argued, a 'takeover of the eastern parts of Ukraine requires serious, determined policy and the readiness to sacrifices. Neither from that side, nor from our side could such a serious drive be generated'.

When the Kremlin was ready to come back to the Ukraine issue in autumn 2006, the net damage assessments arrived to the quite unexpected bottom line: the enforced higher gas prices were quite helpful for the Ukrainian economy that had recovered from the post-revolutionary slump and demonstrated healthy growth. Russian economists started even to argue that this 'test' had proven the need to double domestic gas prices, which for the Putin's team remained an experiment too far despite lobbying from GAZPROM (Gavrilenkov, 2006). It was still possible to tighten the energy squeeze on Ukraine and stifle its 'unnatural' growth, but that required first to settle the 'market' pattern of gas relations with Belarus, which, as described above, has turned out to be far more troublesome that Putin's lieutenants hoped for.

Ukraine has been reluctantly left alone because it was one thing to entertain ideas about demonstrating Russia's 'greatness' by extending its embrace to the parts of unfortunate state collapsing under the pressure generated by the irresistible pull of the successful 'Civilization'. It is, however, an entirely different matter to manage the geopolitical crisis of such proportions. Putin's team have never shown any skill in, or indeed ardour for, crisis management; so, most probably, facing a risky choice it would have backed off opting for the safety of

Hydrocarbon foundation   153

status quo even at the expense of missing an opportunity to snatch a 'historic' victory.[35] Every crisis, however, has its own unpredictable dynamics, and the Kremlin set on the economic suffocation of Ukraine could never be sure that it would have a chance to wisely release the energy squeeze. In a possible situation of deepening economic depression and deadlocked political squabbles, the downplayed problem of Crimean separatism could suddenly explode and become the detonator for a wider self-propelling crisis. Russia is far more likely to experience an unravelling of its own state-structures than to harvest territorial benefits from the disaster next door.

Conclusions

The aim of transforming Russia's energy might into the foundation of an expanding 'Civilization' that would engulf Ukraine and Belarus appeared entirely feasible at the start of Putin's second presidential term but met a spectacular fiasco in revolutionary Kiev. Indeed, successful consolidation of a genuinely democratic and Europe-oriented political system in Ukraine would have revealed that uniquely Russian 'sovereign-democratic Civilization' was a fake despite all its energy resources. Charting a course around and across this obstacle, the Kremlin did not notice that it forked into two diverging tracks.

One avenue went towards extracting maximum profits from energy exports and the key point – 'Why should we subsidize the economies of these independent states?' – appeared impeccably pragmatic.[36] Another avenue was directed to maximizing Russia's influence in Ukraine and Belarus and securing the political compatibility of these inseparable allies with the Russian 'civilization core'. It was probably not entirely impossible to advance along these tracks simultaneously by providing limited subsidies and securing tangible political returns on them; such a flexible policy, however, has turned out to be beyond the conceptual and PR talents of Putin's team. During Putin's last year in the Kremlin, Moscow has found itself facing dead-ends in both avenues (Ryabov, 2007). It had to agree on delivering gas to Belarus and Ukraine on prices more than twice lower than to Poland or Germany, while also agreeing on importing gas from Central Asia at about the same prices, so that the margin of profit on that indirect transit has become very low. It also managed to undercut the pro-Russian sympathies in Belarus and Eastern and Southern Ukraine as well as alienate the political forces that used to support integration but disapproved of Russia's arrogance and greed.

Fundamentally, the success of designing and 'selling' a political project with an ambition as high as to establish the claim for a distinctive 'Civilization' was dependent upon offering a set of attractive examples and prospects that would both mobilize domestic support and convince the key neighbours to subscribe to Russia's lead. Belarus and Ukraine have remained unconvinced not least because the Russians have hardly shown much mobilization readiness; the proposition for harvesting godsend energy revenues have generated mostly political apathy and increasingly pronounced reluctance to share with ungrateful

154 *Energy power and the quest for 'greatness'*

neighbours. The key pillar of this 'civilization' construct was the restored state control over hydrocarbon resources and production; this re-nationalization has enjoyed broad public support, but even those economists who approved of it added serious reservations. Mikhail Dmitriev (2006) pointed out that the 'efficiency of state control Russia is on the level of African states' and accepted as a sad necessity that 'in the near term, the choice between efficiency and acceptability for the society has to be made for the latter'.[37] This state-controlled stagnation of the oil-and-gas sector inevitably leads to deepening of the latent energy crisis in Russia, which not only devalues the imagined 'Civilization' but also guarantees new 'wars' on the Western front, since Belarus and Ukraine would be the first to suffer from the pre-determined cuts in the volume of hydrocarbon export from Russia.

Conclusion

The excessive amount of current sources and expert opinions gathered in this book do not converge towards a coherent set of conclusions but only confirm that Putin's 'stabilization' has not produced any unity of views on Russia's immediate future. The amassed facts and figures do not lend themselves to any kind of quantification that could have established a direction of further developments – but the methods of extrapolation, amounting to sophisticated 'more-of-the-same' forecasting, rarely work for Russia. There is no theory-informed model behind the meandering narrative in the 12 inescapably overlapping chapters that are not testing any scientific hypothesis but merely examining the events, seeking to find a logic in their sequences but freely admitting that the interactions between drivers were often quite random. Disappointing as that analytic approach might be for some readers, it still provides plentiful material for constructing a few plausible theses on the possible trajectories of Russia's advance or, perhaps, descend from the watershed marked in Orwellian style by numerals '2008'.

The main framework for these theses is provided by juxtaposing the policies of building the military power and the energy power and by correlating them both with the policy of rebuilding Russia's 'greatness'. This third coordinate axis might appear not entirely organic; indeed, Sergei Ivanov (2006) seeking to prove that his horizon stretched wider than the narrow viewpoint of the defence minister defined the 'new triad of Russian national values' rather differently: 'sovereign democracy, robust economy, and military power'. As Aleksandr Golts (2006f) noted, it would take a colonel-speechwriter to explain how a robust economy could constitute a national value, but Ivanov was in fact struggling to make a point that only economic and military might could secure for a country such a rare feature as 'sovereignty', which in essence is synonymous with 'greatness'.

This obsession with obtaining an exclusive status is not a new political–psychological phenomenon; Dominique Lieven (2002, p. 264) in his outstanding book quotes the newspaper *Novoye Vremya* which argued back in 1914 about the Russian people's 'still terrible thirst for greatness'. Some 90 years later, this ambition has noticeably weakened so that according to a Levada Center opinion poll, only 30 per cent of Russians believed their country to be a 'great power'

156 *Conclusion*

and only 36 per cent wanted it to be one, while 62 per cent preferred to see Russia more affluent rather than more influential ('Social-political situation in Russia in November 2005', 2005). In the political elite, however, the desire for 'greatness' is still burning bright and is typically translated into ambitious discourse (Vladimirov, 2006):

> Nobody out there needs Russia as a particular Orthodox white civilization, super-ethnos and great power, so none of the equal powers and civilizations would help it. We are doomed to civilization loneliness and have to resolve ourselves all the problems of our survival and development.

The pursuit of 'greatness' in various manifestations has therefore strong impact on both the state-dominated energy business and the posture of the Armed Forces so that the dynamic interplays between these three dimensions of Putin's state-building endeavour are rich in conflict. It appears possible to identify the key contradictions – and then to suggest options for their possible resolution, thus constructing abbreviated scenarios for Russia's near-term transfiguration.

The fault-lines in the three interplays

The radical centralization of political decision-making in the huge and hugely complicated country and the extreme concentration of control in the presidential office have not brought coherence to Russian politics, which remains as short-termist and opportunistic as it is non-transparent. Every chapter in this volume exposes discrepancies between aims and means and incompatibilities between particular guidelines; the task here is to select the main lines of conflict.

In the rather straightforward interplay between the energy and military policies (as examined in the three chapters that constitute Part II), the most obvious contradiction is certainly between the pressing demand to channel more resources towards modernizing the Armed Forces and re-assembling the military–industrial complex and the growing need to invest more in upgrading the fixed assets of the over-exploited energy complex. As the domestic energy crises acquire more acute forms, the rationale for reducing the tax pressure on the oil-and-gas industry and expanding investment in electricity production becomes stronger, but the massive rearmament programmes require greater infusion of the 'oil money'. There is also another less fundamental but still politically significant contradiction in the 'energy-versus-security' interplay: traditional approach to enhancing security prescribes building a system of military–political alliances, but the 'energy-first' strategy implies cutting the costs of supporting the allies that have no hydrocarbon resources. In the 'Overview of Russian Foreign Policy' (2007) prepared by the Foreign Ministry, the relations with the Commonwealth of Independent States (CIS) countries are defined as 'the main priority of Russian foreign policy', but the reluctance to pay for the leadership role in this moribund organization has become quite pronounced.

In the traditional interplay between building the military might and asserting

Conclusion 157

'greatness', the contradiction that had taken shape before Putin's arrival at the Kremlin and has remained barely contained throughout his reign involves prioritizing the strategic nuclear forces or the 'rapid-deployment' conventional forces. Modernizing the strategic arsenal appears to be the surest way of maintaining Russia's international prestige, but the tasks of projecting power, first of all in the Caucasus, could not be resolved without combat-capable 'big battalions'. A different and typically latent contradiction exists between the political desire to build usable power instruments for manipulating conflicts to the south of Russia's borders and the Byzantine concern that such instruments would not be entirely controllable and could become an independent force in the incessant court intrigues. Putin has been very careful in marginalizing the 'top brass' with real combat experience on the tightly controlled political arena but that has left the army without generals capable of building and leading high-readiness units.

In the newly emerged and fast-evolving interplay between maximizing the profitability of the 'energy power' and achieving a new kind of 'greatness', two contradictions appear to be of equal significance. The first one is between the desire to strengthen the global role of the leading exporter of energy and the inability to secure sufficient increase in production of oil and gas. It is the state control over the energy sector that makes the role of 'energy super-power' so attractive, but it also brings inefficiency of management and leads to stagnation in the hugely profitable industry. The second contradiction juxtaposes the goal of increasing the financial returns from energy export and the temptation to manipulate the privilege of an irreplaceable supplier for harvesting political dividends. While energy business cannot be separated from big politics, great caution is required for making it into a useful political instrument – but Moscow's experiments with applying the 'big gas stick' have been so awkward that its reputation as 'energy security' provider has been badly damaged with very little gain to show for it.

These six 'binary' contradictions could constitute a matrix that would include no less than 64 different combinations of their possible resolution. In real life, however, one choice typically determines another, and a common logic, if not a strategy or ideology, guides the decision-making, so that the number of logically coherent options is far smaller. It appears possible to construct just three basic scenarios that would represent traceable and significantly diverging political trajectories. The genre of scenario-drawing is a pastime for the Moscow crowd of experts, 'political technologists', and spinmeisters who seek collectively to call into existence an internally mobilized and universally esteemed Russia of Putin's dreams.[1] The intention here is different, and the author expects that none of the described retrogression and self-destruction would come true.

Buying time until there is no more

The first scenario involves not a particular combination of hard choices but the sustained reluctance to make them and the pronounced preference in the leadership for finding palliative solutions and postponing painful decision indefinitely.

158   *Conclusion*

This style of running the state affairs might appear irrational but in fact would signify merely a continuation of Putin's 'pragmatic' approach where the power of making decisions is concentrated heavily in the Kremlin, but the result is not a swiftly operating mechanism of directing the colossal bureaucracy but a paralysing overload aggravated by court intrigues. The reform of the government launched with Mikhail Fradkov's appointment as the Prime Minister in March 2004 was abandoned halfway, and the current composition with two First Deputy Prime Ministers might look balanced from the point of view of electoral positions of two semi-official presidential candidates – Dmitri Medvedev and Sergei Ivanov – but hardly makes much administrative sense. The list of reforms launched half-heartedly and curtailed after encountering bureaucratic resistance or public disapproval is too long, and the year 2006 added to it further as expected 'fateful decisions' failed to materialize leaving commentators pondering over the question: did that year happen at all? (Butrin, 2006e). In retrospect, the only proactive initiative that the Kremlin implemented with iron determination was the destruction of the oil company *Yukos* and the prosecution of its management starting with Mikhail Khodorkovsky.

Quite possibly, this pattern of procrastination and advancing by incremental steps reflects personal preferences of Vladimir Putin, by no means a natural leader or a 'political animal'. What has made it feasible, however, to sustain the chain of bureaucratic compromises on the basis of lowest common denominators throughout Putin's second presidential term was the spectacular increase of budget revenues, primarily from oil-and-gas export. That godsend fortune may suffice for orchestrating the transition of power in 2007–2008 as the key groupings of courtiers have enough loot while the population is pacified by generous social spending. It is quite clear, however, that the already visible shrinking of the 'oil rent' would make it impossible to deliver on all promises and commitments that are currently confidently issued with target dates into the middle of the next decade. The elementary calculation of the balance of expected income and promised expenditures may be one of the key factors behind Putin's firm insistence on retiring from the 'throne', while it would have been far easier to 'organize' for him the third term than to hammer out an agreement on successor (Piontkovsky, 2007).

The probability that such a deal between the Kremlin clans would bring to the summit of power a competent and dynamic leader appears slim; the risks of losing privileged access to power could only be lowered by agreeing on a compromise figure who can play the role of arbiter but would not claim executive authority. That means that the most natural course for the start of the post-Putin 'era' is 'more-of-the-same', but the technique of converting the oil-and-gas revenues into political stability will stop delivering the desired results. Conflicts of interest within the ruling bureaucracy might escalate as the new president would inevitably lack Putin's grasp on cadre; more troublesome, however, could be the escalation of public protests that would be difficult to quell by disbursing extra funds available in a short supply. The reserves accumulated in the economy would probably suffice to sustain the political system until the next electoral

Conclusion 159

cycle in 2011–2012, but the well-tested methods of political manipulations could fail that test, and a breakdown following the model of 'coloured revolutions' (typically triggered by elections) could happen.

The scale of this revolutionary upheaval is impossible to predict, and some of its driving forces could look disturbingly ugly in their nationalistic zeal; what is significant for the development of this crisis, however, is the extreme rigidity of the over-centralized system of power that is set to survive the current transition. The progressive shrinking of the resource base could cause cracks in this bureaucratic pyramid, but its key structures could not be altered without a profound political crisis (Shevtsova, 2007). Elections are by no means the necessary setting for such a meltdown that could be unleashed by various triggers, including interruptions in energy supply of major cities, hence the permanent insecurity in the mindset of ruling elite. One manifestation of that 'insecurity complex' was the emotional condemnation of the February 1917 revolution on its ninetieth anniversary; the tone was set by Aleksandr Solzhenitsyn's (2007) lengthy article, and the key address was delivered by Surkov who argued: 'Revolution is first of all devastation and destruction …. We must exclude forever revolutions from out political practice'.[2]

The spontaneous collapse of the apparently solid but deeply rotten autocratic regime might indeed be conceptualized as the 'mother of coloured revolutions', but the 'lessons learned' by the Putin's court speak mostly about exterminating the opposition and crushing protests – but not about checking the rot. 'Putinism' without Putin might continue living on borrowed time for only a short time, and its credit could suddenly expire in a more or less spectacular fashion; this bankruptcy could lead to a healthy recovery – but could also degenerate into chaotic disintegration.

No power like the 'hard power'

This scenario is centred on the strategic choice for prioritizing the traditional military-security dimension of power that determines the general pattern of resolving the key contradictions left over from Putin's 'era'. It is certainly incorrect to portray the so-called *siloviki* (literally, 'power-guys') in the Kremlin court as a tightly knit network or a corporation pursuing a militaristic agenda; in fact, most of the 'professionals' from secret services are quite ambivalent about the Armed Forces besides being often at one another's throats. Nevertheless, the underlying logic of concentration of power in the small group of 'colleagues' who ultimately believe only in forceful expropriation of wealth and see international relations as a chain of conspiracies driven by geopolitical interests leads directly to a 'fortress Russia' model.[3]

The significant redistribution of resources from the energy complex to the military–industrial complex could be sustained only if the export revenues are sufficiently high to prevent the stagnation of oil-and-gas production, so this scenario is incompatible with a significant drop of world prices on primary commodities. It also requires a profound internal mobilization that could hardly be

160 *Conclusion*

achieved just by the means of propaganda but implies a serious deterioration of security situation beyond another escalation of the currently quelled 'war on terror'. Such a shift in security posture could recrudesce as an indirect result of the increasingly probable failure of the US intervention in Iraq, which could not only seriously disrupt stability in the Gulf area but also make military might into a practically usable instrument of policy for many states no longer deterred by the US hegemony.

For Russia, the most obvious target for an application of military instruments would be Georgia which has seen too many demarches, provocations, and ultimatums – invariably followed by awkward back-pedalling – from Moscow during this decade. It is Georgia's Black Sea coast that presents the most accessible direction for a *blitzkrieg* offensive, making even a symbolic support from the North Atlantic Treaty Organization (NATO) quite impossible and adding the destruction of the Baku–Tbilisi–Ceyhan (BTC) pipeline as an extra bonus for Moscow. Russia would not be too worried about the 'counter-measures' from the Atlantic Alliance assuming that its integrity would be weakened by the fiasco of the intervention in Afghanistan, while Turkey would have its hands quite full in the collapsing Iraq. Such a decisive action would certainly constitute a break with Putin's cautious temporizing, but it might be driven by desperation more than by boldness. As Dominique Lieven (2002, p. 266) reminded,

> What seemed like aggression and expansion to foreigners might in fact be born of a sense of weakness and vulnerability. Indeed, looking at Russian foreign policy over the centuries, vulnerability and weakness were often at least as powerful a factor as an instinct for territorial expansion.

Such a 'small-and-victorious' operation quite possibly will bring deep deterioration of relations with the West, so that Putin's Munich address would truly become a self-fulfilling prophecy. For his hard-line successors, that replay of the Cold War without the burden of a real arms race and with low risk of confrontation could be quite helpful in sustaining internal mobilization, including, for instance, the restoration of the two-year compulsory draft service. The pumping up of the conventional military muscle could go hand in hand with strengthening defence alliances, first of all with Belarus, which would be again exempted from 'market' energy prices. Ukraine, however, will constitute a massive challenge for this neo-imperial course, notwithstanding the predictably feeble support from the European Union (EU). The proactive steps of the newly securitized Russia towards Georgia and Belarus would hardly convince Kiev to embark on the course of rapprochement, and the cuts in energy export from Russia, necessitated by the shortage of supply, could bring sharp political conflicts.

The main shortcoming of this scenario and the easily distinguishable breaking point on the 'back-to-the-USSR-lite' trajectory is the crumbling economic foundation, since abundance of resources cannot compensate for fragmentation of the industrial base, while the demographic situation makes it impossible to follow the traditional course of extensive growth. The 'Empire' can strike back,

Conclusion   161

but it cannot roll back the retreat caused by internal feebleness rather than by external pressure. Mobilization impulse most probably would dissipate after the first setback, and the inability to meet public demands for upholding the 'social sphere', from communal housing to health care, would compromise the new 'Putin-tough' regime. The attempt to reconstitute the Soviet model (minus the Communist ideology) might result in a new break-up of the state that in fact had never existed in such peculiar borders throughout its long history.

Energy is an eternal delight

This quote from William Blake would appeal to a large part of the Russian political elite that has discovered the enormous material rewards to be gained from controlling the energy flows but is yet to discover the pestilence that this control breeds. The 'energy-first' scenario involves the fundamental shift of strategic priorities towards the maximization of the hydrocarbon rent and further centralization of its redistribution in the Kremlin. It is generally less dependent upon the world oil prices climbing to new peaks between high plateaus and could maintain viability if they tumble down by some 30 per cent from the present level (close to US$70 per barrel), while a deeper drop could be defined as a catastrophic event with unforeseeable consequences. This resilience would be achieved partly by cutting down the redundant expenditures, for instance on conventional forces or on subsidizing alliances, and partly by the possibility to quell the public discontent by the easily available explanation for the 'temporary difficulties'.

A crucial precondition for this scenario is a relatively benign international situation where external challenges to Russia's security would remain low (as they in fact have been since mid-1990s). Moscow, accordingly, would try to preserve 'neutrality' and refrain from entanglement in conflicts that might negatively impact on its energy interests; at the same time, it would prioritize resource allocation to strategic nuclear forces as the 'ultimate' security guarantee. Relations with the CIS would be organized primarily on bilateral basis (this organization quite probably would be disbanded) and have a pronounced 'mercantilist' character centred on the issues of energy trade and transit. One important exception could be Turkmenistan: preserving the monopoly on importing natural gas from this richly endowed state would be considered so important for preventing a full-blown energy crisis in Russia that a 'preventive' or 'peacekeeping' military intervention might be undertaken, despite the reluctance to take security risks and spend money on the military needs.

The main content of state policy in this scenario is strategic development of the energy complex, but this concentration of political attention does not guarantee a steady growth of Russia's leverage as an 'energy super-power'. Investments in expanding production, even if sustained on the level planned for 2007, could bring fruit only in the second half of the next decade, while the inefficiency of state control would manifest itself with increasing misappropriation of resources. Excluding Western (as well as Chinese) companies from partaking in

162 *Conclusion*

large-scale projects aimed at developing new oil-and-gas fields, Russia would deny itself the stimuli of competitive environment and access to new technology. Even the nuclear industry that is perceived as an important complementary element of the energy complex would begin to suffer from technological backwardness that would put Russia at disadvantage on key external markets. In this situation of stagnating production, new 'strategic' pipelines would play the role of boosters for political bargaining making it possible to switch export flows from Europe to China and to play transit countries (for instance, Turkey and Ukraine) one against another.

The well-known 'resource curse' that condemns the oil-rich states to increasing dependency upon export revenues and declining growth would thus intertwine with the 'state curse' (as suggested by Andrei Illarionov, 2005a) that steadily undermines the quality of institutions involved in managing and redistributing the oil wealth (Baev, 2007f). The mechanism of this 'curse' combines the erosion of property rights and legal system due to arbitrary enforcement of state control (as observed in the dismemberment of *Yukos*) and the corruption of the system of governance where political expediency triumphs over economic common sense, while the price of mistakes appears deceivingly low. The end result of this politicization of the oil-and-gas business inevitably is the progressive paralysis of both the energy complex and the state.

The 'resource nationalism' and 'energy egoism' that blossom so richly in this scenario could go hand in hand with claims for Russia's 'unique way' and 'civilization mission' that have already made strong inroads into the contemporary political discourse. While the 'imperial' ambitions could be discarded as too costly and not too popular (as the pathetic 'Imperial march' in Moscow in April 2007 demonstrated), the 'civilization' rhetoric could be usefully employed for shielding the post-Putin political regime from unwarranted Western interference. This rhetoric could gain momentum and become a driver for the policy of self-isolation that would perhaps not reach such extremes as described in the novel *Den oprichnika* (Day of the Oprichnik) by Vladimir Sorokin (2006) but would still effectively condemn Russia to political and social degradation. The inescapable flaw in this scenario is that Russia is too populous, complex, and culturally advanced to be reduced to a 'petro-state', and so an implosion of this model is only a matter of want of a barrel of oil to quell one too many social squall.

None of the three scenarios described above – the 'February 1917', the 'Empire strikes back', and the 'Day of the Oprichnik' – contains much of a promise for a 'Russian miracle' or *chudo* as described by Yergin and Gustafson (1993) in an excellent futuristic research nearly 15 years ago. This author, nevertheless, remains a firm believer in a possibility of such a breakthrough in rediscovering democracy and re-unification with Europe. This narrative digging through layers of economic contradictions and security shortcomings might appear short on positive thinking; the driving intention, however, always was to draw the line under Putin's episode in Russia's never-ending story.

Notes

Introduction

1 Among the key books that captured the main trends in Putin's leadership and significantly influenced this book project, the author should list Kuchins (2002), McFaul (2001), Sakwa (2004), Shevtsova (2003), and Yasin (2005).
2 This vision was never elaborated in anything resembling a consistent strategy, but it was clearly presented in Putin's programmatic article 'Russia on the Threshold of a New Millennium', published, surprisingly, on a newly launched website (Putin, 1999); it also came out strongly in a series of interviews that he granted to three journalists who compiled a captivating book (Gevorkyan *et al.*, 1999).

1 The military reform that never happened

1 The gist of these assessments loaded with much propaganda was presented in the colourful booklet *Soviet Military Power* (1981) produced by the US Department of Defence annually from 1981 to 1989.
2 Extensive and competent analysis of the disastrous transformation of the Soviet military in the Gorbachev era can be found in Odom (1998); see also Taylor (2003); my evaluation is elaborated in Baev (1996).
3 Brian Taylor (2001) provided a sharp examination of the role played by the military under Defence Minister Pavel Grachev in resolving the October 1993 violent political crisis in Moscow.
4 This trajectory is thoroughly researched in McFaul (2001); an early diagnosis was given by Blank (1995, p. 32), who concluded that 'Russia is regressing in civil-military affairs and democracy.'
5 Anatol Lieven's (1998) monumental volume *Chechnya: Tombstone of Russian Power* remains the best account of the impact of the First Chechen War on the Russian military.
6 Competent evaluation of these consequences can be found in the compact monograph 'Chechnya and the posture of the Russian Army' (1999).
7 Baturin and Kokoshin held the positions of secretaries of the Defence Council and Security Council; interesting reflections on their corridor battles can be found in Chapter 10 of the collective memoir *Epokha Eltsina* (2001). Good examples of the civilian debates at that time are Arbatov (1998) and the lengthy report prepared by the Council on Foreign and Defence Policy 'Military reform in the Russian Federation' (1997) that was accompanied by the Council's statement characterizing the situation in the army as 'looming national catastrophe' ('Current status of the Russian army as a looming national catastrophe', 1997).
8 My assessment of the scope of immediate problems created by the Second Chechen War was presented in Baev (2001b).

164 *Notes*

9   I examined these intrigues and Putin's attempts to present himself as a 'military man' in Baev (2000).
10 For a sympathetic view on Sergeev's lost cause, see Golts (2000); on Ivanov's limited clout, see Khodarenok (2001).
11 A critical assessment of the 'Prussian' role of the General Staff can be found in Shlykov (2000).
12 Troshev's removal from a command position in Chechnya in late 2002 triggered a minor scandal, which was promptly extinguished by his 'promotion' to the Kremlin, where his advice was hardly ever asked for, see Poroskov and Shpak (2003).
13 Many military experts pointed out that the only real experiment in organizing military operations could be conducted during a war, while all other 'experiments' tend to provide exactly the outcome that the High Command ordered; for sharp criticism of Baluyevsky's plan, see Kolyvanov (2006).
14 In mid-2006, Putin issued an order to cut 300 positions with the rank of general/admiral, thus bringing down their total number to 1,100; the timeframe, however, was not firmly set, see Babakin (2006c).
15 As one economist (Gritsenko, 2004) thoughtfully argued:

> In the modern society, most of the physical obligations have become archaic myths that were replaced by financial taxes long time ago; the delivery of recruits, however, has remained as a way to pay taxes by physical means. One of the rational explanations for this odd feature that should not be observed in the XXI century is that our country is too poor to afford an army that would be totally supported from the state budget.

16 The Levada Center opinion polls (Sedov, 2005) showed that in 1997 and 2000 the share of the population supporting the draft system remained on the level of 33–34 per cent and 55–56 per cent were in favour of the contract service; in 2002, these figures changed to respectively 27 per cent and 64 per cent.
17 I examined this transformation of military culture in Baev (2002f); for a perceptive analysis of Putin's bureaucratic mind-frame, see Herspring (2002).
18 In 2003, only 23 per cent of respondents supported draft, and 71 per cent were in favour of contract service (Sedov, 2005). Aleksandr Golts (2004a, p. 85) acknowledged that 'The SPS plan was both controversial and not entirely realistic. Nevertheless, when presented to Putin in the fall of 2001, it helped to move the issue of military reform to front burner.' A good presentation of that plan can be found in Tsimbal (2004a).
19 As quoted in Bogatirov (2003). The 76th Pskov Airborne Division was chosen as the subject for the 'experiment', which involved significant costs but did not produce corresponding improvement in performance, see Poroskov (2003).
20 One good analysis of this problem is Van Bladel (2003); Voronov (2003) vividly described the problem of desertion pointing out that Sergei Baev became the first Russian general killed by deserters since 1917, see also Golts (2004a). In April 2006, the Parliamentary Assembly of the Council of Europe approved a Recommendation on the Human Rights of Members of the Armed Forces, which focused particular attention on *dedovshchina* in the Russian army; the relevant parts of the document were published in *Nezavisimoe voennoe obozrenie*, see Ivanov (2006a).
21 According to the Levada Center poll (Sedov, 2005), support for the draft jumped by 16 points to 39 per cent, while 52 per cent still remained in favour of the contract-based system. A good example of the liberal counter-propaganda efforts is Dolgin (2005).
22 Commenting on the undermining of Sychev's case in the court, Aleksandr Golts (2006d) argued:

> Officials from the MoD are perfectly aware that incidents like the one with Sychev are happening in the army every day. They perceive it as vitally important

Notes 165

to send the society a clear message: Do not dare to fight for the rights of soldiers, nobody would ever find the truth.

23 The presentation was published as an article in *Russia in Global Affairs* (Ivanov, 2004); the English version of the text is noticeably less colourful. For an extensive comment, see Mukhin (2003b).

24 Chief of the General Staff Kvashnin told the Duma Committee on Defence with characteristic bluntness: 'It would be unethical to call the on-going transformations in the Armed Forces a military reform.' See 'Anatoly Kvashnin on ethics' (2003).

25 I examined the options available to Putin at the start of the first presidential term in Baev (2001c) and the possibility of a breakthrough in the second term in Baev (2004d).

26 On the debates around the 2003 budget, see Latynina (2002); in mid-2003, the Finance Ministry sent preliminary signals about possible cuts in the 2004 military budget, see Korotchenko (2003).

27 In 2006, Sergei Ivanov received new authority as Deputy Prime Minister to reorganize the system of state defence order aiming at securing better returns on the massive new investments; his innovations, however, remained limited to centralizing the flow of money and cadre reshuffling, see Ivanov (2006a).

28 As Anatoly Tsyganok (2005a) argued, 'In essence, the tank industry works for India, the APCs are produced for the Middle East and Africa, the aircraft industry works for China and India, and the naval shipbuilding serves mostly India and to a lesser degree – China.'

29 Military experts pointed out that delivering a 'battalion set' of T-90C tanks to a regiment equipped with T-80 (of which there are close to 5,000 in the Ground Forces units) doubles the technical and logistic problems since compatibility is quite low, see Tsiganok (2005b).

30 The irony in that parallel is that Peter I dissolved the professional military units of *streltsy*, who showed propensity to mutiny, and formed his guard regiments on the basis of newly institutionalized draft. Renown Russian military thinker Aleksandr Svechin (2002/1937, p. 252) argued that it was the Narva defeat (1700) that convinced Peter I to stop copying European models and 'introduce the military conscription that had been prepared by the course of Russian history'.

31 The federal programme for building the 'permanent readiness' units remains seriously underfinanced and appears on track for a pre-planned failure, see Vorobyev and Tsymbal (2006).

32 Putin's particular attention to the military issues in the 2006 address to the parliament did not positively resonate in the officer corps; according to the internal sociologic research, 70 per cent of officers saw no prospect in the service and up to 100,000 officers were awaiting early retirement after submitting their resignation letters, see Solovyev and Ivanov (2006).

2 The oil-and-gas dividend that was too low – and has become too high

1 The long neglect of oil and natural gas is examined in Campbell (1983) and Ebel (1970). The CIA analysts obviously underestimated the ability of the Soviet leadership to adjust to the new environment and shift investment priorities when they predicted that the USSR oil production would fall sharply from the peak in 1980 ('Prospects for Soviet oil production', 1977). In hindsight, that blunder was presented as an instance when the CIA convinced the Soviet leaders to make changes that 'have real implications for Russian energy production today'. See Tenet (2001).

2 The malignant development of Soviet dependency on export oil-and-gas revenues is thoroughly examined in Egor Gaidar's latest book *Death of the Empire* (2006a), see also Gustafson (1989).

166 *Notes*

3 The doubts in the Soviet leadership concerning the 'big gas' policy were abandoned only after Brezhnev's handshake with Chancellor Willy Brandt in July 1980; convincing analysis is Hewitt (1984). In retrospect, the choice for prioritizing natural gas was one of the greatest moments of the Brezhnev era.

4 One of the strong early influences on Gorbachev was the report by Tatyana Zaslavskaya, a sociologist from Novosibirsk, that had been commissioned by Andropov but discarded as too alarmist by his successor Konstantin Chernenko, see on that Goldman (1994).

5 One important work here is Gustafson (1989); Gaidar (2005, pp. 336–360, 2006a) provides an insightful and informed diagnosis. Putin expressed this questionable view in the annual address to the parliament in April 2005; for a sharp comment, see Bigg (2005).

6 Russian experts believe that these disasters were orchestrated by the United States and Saudi Arabia; thus Gaidar (2006b) argues that:

> the speed and scale of price decline could only be understood in the context of dialogue between US and Saudi Arabia driven by the concerns that events in Afghanistan were just the first step in Soviet expansion in the Middle East.

His bitter opponent Mikhail Leontyev (2006b) concurs:

> The adversary used the chance to set us on this needle and then stopped the drug. In the agony we destroyed our country. I agree with Gaidar that the graph of the oil prices is the history of the illness and death of the Soviet Union.

7 It was estimated that investment in oil production rose by 40 per cent during Gorbachev's first four years, see Gustafson (1989, p. 119).

8 Becoming middle-aged living legends, they popularized their part of the story (Gaidar, 1998; Chubais, 1999); valuable insights can also be found in Boyko *et al.* (1995) and Åslund (1995). Academic literature evaluating Gaidar's mistakes is vast and diverse; useful titles in these bookshelves are Klein and Pomer (2001); Reddaway and Glinsky (2001); Stiglitz (2002); and Shmelev (1999).

9 On GAZPROM's irreducible monopoly, see Kryukov and Moe (1996); also useful is Rutland (1996); on Chernomyrdin's role, see Goldman (2003, pp. 105–116).

10 Gaidar tried to prevent this scheme of privatization which formally guaranteed the interest of the workforce against external buyers but in fact allowed the management to secure ownership with no investment of capital – but lost the political battle to the 'red directors' (Kokh, 1998).

11 Detailed analysis of this initial disintegration and following consolidation in the structures of ownership can be found in Lane (1999).

12 One penetrating account of this murky saga known as the 'loans-for-shares' affair is Freeland (2000).

13 The term 'virtual economy' was popularized by Gaddy and Ickes (1998) in an article that by a striking coincidence appeared just a couple of weeks after the financial meltdown.

14 Good narrative on the making of Russia's second president is Shevtsova (2003), and Sakwa (2004) provides a more substantial analysis.

15 There were certainly many forces at work making that turnaround possible, but as Gaddy (2002, p. 131) noted, 'The statistical relationship between oil prices and industrial output is so close that it is tempting to ascribe virtually all of Russia's post-August 1998 economic performance to oil.'

16 On the *Sidanco* controversy, see Whalen (2001); the overall reshaping and reinvigoration of the oil business is examined in Hill and Fee (2002).

17 Khodorkovsky also adopted a modest personal style strikingly different from typical 'new Russians' with their extravagant spending habits, see Khlebnikov (2002).

18 Even in the Siberian labour camp, Khodorkovsky (2005) was proud to recite that

Notes 167

story, but his presentation in the Carnegie Endowment for International Peace exemplified a totally unclouded vision (Khodorkovsky, 2002).

19 It was Boris Fedorov (2001), a member of the GAZPROM board and former finance minister, who started a public attack against Vyakhirev with the Kremlin's tacit support.

20 Yakov Goldovsky, the president of petrochemical company *Sibur*, was arrested in Miller's office and held in jail for several months, while the company was swallowed by GAZPROM, see Rozhkova (2005).

21 A good collection of impeccably constructed arguments in favour of such a reform can be found in the proceedings of the conference 'Energy security: The role of Russian gas companies' (2003) organized by the International Energy Agency in late 2003.

22 The 'Energy strategy of Russia for the period to 2020' (2003), even if it clearly needs serious revisions, is still available at the Ministry of Industry and Energy website.

23 The main contents of the report were published in the high-circulation tabloid *Komsomolskaya pravda*.

24 This remarkable document reads in retrospect as the last desperate attempt of Aleksandr Voloshin, the head of presidential administration, who resigned a week after Khodorkovsky's arrest, to dissuade Putin by selling him an alternative conspiracy theory.

25 Plenty of factual information and a good amount of sympathetic domestic and international commentary can be found at Khodorkovsky's personal website (www.khodorkovsky.ru).

26 A sharp insight on Putin's transformation into a president-oligarch driven by envy is Gevorkyan (2004); my reflections are in Baev (2005a).

27 Evgeny Yasin (2005, pp. 191–192), the doyen of Russian economists, called the allegations against *Yukos* 'laughable' and its destruction – 'a shameful victory'; elaborate examination of the case was done by Privalov (2005a); and the conclusion about the political nature of this 'show trial' was beyond doubt.

28 The *World Energy Outlook 2006* (2006, p. 92) estimated Russia's production in 2005 at 9.2 million barrels a day, while according to Vladimir Milov (2007a), without the '*Yukos* effect', the still elusive benchmark of ten million barrels a day could have been reached that year.

29 The World Bank report widely cited in the Russian media suggested that state interference caused some worsening of the investment climate but still praised the macroeconomic performance ('World Bank report on Russia's economy', 2004); an editorial in *Expert* argued that the forceful re-distribution of property across the whole country made a mockery of the economic policy ('Caesars and comrades', 2005), see also Hill (2004), while Kasyanov (2006) is of interest as a measured political attack.

30 Illarionov (2004) attached this label at a press conference in late December 2004; Putin had to make reassuring comments at a press conference with German journalists earlier that month (Berger, 2004).

31 Putin's irreducible dependency, more psychological than political, upon this group is analysed by Latynina (2005a).

32 Piontkovsky (2005) speculated that Putin's anger was driven by his personal interest. Some analysts argued that the timing of the attack against Khodorkovsky was determined by his intention to start negotiations with *ExxonMobile* on selling a half of his company following the TNK-BP example (Volkov, 2003).

33 On *Lukoil*'s 'transnationalization' strategy, see Sivakov (2006).

34 Mastepanov and Shafranik (2003) warned that the stable production plateau at 450 million tons a year could be reached by the end of the decade if tens of billions of US dollars were invested in new oilfields. It is worth noting that the reduction of investment in the early 1980s brought a drop in Soviet oil production from 616 million tons

168   *Notes*

in 1983 to 595 million tons in 1985; emergency measures taken by Gorbachev who visited Tyumen in September 1985 helped in reaching a new peak of 624 million tons in 1988, of which 569 millions tons were produced in Russia (Gustafson, 1989, pp. 107–123).

35 Prime Minister Fradkov visiting East Siberia in spring 2007 promised to put the oil companies 'on the ears' discovering that in 2005, they invested 4.2 billion roubles instead of planned 189 billions, and in 2006 – only six billions. See Netreba and Rebrov (2007).

36 An editorial in *Financial Times* suggested that the US$1 billion tax claim on TNK-BP was not approved by Putin:

> The implications for Russia's political and economic future are serious because they suggest that Mr. Putin is no longer in full control of the many-headed monster that is Russia's bureaucracy. Having feasted on the riches of *Yukos*, the beast is hungry and wants to eat again.

See 'Another *Yukos*?' (2005).

37 The real point in this sabotage was that the failure to start development could have resulted in the cancellation of the TNK-BP license on Kovykta by the Ministry of Environment. It is entirely possible that Putin's decision to change the Irkutsk oblast governor in July 2005 was lobbied by GAZPROM (Makarkin, 2005).

38 The questionable rationale for the *Sibneft* deal was examined in Milov (2005); Latynina (2005b) suggested that Roman Abramovich was only a front figure for the real beneficiaries in the Kremlin.

39 There is an obvious contradiction between the 'Soviet' profile of GAZPROM and its declared strategy of transforming itself into a transnational energy giant on par with, for instance, *ExxonMobil*, which in the 'patriotic' discourse remains a symbol of US 'imperialism', see Rubanov and Sivakov (2005).

40 The key parameters of the 2007–2008 investment programme (amounting respectively to 623.73 and 702.95 billion roubles) were approved by the GAZPROM board in January 2007 and were presented at the company website (www.gazprom.ru/eng/news/2007/01/22219.shtml).

41 Presenting his revised reform plans, Chubais expressed a 'private opinion' that GAZPROM's strategy of expansion in every direction from media to coal with the single exception of gas production was not 'entirely correct'; he also asserted that 'state capitalism is a dead-end that would soon become apparent for all state capitalists'. See Gorelov (2007a).

42 The bureaucrats of 'United Russia' who were discussing parameters of this concept were hardly able to master the reformist energy of Comandante Che but could indeed appreciate his ideas on protecting the national economy against the penetration of transnational corporations, see Rudneva and Nikolaeva (2006).

43 In Illarionov's diagnosis, the 'Dutch disease' affects the economy through currency appreciation and high inflation; the 'Argentinean disease' involves an industrial policy of supporting non-competitive sectors by redistributing the resource rent; the 'Venezuelan disease' spreads through nationalization of the key industries; the 'Saudi disease' means political application of the 'oil weapon'; and the 'Zimbabwean disease' signifies a total bureaucratic control over the public life.

3 The dream of a new 'greatness' that has come truly false

1 In the interview with *Expert*, Medvedev (2006) mentioned that additional definitions to the term 'democracy' created 'odd aftertaste'; he reiterated that point at the 2007 World Economic Forum in Davos, see Baev (2007d) and, for an ironic parody, Belkovsky (2007). Putin distanced himself from these debates at the meeting with selected Western experts in August 2006, see Sheglova (2006).

Notes 169

2 That assertion was delivered at the meeting of activists of the pro-Kremlin 'United Russia' party, hardly a sophisticated audience; for a sharp comment, see Golts (2006a). Surkov added more polish to his concept in the article 'Nationalization of the future' (Surkov, 2006b), examined by Rudensky (2006).

3 As one respected economist pointed out, the widespread obsession with fluctuations in the energy sector amounted to a 'Dutch disease in heads', see Guriev (2006).

4 One precise comparison between Russian 'greatness' and French *grandeur* is in Lukyanov (2005a).

5 Sergei Medvedev (1999) explored brilliantly the political dimension of Russian space.

6 Drawing a line 'from Ivan III's 500-year-old campaign to be recognized as the peer of Holy Roman Emperor to Putin's ongoing campaign to be recognized as the peer of Chancellor Gerhard Schröder and President Jacques Chirac', Iver Neumann (2005, p. 25) argued that 'the question of Russian status in relation to other European powers is still with us'.

7 The fortieth anniversary of that flight in April 2006 invited many sentimental reflections but few sober assessments of the status of the Russian space programme, see Bruni (2006).

8 A good example of the focusing on Russia's allegedly unstoppable expansionist drive is Pipes (1996); for a sharp criticism, see Lieven (2000/2001).

9 Dugin (2004a) develops in his many books and articles a rather straightforward variation of classical geopolitics; Leontyev (2006a) has a personal programme *Odnako* on the first channel of Russian television (www.1tv.ru). Thoughtful analysis of the trajectory of the Russian empire can be found in a lecture of Alexei Miller (2005); a solid and original research is in Dominique Lieven (2002).

10 An explicit argument is in Leontyev (2006b); the so-called 'Imperial march' in Moscow in April 2007 was supposed to demonstrate the mass appeal of these ideas, see Gevorkyan (2007).

11 As Iver Neumann (1996, pp. 25–27) argued, the 'formula' was hammered out in the period when Russia's belonging to Europe was not in doubt, and the proposition on the unbridgeable gap was advanced only in the 'remarkable' decade of the 1840s. For a relevant interpretation, see Miller (2007).

12 The latter position gained in popularity in the course of revolts in Paris' ethnic suburbs in autumn 2005 and angry protests in many Muslim states against 'offensive' Danish cartoons in early 2006, see Privalov (2005b).

13 This radical 'civilizational' argument was elaborated in a lengthy memo that found much support in the Kremlin and shocked Putin's more liberal fans after an unauthorized publication, see Yuriev (2004).

14 The article, known as the 'Millennium Manifesto', was not transferred to the relaunched website (http://president.kremlin.ru/mainpage.shtml); a sharp analysis (and a perfect translation in the appendix) can be found in Sakwa (2004).

15 Yeltsin was so shocked by that plain irrelevance of Russia's nuclear arsenal that he ordered the Security Council to develop an emergency programme for upgrading it to a 'usable' instrument, see Sokov (2000a).

16 After the initial surprise, the isolated company of Russian paratroopers had to rely on the NATO forces for supplies, since the Bulgarian, Hungarian, and Romanian airspace was closed for Russian transport planes, see Allison (2004a) and Gobarev (1999).

17 An editorial in *New York Times* reflected on that test: 'It is time to let Mr. Putin know that we are looking hard into his soul, and we don't like what we see' ('Revisiting Putin's soul', 2006).

18 My assessments of the instrumental character of that commitment and its inevitably limited scope can be found in Baev (2003a).

19 Khodorkovsky's (2002) presentation at the Carnegie Endowment for International Peace, Washington, DC, is a perfect example of his grandiose plans.

170 Notes

20 Putin's blunt statement that 'military action against Iraq was a great political mistake' unleashed a storm of vicious anti-American commentary in the mainstream media that was only partly extinguished with his follow-up statement that 'Russia is not interested in a US defeat', see, for instance, Tretyakov (2003).
21 The catchy quote was ascribed to Condoleezza Rice; on the US self-restraint in 'punishing France', see 'Which way now for French policy?' (2003). Perry Anderson (2006) argued impeccably that 'European hostility to the war was broad but not deep' in his review of Francis Fukuyama's *America at the Crossroads*, who emphasized the gross damage to the allied ties.
22 That ambitious but not very successful initiative was praised by as 'the start of the era of a new Eurasian economic empire', see Dugin (2004b).
23 Both crises are examined more thoroughly in Chapter 11; for a broad overview, see Markedonov (2004).
24 According to Lilia Shevtsova (2005), 'For the Russian elite, the possibility of Ukraine's escape to the West through a change of political regime has become a shock nearly equal in pain to the break-up of the USSR.'
25 Arkady Moshes (2004a), one of the best Russian experts on Ukraine, warned about mistakes originating in simplistic perceptions of splits in the Ukrainian political elite and about the risks of pushing the limits of Russia's influence.
26 Spectacular first-hand impressions from the 'orange revolution' are presented in Kolesnikov (2005a).
27 Jonathan Steele (2004) added some credibility to these claims arguing that 'Yushchenko got the western nod, and floods of money poured in to groups which support him.'
28 An interpretation of this idea was offered by Yury Baluyevsky (2007a, p. 30), the chief of General Staff, who pointed that 'it took centuries for Russian civilization to develop', argued 'against the imposition of European civilization upon Russia', and asserted that 'Russia is not Europe, not Asia, and not even Eurasia. I'd like to emphasize, it is Russia!'
29 Meeting with Uzbekistan's President Islam Karimov in June 2005, Putin confirmed the fact of external involvement in the Andijan 'events' and concluded that 'we are satisfied that the situation has successfully been brought under control', see Gabuev (2005).
30 In the Moscow expert community, in April 2005, 58 per cent believed that a revolutionary crisis was possible in Russia, compared with only 28 per cent in December 2004, see Glikin and Saidukova (2005). In the stream of alarmist forecasts, one keen observer argued: 'Russia is not threatened by a revolution. Russia is threatened by fear of a revolution in the Kremlin', see Cherkasov (2005).
31 Vladislav Surkov, asserting himself as the main ideologist of *Putinism*, spelled this idea in February 2006; for a withering evaluation, see Golts (2006a).
32 Leonid Radzikhovsky (2006a), one of the sharpest Moscow political commentators, argues that:

> the class envy is the nightmare for the ruling elite. The main ideological task in the society rigidly split into antagonistic classes (always the case in the raw materials economies) is to prevent the emergence of the class consciousness. The way to do it is to replace the wedge of class envy (hatred) with the wedge of race envy (hatred).

33 That occasion, remarkably, was his short visit to Grozny in December 2005 for the first session of the newly elected Chechen parliament, see Baev (2005c).
34 Alexei Makarkin (2006) suggested that the resonance of that Declaration had more to do with Kirill's personal ambitions than with the church's role in shaping a new state ideology.
35 More liberal commentators argued that the church should not forget the bitter lessons of its previous close alliances with the state and pointed out that the proposed 'draft

Notes 171

of the human rights declaration is surprisingly close to the Kremlin's postulates of "managed sovereign democracy"', see Novoprudsky (2006).

36 This assessment was given in Putin's April 2005 address to the parliament, where he also insisted that 'Russia was, is and will of course be a major European power'; for thoughtful criticism, see Leibin (2005).

37 Dmitri Medvedev (2005), argued with the authority of the head of the presidential administration: 'If we fail to consolidate the elites, Russia could disappear as a unified state .... Break-up of the USSR might look like a kindergarten party comparing with state collapse of the contemporary Russia.' Vladislav Surkov (2004) directly applied the 'fifth column' label to the opposition, accused in cherishing 'hatred not to Putin's Russia but to Russia as such'. A clear parallel with the developments in Belarus is drawn in Milov (2007c).

38 That speech at the high-level conference in Vilnius marked a significant change of tone in US–Russian relations, see Golts (2006b), McFaul (2006), Privalov (2006b), and for my evaluation, Baev (2006a).

4 The trickle of the oil money for the military

1 An extensive research into the scale and consequences of that breakdown can be found in Genin (2001).

2 Galloping inflation and irregular disbursement of funds make it impossible to produce a meaningful estimate of the devastating drop in military funding in 1990–1993, but competent evaluations (Cooper, 1998) show that the amount of money available for military needs was further cut by more than a third in 1995. As Steven Miller (2004, p. 11) argued:

> this budgetary reality has been regarded as a powerful motivating force for reform. On its face, it seemed simply untenable to retain anything like the inherited military force while spending anything like the amounts that Russia was able to devote to defence.

3 Kiriyenko's government made a half-hearted effort to increase the transparency of military spending, placing its hopes on General Georgy Oleinik, the head of the main Directorate for Military Budget and Financing in the MoD, who was later convicted for embezzlement, see Statsky (2003).

4 According to Trenin and Malashenko (2004, p. 158), the peak of direct expenses came in 2000 when up to 20 per cent of the military budget went to war; the 'reconstruction' funds that went up from US$300 million in 2000 to US$500 million in 2001 were mostly spent on infrastructure supporting the fighting force.

5 General Anatoly Sitnov, the chief of armaments of the Armed Forces, asserted that expenditures in the scale of US$16 billion were necessary for 'normal rearmament' of the army, which would amount to delivering 300–350 tanks, 150–200 aircraft, and 50–70 helicopters a year; that 'target' sum was in fact twice larger than the whole military budget, see 'Prospects and plans for armament modernization' (2000).

6 The Security Council approved at that meeting the Guidelines for Military-Industrial Policy to 2015, which did not envisage any large-scale purchases in the near future, see Mukhin (2003a).

7 Aleksandr Golts (2004b) pointed out that the allocation of US$18 billion for 2005 would be beyond the wildest dreams of Igor Sergeev (the sum total in 1999 was five times lower), but the High Command accepted it as the 'minimal level' insisting on the target figure of 3.5 per cent of GDP (instead of 2.7 per cent). On the investigations of the Account Chamber, see Solovyev and Elensky (2004).

8 Finance Minister Alexei Kudrin (2006) explained that the particular needs of the pre-election year determined such a growth but confirmed that 'in principle' the budget should increase proportionally to the overall economic growth of 5–6 per cent.

172 *Notes*

9 Vitaly Tsimbal (2004b) pointed out that the necessary increase of funding in the 2005 budget was completely hidden behind secretive headings like 'counter-terrorist activity', arguing further that such lack of transparency was a recipe for inefficiency.
10 In the 2006 acquisition budget, the funding for research and development was frozen, since too much of it had been channelled towards supporting 'free capacity' at numerous 'strategic' enterprises; the effect, however, was far from stimulating, see Myasnikov (2005b).
11 As Vitaly Shlykov (2001) argued, up to 90 per cent of the 1,700 enterprises with some two million employees for years received no orders whatsoever from the armed forces, so the notion of VPK was simply a myth.
12 Ruslan Pukhov as quoted by Aron Tsypin (2004), who also pointed out that the initial increases in the defence order did not register at all in the balance sheets of the key companies and brought no corresponding increases in the delivery of modern weapon systems.
13 Bitter competition continued inside the formally integrated 'holding' *Sukhoi*, while the enforced merger of *Almaz* and *Antei*, the two key producers of air defence systems, resulted in a series of contracted killings, including the newly appointed General Director Igor Klimov, see Aleksandrov (2003).
14 Pointing to the lack of transparency in distributing funding and sharing revenues, Irina Savitskaya (2004) concluded: 'All this scramble for the Defence Ministry money resembles more criminal *razborki* (clashes) for spheres of influence rather than state building.'
15 By the end of 2005, experts had expected a decline from the very high result of 2004 (US$5.8 billion), but some undisclosed deals added up to an additional one billion, see Khazbiev (2006a).
16 Thus, the price for the T-90 main battle tank was 42 million roubles in 2006 but increased to 58 million in the 2007 defence order, see Kulikov (2006).
17 The list of 'strategic' enterprises was reduced to about 1,000, of which some 150 were technically bankrupt and another 150 had negative balance of payments; the average margin of profit in the industry was only about 3 per cent. The average use of industrial potential was only 40 per cent, so maintaining the 'free capacity' was one of the key handicaps, see Kirillov (2006) and Myasnikov (2006c).
18 The total value of this programme was set at approximately five trillion roubles, which should cover the purchase of 3,000 new and modernization of 5,000 existing weapon systems; the bulk of deliveries, however, was planned for the next decade, see Ivanov and Myasnikov (2006) and Babakin (2006b).
19 In August 2006, Putin gathered all the 'captains' of the air industry in his summer residence near Sochi in order to impress upon them the need in joining efforts; there was hardly any agreement, however, on the strategy for developing the sector except for introducing protective barriers against 'unpatriotic' imports, see Khazbiev (2006b) and Plugatarev and Myasnikov (2006).
20 An editorial in business-oriented *Vedomosti* stated: 'Five years in the job of Defence Minister, Sergei Ivanov has achieved no results of significance in reforming the army and strengthening defence posture', see 'Aggressive helplessness' (2006).
21 Lilia Shevtsova (2006b), one of the sharpest analysts of 'Putinism', pointed out in mid-2006 that the traditional tussle of courtiers who sought to push one another down from the Kremlin wall betrayed 'doubts in Russia's political class about the ability of the closed system controlled from one command centre to secure stability and its own survival'.
22 As Shevtsova (2003, pp. 105, 109) argued, 'Yeltsin regarded the oligarchy as the natural base for his regime.' Putin wanted nothing of that and was convinced that 'all the Russian oligarchs had received property because of their access to Yeltsin entourage. Now the new regime wanted to restore control over them and their activity by blackmailing big business.'

Notes 173

23 Radzikhovsky (2006b) portrayed Berezovsky as 'the most talented schemer of our post-Soviet epoch'.
24 Yulia Latynina (2005g) pointed out that Kukura was 'the only person with full information on the complicated off-shore networks of the oil company' and speculated that the lack of any ransom demands suggested a different kind of deal with the kidnappers.
25 Many experts argued that the increased taxation reduced the disposable profits the oil sector which invested only US$12 billion in 2005 and some US$13 billion in 2006; in fact, the privately owned companies could have doubled the rate of investments but were discouraged by the expansion of state control, see Berezinskaya and Mironov (2006).
26 Soon after establishing the National Anti-Terrorist Committee in early 2006, the Kremlin issued a confidential letter to key business associations encouraging 'volunteer contribution' for supporting its activity, see Butrin (2006b).
27 As these words were written, the Internet delivered brief information about the fire on the nuclear submarine *Daniil Moskovsky* with the loss of two lives, see 'Fire on nuclear submarine *Daniil Moskovsky*' (2006).

5 Counter-terrorism and the Caspian oil games

1 Speculative and alarmist interpretations of the risks in the 'Great Caspian Game' were aplenty; for a sober and balanced analysis, see Müller (2000); for a captivating travelogue, see Kleveman (2003).
2 Important as that meeting was, I cannot quite agree with Oksana Antonenko (2004, p. 247) who presented it as a 'pivotal event' after which 'economic interests became paramount', whereas before 'Russian policy in the Caspian had been motivated primarily by political and security considerations.'
3 Oliker and Szayna (2003, pp. 356–357) also argued that 'a critical determinant of the potential for US involvement in the near future will be the evolution of the counter-terrorist campaign …. A lower level of success will probably mean an increased US presence in the Caspian region'.
4 Anticipating the Iraq turmoil, Rajan Menon (2003, p. 191) argued:

> Resolve and staying power have become paramount in the war against terrorism, and the American leadership will worry that a hasty departure from greater Central Asia will send the wrong message and invite more acts of terror. Accordingly (if paradoxically), the more unstable greater Central Asia becomes, the more pronounced America's nervousness about disengagement will be.

5 Detailed examination of this loaded issue can be found in Polat (2002, pp. 151–166).
6 That was hardly an impressive 'show of force' as Russia was able to deploy only a fraction of forces that were used in the assault on Baku in January 1990, see 'Uneasy aftermath of Putin's Azerbaijan's visit' (2001).
7 That isolated episode is put in a broader perspective in Katik (2004).
8 Comments in Russian media emphasized that 'the Caspian summit was not fruitless: its result was the serious revision by the Kremlin of its power politics in the region' (Golotuyk, 2002).
9 Sokut (2002a) provided a detailed description of these exercises.
10 In June 2004, large-scale military exercises were conducted in the Far East showing the ability to deploy troops by air over huge distances; in my opinion, 'instead of setting off a tsunami wave of alarmist comments in the West with another exercise in the Caspian area, on par with those in summer 2002, Moscow makes the point in a subtler but no less efficient way' (Baev, 2004f).
11 On the naval build-up, see Mukhin (2004a); on the new series of gunboats, see Timchenko (2006).

174 *Notes*

12 As Roger McDermott (2006a) observed in this case, 'all too often, the initiatives and foreign aid programmes are not supported by the authorities in Astana that are responsible for taking the necessary decisions to boost Caspian security'.

13 For the tense but essentially hollow debates on a hypothetic US base, see Ismail (2005) and Mamedov (2006); for a reaction on Donald Rumsfeld's visit to Baku in April 2005, see Talyshli (2005); the adoption of some NATO standards in the Azerbaijan's army in 2006 was interpreted by many commentators as a sure sign of going to the 'other' side, see Panfilova (2006).

14 As Steven Main (2005, p. 7) argued in an excellent study:

> Whether we in the West like to admit it or not, Russia's military presence in the Caspian Sea not only ensures that the Russian interests in the region are safeguarded, but also guarantees that the other littoral states derive security benefits from having a creditable military force in the region, large enough to act as a deterrent, which they do not have to pay for and which ensures a degree of stability in the region as a whole.

15 I examined these low-content interactions in Baev (2001a), for my more recent analysis that informs the narrative in this section, see Baev (2006c).

16 One characteristic example is Khodarenok (2002a); that view correlated nicely with the argument that the main goal for the US intervention in Iraq was establishing control over its oil reserves, see Bykov (2003).

17 See, for instance, Fairbanks (2002); one more recent example can be found in Cohen (2005).

18 It is unclear to what degree drug trafficking was a part of that deal, and there is very little data on the present-day situation on the Afghan-Turkmen border, which opium caravans reportedly cross with little harassment, see Khohlov (2005).

19 In early 1999, Turkmenistan after due consultations with Turkey signed an agreement with PSG International, a branch of *Bechtel* Corp., on launching the Transcaspian pipeline project with the estimated cost of US$2.5 billion; the information is still available at the *Bechtel* website, see 'PSG secures lead role in US$2.5 billion Transcaspian pipeline project' (1999). At the OSCE summit in Istanbul in December 1999, Azerbaijan, Georgia, Turkmenistan, and Turkey signed a letter of intent on this project.

20 An insightful analysis can be found in 'Cracks in the Marble' (2003).

21 Ashgabat demanded a significant increase in price from 1 January 2005, but GAZPROM flatly refused referring to clear contract obligations, see Shahinoglu *et al.* (2005). Niyazov had to back off, but he got his wish the next year when Moscow had to agree on doubling the import prices in the aftermath of its 'gas war' with Ukraine, see Milov (2007b).

22 Gleb Pavlovsky (2005b), one of the masterminds of Russia's disastrous interference in Ukraine, formulated the thesis on 'punching a revolution in the face'.

23 For an elaborate and insightful analysis of this political breakdown, see Marat (2006).

24 It was Defence Minister Sergei Ivanov who most clearly spelled this message at the meeting of Russia-NATO Council, asserting that an incursion of terrorists from Afghanistan was the main cause of the bloodshed, see Dubnov (2005).

25 Critical analysis of uncoordinated efforts and missed opportunities in US policy towards Uzbekistan can be found in Daly *et al.* (2006).

26 A 'lessons learned' memo from Kazakh Interior Minister Turisbekov to Prime Minister Akhmetov was leaked to the press and caused a no small scandal with its straightforward emphasis on readiness to use armed force against demonstrators, see Solovyev (2005).

27 Becoming the operator on the strategic gas pipelines in Uzbekistan, GAZPROM agreed to invest US$100 million in their modernization in order to increase the transit of Turkmen gas by some 20 per cent (Samedova and Gavshina, 2005); Uzbekistan

Notes 175

exported to Russia 8 bcm of gas in 2005 and 9 bcm in 2006 and agreed to deliver 13 bcm in 2007 (Grivach, 2006a).

28 While Turkmenbashi acted in a direct violation of agreed contract, his position was strengthened by GAZPROM's agreement to pay Kazakhstan a higher price, see Polivanov (2006).

29 Stephen Blank (2006a) suggested that Cheney's visit 'may also signify the administration's increased awareness that its democracy project ran into the sand and was terribly counterproductive in Central Asia'.

30 As I have argued, 'Russia is stuck with its insincere embrace of ungrateful Turkmenbashi knowing too well that this "mad tea party" could end abruptly at any moment leaving it with a pile of broken china' (Baev, 2006g, p. 15)

31 On the Chinese connection, see Torbakov (2006); on the Transcaspian option, see Blagov (2007b); Stanislav Belkovsky (2006) poignantly pointed out: 'Turkmenbashi successfully implemented two concepts that the Kremlin is still painfully polishing – "energy empire" and "sovereign democracy"'.

32 On the motivation and organization of that failed 'crusade', see Derluguian (1999); Lanskoy (2002) is also useful.

33 Abdullaev (1999) provided a precise picture of the shift in attitude in Dagestan; for a competent and detailed description of combat operations, see Blandy (2000).

34 I looked into that deliberate destruction in Baev (2001a); for a background on Chechen oil industry, see Ebel (1995).

35 For an informed analysis of the situation in Dagestan in the early 2000s and useful comparison with Chechnya, see Kisriev (2003); another comparative perspective is Zürcher *et al.* (2005).

36 As Sergei Markedonov (2005b) argued, 'In the largest republic of the North Caucasus we face with terrorism of a higher level and quality than in the neighbouring Chechnya.'

37 Much the same way as the larger 'Kozak Report', the memo was leaked to tabloid press so that the resonance made it impossible for the Kremlin to ignore it, see Deeva (2005).

38 This rather odd, if not bizarre evaluation of the situation, was reported by the press but omitted from the presentation of the trip on the presidential website, see, for instance, Sukhov (2005). As Yulia Latynina (2005f) argued, 'The rebels do not infiltrate into Dagestan, they live here …. To speak in the war-time Dagestan about protecting the holiday-makers in Krasnodar kray essentially means to write Dagestan off.'

39 Garry Kasparov argued after visiting Dagestan that 'an explosion in the North Caucasus is inevitable and the whole region might split from Russia' (Ryklin, 2005), while Boris Sokolov (2006) pointed out that 'there are no rational reasons for keeping the republics of the North Caucasus in Russia'.

40 Nick Paton Walsh (2005) accurately portrayed these 'Sharia enclaves'; for a more complex picture in mid-2006, see Latynina (2006c).

41 Dunlop and Menon (2006, p. 111) suggested that 'if Islamic extremists establish secure footholds across the North Caucasus, the political equation in Muslim Azerbaijan and Central Asia could also be changed'.

42 On the explosions on the pipelines in Dagestan, see Tsyganok (2004); my brief comment on Putin's non-requested pledge to protect Islam is in Baev (2005c).

43 According to local journalists, that 'live event' was organized and controlled like a 'special operation', see Rybina (2006).

6 Alliance-building with virtual commitments and energy power

1 For a broad overview of interstate relations in the 1990s, see Dwan and Pavliuk (2000); Allison (2001) provided a balanced evaluation of Russia's neighbourhood policy.

176 *Notes*

2 Fedor Lukyanov (2006c) argued that *maidan* (as huge rallies in Kiev are known) delivered 'a mortal blow on the shape of the post-Soviet space. The Ukrainian shock has destroyed the remaining illusions about both Moscow's unique role in the former empire and the West's readiness to accept this role.'
3 For informed and thoughtful analysis, see Light (2003).
4 Trying to assess that subtle change of attitude (Baev, 2002e), I pointed out that:

> Putin has shown penchant and skill in using this 'soft' political power to build Russia's dominance over its 'near abroad' (the term is abandoned, not the attitude) .... This personalized networking points to a significant shift in Moscow's modus operandi for the CIS: It now adopts, not the strategy of conflict manipulation of the early 1990s, but that of manipulating presidents.

5 Dmitri Trenin (2004a) argued perceptively that:

> the main problem of the shaping up 'CIS project' is in the absence of a long-term strategy in Moscow, as well as mechanisms of its implementation and people who would drive it forward. That makes the project fragile and unstable.

6 A useful assessment of Kyrgyzstan's post-revolution political trajectory is Marat (2006).
7 I have examined the impact of this summit in Baev (2005j); for an even more sceptical view on the CIS May 2005 summit in Moscow, see Socor (2005); Andrei Kokoshin (2005) confirmed that the Kazan summit ended 'better than expected' since 'even the politicians who proclaim their Euro-Atlantic orientation cannot afford turning their backs to the CIS'.
8 Fedor Lukyanov (2005b) noting that Russia untied its hands in the economic cooperation with the CIS partners concluded: 'It turned out to be quite easy: As the great-power illusions were discarded, it became immediately clear that most CIS states were more interested in Russia than Russia was in them.'
9 The composition of this 'zone of pro-Russian orientation in CIS' was defined differently by Moscow analysts; for instance, Egozaryan and Gromov (2005) included also Azerbaijan, while Belkovsky (2005) suggested a new format of Commonwealth of Russia's Allies (in Russian, the abbreviation was familiar SSSR), assumed that Uzbekistan and Azerbaijan would remain out.
10 Anatoly Kinah, secretary of the Ukrainian Security Council, complained that the CIS had lost its economic functions and become a talk shop, see Solovyev and Sidorenko (2006b).
11 Russian military experts concluded from a series of exercises in summer 2005 that the joint air defence system was the only useful structure in the CSTO, see Babakin (2005a). On the military 'blindness' during the North Korean missile tests, see Blinov *et al.* (2006) and Litovkin (2006).
12 Russian Defence Minister Sergei Ivanov, who observed the exercises, emphasized that they were not linked to political situation in Central Asia. However, Nikolai Bordyuzha, the CSTO secretary general, suggested that the mechanism of the Treaty should have been activated in order to check the violent chaos in Bishkek, see 'CSTO military forces could have helped Kyrgyzstan' (2005).
13 As Stephen Blank (2006b) argued, 'Insinuating the CSTO between NATO and individual Central Asian states would give Moscow considerably more say over the Atlantic alliance's activities in the region, effectively forestalling the ability of regional leaders to forge independent relationships with Brussels.'
14 Lukashenko referred to the joint Russian–Belarussian military exercises 'Shield of the Union-2006' in which the allied forces jointly repelled an 'invasion' into Belarus from the West, see Mukhin (2006) and Timofeeva (2006).
15 Putin, who turned 53 that on weekend, pronounced the merger to be the 'best birthday present' he could have expected. Indeed, during the back-to-back CSTO and EEC

Notes 177

summits in Moscow in June 2005, Kyrgyzstan's Foreign Minister Roza Otunbaeva was not quite sure at one moment the session of which organization she was attending, see Kolesnikov (2005b) and Blagov (2005b).

16 The basis for the organization was the so-called 'Shanghai five' mechanism originating in the Treaty on Deepening Military Trust in Border Regions, signed in 1996 by China, Kazakhstan, Kyrgyzstan, Russia, and Tajikistan, which was supplemented in 1997 by the Treaty on Reduction of Military Forces in Border Regions. Uzbekistan joined the five states in 2001, when their cooperative ties were formalized in the framework of SCO, see Beehner (2006).

17 Characteristically, most of the 'important speeches' presented at the SCO official website (www.sectsco.org) are those of its Secretary General Zhang Deguang.

18 One good evaluation of the consequences of China's 'historically unprecedented' growth for Russia is Vlasova *et al.* (2005); for a geopolitical perspective, see Dugin (2006).

19 An attempt to disprove the 'sceptics' who profess such unpatriotic views can be found in 'SCO and the "Great Game"' (2006).

20 Assessing this potential competition, one Russian expert reminded that 'energy relations between Russia and China are complicated by a whole complex of problems in other spheres of their bilateral relations', see Rubanov (2006).

21 Maksim Shein as quoted by Rubanov (2006), see also Fedorov (2006), and on China's interests in Turkmenistan, see Kimmage (2006).

22 Stephen Blank (2005b) argued that 'these exercises aim to show that the two powers can and will wield substantive and effective military power in critical zones of Asia and that, at least in the SCO multilateralism, also has a military dimension'. He also suggested that 'membership in the SCO compels Moscow to keep up with China and thus adopt stances it might not otherwise take, even as it allows it to leverage Chinese power temporarily for its own behalf in Central Asia'.

23 China for its side remained reluctant to stage the 'Peace Mission – 2007' as joint exercises of SCO and CSTO, see Myasnikov and Ivanov (2007).

24 In hindsight, Karimov's readiness to follow up on that carefully worded proposition with the straightforward demand to withdraw US troops appears entirely predictable, but the shock in Washington was genuine, see Marten (2005).

25 As Richard A. Boucher (2006, p. 15), US Assistant Secretary of State for South and Central Asian Affairs, emphasized at the Kabul conference on Partnership, Trade and Development in Greater Central Asia:

> Nations should not be left with only one market, they should not feel squeezed between two powers .... And we are looking really to maximize the movement of energy, people, goods, of information, from the Kazakh steppes to the Indian ocean.

See also Starr (2005a).

26 Dmitri Trenin (2003) identified this dilemma at the early stage of the war against Taliban and Al Qaeda, but his proposal for a Russian–US partnership in Central Asia remained a voice in Moscow's analytical wilderness.

27 As Ariel Cohen (2006) argues, perhaps seeking to prompt the real-time policy to follow his diagnosis, 'American policymakers are currently working to develop a strategy to blunt the SCO's ability to influence regional developments.'

28 Vladimir Milov (2006b) makes a similar point: 'Russia's policy towards its neighbours is still whimsical and eclectic: Moscow could change its mind from generously subsidizing them to rudely cancelling the subsidies .... Small wonder that run from us in every direction.'

178 *Notes*

7 Virtually extended deterrence of the 'Great Power'

1 This official translation (Putin, 2006b) does not quite convey the praise *molodtsy* (great guys, super) that was repeated twice in Russian. The quote from Ilyin is also from this speech.

2 Very little is known about the three secret decrees approved at that meeting, except for a particular emphasis on developing new tactical nuclear weapons, see Sokut (1999); on the profound impact of the Kosovo crisis on nuclear thinking in Russia, see Sokov (2000a).

3 General Wesley Clark, the commander-in-chief of the NATO forces, ordered coalition troops to take the Pristina airport from the Russians by force, but British General Michael Jackson, who was in charge on the ground, had both brains and guts to challenge that order and refused to launch an assault, earning his entry into the annals of military history with the phrase: 'I am not going to start the Third World War for you.' See 'Confrontation over Pristina airport' (2000).

4 One careful examination can be found in Blank (2001); as I argued earlier about these texts, 'the disconnect between the perceived (and elaborately described) role of the military and Russia's real defence posture was nothing short of surreal' (Baev, 2004d, p. 56).

5 Kvashnin went as far as proposing that Russia did not need the 'artificial' strategic parity with the United States and could effectively deter any aggression with a force as small as 150 ICBMs. Many elaborate counter-arguments were based on a common premise: 'Russia cannot exist as a second-rate power. Due to its position in the world, it could survive only as a great power. Its economic capabilities have sharply declined, so only a reliable nuclear deterrent capability could secure this status' (Rogov, 2000). For a competent overview of the debate, see Sokov (2000b).

6 The concept of 'mutual assured destruction' (MAD) made a comeback in early 2006 when *Foreign Affairs* published an article based on old-fashioned quantitative research leading to the conclusion that Russia's strategic arsenal could be wiped out by a disarming strike (Liber and Press, 2006). Dozens of experts and politicians in Moscow rushed to proclaim their confidence that a retaliatory strike would cause the US unacceptable damage; the shallowness of this wishful thinking is captured by Golts (2006c). A sound expert opinion on this issue is Sokov (2007); detailed discussion can be found in Pavel Podvig's blog (Podvig, 2006).

7 These intrigues are carefully examined in Main (2003); for a sympathetic view on Sergeev's uphill battles, see Golts (2000).

8 The Moscow Treaty on Strategic Offensive Reductions signed in May 2002 was merely three pages long, as compared with some 500 pages of the START I, and, according to some US experts, 'makes the world no safer than it was before, and much the worse for failing to achieve a genuine reduction in nuclear weapons', see Daalder and Lindsay (2002). For a useful analysis of the START I and START II treaties, see Graham and LaVera (2003).

9 The conclusion of the report was that by 2010, the United States, which 'continue to perceive Russia as the main enemy' and 'cannot tolerate the risk of Russia's revival', would acquire the capability for destroying all Russian nuclear assets in one strike, see Anisimov and Baranets (2003).

10 A precise evaluation concluding that 'the Ministry of Defense seems to believe that nothing but military power can guarantee Russia's security and interests, especially given the suspected propensity of the United States for unilateral, often not fully logical military escapades' can be found in Sokov (2003).

11 In April 2004, Putin invited French President Chirac to a secret Russian space centre in Krasnoznamensk in order to advance the strategic agenda of the faltering Moscow–Berlin–Paris 'axis', which did not get him very far, even if 'one unusually high-ranking source in the Kremlin confirmed that behind the closed doors in

Notes 179

Krasnoznamensk and then in Novo-Ogarevo (the talks ended late in the night), the French had showed very serious interest in the new Russian missiles', see Kolesnikov (2004).

12 At the meeting with the top brass in November 2004, bragging about research and tests of missile systems that would not appear anytime soon in other nuclear states, Putin emphasized that 'if we reduce attention to such elements of our defence as the nuclear-missile shield, new threats would arise'. English translation of these remarks is not available on the presidential website, see Petrovskaya (2004), my reflections are presented in Baev (2004e).

13 The firm tone of Cheney's speech convinced many experts that the period of 'strategic partnership' had come to an end (McFaul, 2006), while for the Kremlin's propagandists, it was a 'deliberate nasty provocation' (Pavlovsky, 2006a). I looked into the content of Putin's 'answer' in Baev (2006b).

14 For a characteristically upbeat comment on this speech, see Bykov and Vlasova (2007), a sober view is 'Not a cold war, but a cold tiff' (2007).

15 On the nuclear part of new doctrine, see Korobushin (2007); on the need to preserve the INF Treaty, see Arbatov (2007); on Serdyukov's promotion, see Golts (2007b).

16 One of the elaborate presentations of the 'hostile collision' theory is Aleksin (2000).

17 Putin's decisiveness was acknowledged by Latynina (2005c); my comment is in Baev (2005h). On the *Kursk* catastrophe, see Kramer (2000) and Baev (2002c); an insightful exposé of degraded professional culture in the Navy can be found in Pokrovsky (2004).

18 Detailed examination of these exercises can be found in Sokov (2004).

19 On the risks related to the rushed development and insufficient testing of the *Bulava* project, see Myasnikov (2006a); on the failed tests, see Myasnikov (2006b). Pavel Felgengauer (2006a) argued that the Russian posture with two types of active duty subs armed with two different missiles and another class of subs also with different missiles to enter service in the near future made a truly 'asymmetric' comparison with the US posture with one type of subs (*Ohio* class) and one type of missiles (*Trident* II D-5).

20 The plane, which was one of the eight Tu-160s acquired from Ukraine in 1999, disintegrated in the air so fast that the four pilots did not have a chance to leave it, see Mukhin *et al.* (2003).

21 Putin (2005b) also suggested, perhaps not quite coherently, that:

> certainly, in the possible future – God forbid – conflicts, we know that in today's world the Air Force occupies a special place. Unfortunately, I can say that up until know we have not given due attention to this aspect of our activity.

22 Khvorov also promised that two new Tu-160s would be delivered to his army in 2006, see 'Canadian radars did not detect Russian strategic bombers' (2006). North American Airspace Defence Command launched its F-15C and CF-18 fighters to intercept Russian bombers during the next exercise in September 2006, see 'NORAD intercepts Russian aircraft' (2006).

23 Putin proudly revealed this deal at the meeting with the top brass in November 2004 centred on the 'White paper', see note 12. Alexei Arbatov, speaking at the experts round-table on strategic stability in April 2006, argued convincingly that the only way to maintain the minimal level of 'reasonable sufficiency' of the strategic forces was to increase the acquisitions of Topol-M to the level of 25–30 a year, see Kadrmatov (2006).

24 The accuracy of this warhead is significantly lower than the benchmark for the old ones, so its deployment makes sense only from the point of view of penetrating the yet-to-be-deployed US strategic defence system, see on that Felgengauer (2006b).

25 In late 2005, Ukraine raised the issue of increasing the fee for the use of these early warning stations and was not satisfied with the offer to adjust for inflation the rate of US$1.2 million a year, see 'Ukraine is preparing an asymmetric response' (2005).

180 *Notes*

26 In early May 2006, Russia found itself without operational intelligence satellites since the schedule of launches had been altered to accommodate more commercial projects, see 'Russia has no intelligence satellites on orbit' (2006); the optical reconnaissance satellite *Kobalt-M* that was launched to fill the gap had only 120 days of expected orbit life, see Safronov (2006). Another intelligence satellite *Sputnik*-2423 (the *Don* series) was launched in mid-September but terminated already in mid-November well before the 120 days of its 'life expectancy', see Lantratov and Safronov (2006).

27 As one expert argued,

> The main problem of the Glonass system, however, is not the satellites. Rather, it is the very thin customer base and the lack of clear incentives to develop all kinds of applications (commercial and otherwise) that the system can support.
>
> ('Glonass is getting presidential attention', 2005)

Putin indicated that the 'healthy patriotism of state users' would take care of this problem, see Romanov (2007).

28 The origin of and the driving forces behind that provocations still remain unclear, see Leibin (2005b) and Podvig (2005); on the prospects for Cooperative Threat Reduction (CTR) programmes, see Gottemoeller (2005).

29 On the former, see Pollack (2004); on the latter, the hugely provocative article of Mearsheimer and Walt (2006) has established a new framework for debates.

30 Insightful and balanced analysis can be found in Orlov and Vinnikov (2005); another good source is Arbatov (2006b).

31 The agreement, commonly known as the Gore–Chernomyrdin protocol, formalized Yeltsin's promise to Clinton in 1994 not to conclude any new deals with Iran but to deliver all weapons covered by the existing contracts. Putin took the calculated risk of cancelling it in late November 2000 when it became clear that Gore was defeated in the tight presidential race, for a detailed review, see Shaffer (2001); Migranyan (2001) advocated for setting a new agenda for rapprochement with Iran.

32 Putin (2005c) assured that 'We categorically oppose any attempts by Iran to acquire nuclear weapons. Our position fully coincides with that of Israel on this issue' and added further that 'Our Iranian partners must renounce setting up the technology for the entire nuclear fuel cycle and should not obstruct placing their nuclear programmes under complete international supervision.'

33 My view at that time was that:

> Britain, France, and Germany are trying to put together a package of incentives in order to dissuade Iran from advancing its project on uranium enrichment – but Moscow's readiness to strike its own deal despite the deadlock in European negotiations is a strong counter-incentive.
>
> (Baev, 2005i)

34 As Dmitri Trenin (2006a) argued, the West had completed the re-evaluation of relations with Russia by summer 2006 and Iran remained the only option for cooperative action, since 'there is neither time nor sense to discuss other question'.

35 This net assessment is generally not that far from the sober conclusion of Barry Posen (2006) that 'there is reason to believe that we could readily manage a nuclear Iran'.

36 The limited efficiency of air strikes against Serbia and the repeated failures to hit targets in Afghanistan pointed to a strong possibility of a US military 'bluff', see Cirincione (2006) and 'Military fantasies on Iran' (2006).

37 Russia's objections against this plan and the 'moratorium' were stated by Putin (2007d) in his address to the parliament and elaborated by Baluyevsky (2007b).

38 Orlov and Fugfugosh (2006, p. 42) argued that 'in contrast with previous summits, Moscow does not intend to worry about its nuclear inheritance, just as it does not plan to reject it'.

Notes 181

8 The Army and power-projection in the new 'Empire'

1 Dominique Lieven (2002, p. 267) in his excellent research on the Russian Empire, quotes Prince Aleksandr Baryatinsky, who brought the Great Caucasian War to the victorious end in 1859: 'England displays its power with gold. Russia which is poor in gold has to compete with the force of arms.'

2 One of the first systematic examinations of these policies that often moved ahead of concept drafting was Jonson and Archer (1996); Allison and Bluth (1998) provided a useful combination of different perspectives; a more considerate evaluation is Allison (2004a); my first assessment was in Baev (1994).

3 My detailed evaluation of these plans is in Baev (1996); for a clear-cut presentation, see Hall (1993).

4 That episode in the Chechen War was given a huge propaganda spin and provided the story for two television serials; for a sound analysis of mistakes that brought that unit into the trap, see Cherkasov (2006).

5 As Roy Allison (2004a, p. 152) pointed out, 'The type of warfare in the US operations in Afghanistan undoubtedly astonished the Russian military as much as they were shocked by the rapid collapse of the Taliban regime.' I examined the impact of Chechnya and Afghanistan in Baev (2003c).

6 Military thinking about such operations was clearly struggling to escape from a conceptual dead end where the armed forces had to perform missions for which they had neither the capabilities nor the training; see, for instance, Nikolaev (2002).

7 A rather inflated assessment of Lebed's political prospects can be found in Lambeth (1997).

8 In early 2005, the question of gathering together various *Spetsnaz* units in new Special Operations Forces was discussed by the Security Council, but no decision was reached, see Litovkin (2005).

9 A good journalistic portrait of Shpak can be found in Loriya (2003).

10 The 76th Pskov Airborne Division conducted the most radical experiment, and since 2004 has become the first division-size unit that has no draftees; it has not, however, improved its combat performance in any testable way; see Babakin (2006a). In mid-2006, the first few armoured vehicles BRD-4 arrived to the 137th Ryazan Airborne Regiment, see 'Ryazan blue berets get a gun-armed APC' (2006).

11 Aleksandr Golts (2005b) competently argued:

> This weapon is designed not for delivering a high-precision strike but for penetrating through a strong air-defence system. It is hard to believe that Russian military authorities are serious about waging a war against the US. The issue is that our strategists know no other scenario and do not want to develop it. Any other exercises would have inevitably shown the shortcomings in combat training and the waste of resources.

12 One of the best research on that intervention is Jonson (1998); Andrei Nikolaev (1998), the Director of the Federal Border Service in 1993–1997, provided a vivid account of the struggle for sealing off the border with Afghanistan in his memoirs.

13 As Amin Saikal (2000, p. 51) accurately pointed out:

> Russia has also been incensed at the reception that the Taliban have given to the Chechen Islamic fighters, allowing them to open a mission in Kabul and use Afghanistan as a training and conduit base for their anti-Russian resistance in Chechnya.

14 The meeting took place in Dushanbe, Tajikistan, and the third party present was Iranian Foreign Minister Kamal Kharrazi; see Dubnov (2000).

15 Russia continued until 2006 to supply arms to Afghanistan making sure that the deliveries go to its clients in the former Northern Alliance, first of all to General

182 *Notes*

Mohammed Fahim, who up until the end of 2004 held the post of defence minister, see Allison (2004a, p. 151). Explaining the termination of the programme that amounted to nearly US$100 million for five years, a Russian official pointed out that 'Kabul has reoriented towards the US in building the national armed forces.' See 'Russia discontinues free supply of arms to Afghanistan' (2005).

16 The first steps in the implementation of this plan are evaluated in Allison (2004b).

17 A local expert expressed the opinion that the base was 'a good deterrent factor for Uzbekistan's President Karimov who would have otherwise grabbed our land long time ago', see Karshiboev *et al.* (2004).

18 Russia invested meagre US$10.5 million in reconstructing Kant in 2004–2005, so by the end of 2005, only some 250 troops were permanently deployed there in support of five to six Su-27 and Su-25 fighters which made only irregular training flights; the base was unable to receive heavy planes, see Plugatarev (2005b).

19 In early 2005, Karimov still argued against militarization of the region and competition of super-powers, emphasizing that 'I do not understand why in Kyrgyzia two air-bases – Russian and American – are located 30 kilometres from one another. It is not just a demonstration of force, it is simply unnatural.' See Panfilova (2005).

20 As Daly *et al.* (2006, p. 61) argued, 'The alliance treaty of Russia and Uzbekistan, signed on November 14 in Moscow, painfully illustrated Washington's declining plausibility as a buttress of security and stability in Central Asian perceptions, particularly that of the region's strategic linchpin country Uzbekistan.'

21 That strategic assessment led Stephen Blank (2006c) to the conclusion that 'the fact remains that with regard to foreign bases, the most potent symbol of power projection capability, an intense rivalry is growing every day'.

22 Valery Panyushkin (2006) found out that the street price of one gram of high-quality Afghan heroin in Moscow was as low as 1,000 roubles, concluding that 'the price and quality of heroin confirm that a large permanent low-risk delivery channel has been established'.

23 President Putin's remark that 'they do next to nothing to reduce the drug threat even a little' was replayed many times by Russian officials, see Alekseeva (2004). On the EU programme, see 'Central Asia: What role for the European Union?' (2006).

24 An article in *The Onion* ironically described the disappointment of 'revolutionaries' who had prepared to become 'martyrs' in the bloody and hopeless fights against the troops loyal to the regime, see 'Bloodless coup a real letdown' (2005).

25 The Kyrgyz military deployed some 300 troops to the area and suffered 12 casualties before killing four rebels, see Valiev and Orozobekova (2006).

26 A good overview of Russian–Georgian relations at that time can be found in Devdariani (2005).

27 This barely hidden pro-active policy alarmed some US experts who argued that Washington should draw a 'red line' on the issue of Georgia's independence, see Haig and Sicherman (2001). On worries in Tbilisi concerning Giorgadze and the activities of Russian special services, see Dzhorbenadze (2005).

28 At that time, I argued that the switch-offs, painful as they were, appeared too haphazard to qualify as evidence of a consistent policy (Baev, 2001a); the EU, however, criticized Russia for exploiting Georgia's energy dependency to political ends, see Jack (2001). On Georgia's balancing on the brink of failure, see Lieven (2001).

29 David Darchiashvili (2005, p. 132) in his competent evaluation of military reforms in Georgia stated that by the end of 2003, it 'had acquired four professional battalions trained for anti-terrorist and counter-insurgency warfare'. I presented my view on the possible impact of the GTEP programme in Baev (2002a).

30 As I argued at that time:

> Sensing Putin's dissatisfaction with Shevardnadze's desperately pro-US behavior, the rank and file of Moscow's political elite rushed to attack Georgia with every

Notes 183

available PR weapon …. Even being a quintessential control-freak, he finds it difficult to restrain his over-enthusiastic entourage, and so again and again finds himself in situations where armed conflict appears to be a logical next step.

(Baev, 2002b)

31 A rare voice of sober criticism in Moscow, swept by jingoist propaganda, was Yavlinsky (2002).
32 Nikolai Sokov (2002) perceptively argued: 'Apparently, the Moscow political establishment expected that, as an ally of the United States in the war against terror, Russia would be given greater leeway in the former Soviet Union.'
33 See 'Georgia keeps sights set on the West' (2003); at the same time, Putin initially was inclined to give Saakashvili the benefit of the doubt, particularly since at a face-to-face meeting in February 2004, Saakashvili expressed his admiration for his strategic vision and political style, see Torbakov (2004).
34 Good account of that narrowly avoided separatist war can be found in the International Crisis Group report 'Saakashvili's Ajara success' (2004). My explanation for the inept passivity of the Kremlin in that crisis was centred on miscalculations, see Baev (2004b). Bruno Coppieters (2005, pp. 362–363) made an interesting argument that Moscow preferred to stay away because of the 'fear of a total destabilization of Georgia, which would be a far greater risk if Russia intervened in intra-Georgian disputes than in secessionist conflicts'.
35 The International Crisis Group assessed that the re-militarization of conflict reversed a decade of relative progress, see 'Georgia: Avoiding war in South Ossetia' (2004). Many Western experts were alarmed by 'Saakashvili's saber rattling policy' (Zürcher, 2005, p. 114).
36 On Georgia's Military Doctrine, see Novikov (2005); many Russian experts warned at that time that Saakashvili had become a hostage of his rhetoric and could attempt to win back the lost territories, see Markedonov (2005a).
37 For two weeks, various mobile units, including two airborne battalions, a marine battalion, and a *Spetsnaz* brigade, with the total strength of 6,000 troops supported by some 250 tanks, APCs and artillery were engaged in intensive manoeuvring in Dagestan, North Ossetia, and Stavropol kray, see Poroskov (2006) and Plugatarev (2006b).
38 Reflecting on that vote, Latynina (2007) pointed out that every step in Russia's policy had brought results opposite to the declared aims, primarily because the overzealous minions were confident that they would not be fired for whatever damage their blunders would inflict to Russia's reputation as long as they would answer the 'particular psychological complexes of President Putin'.
39 As one sober comment pointed out, 'The problem is that in Russia today, much the same way as in the early 1990s, there are no restraining factors that could stop a military adventure.' See 'Fancying a "small and victorious" one' (2006).

9 Internal order and security in the 'civilization'

1 Poe argued that the Russian history should not be viewed as 'a fruitless exercise in oppression' since the state with its unique 'Russian moment' was in fact able 'to fend off Europe and to build a massive empire'.
2 For my earlier detailed analysis, see Baev (2003b); a researcher can hardly find a more thorough and thoughtful examination than Kramer (2004/2005).
3 Matthew Evangelista (2002) provided a careful assessment of Chechnya's limited but often overrated impact on Russia's territorial integrity.
4 In the same Levada Center polls, 23 per cent in 2000 and 19 per cent in 2006 confirmed that they would be only glad if Chechnya indeed seceded, while respectively 9 per cent and 13 per cent were certain that the secession had already taken place, see 'Social-political situation in Russia in June 2006' (2006).

184   *Notes*

5 As Dmitri Trenin and Alexei Malashenko (2004, p. 155) argued, 'The second Chechen campaign marked a turning point in the public's attitude towards the armed forces ... the army was once again regarded as the ultimate protector.'

6 Assessing the crude falsifications in those elections, Aleksei Malashenko (2003) emphasized the role of fear factor and suggested that 'the split in the Chechen society could deepen'.

7 As Malashenko (2006, p. 40) pointed out in a postscript to his earlier analysis:

> The ruling elite today consist primarily from former separatists who have understood the lack of prospect in their cause. In a no small degree, this understanding was driven by the spread among the extremists in the *mojahed* camp of the ideology of Wahhabism which was not compatible with the traditional Chechen Islam.

8 Georgi Derluguian (2005b) reflected in an obituary: 'In February 1997, Maskhadov became the president with triple legitimacy – national hero, clear winner in real elections, and most importantly symbol of the return to orderly life. The sad irony was that he remained a too decent officer indeed.'

9 His career was succinctly summed up by Thomas de Waal (2006):

> Basayev was a talented warrior and brilliant propagandist, and a very twisted and cruel human being. Very few will mourn his demise, with most Chechens breathing a sigh of relief that someone who blackened their reputation round the world is dead.

10 Dmitri Oreshkin (2005) pointed out that this attempt to buy loyalty of 'parasitic' local elites could lead only to their rapid degradation.

11 I advanced this thesis in Baev (2004h) and developed it further in Baev (2005k) and Baev (2006c); a contrasting view can be found in Stepanova (2005).

12 Vladimir Kara-Murza (2006) reflecting on the closure of the last independent television channel (TVC) in June 2003 suggested: 'On that day, quite possibly, Russia has lost the right to be called a democratic country', see also Albats (2006).

13 A well-assembled collection of complementary analyses of the dynamics of regional processes in Russia at the start of Putin's era can be found in Herd and Aldis (2003).

14 My understanding of these complex transformations is strongly influenced by Nikolai Petrov who has produced a body of perceptive and penetrating analyses of Russian regionalism, see, for instance, Petrov (2002). He described the seven 'presidential districts' as an element of infrastructure of the police state (Petrov, 2001).

15 Andrei Kolesnikov (2006d) ironically examined the 'special aura' of the sprawling Central Committee building on Staraya Ploshchad that triggers 'the biological instincts of the Russian authorities who run to the habitual spawning place near the Kremlin'.

16 Olga Kryshtanovskaya (2002) pioneered sociological analysis of this phenomenon; for her more elaborate research, see Kryshtanovskaya (2005); for a sharp political comment, see Karatnycky (2003).

17 In the official statement on this 'friendly takeover', Putin emphasized the need in increasing efficiency and coordination in the fight against terrorism, see Galeotti (2003).

18 There was plentiful evidence that the FSB remained able both to closely supervise the operations in Chechnya and to control the deployment of GROUs; Kramer (2004/2005) examined the role of the FSB most carefully, see also Gromov (2005).

19 The need in assigning to the FSB the permanent leadership in this high-profile Committee by a special presidential decree was no means evident, see Soldatov (2006).

20 That agenda was the subject of my analysis in Baev (2004i).

21 For a precise analysis of Putin's speech, see Dolgin (2004); a peculiar phenomenon identified by Mikhail Fishman (2005) can be traced back to that speech: 'The notion of "security of the state" has acquired a distinctively sacral character. The key feature of this security is that it cannot be achieved in principle.'

Notes 185

22 Seeking to invent the missing connection, Vitaly Tretyakov (2004a) argued:

> Russia's national security crisis recognized by the society and authorities after Beslan overlapped with the deep and long-developing (under the cover of stability) political crisis, which the officials prefer to call a crisis of controllability. These two crises aggravate one another – the more terrorist attacks, the more uncontrollability; and the more uncontrollability, the more opportunities for terrorists.

23 As one observer of the 300 years anniversary festivities in St. Petersburg noted: 'The sudden unannounced appearance of armed soldiers and cops and armored vehicles painted desert camouflage at a civic celebration caused no real surprise' (Fraizer, 2003, p. 47).

24 The revisions to the Law on Countering Extremism approved by the State Duma in July 2006 expanded the definition in such a way that, in the words of Vladimir Ryzhkov (2006), 'political opponents of the regime are now the target instead of terrorists and extremists'. In the last address to the parliament, Putin (2007d) requested a further tightening of this law.

25 I looked into the murder of Movladi Baisarov in Baev (2006i) and into the terrorist alerts in Baev (2007b).

26 A good overview of the political and security developments in the North Caucasus at the start of this decade can be found in Derluguian (2005d).

27 On Aushev's outstanding performance, see Derluguian (2001); Evangelista (2004) provides an excellent evaluation of the intrigue around his removal.

28 As Pavel Felgengauer (2004) pointed out, even carefully prepared operations of this kind had high risk of failure, but the support from local population helped several groups of rebels to find their targets and then to disperse without any trace, see also Politkovskaya (2004).

29 A thorough examination of that shocking tragedy can be found in Dunlop (2005); David Remnick (2004) insightfully evaluated Putin's hard choices in the North Caucasus.

30 The so-called 'Kozak Report' was leaked to tabloid *Moskovsky komsomolets*, quite possibly, deliberately, see Khinshtein (2005); for a good analysis, see Blandy (2005).

31 On the stalled investigation and political ramifications of this crisis, see Smirnov (2005); for an informative background, see Latynina (2005d).

32 Characteristically, when Interior Minister Rashid Nurgaliyev proudly reported about successful operations in the North Caucasus, Putin reprimanded him for using confusing terms like *jamaat* and ordered to call the terrorists by their only real name; I have looked into that in Baev (2005l).

33 For an independent journalistic investigation, see Borogan and Soldatov (2006); for a brief and insightful analysis, see Derluguian (2005a).

34 On the intrigue around Magomedov's replacement, see Latynina (2006b).

35 I looked into that issue in Baev (2006d); Sovmen quietly retired in early 2007.

36 As Dunlop and Menon (2006, pp. 109–110) argued, 'this policy could overload the centre, while also provoking a backlash from local elites determined to defend a status quo that gives them wealth and power'.

37 The share of direct transfers from the federal centre in the budgets of republics of the North Caucasus was between 75 per cent and 90 per cent, see Nikitina *et al.* (2005).

38 Georgi Derluguian (2005c) convincingly examined this trajectory.

39 Only 24 per cent expressed the opinion in the July 2006 Levada Center poll that a breakthrough was achieved, while 59 per cent were certain that the struggle with the rebels would continue for long years, see 'Russians on the death of Shamil Basaev' (2006).

186 *Notes*

10 Applying the gas lever for qualifying as a 'great power'

1 Vyakhirev expected that his personal involvement in the hostile takeover of the independent television channel NTV by GAZPROM would be rewarded by an extension of his contract; Putin allegedly gave him certain promises at the lengthy face-to-face meeting on 4 March 2001, only to deliver a coup de grace in late May. Miller for a short time was a deputy minister of energy but before that had presided over the Baltic Pipeline System company with the total staff of 22, see Portnikov (2001) and Goryaev (2001a).

2 At that time, numerous leaks signalled that Miller was engaged in conflicts not only with the Vyakhirev's team of top managers but also with Medvedev, see Goryaev, 2001b.

3 Medvedev and such key GAZPROM 'curators' in the government as Prime Minister Mikhail Kasyanov and Minister for Economic Development German Gref were in favour of reaching a compromise with *Sibur*, but Miller concluded that he could wrestle control out of hands of CEO Yakov Goldovsky by throwing him in jail, see Goryaev (2002).

4 See Romanova and Mukhin (2001); the share of E.ON *Ruhrgas* was eventually increased to 6.8 per cent. Burckhard Bergmann, the chairman of the executive board of E.ON *Ruhrgas* AG, has been a member of GAZPROM Board since 2000; while having close ties with Vyakhirev, he wisely refused to take a stand during the feud in the management in 2001, see Starobin (2001).

5 Expert estimates showed that the coordinated cuts led to the increase of oil prices from US$18 to US$26 per barrel, but the abundance of oil on the domestic market caused a drop in prices so that the net result of that 'experiment' were losses close to US$270 million, see Tymenev (2002).

6 Arguing against the temptations for further deals with OPEC, Aleksandrov and Orlov (2002) concluded: 'The period of unfavourable prices on energy is a good time for a rapprochement with the US …. It would be an unforgivable fault for the Kremlin to miss this chance.'

7 As quoted in the remarkably upbeat Baker Institute paper 'US–Russia Commercial Energy Summit' (2003). Other analysis suggested that:

> The Russians are stealing the mantle of reliable oil supplier of choice to the United States, European Union nations, and other industrialized countries. And, if this reputation is gained, increased Western dependence on Russian oil and gas would do more than anything to stimulate Russian integration with the international community.
>
> ('Two geopolitical shifts', 2002)

8 Some two million barrels of crude were delivered to Houston by *Yukos* in July 2002 by a super-tanker, see Koliandre (2002). For the Murmansk project, Khodorkovsky secured partnership with *Lukoil* but insisted that the 60 million tons a year pipeline should be private and not controlled by the state-owned *Transneft*, see Ignatova *et al.* (2002).

9 It was Sergei Parkhomenko (2006) who emphasized that yet another harsh and blatantly unjust court verdict against Svetlana Bakhmina, a *Yukos* lawyer, brought back the Soviet term 'repression'. On the new accusations against Khodorkovsky and Lebedev, see Nikitinsky (2007) and Gaidar (2007).

10 The proposal prepared in the Ministry of Economic Development and Trade under Gref's supervision aimed at dividing GAZPROM into five to six independent producing companies; it was turned down by Putin who by the end of 2002 had developed the habit of close monitoring of the gas sector and concluded that only monopoly would answer his ideas about management, see Milov (2005c).

11 In that noisy squabble, the voices of economic reasoning were completely drowned;

Notes 187

still Gref raised objections against GAZPROM's 'hyper-monopoly' and suggested that 'if the anti-monopoly legislation is not modernized, the country is finished', see Frumkin (2004) and, for my assessments, Baev (2004c, 2005e).

12 The latest figure available from the GAZPROM not particularly informative website (www.gazprom.ru/articles/article20153.shtml).

13 This manoeuvring is meticulously examined in Stern (2005, pp. 129–139).

14 The path-breaking deal between GAZPROM and ENI on direct deliveries of Russian gas to Italian consumers was signed in May 2005 but collapsed already in October when a parliamentary investigation in Italy found evidence of corruption leading directly to Berlusconi, see Ratnikova (2005) and Baev (2005f).

15 On the continuing usefulness of Putin's old contacts, in particular with Mattias Warnig, see Benoit *et al.* (2005); on the intersecting activities of Boris and Nicholas Jordan, see Alyakrinskaya (2004); my view is in Baev (2005g).

16 Putin (2004a) singled out this project in his 2004 address to the Federal Assembly: '... construction of the North European gas pipeline is most important. It will make it possible to diversify export flows, directly linking the networks of Russia and countries of the Baltic region with the total European gas network.'

17 As Pekka Sutela (2005) precisely pointed out, 'For the EU the problem isn't too much Russian energy …. Competition among buyers, not overwhelming market share, will give Russia leverage.'

18 Except for Putin's (2005a) opening speech, no other information about deliberations at that meeting was released, see Tatarinov (2005). The tone of the mainstream commentary was that 'Russia's positions in the conflict with Ukraine are strong precisely because the gas policy is determined not by muddled political calculations but by the strategy of world energy leadership', see 'The supplier of energy security' (2005).

19 As Alexei Miller (2006) pointed out:

> Russia would have welcomed a power shift in Ukraine through a major victory of the Yanukovich party. But even the most pro-Russian government in Ukraine would not be able to reverse the situation radically since a reduction of the increased prices appears improbable.

20 In April 2006, under the pressure from US Justice Department, little-known Ukrainian entrepreneurs Dmitri Firtash and Ivan Fursin were named as beneficiaries, but the real money flows proved impossible to trace, see Berezhnoi (2006).

21 Fedor Lukyanov (2006a) proposed that Russia's elite was 'genetically and mentally' rooted in the Soviet 'epoch of deficit', so that control over high-demand raw materials translated into recklessness and the unwillingness to assess the consequences.

22 Commenting on this Green Paper, *The Economist* concluded: 'The EU is rightly castigated for meddling in the areas where it is not needed. How rare, almost refreshing, to find a business in which its intervention can, at least partly, be justified' ('Energetic debate', 2006).

23 As one Russian commentator pointed out, Putin, Miller, and other officials tried to 'add some steel to their voices', but it was still easy to hear 'barely suppressed irritation and personal offence' (Todres, 2006).

24 Lord Browne, chief executive of the BP, tried to resolve the problem by cultivating personal relations with Putin but was not able to dissuade GAZPROM from its plan aimed at securing the withdrawal from 'foreign hands' the license issued by the National Resources Ministry to develop the Kovykta field, see Belton (2007).

25 Hard pressed in the bargaining, GAZPROM agreed to give BASF also 10 per cent of non-voting 'privileged' shares in *Severneftegazprom* but was not happy with the E.ON offer of 40 per cent shares in Hungarian gas distribution company MOL. A long-term partner of GAZPROM and often its 'friend-in-need', E.ON was initially eager to maximize the politicized business opportunity – but then apparently developed second thoughts. For an evaluation of E.ON position, see Grib (2006a).

188 *Notes*

26 That statement by Vice President Cheney (2006) was in tune with remarks of State Secretary Rice (2006) who saw an 'obvious political motive' in Russia's behaviour, which was far from 'what would be expected of a responsible member of the G-8'.

27 Moscow hired *Ketchum*, a US company specializing in PR, for providing positive media coverage of the Strelna summit, and this campaign received a prestigious international award (Kaftan, 2007).

28 Dmitri Butrin (2006d) summarized this Action Plan as: 'We should think about what to do but in any case hardly anything can be done.'

29 The painstaking work of forging that platform was exposed in a set of confidential memos discarded by Spanish Foreign Ministry and published by *El Pais* (Kobo, 2006).

30 Vladimir Milov (2006d, p. 9) argued that 'it is time to recognize that leaving the Russia–EU energy dialogue to European downstream gas monopolies and the various governments that back them is an approach that is doomed to failure'.

31 In the debates in US Congress, the 'gas OPEC' was described as 'an organization for extortion and racketeering', see Sidorov (2007); for a sober comment, see Bush (2007).

11 Reconstituting the 'Empire' as an oil-and-gas cartel

1 Svyatoslav Kaspe (2005) accurately pointed out that 'even those who see Chubais as enemy No. 1 and take everything he says for satanic seduction' still have to define their position towards the 'Liberal Empire' slogan. For concise criticism, see Hestanov (2004).

2 This slow-moving project constitutes a part of the package deal approved by Putin and Rakhmonov in October 2004 that included also the construction of an aluminium plant and the permanent leasing of the Nurek space control station, as well as cancellation of a large part of Tajikistan's dept to Russia, see Blagov (2006a).

3 On Putin's readiness to go the extra mile for reaching concord with Aliev, starting with resolving the maritime border problem, see Shermatova (2001); on Aliev's worries about the attitude in Washington, see Pravosudov (2001).

4 See on that Chapter 5, footnote 2.

5 This pipeline had enjoyed great support in the last years of the Clinton administration but opinions in the republican team were quite mixed, as it was shown by a Cato Institute report (Kober, 2000).

6 Starr (2005b, p. 9) reflected upon the prevailing mood in mid-2000: 'Skeptics regrouped to warn that huge overruns of construction costs would be inevitable, and that even if construction was miraculously completed within budget, there would not be enough oil to keep the big tube filled.'

7 No detailed accounts of that meeting have emerged so far; some insightful reflections can be found in De Waal (2003a, pp. 279–280, 2004). Apparently, the freshly inaugurated President George W. Bush rushed that initiative seeking to start his presidency with a success story; disappointed in the failure, he has erased Nagorno Karabakh from his metal map.

8 Despite protests from the Armenian lobby, President Bush did sign a waiver of Section 907 of the Freedom Support Act ending restrictions on US economic assistance to Azerbaijan that had been approved by the Congress in October 1992 during the escalation of the Nagorno Karabakh conflict, see O'Lear (2002).

9 On Alekperov's role in shaping the rapprochement policy, see Kasaev *et al.* (2001); on *Lukoil*'s sell-off of potentially profitable assets in Azerbaijan, see Blum (2003).

10 A RAND study confidently asserted: 'Kazakh crude, transported by tanker or pipeline from Tengiz to Baku to supplement Azeri crude, would help to ensure the economic viability of the project by reducing the risks from potential Azeri production shortfalls.' Considering Tengiz to be 'potentially crucial to the future success of the

Notes 189

project', the authors even changed the abbreviated name of the pipeline to TBTC, see Oliker and Szayna (2003, p. 117).

11 See Kashavtsev (2004); I examined these assessments in Baev (2004a).

12 His 20-minute video 'Oil Odyssey 2000' made a strong impression at several academic seminars, see Goltz (2001).

13 Russian authorities preferred to ignore the festivities both in 2005 and in 2006, see Gulieva and Abasov (2005).

14 BP and its partners took calculated (but not really calculable) risk as in the first year of construction (until mid-2003) doubts persisted about the availability of necessary volumes of oil to pump one million barrels a day through the pipeline, see Roberts (2004). An editorial in *Wall Street Journal Europe* ('BP's big bet', 2003) argued: 'BP is a trailblazer; everyone is watching to see which way the gamble goes.'

15 They did not, however, deliver as much as a hint of a possible change in the position on Nagorno Karabakh, see Marchuk and Babaeva (2003).

16 Opposition protests in the streets of Baku were crushed with considerable violence, see Rzayev (2003). Heidar Aliev died in December the same year at the age of 80; Ilham Aliev carefully cultivates his 'great statesman' cult; for a balanced life assessment, see De Waal (2003b).

17 As *The Economist* ('Use a long spoon', 2006) argued:

> This public validation will be bad for Azerbaijan, but ultimately for America too …. America may one day be faced with an oil-rich Muslim country in a volatile region that is disillusioned with democracy and the West, and susceptible to other ideas.

18 Aliev Jr had good reasons to worry about the consequences of the building confrontation between the United States and Iran but saw few benefits in siding with opportunistic Russia, see Mustafaev and Zygar (2006).

19 Characteristically, at the Kremlin reception on the occasion of Boris Yeltsin's seventy-fifth birthday in February 2006, Nazarbaev made a toast: 'For our dream, Vladimir Vladimirovich, the Eurasian union – that will come true!' See Kolesnikov (2006b).

20 In early 2006, the Kremlin granted the right to manage its share in the CPC to *Transneft*, which greatly alarmed the management of the Consortium due to the clear conflict of interests since *Transneft* was 'a direct competitor in transporting the Kazakh oil', see Skornyakova (2006).

21 An overview of the CPC project that 'has offered a unique prism through which to assess how extraordinarily far apart two philosophies of building oil-related structures evolved in parallel fashion over the 20th century' can be found in 'Caspian pipeline' (2002).

22 For a thorough evaluation of this approach aimed at avoiding dependency, see Olcott (2002); very useful is also Bukkvoll (2004).

23 This ambitious but not very successful initiative was praised by Aleksandr Dugin (2004b) as 'the start of the era of a new Eurasian economic empire'.

24 Stephen Blank (2005a), while complaining about 'woeful ignorance of American politics and policy', has to acknowledge that 'American policy continues to push Nazarbaev away from America and closer to Russia and China.'

25 Kashagan's recoverable reserves are estimated at seven to nine billion barrels, but difficult conditions for development have brought the estimated costs to US$30 billion; *Agip* is the main operator, but *KazMunaiGaz* is pushing for increasing its share and operational control, see Shahnazaryan (2005).

26 Thus, Seymour Hersh (2001, p. 48) argued: '*Mobil*'s activities in Russia and Kazakhstan were not driven entirely by a desire for quick profit. The company also had a strategic goal: access to Kazakhstan's rich Tengiz oil field.'

27 Despite its successes in economic reforms, Kazakhstan is placed in the second

190   *Notes*

hundred of the *Corruption Perception Index* (2004, 2005, 2006) compiled by Transparency International (111–120 place in 2006, 107–117 place in 2005, and 122–128 place in 2004).

28 I looked into that lull in business activity in Baev (2004g).

29 The two companies announced the plan to invest up to US$1 billion in the project, see '*Lukoil* and *KazMunaiGas* will develop the Caspian together' (2005); for a balanced assessment, see Marten (2006).

30 That public offering was quite popular on the domestic market but triggered 'undesirable' international controversy. As *The Economist* ('Thou shalt not steal', 2006) argued:

> Since the fall of communism, Russian businessmen, including Mr Khodorkovsky, have repeatedly gambled on the amnesia of foreigners – betting that the greed of investors and a bit of public relations would obscure memories of malfeasance and instability …. This time, the gamble should fail.

Major new loans (amounting to US$22 billion) were taken by *Rosneft* in March 2007 in order to wrap up the *Yukos* 'affair', see Topalov (2007).

31 *Lukoil* tried to challenge the acquisition but found no support in international courts, see Rebrov (2005).

32 Russian commentators did not miss that change of tone indicating the renewed US eagerness to cultivate this 'strategic partnership', see, for instance, Dubnov (2006).

33 The initially small volumes of oil could be transported by tankers, but the full-scale implementation of this agreement is dependent upon the construction of a pipeline across the Caspian Sea, which Russia could still find many ways to block, see Denison (2006).

34 The disappointingly hollow CIS summit in Minsk in November 2006 added another drop to Nazarbaev's bitter personal reflections on the collapse of the USSR 15 years prior, see Satpaev (2006).

35 A good example of this thinking is *Belaya Kniga* (1996), but it was quite widespread and accentuated by the feeling of vulnerability after the defeat in the First Chechen War.

36 A few weeks after that meeting, General Tuncer Kilinc, secretary of the powerful National Security Council, triggered a political earthquake with the suggestion, obviously driven by frustration over the slow-moving negotiations with the EU, that Turkey should start looking eastward for new allies, singling out Russia as the most promising partner, see Smith (2002) and Torbakov (2002).

37 The GAZPROM–ENI joint venture for constructing this deepest (down to 2,150 m) underwater pipeline was formed in 1996, but only in 2000, after Moscow guaranteed sufficient funding, the work moved ahead at *Stakhanov* speed, see Lelyveld (2002).

38 The provisional compromise reached by the end of 2003, making it a year of significant underperformance of the pipeline, envisaged delayed returns on the investment, see Burtin (2003) and Orehin and Skornyakova (2003).

39 The visit was originally scheduled for early September 2004 but was postponed due to the Beslan terrorist attack; one noteworthy point in the public exchanges was Putin's emotional objections against dividing Europe into 'the first and the second categories', with the explicit reference to internal divisions in Germany, see Grigoryeva (2005).

40 Earlier proposals for opening an export route to Israel were abandoned as unfeasible, but the close personal relations between Putin and Berlusconi were perceived in the Kremlin as a solid foundation for the 'offensive' towards Italy – until Berlusconi's defeat in the April 2006 parliamentary elections, see Baev (2004k).

41 The issue was hotly debated at the EU energy summit in March 2006 (O'Rourke, 2006) and then discussed in detail during President Aliev's visit to Brussels in November (Lobjakas, 2006).

Notes 191

42 The deal was signed with much fanfare during Putin's visit to Greece in March 2007, but Nazarbaev immediately pointed out that without Kazakhstan's participation the arrangement would hardly make much sense, see Gritsenko (2007).
43 A confidential report on this issue by a NATO economic experts group was popularized by *Financial Times* (Dombey *et al.*, 2006) but shrugged off by Russian officials (Grivach and Shpakov, 2006).

12 Hydrocarbon foundation for the imagined 'civilization'

1 As Fedor Lukyanov (2005a) argued:

> 'Energy superpower' or 'world energy leader for the XXI century' – such statements are music to the ears but there is also an aftertaste. There is hardly any achievement in preserving influence in such a way; it may even appear shameful that we have only the energy lever and no other instruments. One might ask, but what about our great history, culture and science? Can the pipe tip the balance over everything else?

2 In a testimony for the US Senate Foreign Relations Committee, Trenin (2006c) also emphasized that Moscow was not interested in any return to a bi-lateral Cold War-type confrontation but sought for a role similar to what Russia had had at the start of the XX century: 'It is tsarist, capitalist, open, relatively free in many respects (though not in the political sphere), increasingly nationalist (the last former Communist country to have discovered nationalism, though of a peculiar post-imperial variety), and assertive internationally.'
3 Examining this European 'appeasement' on the eve of the G8 event in St. Petersburg, Diehl (2006) concluded: 'Faced with such European fecklessness, US officials appear to have resigned themselves to a summit where Putin will portray himself as a ruler of a resurgent superpower.'
4 Mikhail Delyagin (2005a) argued for adopting a strategic plan for modernizing the oil-and-gas sector, without which 'the ruling bureaucracy would continue to saw the oil branch on which not only itself (in that case it should have been only encouraged) but the whole Russia is sitting'. Quite in tone, Sergei Guriev (2005), who would probably disagree with Delyagin in most economic assessments, reasoned: 'We should not feel any joy about the inefficiency of the bureaucratic machine built by the Kremlin – we would pay dear for that inefficiency when the current rulers would be out of business.'
5 Friedman (2006) took Russia as one of the key examples that proved his proposition: 'If Bush looked into Putin's soul today – Putin II, the Putin of $60 a barrel – it would look very black down there, black as oil.'
6 Egorov *et al.* (2006) argued that every authoritarian ruler had to keep a balance between informing the public and informing himself, which determined the level of control over media. Putin, with his background in the KGB, was perfectly aware of the risk of not getting adequate information about the hidden tensions in the society; nevertheless, the oil factor caused the progressive contraction of the free media space.
7 These poll numbers added up to a firm conclusion: 'None of the potential candidates from the party of power can prove the substance of his claim for the Kremlin' ('Heritage without heirs', 2006).
8 That reasoning was based on many opinion polls showing strong preferences for immediate spending of the oil rent by increasing salaries and pensions as well as channelling funding towards health care but not for accumulating it in the Stabilization Fund (Balatskii, 2005). As Igor Mintusov (2005) argued, 'the information about money in the state coffers accumulates faster comparing with the growth of real income'.
9 Hisamov (2006) pointed out the similarities of thinking about the 'crucial link in the

192   *Notes*

chain' in Putin's team and 'the group of intellectuals that gathered some hundred years ago around Vladimir Lenin' and suggested that Putin's projects would enter the history records under the same category of big follies as Khrushchev's *Sovnark-hoz*.

10 Levada Center opinion polls from March and September 2006 showed that 57–58 per cent of respondents assumed that the national projects would not have any impact on their lives; 43 per cent and 47 per cent respectively were sure that the funds would be used inefficiently, while 31 per cent and 30 per cent respectively expected them to be stolen ('Would the "national projects" improve life of Russians?' 2006; 'Russians on the "national projects"', 2006).

11 Russian economy consumes two times more electricity per unit of GDP than the Chinese, while in the United States, this indicator is seven times lower ('Non-competitive advantage', 2006); on the vulnerability of Moscow energy networks, see 'Social-political blackout' (2005).

12 As Vladimir Milov argued, 'Trying to be a Kuwait or a Norway while having a population of nearly 150 million is not just a crime, it is a mistake', see 'Not enough for everyone' (2006).

13 On the shortcomings of the course of creating state-controlled 'holdings', see Khaz-biev (2007); on the 2006 record in air catastrophes, see 'Deadly record' (2007). On the politicization of the innovation strategy, see Medovnikov *et al.* (2007).

14 As Dmitri Furman (2006) insightfully argued:

> He is a rather naive man, he did not understand for a long time that integration with Russia is a loss of power. Lukashenko's logic of action reminds me of a young Qaddafi …. He was just deeply convinced that he was so good and clever leader, so he would certainly be the head of that union …. Now, apparently, he has understood what the union would mean for him.

15 The ironic joke at June 2002 St. Petersburg summit was a response to the suggestion from Lukashenko for a union of two equal parts; Putin's counter-proposal to join Russia as one of its subjects was rejected by Lukashenko as 'insulting', see Plu-gatarev and Nezvanov (2002).

16 Russian Foreign Ministry responded with a statement accusing Lukashenko in 'systemic mistakes in domestic and foreign policy', see Grivach and Dzaguto (2004).

17 Sergei Karaganov (2004) argued that the 'theology of integration' provided a camouflage for the fact that the project of Union States was in the dead end. He also warned against a prolongation of Lukashenko's term which 'would not stop the degradation of the country but inevitably increase the repressive character of the regime'.

18 According to Vitali Silitski (2005), for Lukashenko the question was only about finding 'the right moment', that came days after the Beslan tragedy, 'which was exploited by the Belarus leader to contrast Belarus' stability with Russia's chaos'.

19 Gleb Pavlovsky (2006b) ventured also an opinion that both leaders put high premium on preserving stability, which left only a narrow corridor of available options. At the St. Petersburg summit, Lukashenko emphasized that the integration had acquired 'an irreversible character' over ten years but refused to move one step in approving the Constitutional act, see Nikolaeva (2006).

20 As Kirill Koktysh (2006, p. 111) argued in a noteworthy article, 'on a close examination, the "Belarus miracle" turns out to be merely a miracle of manoeuvring but not a real or sustainable growth'.

21 Andrei Piontkovsky (2006) noting the readiness of Putin's team to move ahead against this resistance warned: 'Apparently, the "Reunification with Belarus" issue has moved from the plane of political calculations to a sacral sphere where rational arguments are powerless.'

22 Arkady Moshes (2006b) argued that the oil-and-gas crisis with Belarus reminded Russian political class that national interest could not be reduced to national egoism

Notes 193

and that it should be internalized by the whole nation – and not only by a small group of executives.

23 Arkady Moshes (2001) estimated that besides non-payments for registered import, on average 10 bcm a year (equivalent to US$800 million) simply disappeared from the pipelines in Ukraine, but 'the Russian leadership failed to provide efficient political support to GAZPROM in order to stop that fallacious activity'. He pointed out that Moscow's attitude could hardly be rationally explained but referred to the 'integrationist temptations' related to indefinite and 'possibly phantom goals'.

24 Immediately after that declaration of intentions by Putin, Kuchma, and Schröder, Russia and Ukraine signed an agreement on mid-term transit, according to which the price for transporting some 110 bcm of Russian gas would be agreed on the annual basis, see Aglamishyan (2002).

25 Political enthusiasm contrasted with scepticism of economists who warned that 'disagreements in mutual relations between Russia, Ukraine, Belarus, and Kazakhstan are too profound for their economic union to be effectual', see Shokhina (2003).

26 For sharp journalistic reflections, see Kolesnikov (2005a); a wide spectrum of expert opinions is in Pogrebinsky (2005); for the first draft of 'lessons learned' in Moscow, see Zatulin (2005).

27 As Andrei Illarionov (2005c) argued, it was not a coincidence that the agreement covered the five years of expected presidential term of Viktor Yanukovich whom Moscow was ready to subsidize as a political ally. Illarionov concluded that the dangerous ideas of 'national greatness' that always demanded sacrifices had nothing to do with national interests.

28 The source also asserted that the new policy was not aimed at restoring Russia's influence 'allegedly lost as a result of orange revolutions. There has never been such an influence, only wasted money and stealing of Russian gas.' See Samarina (2005).

29 Both Putin and Yushchenko praised the agreement as 'fully transparent', but the number of unknown beneficiaries was even more than in the previous arrangements, see Butrin (2006a) and Shleinov (2006).

30 The agreement resulted in the government crisis in Ukraine as the various opposition groups blamed the negotiators in 'betrayal of the national interests', see 'The head of Ukrainian MFA called the agreement with GAZPROM the "fiasco of Russian policy"' (2006).

31 Thus Vladimir Milov (2005b) argued: 'Behind Russia's lack of readiness to any compromises there is nothing but the blind desire of the Russian leadership and, apparently, Putin to take revenge on the Ukrainian authorities for the last year defeat.'

32 Positive attitude towards Ukraine was overwhelming in November 2004 (79 per cent – against 16 per cent with negative attitude); it slipped to 68 per cent in November 2005 (against 24 per cent) and declined to 52 per cent in February 2006 (against 39 per cent), see Sedov (2006).

33 That rhetorical question was spelled to the journalists (Putin, 2006c), but apparently it had been posed at the Russia–EU summit a week prior, see Cullinson (2006).

34 As Arkady Moshes (2006a) argued, 'The multi-tier system of compromise, checks and balances of today does not resemble what was in place one and a half years ago and is more in sync with the tasks of systemic reform.'

35 Thus, Gleb Pavlovsky (2006c), leaving behind his fiasco in 'orange' Kiev, started to argue in mid-2006: 'The break-up of Ukraine is a scenario we must prevent by any means. We have to cooperate with the Europeans in that as the Americans are playing a destructive role and it is difficult to cooperate with them.'

36 Vladimir Milov (2007d) pointed out that the argument about the scale of these subsidies was seriously overblown by the official propaganda.

37 Mikhail Arsenin (2006) commenting on this article argued that the process of 'nationalization' (in real terms, just a redistribution of property) involved more serious distortions in the economic system than the widely condemned process of privatization.

194 *Notes*

Conclusion

1 One of more thoughtful works in this genre is the book *Mir vokrug Rossii: 2017* (2007) published by the Council on Foreign and Defence Policy; the key theses of this prognosis were criticized by Foreign Minister Lavrov (2007) as insufficiently optimistic; a noteworthy collection of forecasts is Khodorkovsky (2007); a recent example of positive thinking is Kortunov (2007).
2 A thoughtful reflection on 'the historical experience of the crash of the monarchy', which is 'scary for the present-day rulers of the state', is in Sokolov (2007), see also Radzikhovsky (2007).
3 Olga Kryshtanovskaya (2007), a key expert on *siloviki* as a sociological phenomenon, argues that 'the position of *chekists* is now fantastically stable primarily because this system of power is based on the ages-old tradition of autocratic state'.

References

Abdullaev, Nabi, 1999. 'Dagestan turns its back on Chechnya', *IWPR Caucasus Reporting Service*, (hereafter, *CRS*) 10 December (www.iwpr.net/?p=crs&s=f&o=158933&apc_state=henicrs1999).

'Aggressive helplessness', 2006. *Vedomosti*, 16 February.

Aglamishyan, Varvara, 2002. 'Moscow-Kiev: The bargaining is over', *Nezavisimaya gazeta*, 18 June.

Albats, Evgenia, 2006. 'Five years ago there was an NTV', *Ezhednevny zhurnal*, 14 April (www.ej.ru/?a=note&id=3556).

Aleksandrov, Vladimir, 2003. '*Chekist* from St. Petersburg will preside over the air defense consortium', *Nezavisimoe voennoe obozrenie* (hereafter, *NVO*), 15 August.

Aleksandrov, Yuri, 2002. 'Baku-Ceyhan: Where is the oil?' *Politcom.ru*, 12 September (www.politcom.ru/2002/p_neft11.php).

Aleksandrov, Yuri and Dmitry Orlov, 2002. 'OPEC or Russia?' *Nezavisimaya gazeta*, 28 February.

Alekseeva, Natalya, 2004. 'Putin points to NATO's mistakes', *Izvestia*, 24 September.

Aleksin, Valery, 2000. 'Most probably, *Kursk* was rammed by a foreign submarine', *NVO*, 15 September.

Aliyev, Ali, 2007. 'Energy dreams', *Expert*, 6 April.

Allison, Roy, 2001. 'Russia and the new states of Eurasia', pp. 443–452 in Archie Brown (ed.), *Contemporary Russian Politics: A Reader*. Oxford: Oxford University Press.

—— 2004a. 'Russia, regional conflict, and the use of military power', pp. 121–156 in Steven E. Miller and Dmitri Trenin (eds), *The Russian Military: Power and Policy*. Cambridge, MA: The MIT Press.

—— 2004b. 'Strategic reassertion in Russia's Central Asia Policy', *International Affairs*, vol. 80, no. 2, pp. 277–293.

—— 2004c. 'Regionalism, regional structures and security management in Central Asia', *International Affairs*, vol. 80, no. 3, pp. 463–483.

Allison, Roy and Christoph Bluth (eds), 1998. *Security Dilemmas in Russia and Eurasia*. London: RIIA.

Alyakrinskaua, Natalya, 2004. 'Brothers in mind', *Moskovskie novosti*, 3 December.

'Anatoly Kvashnin on ethics', 2003. *Grani.ru*, 10 February (http://grani.ru/War/m.22429.html).

Anderson, Perry, 2006. 'Inside man', *The Nation*, 24 April (www.thenation.com/doc/20060424/anderson).

Anisimov, Evgeny and Viktor Baranets, 2003. 'Will America attack Russia in 2010?' *Komsomolskaya pravda*, 21 May.

196 *References*

Anjaparidze, Zaal, 2006. 'FSB claims Georgia planning "provocation" during G8 meeting', *Eurasia Daily Monitor* (hereafter, *EDM*) 14 July (www.jamestown.org/edm/article.php?article_id=2371271).

'Another *Yukos*?', 2005. *Financial Times*, 13 April.

Antonenko, Oksana, 2004. 'Russia's policy in the Caspian region', pp. 244–262 in Shirin Akiner (ed.), *The Caspian: Politics, Energy and Security*. London and New York: RoutledgeCurzon.

Aptekar, Pavel, 2000. 'Lessons from the conqueror of the Caucasus', *Vesti.ru*, 27 April (http://vesti.lenta.ru/daynews/2000/04/27/65baryatinsky/).

Arbatov, Alexei G., 1998. 'Military reform in Russia: Dilemmas, obstacles, and prospects', *International Security*, vol. 22, no. 4, pp. 83–134.

—— 2004. 'Military reform: From crisis to stagnation', pp. 95–119 in Steven E. Miller and Dmitri Trenin (eds), *The Russian Military: Power and Policy*. Cambridge, MA, and London: The MIT Press.

—— 2006a. 'Russian military policy adrift', *Briefing Paper*, vol. 8, no. 6, November, Moscow: Carnegie Moscow Center.

—— 2006b. 'Russia and the Iranian nuclear crisis', *Web Commentary*, 23 May (www.carnegieendowment.org/publications/index.cfm?fa=view&id=18364&prog=zgp&proj=znpp).

—— 2007. 'A dangerous and useless step', *NVO*, 2 March.

Arbatov, Alexei and Petr Romashkin, 2003. 'The budget as a mirror of the military reform', *NVO*, 17 January.

Arsenin, Mikhail, 2006. 'Essays in applied research on literature', *Polit.ru*, 13 February (www.polit.ru/author/2006/02/09/arsenin.html).

Åslund, Anders, 1995. *How Russia Became a Market Economy*. Washington, DC: Brookings.

Åslund, Anders, 2002. *Building Capitalism: The Transformation of the Former Soviet Block*. Cambridge: Cambridge University Press.

—— 2005. 'Russian resources: Curse or rents?' *Eurasian Geography and Economics*, vol. 46, no. 8, pp. 610–617.

—— 2006. 'Russia's energy policy: A framing comment', *Eurasian Geography and Economics*, vol. 47, no. 3, pp. 312–328.

Babakin, Aleksandr, 2005a. 'The funeral of the joint air defense system would have to wait', *NVO*, 2 September.

—— 2005b. 'The numbers of air carriers are declining', *NVO*, 1 July.

—— 2005c. 'Trotskyst ideas has penetrated into Genshtab', *NVO*, 16 December.

—— 2006a. 'Flying infantry must remain a separate branch', interview with General Aleksandr Kolmakov, Commander of the VDV, *NVO*, 26 May.

—— 2006b. 'Or we will not have modern weapons', *NVO*, 4 August.

—— 2006c. 'Redundant commanders', *NVO*, 7 July.

Baev, Pavel K., 1994. 'Russia's experiments and experience in conflict management and peacekeeping', *International Peacekeeping*, vol. 1, no. 3, pp. 245–260.

—— 1996. *The Russian Army in a Time of Troubles*. London: Sage.

—— 2000. 'Putin's court: How the military fit in', *PONARS Memo* 153, Washington, DC: Council on Foreign Relations, December.

—— 2001a. 'Russia's policies in the Caucasus and the Caspian area', *European Security*, vol. 10, no. 2, pp. 95–110.

—— 2001b. 'The Russian army and Chechnya: Victory instead of reform?' pp. 75–95 in Stephen J. Cimbala (ed.), *Russia's Military into the Twenty-First Century*. London and Portland, OR: Frank Cass.

References 197

—— 2001c. 'Russian military: The best case', pp. 35–45 in Mark Galeotti and Ian Synge (eds), *Putin's Russia: Scenarios for 2005*. London: Jane's Special Report, February.

—— 2001d. 'Russian military: The worst case', pp. 99–108 in Mark Galeotti and Ian Synge (eds), *Putin's Russia: Scenarios for 2005*. London: Jane's Special Report, February.

—— 2002a. 'Could the Pankisi gorge decide the fate of the Caucasus?' *CACI Analyst*, 24 April (www.cacianalyst.org/view_article.php?articleid=25).

—— 2002b. 'Russia's virtual war against Georgia: Risks of a PR offensive', *PONARS Memo* 251, Washington, DC: CSIS, October (www.csis.org/media/csis/pubs/pm_0251.pdf).

—— 2002c. 'The Russian navy after the *Kursk*: Still proud but with poor navigation', *PONARS Memo* 215, Washington, DC: CSIS, January.

—— 2002d. 'Gunboats in the great anti-terrorist game', *CACI Analyst*, 28 August (www.cacianalyst.org/view_article.php?articleid=17&SMSESSION=NO).

—— 2002e. 'The CIS: Refusing to fade away', *Russia and Eurasia Review*, 22 October (www.jamestown.org/publications_details.php?volume_id=15&&issue_id=608).

—— 2002f. 'The plight of the Russian military: Shallow identity and self-defeating culture', *Armed Forces & Society*, vol. 29, no. 1, pp. 129–146.

—— 2003a. 'Putin's western choice: Too good to be true?' *European Security*, vol. 12, no. 1, pp. 1–16.

—— 2003b. 'Examining the "terrorism-war" dichotomy in the "Russia-Chechnya" case', *Contemporary Security Policy*, vol. 24, no. 2, pp. 29–46.

—— 2003c. 'The challenge of "small wars" for the Russian military', pp. 189–208 in Anne Aldis and Roger McDermott (eds), *Russian Military Reform 1992–2002*. London: Frank Cass.

—— 2004a. 'Russia's happiness in multiple pipelines', *CACI Analyst*, 16 June (www.cacianalyst.org/view_article.php?articleid=2452).

—— 2004b. 'Ajaria's failed secession and Russia's Caucasian choices', *CACI Analyst*, 19 May (www.cacianalyst.org/view_article.php?articleid=2377).

—— 2004c. 'Greed, GAZPROM, and Gref: The making of a super-monopoly', *EDM*, 8 December (www.jamestown.org/edm/article.php?article_id=2368969).

—— 2004d. 'The trajectory of the Russian military: downsizing, degeneration, and defeat', pp. 43–72 in Steven E. Miller and Dmitri Trenin (eds), *The Russian Military: Power and Policy*. Cambridge, MA, and London: The MIT Press.

—— 2004e. 'Putin's "wonder" missiles: Bluff, threat or pep talk?' *EDM*, 22 November (www.jamestown.org/edm/article.php?article_id=2368892).

—— 2004f. 'Kremlin launches military exercises in Russian far east', *EDM*, 10 June (www.jamestown.org/edm/article.php?article_id=2368077).

—— 2004g. 'The destruction of *Yukos* and the slowdown of Russian Caspian projects', *CACI Analyst*, 3 November (www.cacianalyst.org/view_article.php?articleid=2798).

—— 2004h. 'Instrumentalizing counter-terrorism for regime consolidation in Putin's Russia', *Studies in Conflict & Terrorism*, vol. 27, no. 4, pp. 337–352.

—— 2004i. 'The evolution of Putin's regime: Inner circles and outer walls', *Problems of Post-Communism*, vol. 51, no. 6, pp. 3–13.

—— 2004j. 'The decline of the general staff leaves reform in limbo', *Jane's Intelligence Review*, vol. 16, no. 10, pp. 48–49.

—— 2004k. 'Putin and Berlusconi: An odd friendship between President Bush's best friends', *EDM*, 8 November (www.jamestown.org/edm/article.php?article_id=2368814).

198   *References*

—— 2005a. 'Public sentiment turns towards Khodorkovsky', *EDM*, 27 May (www.jamestown.org/edm/article.php?article_id=2369808).

—— 2005b. 'Russian newly invented holiday becomes a day of Nazi unity', *EDM*, 9 November (www.jamestown.org/edm/article.php?article_id=2370446).

—— 2005c. 'Putin protects Islam and praises democracy in Grozny', *EDM*, 14 December (www.jamestown.org/edm/article.php?article_id=2370597).

—— 2005d. 'What is wrong with Andrei Illarionov?' *EDM*, 7 January (www.jamestown.org/edm/article.php?article_id=2369060).

—— 2005e. 'GAZPROM's crisis of overgrowth', *EDM*, 31 January (www.jamestown.org/edm/article.php?article_id=2369173).

—— 2005f. 'GAZPROM loses Italian deal, corruption could cause more upsets', *EDM*, 24 October (www.jamestown.org/edm/article.php?article_id=2370379).

—— 2005g. 'Disentangling the Moscow-Berlin axis: Follow the money', *EDM*, 1 August (www.jamestown.org/edm/article.php?article_id=2370085).

—— 2005h. 'Putin's sinking presidency: What efficiency?' *EDM*, 8 August (www.jamestown.org/edm/article.php?article_id=2370120).

—— 2005i. 'Moscow insists on seeing no evil in Iran', *EDM*, 3 March (www.jamestown.org/edm/article.php?article_id=2369360).

—— 2005j. 'Russia evolves its commonwealth policy', *Jane's Intelligence Review*, vol. 17, no. 11, pp. 44–45.

—— 2005k. 'Counter-terrorism as a building block for Putin's regime', pp. 323–344 in Jakob Hedenskog, Vilhelm Konnander, Bertil Nygren, Ingmar Oldberg and Christer Pursiainen (eds), *Russia as a Great Power: Dimensions of Security under Putin*. London: Routledge.

—— 2005l. 'The North Caucasus slips out of control', *EDM*, 4 April (www.jamestown.org/edm/article.php?article_id=2369543).

—— 2005m. 'Sergei Ivanov challenges new political generation', *EDM*, 13 June (www.jamestown.org/edm/article.php?article_id=2369871).

—— 2005n. 'Putin's team in disarray over oil money', *EDM*, 21 March (www.jamestown.org/edm/article.php?article_id=2369450).

—— 2006a. 'After Vilnius, Putin has to reconsider his prospects', *EDM*, 8 May (www.jamestown.org/edm/article.php?article_id=2371059).

—— 2006b. 'Russia's virtual military shield against US criticism', *EDM*, 15 May (www.jamestown.org/edm/article.php?article_id=2371085).

—— 2006c. 'Putin's counter-terrorism: Parameters of a strategic dead-end', *Small Wars & Insurgencies*, vol. 17, no. 1, pp. 1–21.

—— 2006d. 'Russian quasi-federalism and Georgia's non-existent territorial integrity', *CACI Analyst*, 3 May (www.cacianalyst.org/view_article.php?articleid=4201).

—— 2006e. 'Shifting battlefields of the Chechen war', *Chechnya Weekly*, 20 April (www.jamestown.org/publications_details.php?volume_id=416&issue_id=3697&article_id=2371008).

—— 2006f. 'Ustinov's firing reveals clan maneuvering inside Kremlin', *EDM*, 5 June (www.jamestown.org/edm/article.php?article_id=2371148).

—— 2006g. 'Turning counter-terrorism into counter-revolution: Russia focuses on Kazakhstan and engages Turkmenistan', *European Security*, vol. 15, no. 1, pp. 3–22.

—— 2006h. 'Russia ignores the Riga summit and expects NATO to fail in Afghanistan', *EDM*, 4 December (www.jamestown.org/edm/article.php?article_id=2371704).

—— 2006i. 'The Chechen execution squad comes to Moscow', *EDM*, 22 November (www.jamestown.org/edm/article.php?article_id=2371665).

References 199

—— 2006j. 'The Russian march that wasn't: Moscow avoids a holiday porgom', *EDM*, 6 November (www.jamestown.org/edm/article.php?article_id=2371616).

—— 2006k. 'Is Putin becoming desperate about being "best friends" with Germany?' *EDM*, 19 October (www.jamestown.org/edm/article.php?article_id=2371552).

—— 2007a. 'Putin plans to "stay the course" for 2008', *EDM*, 5 February (www.jamestown.org/edm/article.php?article_id=2371875).

—— 2007b. 'Moscow is reminded that "war on terror" is not over', *EDM*, 22 January (www.jamestown.org/edm/article.php?article_id=2371825).

—— 2007c. 'Russia's military PR part of Kremlin intrigues', *EDM*, 19 March (www.jamestown.org/edm/article.php?article_id=2372017).

—— 2007d. 'Putin is lost between East and West, but Medvedev shines in Davos', *EDM*, 29 January (www.jamestown.org/edm/article.php?article_id=2371844).

—— 2007e. 'Putin expands the government and derogates the military', *EDM*, 20 February (www.jamestown.org/edm/article.php?article_id=2371922).

—— 2007f. 'Russian economic dynamism undermined by "state curse"', *EDM*, 9 April (www.jamestown.org/edm/article.php?article_id=2372082).

—— 2007g. 'The Iranian test for Putin's new course', *EDM*, 26 February (www.jamestown.org/edm/article.php?article_id=2371946).

—— 2007h. 'Putin's double triumph not yet in the bag', *EDM*, 14 May (www.jamestown.org/edm/article.php?article_id=2372161).

Balatskii, Evgeny, 2005. 'Petro-dollars: What the people want', *Vedomosti*, 8 September.

Baluyevsky, Yury, 2007a. 'Security index of a globalized world: The Russian dimension', *Security Index*, vol. 13, no. 1 (81), pp. 27–38.

—— 2007b. 'On anti-missile defence', *Rossiiskaya gazeta*, 4 May.

Beehner, Lionel, 2006. 'The rise of the Shanghai Cooperation Organization', *Backgrounder*, Council on Foreign Relations, 12 June (www.cfr.org/publication/10883/rise_of_the_shanghai_cooperation_organization.html).

Belaya Kniga Rossiiskih Spetssluzhb (The White Book of Russian Special Services), 1996. Moscow: Obozrevatel.

Belkovsky, Stanislav, 2005. 'SSSR – the future of Russia', *Lenta.ru*, 12 April (http://vip.lenta.ru/doc/2005/04/11/ussr/).

—— 2006. 'The master of the gas sands', *Kommersant*, 26 December.

—— 2007. 'The empire of small evil', *Ezhednevny zhurnal*, 12 March (www.ej.ru/?a=note&id=6369).

Belton, Catherine, 2007. 'BP under pressure on the Kovykta field', *Financial Times*, 28 February.

Benoit, Bertrand, Neil Buckley and Patrick Jenkins, 2005. 'E-spy who helped Dresdner gain influence in the Kremlin', *Financial Times*, 22 December.

Berezhnoi, Vladimir, 2006. 'Who owns Ukrainian gas', *Izvestia*, 26 April.

Berezinskaya, Olga and Valery Mironov, 2006. 'The most important industry', *Kommersant*, 22 August.

Berger, Mikhail, 2004. 'It looks like they got scared', *Ezhenedelny zhurnal*, 21 December (http://supernew.ej.ru/149/life/ispug/index.html).

Bigg, Claire, 2005. 'Was Soviet collapse last century's worst geopolitical catastrophe?' *RFE/RL Newsline*, 29 April (www.rferl.org/featuresarticle/2005/4/725C2B55-E0C0–488F-B720–0283BDF98C10.html).

Blagov, Sergei, 2005a. 'Russia eyes stronger clout in Caspian region', *Eurasia Insight*, 17 July (www.eurasianet.org/departments/insight/articles/eav071505.shtml).

200   References

—— 2005b. 'CACO and EEC merge to eliminate overlapping goals', *EDM*, 11 October (www.jamestown.org/edm/article.php?article_id=2370322).

—— 2006a. 'Russia renews diplomatic-economic offensive in Central Asia', *Eurasia Insight*, 19 April (www.eurasianet.org/departments/business/articles/eav041906.shtml).

—— 2006b. 'Deal with Turkmenistan enhances Russia's energy positions in Central Asia', *Eurasia Insight*, 3 July (www.eurasianet.org/departments/insight/articles/eav012406.shtml).

—— 2007a. 'Russian economic ties with Uzbekistan hit turbulence', *EDM*, 8 March (www.jamestown.org/edm/article.php?article_id=2371978).

—— 2007b. 'Itera suggests reviving Zarit consortium for Caspian exploration', *EDM*, 14 March (www.jamestown.org/edm/article.php?article_id=2372001).

Blandy, C.W., 2000. 'Dagestan: The storm. Part I: The invasion of Avaristan. Part II: The federal assault on the Kadar complex', *Caucasus Series* P30, Conflict Studies Research Centre, Royal Military Academy Sandhurst, Camberley, March.

—— 2005. 'North Caucasus: On the brink of far-reaching destabilisation', *Caucasus Series* 05/36, Conflict Studies Research Centre, Defence Academy of the UK, Camberley, August.

Blank, Stephen J., 1995. *Russian Defense Legislation and Russian Democracy*. Carlisle, PA: US Army War College.

—— 1998. *Russia's Armed Forces on the Brink of Reform*. Carlisle, PA: US Army War College.

—— 2001. 'The new turn in Russian defense policy: Russia's Defense Doctrine and National Security Concept', pp. 53–74 in Stephen J. Cimbala (ed.), *The Russian Military into the Twenty-First Century*. London: Frank Cass.

—— 2005a. 'Kazakhstan's foreign policy in a time of turmoil', *Eurasianet*, 27 April (www.eurasianet.org/departments/insight/articles/eav042705.shtml).

—— 2005b. 'The Central Asian dimension of Russo-Chinese exercises', *CACI Analyst*, 21 September (www.cacianalyst.org/view_article.php?articleid=3662).

—— 2006a. 'America strikes back? Geopolitical rivalry in Central Asia and the Caucasus', *CACI Analyst*, 17 May (www.cacianalyst.org/view_article.php?articleid=4233&SMSESSION=NO).

—— 2006b. 'Russia looks to build a new security system in Central Asia', *Eurasia Insight*, 4 January (www.eurasianet.org/departments/insight/articles/eav010406.shtml).

—— 2006c. 'Beyond Afghanistan: The future of American bases in Central Asia', *CACI Analyst*, 26 July (www.cacianalyst.org/view_article.php?articleid=4349).

Blinov, Artur, Vladimir Ivanov, Aleksandr Babakin and Igor Verba, 2006. 'Under the fire of friendly missiles', *Nezavisimaya gazeta*, 6 July.

'Bloodless coup a real letdown', 2005. *The Onion*, 16 February (www.theonion.com/content/node/30906).

Blum, Douglas W., 2003. 'Why did Lukoil *really* pull out of the Azeri–Chirac–Guneshli oilfield?' *PONARS Memo* 286, January, Washington, DC: CSIS.

Bogatirov, Aleksandr, 2003. 'Our profession is to serve the Motherland', *Krasnaya zvezda*, 2 April.

Borogan, Irina and Andrei Soldatov, 2006. 'Basaev left the rebels in distress', *Novaya gazeta*, 22 June.

Boucher, Richard A., 2006. 'Keynote speech', pp. 13–18 in Nicklas Noring (ed.), *First Kabul Conference on Partnership, Trade and Development in Greater Central Asia*, CACI Paper, Washington, DC: Johns Hopkins University-SAIS, April.

References 201

Boyko, Maxim, Andrei Shleifer and Robert Vishny, 1995. *Privatizing Russia*. Cambridge, MA: The MIT Press.

'BP's big bet', 2003. *Wall Street Journal Europe*, 13 February.

Bremmer, Ian, 2005/2006. 'Who is in charge in the Kremlin?' *World Policy Journal*, vol. XXII, no. 4, pp. 1–6.

Brodsky, Joseph, 1996. 'The main enemy of mankind is vulgarness in the heart', interview with *Gazeta Wyborcza*, reprinted in *Izvestia*, 3 February.

Bruni, Lev, 2006. 'The first one, the most loved', *Vermya novostei*, 12 April.

Buckley, Neil, 2006. 'Russia's energy minister hits back at Cheney', *Financial Times*, 7 May.

Bukkvoll, Tor, 2004. 'Astana's privatized independence: Private and national interests in the foreign policy of Nursultan Nazarbaev', *Nationalities Papers*, vol. 32, no. 3, pp. 631–650.

Bush, Jason, 2007. 'A "Gas OPEC"? Mostly a pipe dream', *Business Week*, 2 February.

Butrin, Dmitri, 2003. 'GAZPROM has corrected the Turkish mistake', *Kommersant*, 21 November.

—— 2006a. 'Miller's cocktail', *Kommersant*, 10 January.

—— 2006b. 'Anti-terror-invest', *Kommersant*, 9 March.

—— 2006c. 'Ilham Aliev changes the travel plans', *Kommersant*, 9 November.

—— 2006d. 'The three-mice summit', *Kommersant*, 18 July.

—— 2006e. 'The lost year of the puzzled country', *Gazeta.ru*, 18 December (www.gazeta.ru/column/butrin/1166048.shtml).

Butrin, Dmitri and Petr Netreba, 2007. 'The state will go on an oil-&-gas diet', *Kommersant*, 12 March.

Bykov, Pavel, 2003. 'The price of the issue', *Expert*, 31 March.

Bykov, Pavel and Olga Vlasova, 2007. 'Who would like that?' *Expert*, 19 February.

'Caesars and comrades', 2005. *Expert*, 11 April.

Campbell, Robert W., 1983. *The Economics of Soviet Oil and Gas*. Baltimore, MD: Johns Hopkins University Press.

'Canadian radars did not detect Russian strategic bombers', 2006. *Lenta.ru*, 22 April (http://lenta.ru/news/2006/04/22/fly/).

'Caspian pipeline: A history of square pegs into round holes', 2002. *News & Trends: Central Asia*, vol. 7, no. 12, Alexander's Gas & Oil Connections (www.gasandoil.com/goc/news/ntc22449.htm).

'Central Asia: What role for the European Union?', 2006. *Asia Report* 113, International Crisis Group, 10 April (www.crisisgroup.org/home/index.cfm?id=4065&l=1).

Chadova, Elena, 2006. 'Negotiations on US military base in Kyrgyzstan raise transparency concerns', *Eurasia Insight*, 5 June (www.eurasianet.org/departments/insight/articles/eav060506.shtml).

'Chechnya and the posture of the Russian Army', 1999. *Voenny Vestnik*, no. 6, October (www.mfit.ru/defensive/vestnik/vestnik6_1.html).

Cheney, Richard, 2006. 'Remarks at the 2006 Vilnius conference', 4 May (www.whitehouse.gov/news/releases/2006/05/20060504–1.html).

Cherkasov, Aleksandr, 2006. 'PR on the blood of paratroopers', *Polit.ru*, 8 March (www.polit.ru/author/2006/03/07/6_rota.html).

Cherkasov, Gleb, 2005. 'Loons and the forthcoming storm', *Gazeta.ru*, 16 February (www.gazeta.ru/comments/2005/02/16_a_240466.shtml).

Chow, Edward C., 2003. 'U.S.-Russia energy dialogue: policy, projects, or photo-op?' *Foreign Service Journal*, December (www.afsa.org/fsj/dec03/chow.pdf).

202 References

Chubais, Anatoly B. (ed.), 1999. *Privatizatsiya po rossiiski* (Privatization Russian Style). Moscow: Vagirus.

Cirincione, Joseph, 2006. 'No military options', *Issue Brief*, Washington, DC: CEOP, February (www.carnegieendowment.org/publications/index.cfm?fa=view&id=18006& prog=zgp&proj=znpp).

Cohen, Ariel (ed.), 2005. *Eurasia in Balance: The US and the Regional Power Shift*. Aldershot: Ashgate.

—— 2006. 'Washington ponders ways to counter the rise of the Shanghai Cooperation Organization', *Eurasia Insight*, 15 June (www.eurasianet.org/departments/insight/articles/eav061506.shtml).

'Confrontation over Pristina airport', 2000. *BBC World News*, 9 March (http://news.bbc.co.uk/2/hi/europe/671495.stm).

Cooper, Julian, 1998. 'The military expenditures of the USSR and Russian Federation', in *SIPRI Yearbook 1998*, Oxford: Oxford University Press.

Coppieters, Bruno, 2005. 'Locating Georgian security', pp. 339–387 in Bruno Coppieters and Robert Legvold (eds), *Statehood and Security: Georgia after the Rose Revolution*. Cambridge, MA: The MIT Press.

Cornell, Svante E., 2006. 'Eurasia: Crisis and Opportunity', *The Journal of International Security Affairs*, no. 11, Fall, pp. 29–38.

Corruption Perception Index, 2004. Transparency International (www.transparency.org/policy_research/surveys_indices/cpi).

—— 2005. Transparency International (www.transparency.org/policy_research/surveys_indices/cpi).

—— 2006. Transparency International (www.transparency.org/policy_research/surveys_indices/cpi).

'Cracks in the marble: Turkmenistan's failing dictatorship', 2003. *Asia Report* 44, Brussels: International Crisis Group, January (www.crisisgroup.org/home/index.cfm?id=1445&l=1).

'CSTO military forces could have helped Kyrgyzstan', 2005. *NVO*, 8 April.

Cullinson, Alan, 2006. 'Russia tests Ukraine gas truce', *Wall Street Journal*, 7 June, p. A8.

'Current status of the Russian army as a looming national catastrophe', 1997. Statement of the Council on Foreign and Defense Policy, 14 February (www.svop.ru/live/materials.asp?m_id=6973).

'Customer relations, *Gazprom*-style', 2006. *The Economist*, 27 April.

Daalder, Ivo H. and James M. Lindsay, 2002. 'One-day wonder: The dangerous absurdity of Bush-Putin arms treaty', *The American Prospect*, vol. 13, no. 15, 26 August (www.prospect.org/cs/articles?article=oneday_wonder).

Daly, John C.K., Kurt H. Meppen, Vladimir Socor and S. Frederick Starr, 2006. 'Anatomy of a Crisis: US–Uzbekistan relations, 2001–2005', *Silk Road Paper*, Washington, DC: Johns Hopkins University SAIS, February.

Darchiashvili, David, 2005. 'Georgia defense policy and military reform', pp. 117–151 in Bruno Coppieters and Robert Legvold (eds), *Statehood and Security: Georgia after the Rose Revolution*. Cambridge, MA: The MIT Press.

De Waal, Thomas, 2003a. *The Black Garden: Armenia and Azerbaijan Through Peace and War*. New York and London: New York University Press.

—— 2003b. 'Heidar Aliev: A political colossus', *IWPR CRS*, 18 December (www.iwpr.net/?p=crs&s=f&o=158717&apc_state=henicrs2003).

—— 2004. 'Karabakh: The ceasefire's troubled anniversary', *IWPR CRS*, 12 May

References 203

(www.iwpr.net/?p=crs&s=f&o=160731&apc_state=henicrsce0aecfe19308d0fa0c4416 708e1a01b).

—— 2006. 'Basaev: From rebel to vicious extremist', *IWPR CRS*, 11 July (www.iwpr.net/?p=crs&s=f&o=322196&apc_state=henpcrs).

'Deadly record', 2007. *Lenta.ru*, 14 March (http://lenta.ru/articles/2007/03/14/crash/).

Deeva, Ekaterina, 2005. 'How Dagestan will be exploded', *Moskovskii komsomolets*, 8 July.

Delyagin, Mikhail, 2005a. 'How not to break the oil-&-gas spine', *Polit.ru*, 29 November (www.polit.ru/author/2005/11/25/neftgaz.html).

—— 2005b. 'After CIS: Russia's loneliness', *Russia in Global Affairs*, July–August, pp. 142–151.

Dempsey, Judy, 2006. 'Gazprom's grip on Western Europe tightens with pipelines to Hungary', *International Herald Tribune*, 22 June.

Denison, Michael, 2006. 'Kazakh decision to join BTC pipeline may alter delicate regional dynamics', *CACI Analyst*, 28 June (www.cacianalyst.org/view_article.php?articleid=4290&SMSESSION=NO).

Derluguian, Georgi M., 1999. 'Che Guevaras in turbans', *New Left Review*, no. 237, September–October, pp. 3–27.

—— 2001. 'A Soviet general and nation-building', *Chicago Tribune*, 28 October.

—— 2003. 'Whose truth?' Introduction to Anna Politkovskaya, pp. 1–25 in *A Small Corner of Hell: Dispatches from Chechnya*. Chicago: University of Chicago Press.

—— 2005a. 'Nalchik as the Russian Andijan', *Izvestia*, 18 October.

—— 2005b. 'The last Chechen soldier of the Soviet empire', *Izvestia*, 10 March.

—— 2005c. 'The coming revolutions in the North Caucasus', *PONARS Memo* 378, Washington, DC: CSIS, December.

—— 2005d. *Bourdieu's Secret Admirer in the Caucasus: A World-System Biography*. Chicago: University of Chicago Press.

Devdariani, Jaba, 2005. 'Georgia and Russia: The troubled road to accommodation', pp. 153–203 in Bruno Coppieters and Robert Legvold (eds), *Statehood and Security: Georgia after the Rose Revolution*. Cambridge, MA: The MIT Press.

Diehl, Jackson, 2006. 'Crumbling before Putin', *Washington Post*, 19 June.

Dmitriev, Mikhail, 2006. 'In defense of nationalization', *Kommersant*, 30 January.

'Doklad premier-ministra SSSR V.S. Pavlova na V sessii Verhovnogo Soveta SSSR' (Report of Prime Minister V.S. Pavlov at the V session of the Supreme Council of the USSR), 1991. *Izvestia*, 23 April.

Dolgin, Boris, 2004. 'What has Vladimir Putin re-evaluated?' *Polit.ru*, 6 September (www.polit.ru/analytics/2004/09/06/quest.html).

—— 2005. 'Let's stand for our boys', *Polit.ru*, 14 January (www.polit.ru/author/2005/01/14/army.html).

—— 2006. 'The end of a gold-plated era', *Polit.ru*, 22 December (www.polit.ru/author/2006/12/22/turkmen.html).

Dombey, Daniel, Neil Buckley and Carola Hoyos, 2006. 'NATO fears Russian plans for "gas OPEC"', *Financial Times*, 13 November.

Dubnov, Arkady, 2000. 'The plan of the marshal', *Vremya novostei*, 27 October.

—— 2005. 'Discontent on Andijan', *Vremya novostei*, 10 June.

—— 2006. 'Listen to Cheney but don't pick up your nose', *Vremya novostei*, 11 May.

—— 2007. 'Lukewarm atmosphere in Russian–Kazakhstan summit', *Vremya novostei*, 20 March.

Dugin, Aleksandr, 2004a. *Proekt 'Evraziya'* (Project Eurasia), Moscow: EKSMO.

204 *References*

—— 2004b. 'They started an Empire', *Politcom.Ru*, 21 January (www.politcom.ru/2004/pvz341.php).

—— 2006. 'It is logical for Peking to stay on the Eurasian side of barricades', *KM.ru*, 26 April (www.km.ru/comment/index.asp?data=26.04.2006%2012:00:00&archive=on).

Dunlop, John, 2005. *Beslan: Russia's 9/11?* Washington, DC: Jamestown Foundation.

Dunlop, John B. and Rajan Menon, 2006. 'Chaos in the North Caucasus and Russia's future', *Survival*, vol. 48, no. 2, pp. 97–114.

Dwan, Renata and Oleksandr Pavliuk, 2000. *Building Security in the New States of Eurasia: Subregional Cooperation in the Former Soviet Space*. New York and London: M.E. Sharpe.

Dzhorbenadze, Irina, 2005. 'Tbilisi expects a counter-revolution from Moscow', *Rosbalt*, 2 December (www.rosbalt.ru/2005/12/04/236656.html).

Ebel, Robert E., 1970. *Communist Trade in Oil and Gas*. New York: Praeger.

—— 1995. 'The History and Politics of the Chechen Oil', *Caspian Crossroads*, vol. 1, no. 1, Winter (http://ourworld.compuserve.com/HOMEPAGES/USAZERB/3.htm).

Efremov, Gerbert A., 2006. 'Rearmament with *Topol*-M appears to be an anachronism', *NVO*, 26 May.

Egorov, Georgy, Sergei M. Guriev and Konstantin Sonin, 2006. 'Media freedom, bureaucratic incentives, and the resource curse', paper of the Center for Economic Policy Research, June (http://papers.ssrn.com/sol3/papers.cfm?abstract_id=898888).

Egozaryan, Valery and Andrei Gromov, 2005. 'After the divorce', *Expert*, 4 April.

'Energetic debate', 2006. *The Economist*, 11 March, p. 30.

'Energy security: The role of Russian gas companies', 2003. Conference proceedings, the International Energy Agency, 25 November (www.iea.org/textbase/work/2003/soyuzgaz/proceedings/programme.htm).

'Energy strategy of Russia for the period to 2020', 2003. Ministry of Industry and Energy (www.minprom.gov.ru/docs/strateg/1).

Epokha Eltsina (Yeltsin's Epoch), 2001. Moscow: Vagirus.

Evangelista, Matthew, 2002. *The Chechen Wars: Will Russia Go the Way of the Soviet Union?* Washington, DC: Brookings Institution.

—— 2004. 'Ingushetia as a microcosm of Puitn's reforms', *PONARS Memo* 346, Washington, DC: CSIS, November.

Fadeev, Valery, 2006. 'Coming back to Russia', *Expert*, 16 January.

Fairbanks, Charles, 2002. 'Bases of debate: America in Central Asia: Being there', *The National Interest*, No. 68, January, pp. 39–53 (www.nationalinterest.org/General.aspx?id=92&id2=11172).

'Fancying a "small and victorious" one', 2006. *Gazeta.ru*, 4 August (www.gazeta.ru/comments/2006/08/02_e_725241.shtml).

Fedorov, Boris, 2001. 'Gazprom: A test case for President Putin', presentation at the Carnegie Endowment for International Peace, Washington, DC, 18 April (www.carnegieendowment.org/events/index.cfm?fa=eventDetail&id=310).

Fedorov, Yuri, 2006. 'The Shanghai knot: Russian-Chinese cooperation is in fact competition', *Kommersant*, 10 April.

Felgengauer, Pavel, 2004. 'Nazran: Rebels win by skill not quantity', *Novaya gazeta*, 28 June.

—— 2006a. '*Bulava* is no headache for smart alecks', *Novaya gazeta*, 30 October.

—— 2006b. '*Kuzkina mat* modernized', *Novaya gazeta*, 9 February.

—— 2007. 'Russian Security Council plans to draft military doctrine', *EDM*, 22 March (www.jamestown.org/edm/article.php?article_id=2372031).

References 205

'Fire on nuclear submarine *Daniil Moskovsky*', 2006. *Newsru.com*, 7 September (http://newsru.com/russia/07sep2006/submarin.html).

Fishman, Mikhail, 2005. 'Security as sickness', *Gazeta.ru*, 26 May (www.gazeta.ru/column/fishman/291264.shtml).

Fraizer, Ian, 2003. 'Invented city', *The New Yorker*, 28 July, pp. 37–47.

Freedman, Robert, 2002. 'Putin and the Middle East', *Middle East Review of International Affairs*, vol. 6, no. 2, pp. 1–16.

Freeland, Chrystia, 2000. *Sale of the Century*. Toronto: Doubleday.

Friedman, Thomas L., 2006. 'The first law of petropolitics', *Foreign Policy*, May/June, pp. 28–36.

'From Koptsev to Kondopoga', 2006. *Kommersant*, 28 December.

Frumkin, Konstantin, 2004. 'Gref promised the end to the country', *Izvestia*, 25 November.

Fuller, Liz, 2005. 'Georgia/Russia: Withdrawal agreement clears first hurdle', *Eurasia Insight*, 22 June (www.eurasianet.org/departments/insight/articles/pp.062205.shtml).

Furman, Dmitri, 2004. 'Inevitable growing up', *Polit.ru*, 29 December (www.polit.ru/analytics/2004/12/26/furm.html).

—— 2006. 'I am not sure our authorities know what they want', interview with *Polit.ru*, 12 May (www.polit.ru/analytics/2006/05/10/furman2.html).

Gabuev, Aleksandr, 2005. 'Vladimir Putin justifies his trust in Islam Karimov', *Kommersant*, 30 June.

—— 2007. 'Moscow greets Nursultan Nazarbaev like a foreigner', *Kommersant*, 19 March.

Gaddy, Clifford G., 2002. 'Has Russia entered a period of sustainable economic growth?' pp. 125–144 in Andrew C. Kuchins (ed.), *Russia after the Fall*. Washington, DC: CEIP.

Gaddy, Cliffort G. and Barry W. Ickes, 1998. 'Russia's virtual economy', *Foreign Affairs*, vol. 77, no. 5, pp. 53–67.

—— 2005. 'Resource rents and the Russian economy', *Eurasian Geography and Economics*, vol. 46, no. 8, pp. 559–583.

Gaidar, Egor T., 1998. *Dni porazhenii i pobed* (Days of Defeats and Victories). Moscow: Eurasia (published in English as Jegor Gaidar, *The Days of Defeat and Victory*, Seattle: University of Washington Press, 1999).

—— 2005. *Dolgoe vremya: Rossiya v mire* (Long Time: Russia in the World). Moscow: Delo.

—— 2006a. *Gibel Imperii: Uroki dlya sovremennoi Rossii* (Death of the Empire: Lessons for Contemporary Russia), Moscow: Rossiiskaya politicheskaya entsiklopedia.

—— 2006b. 'Coutry and oil: The price of steel in the voice', *Vedomosti*, 17 May.

—— 2007. 'The rule of outstretched hand', *The New Times*, no. 4, 5 March.

Galeotti, Mark, 2002. 'Moscow dismayed by unfaithful CARs', *Jane's Intelligence Review*, June, pp. 50–51.

—— 2003. 'Putin reintroduces centralised intelligence', *Jane's Intelligence Review*, May, pp. 52–53.

Galich, Aleksandr A., 2003. *Izbrannoe* (Select Works). Anthology of Russian humor and satire, vol. 25, Moscow: Eksmo.

Gavrichev, Sergei, 2004. 'A change of course: Kazakhstan alters the guidelines for developing of the Caspian shelf', *RusEnergy*, 16 April (www.rusenergy.com/politics/a16042004.htm).

206 *References*

Gavrilenkov, Evgeny, 2006. 'Economic growth: We have to become introverts', *Vedomosti*, 7 November.

Genin, Vlad E. (ed.), 2001. *The Anatomy of Russian Defense Conversion*. Walnut Creek, CA: Vega Press.

'Georgia: Avoiding war in South Ossetia', 2004. *Europe Report* 159, Brussels: International Crisis Group, 26 November.

'Georgia keeps sights set on the West', 2003. *BBC News*, 24 November (http://news.bbc.co.uk/2/hi/europe/3232158.stm).

'Gerhard Schroeder's sellout', 2005, *Washington Post*, 13 December.

Gevorkyan, Natalya, 2004. 'Low truth', *Gazeta.ru*, 22 December (www.gazeta.ru/column/gevorkyan/254490.shtml).

—— 2006. 'A group of gods', *Gazeta.ru*, 19 July (www.gazeta.ru/column/gevorkyan/704388.shtml).

—— 2007. 'My friend and the empire', *Gazeta.ru*, 21 March (www.gazeta.ru/column/gevorkyan/1503671.shtml).

Gevorkyan, Natalya, Vladimir Kolesnikov and Natalya Timakova, 1999. *Ot Pervogo Litsa: Razgovory s Vladimirom Putinym* (In the First Person: Talks with Vladimir Putin). Moscow: Vagirus.

Glikin, Maksim and Marina Saidukova, 2005. 'Politologists now believe in changes', *Nezavisimaya gazeta*, 27 May.

'Glonass is getting presidential attention', 2005. *Russian strategic nuclear forces*, 26 December (http://russianforces.org/blog/2005/12/glonass_is_getting_presidentia.shtml).

Glumskov, Dmitry and Artur Shahnazaryan, 2006. 'Splitting a billion', *Expert*, 29 May.

Gnusarev, Aleksandr, 2007. 'Russian navy: The course to modernization', interview with *Rossiiskaya gazeta*, 6 March.

Gobarev, Victor, 1999. 'Russia–NATO relations after the Kosovo crisis: Strategic implications', *Journal of Slavic Military Studies*, vol. 12, no. 3, pp. 1–17.

Goldman, Marshall I., 1994. *Lost Opportunity: Why Economic Reforms in Russia Have Not Worked*. New York: W.W. Norton.

—— 2003. *The Piratization of Russia: Russian Reform Goes Awry*. London and New York: Routledge.

Golotuyk, Yuri, 2002. 'President summed up the results of the summit', *Vremya novostei*, 26 April.

Golts, Aleksandr, 2000. 'The last chance of a technocrat', *Itogi*, 28 July.

—— 2004a. 'The social and political condition of the Russian military', pp. 73–94 in Steven E. Miller and Dmitri Trenin (eds), *The Russian Military: Power and Policy*. Cambridge, MA, and London: The MIT Press.

—— 2004b. 'Drafting money in the autumn', *Ezhenedelny zhurnal*, 27 September (http://supernew.ej.ru/138/tema/05/index.html).

—— 2005a. 'Tank wipes cleans all footprints', *Ezhenedelny zhurnal*, 17 January (http://supernew.ej.ru/150/tema/goltz17/index.html).

—— 2005b. 'According to the old scenario', *Ezhednevny zhurnal*, 22 August (www.ej.ru/?a=note&id=1648).

—— 2006a. 'Forward, to the victory of Putinism', *Ezhednevny Zhurnal*, 3 March (www.ej.ru/?a=note&id=3169).

—— 2006b. 'The change of tone', *Ezhednevny zhurnal*, 5 May (www.ej.ru/?a=note&id=3725).

—— 2006c. 'Unequal fight with own shadow', *Ezhednevny zhurnal*, 26 April (www.ej.ru/?a=note&id=3638).

References   207

—— 2006d. 'Debilitization is on the march', *Ezhednevny zhurnal*, 19 July (www.ej.ru/
?a=note&id=4334).

—— 2006e. 'Minus one division', *Ezhednevny zhurnal*, 15 December (www.ej.ru/
?a=note&id=5638).

—— 2006f. 'Week-end with soft enemies', *Ezhednevny zhurnal*, 15 July (www.ej.ru/
?a=note&id=4308).

—— 2007a. 'Dneprovia against Dvinia', *Ezhednevny zhurnal*, 10 January (www.ej.ru/
?a=note&id=5829).

—— 2007b. 'Civilian control a la Putin', *Ezhednevny zhurnal*, 24 February (www.ej.ru/
?a=note&id=6230).

Golts, Aleksandr and Dmitry Pinsker, 2000a. 'Supreme commander's headquarters',
Itogi, 11 July (www.itogi.ru/paper2000.nsf/Article/Itogi_2000_07_07_213904.html).

—— 2000b. 'Babylonian vertical', *Itogi*, 15 August (www.itogi.ru/paper2000.nsf/
Article/Itogi_2000_08_14_102305.html).

Goltz, Thomas, 2001. 'Sea of instability: Caspian politics and pipelines', seminar at the
Belfer Center for Science and International Affairs, Harvard University, 10 April
(http://bcsia.ksg.harvard.edu/publication.cfm?ctype=event_reports&item_id=79).

Gomart, Thomas, 2006. 'The paradox of inconsistency', *Russia in Global Affairs*,
May–June, pp. 62–71.

Gorelov, Nikolai, 2007a. 'The bird-troika from Chubais', *Vremya novosti*, 14 February.

—— 2007b. 'Dynamic renaissance', *Vremya novosti*, 4 April.

Goryaev, Ivan, 2001a. 'Autumn feast in GAZPROM', *Grani.ru*, 27 September
(http://grani.ru/Politics/Russia/m.3300.html).

—— 2001b. 'No, he will not go completely', *Grani.ru*, 30 October (http://grani.ru/Poli-
tics/Russia/m.3304.html).

—— 2002. 'Gas arestocrasy', *Grani.ru*, 9 January (http://grani.ru/Politics/Russia/
m.3307.html).

Gottemoeller, Rose, 2002. 'New shape of the East–West nuclear relationship', pp.
260–277 in Andrew C. Kuchins (ed.), *Russia after the Fall*, Washington, DC: CEIP.

—— 2004. 'Nuclear weapons in current Russian policy', pp. 183–215 in Steven E. Miller
and Dmitri Trenin (eds), *The Russian Military: Power and Policy*. Cambridge, MA,
and London: The MIT Press.

—— 2005. 'Cooperative threat reduction beyond Russia', *Washington Quarterly*, vol. 28,
no. 2, pp 145–158.

—— 2006. 'The Russia card', *New York Times*, 3 May.

Graham, Thomas and Damien J. LaVera, 2003. *Cornerstones of Security: Arms Control
Treaties in the Nuclear Era*. Seattle: University of Washington Press.

Grant, Charles and Katinka Barysh, 2003. 'The EU-Russia energy dialogue', *CER Briefing Note*, May (www.cer.org.uk/pdf/briefing_eu_russia.pdf).

Grib, Natalya, 2006a. 'Changes on the western front', *Kommersant*, 18 May.

—— 2006b. 'Gas with direct impact', *Kommersant*, 15 November.

Grigoryeva, Ekaterina, 2005. 'Shuttle-traders and tourists pushed Putin and the Turkish
leadership to negotiations', *Izvestiya*, 7 December.

Gritsenko, Grigory, 2004. 'The draft as a physical tax', *Polit.ru*, 8 October
(www.polit.ru/analytics/2004/10/08/army.html).

—— 2007. 'Oil with no intermediaries', *Polit.ru*, 19 March (www.polit.ru/author/
2007/03/19/oil.html).

Grivach, Aleksei, 2006a. 'Central Asian rates for Gazprom', *Vremya novosti*, 23 January.

—— 2006b. 'Miller got rid of Ryazanov', *Vremya novosti*, 16 November.

208 References

Grivach, Alexei and Vladimir Dzaguto, 2004. 'The Union was poisoned by gas', *Vremya novostei*, 20 February.

Grivach, Alexei and Yuri Shpakov, 2006. 'The phantom of "gas OPEC" wanders across Europe', *Vermya novostei*, 15 November.

Gromov, Andrei, 2005. 'Security: A year after Beslan', *Expert*, 29 August.

Gromov, Andrei and Shamsudin Mamaev, 2006. 'The end of Basaev: The epoch of Chechen terrorism came to an end with Basaev's destruction', *Expert*, 17 July.

Gulieva, Gulnaz and Rafat Abasov, 2005. 'Azerbaijan en route to oil riches', *IWPR CRS*, 26 May (www.iwpr.net/?apc_state=henicrs&s=i&o=488f9f4326101ea9edbbe65d3 c90cca3).

Guriev, Sergei, 2005. 'The worse is the worse', *Gazeta.ru*, 16 August (www.gazeta.ru/ comments/2005/08/16_a_355535.shtml).

—— 2006. 'Raw materials mentality', *Kommersant*, 29 March.

Gustafson, Thane, 1989. *Crisis Amid Plenty: The Politics of Soviet Energy under Brezhnev and Gorbachev*, Princeton, NJ: Princeton University Press.

Haig, Alexander M. Jr. and Harvey Sicherman, 2001. 'From Russia without love', *E-Notes*, Washington, DC: Foreign Policy Research Institute, 2 March (www. fpri.org/enotes/russia.20010302.haigsicherman.withoutlove.html).

Hall, Robert, 1993. 'Russia's mobile forces – rationale and structure', *Jane's Intelligence Review*, April, pp. 154–155.

Haran, Olexiy, 2002. 'Ukraine at the crossroads: Velvet revolution or Belarusification', *PONARS Memo* 261, Washington, DC: CSIS, October.

Herd, Graeme P. and Anne Aldis (eds), 2003. *Russian Regions and Regionalism*. London: RoutledgeCurzon.

'Heritage without heirs', 2006. *Gazeta.ru*, 4 May (www.gazeta.ru/com-ments/2006/05/04_e_631951.shtml).

Hersh, Seymour M., 2001. 'The price of oil', *The New Yorker*, 9 July, pp. 48–65.

Herspring, Dale R., 2002. 'Putin and the armed forces', pp. 173–194 in Dale R. Herspring (ed.), *Putin's Russia: Past Imperfect, Future Uncertain*. Lanham, MD: Rowman & Littlefield.

Hestanov, Ruslan, 2004. 'Regional empire', *Russkii zhurnal*, 14 January (http://old.russ. ru/politics/20040114-hest.html).

Hewett, Ed A., 1984. *Energy, Economics and Foreign Policy in the Soviet Union*. Washington, DC: Brookings.

'Hidden threat', 2006. *Vedomosti*, 28 March.

Hill, Fiona, 2003. 'Seismic shifts in Eurasia: The changing relationship between Turkey and Russia and its implication for the South Caucasus', *Journal of Southeast European and Black Sea Studies*, vol. 3, no. 3, pp. 55–75.

—— 2004. 'Putin, Yukos and Russia', *The Globalist*, 1 December (www.brookings.edu/ views/articles/hillf/20041201.htm).

Hill, Fiona and Florence Fee, 2002. 'Fuelling the future: Prospects for Russian oil and gas', *Demokratizatsiya*, vol. 10, no. 4, pp. 462–487.

Hisamov, Iskander, 2006. 'A meeting with reality', *Kommersant*, 7 March.

Ignatova, Maria, Ekaterina Kravchenko and Alexei Tihonov, 2002. 'The first private pipeline will appear soon', *Izvestia*, 27 November.

Ilf, Ilya and Evgeny Petrov, 2006. *Zolotoi Telenok* (The Golden Calf). Moscow: Eksmo.

Illarionov, Andrei, 2004. Interview with *Moscow echo*, 30 December (www. echo.msk.ru/interview/33755/).

—— 2005a. 'Dangerous turn', *Rossiiskaya gazeta*, 23 September.

References 209

—— 2005b. 'Russian economy becomes state-run', *Newsru.com*, 11 November (http://newsru.com/finance/11nov2005/illar.html).

—— 2005c. Interview with *Moscow echo*, 31 December (www.echo.msk.ru/interview/40891/).

—— 2006. 'Political freedom and prosperity', report presented at the conference 'Transitional Economies in Post-Industrial World', Institute for the Economy in Transition, Moscow, 20 March (www.iet.ru/files/text/confer/2006_03_20/Illarionov.pdf).

Isaev, Timur, 2006. '*Lukoil* will develop oil and gas on Dagestan's Caspian sea-shelf', *Kavkazsky uzel*, 27 October (www.kavkaz.memo.ru/newstext/news/id/1094540.html).

Ismail, Alman Mir, 2005. 'A base or not a base for Azerbaijan?' *Eurasia Insight*, 12 September (www.eurasianet.org/departments/insight/articles/eav091205ru.shtml).

Ismailzade, Fariz, 2007. 'Tehran reminds Azerbaijan to keep distance from Washington', *EDM*, 2 March (www.jamestown.org/edm/article.php?article_id=2371967).

Ivanov, Sergei, 2004. 'Russia's geopolitical priorities and armed forces', *Russia in Global Affairs*, January–February, pp. 38–51.

—— 2006. 'The triad of national values', *Izvestia*, 13 July.

Ivanov, Vladimir, 2006a. 'Dedovshchina from the Atlantic to the Pacific', *NVO*, 21 April.

—— 2006b. 'A still-born monster', *NVO*, 7 July.

Ivanov, Vladimir and Viktor Myasnikov, 2006. 'The chosen of the OPK have guaranteed their prosperity', *NVO*, 9 June.

Ivanov, Vladimir and Igor Plugatarev, 2005. 'Moscow's shoot to Khanabad', *NVO*, 9 September.

Izmailov, Vyacheslav, 2006. 'Disbanding the gangs', *Novaya gazeta*, 31 July.

Jack, Andrew, 2001. 'Russia warned over attitude to Georgia', *Financial Times*, 19 January.

Jonson, Lena, 1998. 'The Tajik war: A challenge to Russian policy', *Discussion Paper* 74, London: RIIA, March.

Jonson, Lena and Clive Archer (eds), 1996. *Peacekeeping and the Role of Russia in Eurasia*. Boulder, CO: Westview Press.

Kadrmatov, Ruslan, 2006. 'Power and feebleness', *Lenta.ru*, 14 April (http://lenta.ru/articles/2006/04/14/strateg/).

Kaftan, Larisa, 2007. 'The G8 success is recognized in the West', *Komsomolskaya pravda*, 14 March.

Kalabugin, Valery, 2005. 'Azerbaijan: What color will a revolution take?' *Nezavisimaya gazeta*, 3 June.

Karaganov, Sergei, 2004. 'Russia and Belarus: Getting rid of the myths', *Rossiiskaya gazeta*, 12 February.

Kara-Murza, Vladimir, 2006. 'Three years in the dark', *Ezhednevny zhurnal*, 22 June (www.ej.ru/?a=note&id=4111).

Karatnycky, Adrian, 2003. 'Jobs for the boys: Putin's new militocracy', *Wall Street Journal*, 13 June.

Karshiboev, Nuriddin, Viktoria Panfilova and Igor Plugatarev, 2004. 'Russian military base appeared in Tajikistan', *Nezavisimaya gazeta*, 18 October.

Kasaev, Alan, 2001. 'Russian Security Council has decided to close down the CIS', *Nezavisimaya gazeta*, 7 February.

Kasaev, Alan, Asya Gadzhizade and Dmitry Kosyrev, 2001. 'Russia shapes a new policy for the trans-Caucasus', *Nezavisimaya gazeta*, 11 January.

Kashavtsev, Vladilen, 2004. 'Caspian apple of discord', *Neft Rossii*, no. 10, October (www.oilru.com/nr/137/2744/).

210   *References*

Kasparov, Garry, 2007. 'Putin's gangster state', *Wall Street Journal*, 30 March.

Kaspe, Svyatoslav, 2005. 'Reflections at the entrance to the empire', *Expert*, 17 October.

Kasyanov, Mikhail, 2006. 'Diagnosis: Peace and quiet are prescribed', *Vedomosti*, 24 April.

Katik, Mevlut, 2004. 'Militarization of the Caspian sea', pp. 297–310 in Shirin Akiner (ed.), *The Caspian: Politics, Energy and Security*. London and New York: RoutledgeCurzon.

—— 2006. 'Russian pipeline play poses dilemma for Turkey', *Eurasia Insight*, 27 September (www.eurasianet.org/departments/insight/articles/eav092706a.shtml).

Khazbiev, Aleksei, 2006a. 'Mysterious weapons are eagerly bought', *Expert*, 20 February.

—— 2006b. 'The choice of the target', *Expert*, 13 March.

—— 2007. 'Dinosaurs come back', *Expert*, 15 January.

Khinshtein, Aleksandr, 2005. 'The Caucasus for sale, bargaining encouraged. The sensational report of Dmitry Kozak', *Moskovsky komsomolets*, 16 June.

Khlebnikov, Paul, 2002. 'The oligarch who came in from the cold', *Forbes*, 18 March, pp. 110–114.

Khodarenok, Mikhail, 2001. 'The Grachev effect', *Nezavisimaya gazeta*, 22 August.

—— 2002a. 'The necklace of US bases', *NVO*, 29 March.

—— 2002b. 'Threaten and forget', *NVO*, 4 October.

Khodorkovsky, Mikhail, 2002. 'Stabilizing world oil markets: Russia's role in global recovery', presentation at the Carnegie Endowment for International Peace, Washington, DC, 8 February (www.carnegieendowment.org/events/index.cfm?fa=eventDetail&id=454&&prog=zru).

—— 2005. 'Left turn – 2', *Kommersant*, 11 November.

—— (ed.), 2007. *Mir v 2020 gody* (The World in Year 2020), Moscow: Algoritm.

Khohlov, Igor, 2005. 'Heroin in exchange for democracy', *Lenta.ru*, 20 June (http://lenta.ru/articles/2005/06/20/opium/).

Khristenko, Viktor, 2006. 'Russia's energy strategy: Breakthrough towards the East', *Vedomosti*, 6 February.

Kimmage, Daniel, 2006. 'Turkmenistan-China pipeline project has far-reaching implications', *RFE/RL Newsline*, 10 April (www.rferl.org/featuresarticle/2006/4/55F9574D-407A-4777–9724–944E6C2ECD7B.html).

Kirillov, Nikolai, 2006. 'The Achilles heel of the defense potential', *NVO*, 10 November.

Kisriev, Enver, 2003. 'Why is there stability in Dagestan but not in Chechnya?' pp. 103–126 in Christoph Zürcher and Jan Koehler (eds), *Potentials of Disorder*. Manchester: Manchester University Press.

Klein, Lawrence R. and Marshall Pomer (eds), 2001. *The New Russia: Transition Gone Awry*. Stanford: Stanford University Press.

Kleveman, Lutz, 2003. *The New Great Game: Blood and Oil in Central Asia*. New York: Atlantic Monthly Press.

Kober, Stanley, 2000. 'The great game, round 2: Washington's misguided support for the Baku-Ceyhan oil pipeline', *Foreign Policy Briefing* 63, Washington, DC: Cato Institute (www.cato.org/pub_display.php?pub_id=1587).

Kobo, Juan, 2006. 'Stale summit', *Kommersant*, 13 November.

Kokh, Alfred, 1998. *The Selling of the Soviet Empire: Politics and Economics of Russia's Privatization*. New York: Liberty.

Kokoshin, Andrei, 2005. 'CIS cracked a bit but did not fall apart', interview with *Nezavisimaya gazeta*, 14 September.

Koktysh, Kirill, 2006. 'The Belarus identity-building project', *Pro et Contra*, March–June, pp. 105–115.

Kolesnikov, Andrei, 2004. 'Conquest by space', *Kommersant*, 7 April.

References   211

—— 2005a. *Pervyi Ukrainskii* (The First Ukraininan). Moscow: Vagirus.

—— 2005b. 'Aleksandr Lukashenko substituted a revolution with himself', *Kommersant*, 23 June.

—— 2006a. 'Either gay, or the Slavs', *Grani.ru*, 4 May (http://grani.ru/opinion/m. 105244.html).

—— 2006b. 'Boris Yeltsin said good-bye to his epoch', *Kommersant*, 6 February.

—— 2006c. 'Vladimir Putin preferred Islam Karimov to Aleksandr Lukashenko', *Kommersant*, 24 June.

—— 2006d. 'The last march of the Soviets', *Gazeta.ru*, 25 July (www.gazeta.ru/ column/kolesnikov/707654.shtml).

Koliandre, Alexander, 2002. 'Oil trade strengthens US–Russian ties', *BBC News*, 8 July (http://news.bbc.co.uk/1/hi/business/2116133.stm).

Kolyvanov, Georgy, 2006. 'Reduction-generals are in charge of military reform', *NVO*, 17 March.

Korobushin, Varfolomei, 2007. 'There is no alternative yet', *NVO*, 2 February.

Korotchenko, Igor, 2003. 'Finance ministry cuts the military order', *Nezavisimaya gazeta*, 20 June.

Kortunov, Sergei, 2007. 'Military–political context of Russia's economic and social development', paper presented at the VIII Higher School of Economics annual conference, Moscow (http://new.hse.ru/sites/mbd/program.aspx).

Kramer, Andrew E., 2006. 'Russian oil reversal stirs outcry', *International Herald Tribune*, 19 September.

Kramer, Mark, 2000. 'The sinking of the *Kursk*', *PONARS Memo* 145, Cambridge, MA: Harvard University, September.

—— 2004/2005. 'The perils of counter-insurgency: Russia's war in Chechnya', *International Security*, vol. 29, no. 3, pp. 5–63.

Kryshtanovskaya, Olga, 2002. 'Putin's regime: A liberal militocracy?' *Pro et Contra*, Autumn, pp. 158–180.

—— 2005. *Anatomiya rossiiskoi elity* (The Anatomy of the Russian Elite), Moscow: Zakharov.

—— 2007. 'The position of chekists is now fantastically stable', *Kommersant-Vlast*, 19 March.

Kryukov, Valery and Arild Moe, 1996. *Gazprom: Internal Structure, Management Principles and Financial Flows*. London: RIIA.

Kuchins, Andrew C. (ed.), 2002. *Russia after the Fall*. Washington, DC: CEIP.

Kudrin, Alexei, 2006. 'I know better about the financial policy', interview with *Kommersant*, 15 August.

Kulikov, Sergei, 2006. 'Hit by the rouble, very painfully', *NVO*, 4 August.

Kulikov, Sergei and Viktoria Panfilova, 2006. 'Acceleration towards the West', *Nezavisimaya gazeta*, 5 December.

Kuznetsova, Vera, 2000. 'All the best to the Turks', *Vremya novostei*, 24 October.

Lambeth, Benjamin S., 1997. *The Warrior Who Would Rule Russia: A Profile of Aleksandr Lebed*. Santa Monica, CA: RAND.

Lane, David (ed.), 1999. *The Political Economy of Russian Oil*. Lanham, MA: Rowman & Littlefield.

Lanskoy, Miriam, 2002. 'Dagestan and Chechnya: The Wahhabi challenge to the state', *SAIS Review*, vol. 12, no. 2, Summer–Fall, pp. 167–192.

Lantratov, Konstantin and Ivan Safronov, 2006. 'The last Russian spy broke down on the orbit', *Kommersant*, 20 November.

212 *References*

Latynina, Yulia, 2002. 'Black hole in the third reading', *Novaya gazeta*, 25 November.

—— 2005a. 'Yukos measured in deci-rebas', *Ezhednevny zhurnal*, 18 March (www.ej.ru/?a=note&id=473).

—— 2005b. 'Abramovich free-to-go', *Ezhednevny zhurnal*, 29 September (www.ej.ru/?a=note&id=1952).

—— 2005c. 'She sank but he rose up', *Ezhednevny zhurnal*, 8 August (www.ej.ru/?a=note&id=1553).

—— 2005d. 'Mountains come to Magomet', *Novaya gazeta*, 12 September.

—— 2005e. 'The reasons for killings in Dagestan', *Ezhednevny zhurnal*, 3 February (www.ej.ru/?a=note&id=112).

—— 2005f. 'Boots in Dagestan', *Ezhednevny zhurnal*, 18 July (www.ej.ru/?a=note&id=1443).

—— 2005g. 'This is a failure: On the systemic crisis of President Putin's regime', *Novaya gazeta*, 14 February.

—— 2006a. 'New declaration of human rights', *Ezhednevny zhurnal*, 7 April (www.ej.ru/?a=note&id=3495).

—— 2006b. 'Dagestan and political corpses', *Ezhednevny zhurnal*, 20 February (www.ej.ru/?a=note&id=3069).

—— 2006c. 'Dagestan needs an amnesty', *Novaya gazeta*, 15 May.

—— 2007. 'The Georgian Pact-2007', *Ezhednevny zhurnal*, 14 March (www.ej.ru/?a=note&id=6394).

Lavrov, Sergei, 2007. Speech at the XV Assembly of the Council on Foreign and Defense Policy, 17 March (www.mid.ru/brp_4.nsf/2fee282eb6df40e643256999005e6e8c/f3c5edc2dadb268dc32572a10041ed8f?OpenDocument).

Leibin, Vitaly, 2005a. 'Power has limits', *Polit.ru*, 26 April (www.polit.ru/analytics/2005/04/26/ideol.html).

—— 2005b. 'Occupation of Russia: Hidden lessons of the Bratislava summit', *Polit.ru*, 28 February (www.polit.ru/author/2005/02/28/leiba.html).

—— 2005c. 'Nuances of gas imperialism', *Polit.ru*, 12 December (www.polit.ru/author/2005/12/12/gazz.html).

—— 2006. 'The so-called army', *Polit.ru*, 22 February (www.polit.ru/author/2006/02/22/army1.html).

Lelyveld, Michael, 2002. 'Blue stream pipeline: A technological feat but an economic misadventure', *RFE/RL Newsline*, 23 October (www.rferl.org/features/2002/10/23102002155651.asp).

Leontyev, Mikhail, 2006a. 'The restoration of Russia's future', *Komsomolskaya Pravda*, 26 April.

—— 2006b. 'The concept "Russia as energy super-power"', *Russkii zhurnal*, 27 October (http://russ.ru/politics/docs/koncept_rossiya_kak_energeticheskaya_sverhderzhava).

Lieber, Keir A. and Daryl G. Press, 2006. 'The rise of US nuclear primacy', *Foreign Affairs*, vol. 85, no. 2, pp. 42–54.

Lieven, Anatol, 1998. *Chechnya: Tombstone of Russian Power*. New Haven, CT: Yale University Press.

—— 2001. 'Georgia: A failing state?' *Eurasia Insight*, 30 January (www.eurasianet.org/departments/insight/articles/eav013001.shtml).

—— 2000/2001. 'Against Russophobia', *World Policy Journal*, vol. XVII, no. 4, pp. 25–31.

Lieven, Dominique, 2002. *The Russian Empire and Its Rivals*. New Haven, CT: Yale University Press.

References   213

Light, Margot, 2003. 'International relations of Russia and the commonwealth of independent states', pp. 3–10 in *Eastern Europe, Russia and Central Asia 2004*. London and New York: Europa Publications.

Litovkin, Dmitri, 2006. 'Korean missile went towards Vladivostok', *Izvestia*, 10 July.

Litovkin, Viktor, 2005. 'Spetsnaz to be reorganized', *RIA Novosti*, 22 March (http://en.rian.ru/analysis/20050322/39700137.html)

Lobjakas, Ahto, 2006. 'Azerbaijan: EU taking note of Baku's strength', *RFE/RL Newsline*, 7 November (www.rferl.org/features/features_Article.aspx?m=11&y=2006&id=0F418E0F-3F21–4AE3–8F3E-BCEEB1C4BE40).

Loriya, Elena, 2003. 'Our paratroopers can lose to Americans only in basketball', interview with Georgy Shpak, *Izvestia*, 18 March.

'*Lukoil* and *KazMunaiGas* will develop the Caspian together', 2005. *Lenta.ru*, 14 March (http://lenta.ru/news/2005/03/14/sp/).

Lukyanov, Fedor, 2004. 'The anti-gravitation pole', *Gazeta.ru*, 23 July (www.gazeta.ru/comments/2004/07/a_138170.shtml).

—— 2005a. 'Valve's own pride', *Gazeta.ru*, 29 December (www.gazeta.ru/column/lukyanov/508590.shtml).

—— 2005b. 'The shoots of self-control', *Gazeta.ru*, 25 August (www.gazeta.ru/column/lukyanov/360875.shtml).

—— 2006a. 'A view on things', *Kommersant*, 15 February.

—— 2006b. 'The code of the state', *Gazeta.ru*, 16 March (www.gazeta.ru/column/lukyanov/563830.shtml).

—— 2006c. 'The long year in Russia's policy', *Kommersant*, 17 July.

—— 2006d. 'A view on revanchism', *Kommersant*, 1 August.

—— 2006e. 'Vlaues and prices', *Gazeta.ru*, 19 October (www.gazeta.ru/column/lukyanov/946920.shtml).

—— 2007a. 'From Berlin to Munich', *Gazeta.ru*, 15 February (www.gazeta.ru/column/lukyanov/1377298.shtml).

—— 2007b. 'The never-ending construction of integration', *Gazeta.ru*, 18 January (www.gazeta.ru/column/lukyanov/1269504.shtml).

McDermott, Roger, 2004. 'Russia launches large-scale military exercises', *EDM*, 22 June (www.jamestown.org/edm/article.php?article_id=2368134).

—— 2006a. 'Kazakhstan boosting Caspian security', *EDM*, 23 May (www.jamestown.org/edm/article.php?article_id=2371108).

—— 2006b. 'Nazarbaev's Caspian security deals: What can Moscow offer?' *EDM*, 27 June (www.jamestown.org/edm/article.php?article_id=2371222).

—— 2007. 'Russian using CSTO to counterbalance NATO', *EDM*, 6 March (www.jamestown.org/edm/article.php?article_id=2371973).

McDermott, Roger, Pavel Baev and Alex Vatanka, 2002. 'Central Asian states: Split loyalties', *Jane's Defence Weekly*, 16 October, pp. 82–90.

McFaul, Michael A., 2001. *Russia's Unfinished Revolution: Political Change from Gorbachev to Putin*. Ithaca, NY: Cornell University Press.

—— 2002. 'Taking the Russia summit a step further', *New York Times*, 20 May.

—— 2006. 'The end of partnership', *Kommersant*, 11 May.

Main, Steven J., 2003. 'The strategic rocket forces, 1991–2002', pp. 99–123 in Anne C. Aldis and Roger N. McDermott (eds), *Russian Military Reform 1992–2002*. London: Frank Cass.

—— 2005. 'The bear, the peacock, the sturgeon, the eagle and the black, black oil: Contemporary regional power politics in the Caspian sea', Conflict Studies Research

214 *References*

Centre, Defence Academy of the UK, December (www.defac.ac.uk/colleges/ csrc/document-listings/caucasus/).

Makarkin, Aleksei, 2005. 'The Kovykta story', *Ezhednevny zhurnal*, 18 November (www.ej.ru/?a=note&id=2348).

—— 2006. 'The church myth in present-day Russia', *Ezhednevny zhurnal*, 24 April (www.ej.ru/?a=note&id=3627).

—— 2007a. 'Weak Alkhanov and triumphant Ramzan', *Ezhednevny zhurnal*, 13 February (www.ej.ru/?a=note&id=6113).

—— 2007b. 'Two chapels on one island', *Ezhednevny zhurnal*, 17 May (www. ej.ru/?a=note&id=7052).

Malashenko, Aleksei, 2003. 'Chechnya for internal and external consumption', *Briefing* of the Moscow Carnegie Center, September–October.

—— 2006. *How the Elections Were Held in Chechnya*. Moscow: Carnegie Center.

Mamadshoyev, Marat, 2000. 'The Central Asian insurgency raises questions about civilian sympathies and military capabilities', *Eurasia Insight*, 5 August (www. eurasianet.org/departments/insight/articles/eav082500.shtml).

Mamedov, Sohbet, 2006. 'Pentagon builds bridgeheads in Azerbaijan', *NVO*, 17 February.

Marat, Erika, 2006. *The Tulip Revolution: Kyrgyzstan One Year After*. Washington, DC: Jamestown Foundation.

Marchuk, Galina and Usnia Babaeva, 2003. 'Aliev Jr. tells the opposition to brush the streets', *Nezavisimaya gazeta*, 6 October.

Markedonov, Sergei, 2004. 'It is time to act not "concentrate"', *Nezavisimaya gazeta*, 20 December.

—— 2005a. 'Georgian challenge without a Russian response', *Polit.ru*, 30 November (www.polit.ru/analytics/2005/11/30/georgia.html).

—— 2005b. 'Terrorism in Dagestan will become problem no. 1', *Prognosis.ru*, 5 July (www.prognosis.ru/news/region/2005/7/5/markedonov.html).

—— 2007. 'The Russian effect of the Chechen castling', *Polit.ru*, 21 February (www.polit.ru/author/2007/02/21/putin_kadyrov.html).

Marten, Kimberly, 2005. 'Understanding the impact of K2 closure', *PONARS Memo* 401, Washington, DC: CSIS, December.

—— 2006. 'Disrupting the balance: Russian efforts to control Kazakhstan's oil', *PONARS Memo* 428, Washington, DC: CSIS, December.

Mastepanov, Aleksei and Yuri Shafranik, 2003. 'Current tasks of Russia's oil policy', *Mirovaya energeticheskaya politika*, September, pp. 36–39.

Mearsheimer, John and Stephen Walt, 2006. 'The Israel lobby', *London Review of Books*, 23 March.

Medovnikov, Dan, Stanislav Rozmirovich and Irik Imamutdinov, 2007. 'Elephants on a glade', *Expert*, 15 January.

Medvedev, Dmitri, 2005. 'As for the group struggle in the administration ... we are not the CPSU Central Committee ', interview with *Expert*, 4 April.

—— 2006. 'The common prosperity and the individual interests', interview with *Expert*, 24 July.

Medvedev, Sergei, 1999. 'A general theory of Russian space', pp. 15–43 in Jeremy Smith (ed.), *Beyond the Limits: The Concept of Space in Russian History and Culture*. Helsinki: Suomen.

Menon, Rajan, 2003. 'The new great game in Central Asia', *Survival*, vol. 45, no. 2, pp. 187–204.

References 215

Migranyan, Andranik, 2001. 'The Iranian test for Russian foreign policy', *Nezavisimaya gazeta*, 15 March.

Mikhailov, Andreai, Sergei Sokut and Dmitri Gornostaev, 2000. 'It will be hard to get the Taliban', *Nezavisimaya gazeta*, 24 May.

'Military fantasies on Iran', 2006. *New York Times*, 11 April.

'Military reform in the Russian Federation', 1997. Report of the Council on Foreign and Defense Policy, 12 July (www.svop.ru/live/materials.asp?m_id=6974).

Miller, Alexei, 2005. 'Empire and nation as imagined in Russian nationalism', *Polit.ru*, 31 March (www.polit.ru/lectures/2005/04/14/miller.html).

—— 2006. 'Yushchenko has nothing to lose', *Polit.ru*, 3 January (www.polit.ru/analytics/2006/01/03/miller.html).

—— 2007. 'Count Uvarov's triad', *Polit.ru*, 11 April (www.polit.ru/lectures/2007/04/11/uvarov.html).

Miller, Steven E., 2004. 'Moscow's military power: Russia's search for security in the age of transition', pp. 1–41 in Steven E. Miller and Dmitri Trenin (eds), *The Russian Military: Power and Policy*. Cambridge, MA, and London: The MIT Press.

Milov, Vladimir, 2005a. '$13 billion for football players', *Vedomosti*, 6 October.

—— 2005b. 'Gas aggression', *Vedomosti*, 15 December.

—— 2005c. 'The gas president', *Novaya gazeta*, 26 December.

—— 2006a. Interview with *Moscow echo*, 2 March (www.echo.msk.ru/interview/42109/).

—— 2006b. 'What do we want from the neighbors?' *Vedomosti*, 1 June.

—— 2006c. 'The masters of the pipes', *Novaya gazeta*, 27 July.

—— 2006d. 'The EU-Russia energy dialogue: Competititon versus monopolies', *Russie.Nei.Visions* 13, Paris: IFRI, September (www.ifri.org/frontDispatcher/ifri/recherche/russie_et_monde_post_sovi_tique_1040123098618/russie_cei_visions_1111748684650).

—— 2007a. 'The rise of state energy companies and its effect on oil & gas sectors in Russia', presentation at the International Petroleum Week, London, 13 February (www.milov.info/speech.php?id=442).

—— 2007b. 'The economic results of 2006 for the energy sector', presentation of the Institute of Energy Policy report, 18 January (www.milov.info/speech.php?id=421).

—— 2007c. 'The Belorussian mirror', *Vedomosti*, 10 January.

—— 2007d. 'What subsidies?' *Vedomosti*, 24 January.

Mintusov, Igor, 2005. 'Life after oil', *Gazeta.ru*, 27 December (www.gazeta.ru/comments/2005/12/21_x_503055.shtml).

Mir vokrug Rossii: 2017 – Kontury nedalekogo budushchego (World Around Russia: 2017 – The Contours of the Near Future), 2007. Moscow: Council on Foreign and Defense Policy.

Moe, Arild, 2006. 'Sjtokman-beslutningen: Forklaringer og implikasjoner' (The Shtokman decision: Explanations and implications), *Nordisk Østforum*, vol. 20, no. 4, pp. 389–403.

Moshes, Arkady, 2001. 'The Slav triangle: Ukraine and Belarus in Russian foreign policy in the 1990s', *Pro et Contra*, vol. 6, no. 1–2, pp. 107–121.

—— 2004a. 'Ukraine after Kuchma', *Russia in Global Affairs*, September–October, pp. 188–199.

—— 2004b. 'Intangible and virtual', *Moskovskie novosti*, 28 May.

—— 2006a. 'Change in the air in Ukraine', *Russia in Global Affairs*, April–June, pp. 142–155.

216   References

—— 2006b. 'Gas fist and national interest', *Gazeta.ru*, 28 December (www.gazeta.ru/comments/2006/12/28_a_1200572.shtml).

Mukhin, Vladimir, 2003a. 'Military industry survives by exporting arms', *Nezavisimaya gazeta*, 26 February.

—— 2003b. 'Russia defines new defense guidelines', *NVO*, 10 October.

—— 2004a. 'Russia promotes militarization of the Caspian', *NVO*, 20 December.

—— 2004b. 'Mostly special forces are fighting in Chechnya', *NVO*, 12 November.

—— 2006. 'Moscow and Minsk defend the Molotov-Ribbentrop Pact', *Nezavisimaya gazeta*, 19 June.

Mukhin, Vladimir, Igor Plugatarev and Vadim Solovyev, 2003. 'The symbol of Russian military might collapsed', *NVO*, 26 September.

Müller, Friedeman, 2000. 'Energy development and transport network cooperation in Central Asia and the South Caucasus', pp. 177–199 in Renata Dwan and Oleksandr Pavliuk (eds), *Building Security in the New States of Eurasia*, Armonk, NY, and London: M.E. Sharp.

Mustafaev, Rafael and Mihail Zygar, 2006. 'Sheikh from Moscow', *Kommersant*, 22 February.

Myasnikov, Viktor, 2005a. 'Defense expenditures grow but the deliveries of weapons stagnate', *NVO*, 28 August.

—— 2005b. 'The struggle for the defense order money heats up', *NVO*, 11 November.

—— 2006a. '*Bulava* dangerous for us', *NVO*, 13 January.

—— 2006b. 'The short flight of *Bulava*', *NVO*, 3 November.

—— 2006c. 'Another 365 hard days for the military industry', *NVO*, 29 December.

—— 2007a. 'Minister without uniform', *NVO*, 2 March.

—— 2007b. 'Politician on the rise is slowed down', *Nezavisimaya gazeta*, 16 March.

Myasnikov, Viktor and Aleksandr Grigoryev, 2006. 'Super-innovations of the chief of the general staff take no root in the troops', *NVO*, 20 October.

Myasnikov, Viktor and Vladimir Ivanov, 2007. 'Moscow and China will play war game', *Nezavisimaya gazeta*, 1 March.

Netreba, Petr, 2006. 'Ivanov day: Defense minister will form a parallel government', *Kommersant*, 21 March.

Netreba, Petr and Denis Rebrov, 2007. 'The PM has found a pipeline', *Kommersant*, 14 March.

Neumann, Iver B., 1996. *Russia and the Idea of Europe*. London: Routledge.

—— 2005. 'Russia as a great power', pp. 13–28 in Jakob Hedenskog *et al.* (eds), *Russia as a Great Power: Dimensions of Security under Putin*. London and New York: Routledge.

Nikitina, Larisa, Kseniya Veretennikova, Vera Sitnina and Mikhail Vorobyev, 2005. 'Objects of the Fedration', *Vremya novostei*, 20 July.

Nikitinsky, Leonid, 2007. 'Race of the courts: Strasbourg and Basmanny', *Novaya gazeta*, 26 March.

Nikolaev, Andrei, 1998. *Na Perelome: Zapiski Russkogo Generala* (At the Break-Point: Diary of a Russian General). Moscow: Sovremennyi Pisatel.

—— 2002. 'We are in a terrorist war', *Nezavisimaya gazeta*, 15 November.

Nikolaeva, Anna, 2006. 'Endless integration', *Vedomosti*, 25 January.

Nikonov, Vyacheslav, 2002. 'Back to the concert, global this time', *Russia in Global Affairs*, November–December, pp. 78–99.

'Non-competetive advantage', 2006. *Kommersant*, 13 February.

'NORAD intercepts Russian aircraft', 2006. *NORAD Newsroom*, 29 September (www.norad.mil/News/2006/092906.html).

References 217

'Not a cold war, but a cold tiff', 2007. *The Economist*, 15 February.

'Not enough for everyone', 2006. *Kommersant*, 27 April.

Novikov, Vladimir, 2005. 'Georgian military doctrine descended from the mountains', *Kommersant*, 29 November.

Novikova, Evgeniya, 2006. 'FSB in *Rosneft*: Everybody needs money', *Expert*, 14 September.

Novoprudsky, Semyon, 2006. 'Political sexual orientation', *Gazeta.ru*, 5 May (www.gazeta.ru/column/novoprudsky/631903.shtml).

Odom, William E., 1998. *The Collapse of the Soviet Military*. New Haven, CT: Yale University Press.

Olcott, Martha Brill, 2002. *Kazakhstan: Unfulfilled Promise*. Washington, DC: CEIP.

O'Lear, Shannon, 2002. 'Armenia, Azerbaijan and the United States: Power shift in the Caucasus or business as usual?' *Swords and Plowshares*, vol. XIV, no. 1, pp. 13–17 (www.acdis.uiuc.edu/Research/S&Ps/2002-Su/S&P-Su2002.pdf).

Oliker, Olga and Thomas S. Szayna, 2003. 'Sources of conflicts and paths to US involvement', pp. 307–358 in Olga Oliker and Thomas S. Szayna (eds), *Faultlines of Conflict in Central Asia and the South Caucasus*. Santa Monica, CA: RAND.

Orehin, Petr and Anna Skornyakova, 2003. 'GAZPROM tries to save the Blue Stream', *Nezavisimaya gazeta*, 26 August.

Oreshkin, Dmitri, 2005. 'Russia could rely on nobody in Chechnya', *Kavkaz-Forum*, 22 August (www.kavkaz-forum.ru/politic/12412.html).

Orlov, Vladimir A. and Miriam Fugfugosh, 2006. 'The G8 Strelna summit and Russia's national power', *The Washington Quarterly*, vol. 29, no. 3, pp. 35–48.

Orlov, Vladimir A. and Alexander Vinnikov, 2005. 'The great guessing game: Russia and the Iranian nuclear issue', *The Washington Quarterly*, vol. 28, no. 2, pp. 49–66.

O'Rourke, Breffni, 2006. 'Caspian: EU invests in new pipeline', *RFE/RL Newsline*, 27 June (www.rferl.org/features/features_Article.aspx?m=06&y=2006&id=03531B6D-AD4F-4488-B54D-177E9411EB42).

Ostrovsky, Arkady, 2006. 'Gazprom acts as lever in Putin's power play', *Financial Times*, 13 March.

Ostrovsky, Arkady and Isabel Gorst, 2005. 'TNK-BP chief attacks Russia's uncertain investment climate', *Financial Times*, 13 April.

'Overview of Russian Foreign Policy', 2007. Foreign Ministry of the Russian Federation (www.mid.ru/brp_4.nsf/sps/690A2BAF968B1FA4C32572B100304A6E).

Panfilova, Viktoria, 2005. 'Islam Karimov: In the empire, we were considered second class', *Nezavisimaya gazeta*, 14 January.

—— 2006. 'Logical drift towards NATO', *Nezavisimaya gazeta*, 1 December.

Panyushkin, Valery, 2006. 'Political substance', *Kommersant*, 10 July.

Parkhomenko, Sergei, 2006. 'The meaning of events', *Moscow echo*, 28 April (www.echo.msk.ru/programs/sut/43198/).

Pavlovsky, Gleb, 2003. 'On the negative consequences of the "summer offensive" of the minority group opposed to the course of the President', *Russkii zhurnal*, 2 September (http://old.russ.ru/politics/20030902_gp.html).

—— 2005a. 'A European project without Russia: A new draft', *Russkii zhurnal*, 16 June (http://old.russ.ru/culture/20050616_pavl.html).

—— 2005b. 'On the planning of the 2007–2015 election cycle', *Russkii zhurnal*, 27 February (http://old.russ.ru/culture/20050227_gp.html).

—— 2006a. 'It was a deliberately nasty statement', interview with *Strana.ru*, 4 May (www.strana.ru/stories/01/11/14/2017/280734.html).

218   References

—— 2006b. 'Belarus is a nerve point of the European integration', *Kreml.org*, 15 February (http://kreml.org/opinions/110524439).

—— 2006c. 'In the neutral zone', interview with *Nezavisimaya gazeta*, 27 June.

Plugatarev, Igor and Anatoly Nezvanov, 2002. 'Three days that have shaken Belarus and Russia', *Nezavisimaya gazeta*, 20 June.

Petrov, Nikolai, 2001. 'Policization versus democratization: 20 months of Putin's "federal" reform', *PONARS Memo* 241, Washington, DC: CSIS, December.

—— 2002. 'Seven faces of Putin's Russia', *Security Dialogue*, vol. 33, no. 1, pp. 73–91.

—— 2004. 'Putin's anti-federal reform-2: Back to the USSR', *PONARS Memo* 339, Washington, DC: CSIS, November.

Petrovskaya, Yulia, 2004. 'Diplomacy of nuclear incontinence', *Nezavisimaya gazeta*, 18 November.

Piontkovsky, Andrei, 2005. 'The mistake of engineer Khodorkovsky', *Grani.ru*, 21 October (www.grani.ru/opinion/piontkovsky/m.96899.html).

—— 2006. 'Hard to swallow', *Grani.ru*, 17 May (www.grani.ru/opinion/piontkovsky/m.105729.html).

—— 2007. 'The end of history Russian style', *Grani.ru*, 2 March (www.grani.ru/opinion/piontkovsky/m.118752.html).

Pipes, Richard, 1996. 'Russia's past, Russia's future', *Commentary*, June 1996.

Plugatarev, Igor, 2004. 'Defense ministry has enough money only for the "inner circle"', *NVO*, 12 November.

—— 2005a. 'The first five years of CIS anti-terror', *NVO*, 24 June.

—— 2005b. 'Kant airbase: Control over the whole Central Asia', *NVO*, 30 September.

—— 2005c. 'Dushanbe does not have enough forces for guarding the Pyanj border', *NVO*, 2 December.

—— 2006a. 'Reliable military protection for oil', *Nezavisimaya gazeta*, 1 June.

—— 2006b. 'Brinksmanship on the edge of war', *NVO*, 21 July.

—— 2006c. 'General prosecutor made peace with the defense ministry', *NVO*, 11 August.

—— 2007a. 'Accomplishments and Augean stables of Sergei Ivanov', *NVO*, 2 March.

—— 2007b. 'Companies of suicide victims are the results of hundreds of tragedies', *NVO*, 23 March.

Plugatarev, Igor and Viktor Myasnikov, 2006. 'Without presidential efforts the air industry would not unite', *NVO*, 25 August.

Plugatarev, Igor and Anatoly Tsyganok, 2005. 'Russia builds a new army of the old type', *NVO*, 25 March.

Podvig, Pavel, 2005. 'US wants to take over Russian nuclear arsenal?' *Russian Strategic Nuclear Forces*, 11 February (http://russianforces.org/blog/2005/02/us_wants_to_take_over_russian.shtml).

—— 2006. 'Speaking of nuclear primacy', *Russian Strategic Nuclear Forces*, 10 March (http://russianforces.org/blog/2006/03/speaking_of_nuclear_primacy.shtml).

—— 2007. 'Missiles old and new', *Russian Strategic Nuclear Forces*, 28 February (http://russianforces.org/blog/2007/02/missiles_old_and_new.shtml).

Poe, Marshall T., 2003. *The Russian Moment in World History*, Princeton, NJ: Princeton University Press.

Pogrebinsky, Mikhail, 2005. *Oranzhevaya Revoliutsiya: Versii, Khronika, Dokumenty* (The Orange Revolution: Versions, Chronicle, Documents), Kiev: Optima.

Pokrovsky, Aleksandr, 2004. *Rasstrelyat!* (Firing Squad), St. Petersburg: Inapress.

Polat, Necati, 2002. *Boundary Issues in Central Asia*, Ardsley, NY: Transnational Publishers.

References 219

Politkovskaya, Anna, 2004. 'The country of spreading rakes', *Novaya gazeta*, 28 June.

Politov, Yuri, 2005. 'Resource exchange: Putin will try to reunify Cyprus', *Izvestia*, 19 July.

Polivanov, Aleksandr, 2006. 'There is no more cheap gas', *Lenta.ru*, 30 June (http://lenta.ru/articles/2006/06/30/turkmengaz/).

Pollack, Kenneth M., 2004. *The Persian Puzzle: The Conflict Between Iran and America*. New York: Random House.

Poroskov, Nikolai, 2003. 'The Potemkin division', *Vremya novostei*, 25 December.

—— 2006. 'The "Blue" side starts and everybody loses', *Vremya novostei*, 27 July.

Poroskov, Nikolai and Vladimir Shpak, 2003. 'Gennady Troshev is back in the center of an intrigue', *Vremya novostei*, 19 February.

Portnikov, Vitlay, 2001. 'Putin got access to money', *Grani.ru*, 30 May (www.grani.ru/Politics/Russia/m.3293.html).

Posen, Barry R., 2006. 'We can live with a nuclear Iran', *New York Times*, 27 February.

Pravosudov, Sergei, 2001. 'Aliev turned to the northern neighbor', *Nezavisimaya gazeta*, 13 January.

Privalov, Aleksandr, 2005a. 'On the future *Yukos* case', *Expert*, 4 April.

—— 2005b. 'On the Notre Dame mosque', *Expert*, 7 November.

—— 2005c. 'On the gas hysterics', *Expert*, 12 December.

—— 2006a. 'On Voltaire, Rousseau, and prosecutor Ustinov', *Expert*, 18 April.

—— 2006b. 'On the speech of vice president Cheney', *Expert*, 8 May.

—— 2006c. 'On national projects', *Expert*, 6 March.

—— 2007. 'On the Slavic assortment', *Expert*, 26 February.

'Prospects for Soviet oil production', 1977. ER77–10270, Washington, DC: CIA, April.

'Prospects and plans for armament modernization', 2000. Interview with General Anatoly Sitnov, *Krasnaya zvezda*, 10 June.

'PSG secures lead role in US$2.5 billion Transcaspian pipeline project', 1999. *Bechtel News Releases*, 19 February (www.bechtel.com/newsarticles/190.asp).

Puchnin, Vladimir, 2006. 'The sea power comes to the end', *NVO*, 22 December.

Putin, Vladimir V., 1999. 'Russia on the threshold of a new millennium'. Originally published on the official website www.government.gov.ru; currently available in Russian in the Web archive of *Nezavisimaya gazeta*, 30 December (www.ng.ru/politics/1999–12–30/4_millenium.html).

—— 2000. 'The state will pay its debts', speech in Nizhny Novgorod on 21 March, *NVO*, 31 March.

—— 2003a. Address to the Federal Assembly, 16 May.

—— 2003b. Concluding remarks at a meeting with the leading personnel of the Russian Armed Forces, 2 October.

—— 2004a. Address to the Federal Assembly, 26 May.

—— 2004b. Press-conference with the Russian and foreign media, 23 December.

—— 2005a. Opening address at the Security Council session on Russia's role in guaranteeing international energy security, 22 December.

—— 2005b. President's live television and radio dialogue with the nation, 27 September.

—— 2005c. Press statement and answers to questions following talks with President of Israel Moshe Katsav, 28 April.

—— 2005d. Speech at the meeting with the Cabinet Members, the Heads of the Federal Assembly, and State Council Members, 5 September.

—— 2005e. Address to the Federal Assembly, 25 April.

220 *References*

—— 2006a. 'The upcoming G8 summit in St. Petersburg: Challenges, opportunities and responsibility', 1 March.

—— 2006b. Address to the Federal Assembly, 10 May.

—— 2006c. Meeting with the leaders of the news agencies of the G8 countries, 2 June.

—— 2006d. 'SCO – a new model of successful international cooperation', 14 June.

—— 2007a. Speech at the Munich Conference on Security Policy, 10 February.

—— 2007b. Excerpts from the transcript of the meeting with cabinet ministers, 9 January.

—— 2007c. '50 years of the European integration and Russia', 25 March.

—— 2007d. Address to the Federal Assembly, 26 April.

Radzikhovsky, Leonid, 2006a. 'Race/class', *Ezhednevny zhurnal*, 12 April (www.ej.ru/?a=note&id=3524).

—— 2006b. 'Anarcho-oligarch', *Ezhednevny zhurnal*, 24 January (www.ej.ru/?a=note&id=2853).

—— 2006c. 'Strong castling', *Ezhednevny zhurnal*, 29 June (www.ej.ru/?a=note&id=4145).

—— 2007. 'February – crooked roads', *Rossiiskaya gazeta*, 6 March.

Rastopshin, Mikhail, 2007. 'Strategic loss of pace', *NVO*, 9 February.

Ratnikova, Natalya, 2005. 'Friend Silvio turned down the deal with GAZPROM', *Politcom.ru*, 21 October (http://politcom.ru/article.php?id=1548).

Rebrov, Denis, 2005. 'Black line to the under-heaven', *Vremya novostei*, 16 December.

Reddaway, Peter and Dmitry Glinsky, 2001. *The Tragedy of Russia's Reforms: Market Bolshevism Against Democracy*. Washington, DC: US Institute of Peace.

Remnick, David, 2004. 'Prisoner of the Caucasus', *The New Yorker*, 20 September.

'Revisiting Putin's soul', 2006. *New York Times*, 4 December.

Rice, Condoleezza, 2006. Remarks at the State Department Correspondents Association breakfast, 5 January (www.state.gov/secretary/rm/2006/58725.htm).

Roberts, John, 2004. 'Pipeline politics', pp. 77–89 in Shirin Akiner (ed.), *The Caspian: Politics, Energy and Security*. London and New York: RoutledgeCurzon.

Rogov, Sergei, 2000. 'Putting the stake on the nuclear shield', *NVO*, 4 August.

Romanov, Igor, 2007. 'Putin has chosen GLONASS', *Nezavisimaya gazeta*, 13 March.

Romanova, Lyudmila, 2002. 'Five president, six opinions and one scandal', *Nezavisimaya gazeta*, 25 April.

Romanova, Lyudmila and Vladimir Mukhin, 2001. 'Putin and Schröder meet in St. Petersburg', *Nezavisimaya gazeta*, 10 April.

Ross, Michael L., 2001. 'Does oil hinder democracy?' *World Politics*, vol. 53, no. 3, pp. 325–361.

Rotar, Igor, 2006. 'Resurgence of Islamic radicalism in Tajikistan's Ferghana Valley', *Terrorism Focus*, 18 April (www.jamestown.org/terrorism/news/article.php?articleid=2369965).

Rozhkova, Maria, 2005. 'I would like to return to Russia', interview with Yakov Goldovsky, *Vedomsti*, 31 October.

Rubanov, Ivan, 2006. 'China is there to stay', *Expert*, 27 March.

Rubanov, Ivan and Dmitri Sivakov, 2005. 'We want more', *Expert*, 10 October.

—— 2006. 'Skillfully laid trap', *Expert*, 23 January.

Rudensky, Nikolai, 2006. 'Verified democracy', *Grani.ru*, 23 November (www.grani.ru/opinion/rudensky/m.114794.html).

Rudneva, Elena and Anna Nikolaeva, 2006. 'Let's be like Che', *Vedomosti*, 12 July.

'Russia discontinues free supply of arms to Afghanistan', 2005. *Vremya novostei*, 10 November.

References 221

'Russia has no intelligence satellites on orbit', 2006. *Lenta.ru*, 3 May (http://lenta.ru/news/2006/05/03/satellit/).

'Russians on the death of Shamil Basaev, the leader of Chechen separatists', 2006. Levada Center poll, 19 July (www.levada.ru/press/2006071902.html).

'Russians on the "national projects"', 2006. Levada Center poll, 27 September (www.levada.ru/press/2006092700.html).

Rutland, Peter, 1996. 'Russia's natural gas leviathan', *Transition*, 3 May, pp. 6–13.

—— 2003. 'Russia's response to U.S. regional influence', pp. 27–50 in *NBR Analysis: Regional Power Plays in the Caucasus and Central Asia* (www.nbr.org/publications/analysis/pdf/vol14no4.pdf).

Ryabov, Andrei, 2006. 'Power and powerlessness of "petro-state"', *Gazeta.ru*, 18 January (www.gazeta.ru/comments/2006/01/17_x_519295.shtml).

—— 2007. 'There is no cost-free hegemony', *Gazeta.ru*, 10 January (www.gazeta.ru/comments/2007/01/09_a_1238751.shtml).

'Ryazan blue berets get a gun-armed APC', 2006. *Lenta.ru*, 20 June (http://lenta.ru/news/2006/06/20/vdv/).

Rybina, Yulia, 2006. 'Direct line with distortions in some places', *Kommersant-Vlast*, 30 October.

Ryklin, Aleksandr, 2005. 'We are losing it', *Novaya gazeta*, 14 July.

Ryzhkov, Vladimir, 2006. 'The main extremists are in the Kremlin', interview with *Novaya gazeta*, 27 July.

Rzayev, Shahin, 2003. 'Ilham election ends in violence', *IWPR CRS*, 17 October (www.iwpr.net/?p=crs&s=f&o=159347&apc_state=henicrs2003).

'Saakashvili's Ajara success: Repeatable elsewhere in Georgia?', 2004. *Europe Briefing* 34, Brussels: International Crisis Group, 18 August.

Safronov, Ivan, 2006. 'Russian spies back into orbit', *Kommersant*, 5 May.

Saikal, Amin, 2000. 'The role of outside actors in Afghanistan', *Middle East Policy*, vol. 7, no. 4, pp. 50–57.

Sakwa, Richard, 2004. *Putin: Russia's Choice*. London and New York: Routledge.

Samarina, Aleksandra, 2005. 'The West was asked to become more civilized', *Nezavisimaya gazeta*, 24 August.

Samedova, Evlaliya and Oksana Gavshina, 2005. 'Double armor for Gazprom', *Nezavisimaya gazeta*, 28 September.

Satpaev, Dosum, 2006. 'The duo of bear and snow leopard', *Nezavisimaya gazeta*, 11 December.

Savitskaya, Irina, 2004. 'What the army will get?' *Polit.ru*, 26 May (www.polit.ru/country/2004/05/24/order.html).

'SCO and the "great game": Where the Russian pipelines will go', 2006. *America-Russia.net*, 10 June (www.america-russia.net/eng/business/120429934?user_session=f875810c7646564e601660160fb3ac56).

Sedov, Lev, 2005. 'Transformations in the army as reflected in the public opinion', overview of the Levada Center polls, 7 September (www.levada.ru/press/2005090701.html).

—— 2006. 'The country and the world', overview of the Levada Center polls, 6 May (www.levada.ru/press/2006050600.html).

Sergeev, Igor, 2002. 'Agreements with US are within reach', interview with *NVO*, 8 February.

Shaffer, Brenda, 2001. 'Partners in need: The strategic relationship of Russia and Iran', *Policy Paper* 57, Washington, DC: Institute for Near East Policy.

222   References

Shahinoglu, Emin, Olga Mazaeva and Anna Skornyakova, 2005. 'Gas wars in the CIS space', *Nezavisimaya gazeta*, 13 January.

Shahnazaryan, Artur, 2005. 'The mirage of Kashagan', *Expert*, 3 October.

Sharavin, Aleksandr, 2005. 'Thirteen lost years: It is easier to form a new army than to reorganize the one we have', *NVO*, 23 December.

Sheglova, Tatyana, 2006. 'Sovereign philology', *Lenta.ru*, 13 September (http://lenta.ru/articles/2006/09/13/surkov/).

Shermatova, Sanobar, 2001. 'Working on past mistakes', *Moskovskie novosti*, 16–21 January.

Shevtsova, Lilia, 2003. *Putin's Russia*. Washington, DC: CEIP.

—— 2005. 'Russia 2005: The logic of retreat', *Nezavisimaya gazeta*, 25 January.

—— 2006a. 'Crisis of the system is inevitable', *Polit.ru*, 12 January (www.polit.ru/analytics/2006/01/12/shevts2.html).

—— 2006b. 'Transfer of power: The elite breaks the hermetic seal', *Vedomosti*, 31 July.

—— 2007. 'We are present at the end of the life cycle of this political regime', interview with *Polit.ru*, 19 March (www.polit.ru/analytics/2007/03/19/shevtsova.html).

Shleinov, Roman, 2006. 'Who is left on the pipe', *Novaya gazeta*, 16 January.

Shlykov, Vitaly, 2000. 'Does Russia need the general staff?' *Voenny Vestnik*, no. 7, October (www.mfit.ru/defensive/vestnik/vestnik7_1.html).

—— 2001. 'Potemkin complex', *Itogi*, 19 June.

—— 2004. 'The economics of defense in Russia and the legacy of structural militatization', pp. 157–182 in Steven E. Miller and Dmitri Trenin (eds), *The Russian Military: Power and Policy*. Cambridge, MA, and London: The MIT Press.

—— 2005. 'Russian defense economy and structural militarization', *Ezhednevny zhurnal*, 24 January (www.ej.ru/experts/entry/10).

Shmelev, Nikolai P., 1999. 'On the consensus in the Russian economic and social policy', *Voprosy Ekonomiki*, no. 8, pp. 49–63.

Shmelev, Nikolai P. and Vladimir Popov, 1989. *The Turning Point: Revitalizing the Soviet Economy*. New York: Doubleday.

Shokhina, Ekaterina, 2003. 'The space of unfriendliness', *Expert*, 29 September.

—— 2007. 'Oil collapse', *Expert*, 13 April.

Shuvalov, Igor, 2006. 'In the circle of light', interview with *Moscow echo*, 15 July (www.echo.msk.ru/programs/sorokina/44853/).

Sidorov, Dmitri, 2007. 'Russia is targeted in a cartel operation', *Kommersant*, 4 April.

Silitski, Vitali, 2005. 'Internal developments in Belarus', pp. 25–45 in Dov Lynch (ed.), *Changing Belarus*, Chaillot Paper No. 85, Paris: ISS, November.

Sinelnikov, Sergei G., 1995. *Bydzhetnyi krizis v Rossii: 1985–1995* (Budget Crisis in Russia: 1985–1995). Moscow: Eurasia.

Sivakov, Dmitri, 2006. 'Sorry, Russia – and farewell', *Expert*, 30 October.

Skornyakova, Anna, 2006. 'Russia has found a manager for CPC', *Kommersant*, 13 January.

Smirnov, Andrei, 2005. 'Kremlin appoints new government in Karachaevo-Cherkessia', *EDM*, 16 February (www.jamestown.org/edm/article.php?article_id=2369264).

Smith, Mark A., 2002. 'Russia and Turkey', *CSRS Paper* F80, Sandhurst: Conflict Studies Research Centre, September.

'Social-political blackout', 2005. *Gazeta.ru*, 26 May (www.gazeta.ru/comments/2005/05/26_e_291253.shtml).

References 223

'Social-political situation in Russia in November 2005', 2005. Levada Center poll, 8 December (www.levada.ru/press/2005120801.html).

'Social-political situation in Russia in June 2006', 2006. Levada Center poll, 29 June (www.levada.ru/press/2006062901.html).

'Social-political situation in Russia in January–February 2007', 2007. Levada Center poll, 7 March (www.levada.ru/press/2007030702.html).

Socor, Vlad, 2005. 'CIS summit: Decorative yet acrimonious', *EDM*, 12 May (www.jamestown.org/edm/article.php?article_id=2369746).

—— 2006a. 'GAZPROM squeezing Belarus', *EDM*, 7 April (www.jamestown.org/edm/article.php?article_id=2370959).

—— 2006b. 'Uzbekistan accedes to Collective Security Treaty Organization', *EDM*, 27 June (www.jamestown.org/edm/article.php?article_id=2371223).

—— 2006c. 'Russia augmenting air base in Kyrgyzstan', *EDM*, 21 February (www.jamestown.org/edm/article.php?article_id=2370794).

—— 2006d. 'Seven Russian challenges to the West's energy security', *EDM*, 6 September (www.jamestown.org/edm/article.php?article_id=2371410).

Sokolov, Boris, 2006. 'The Caucasus will be given to the "enemies"', *Prognosis.ru*, 15 February (www.prognosis.ru/news/region/2006/2/15/sokolov.html).

—— 2007. 'Lies in the back of the revolution', *Grani.ru*, 15 March (www.grani.ru/Society/History/m.119356.html).

Sokov, Nikolai, 2000a. 'Kosovo syndrome and the great nuclear debate of 2000', *PONARS Memo* 181, Cambridge, MA: Harvard University, November.

—— 2000b. 'Denuclearization of Russian defense policy?' *CNS Report*, 17 July (www.cns.miis.edu/pubs/reports/denuke.htm).

—— 2002. 'Quod Licet Iovi: Preemptive use of military force in Russian foreign policy', *PONARS Memo* 254, Washington, DC: CSIS, October.

—— 2003. 'Russian ministry of defense's new policy paper: The nuclear angle', *CNS Report*, 10 October (www.cns.miis.edu/pubs/reports/sok1003.htm).

—— 2004. 'Military exercises in Russia: Naval deterrence failures compensated by strategic rocket success', *CNS Research Story*, 24 February (www.cns.miis.edu/pubs/week/040224.htm).

—— 2007. 'Second thoughts about a first strike', *Non-Proliferation Review*, vol. 14, no. 1, pp. 139–147.

Sokut, Sergei, 1999. 'Russia's priority state interest', *NVO*, 7 May.

—— 2002a. 'The military return to the Caspian', *NVO*, 16 August.

—— 2002b. 'We will deter terrorists from Bishkek', *NVO*, 6 December.

—— 2002c. 'Defense industry goes into a free cruise', *NVO*, 29 November.

Soldatov, Andrei, 2006. 'Presidential administration will keep an eye on Lubyanka', *Novaya gazeta*, 20 February.

Solovyev, Vadim, 2002. 'It is easier to build a new army that to reform the existing one', *Nezavisimaya gazeta*, 12 September.

—— 2004. 'The north Caucasus: Another 22 June 1941', *NVO*, 25 June.

Solovyev, Vadim and Oleg Elensky, 2004. 'Defense minister loses the trust of the Kremlin', *NVO*, 11 June.

Solovyev, Vadim and Vladimir Ivanov, 2006. 'Quiet mutiny in the officer corps', *NVO*, 2 June.

Solovyev, Vadim and Vitaly Tsimbal, 2007. 'State plans in the military sphere remain non-transparent', *NVO*, 16 March.

Solovyev, Vladimir, 2005. 'The goal justifies the special means', *Kommersant*, 24 June.

224 References

Solovyev, Vladimir and Aleksandr Sidorenko, 2006a. 'Raw materials and democratization', *Kommersant*, 7 June.

—— 2006b. 'Ukraine has found an exit from the CIS', *Kommersant*, 6 May.

Solzhenitsyn, Aleksandr, 2007. 'Thoughts about the February revolution', *Rossiiskaya gazeta*, 27 February.

Sorokin, Vladimir, 2006. *Den oprichnika* (Day of the Oprichnik), Moscow: Zakharov.

Sotsialisticheskie strany i strany kapitlizma v 1986 g (Socialist Countries and Capitalist States in 1986), 1987. Moscow: Goskomstat.

Soviet Military Power, 1981. Washington, DC: US Department of Defense.

Starobin, Paul, 2001. 'Give Gazprom a fresh start, President Putin', *Business Week*, 4 June.

Starr, Frederick S., 2005a. 'A partnership for Central Asia', *Foreign Affairs*, vol. 84, no. 4, pp. 164–178.

Starr, Frederick S., 2005b. 'The Baku–Tbilisi–Ceyhan pipeline: School of modernity', pp. 7–16 in Frederick S. Starr and Svante E. Cornell (eds), *The Baku–Tbilisi–Ceyhan Pipeline: Oil Window to the West*. Washington, DC: Johns Hopkins University.

Statsky, Vladimir, 2003. 'The minefield of the head of the military budgeting', *NVO*, 21 November.

Steele, Jonathan, 2004. 'Ukraine's post-modern coup d'etat', *Guardian*, 26 November.

Stepanov, Andrei, 2007. 'A Caucasian radar', *Rossiiskaya gazeta*, 3 March.

Stepanova, Ekaterina, 2005. 'Russia's approach to the fight against terrorism', pp. 301–322 in Jakob Hedenskog, Vilhelm Konnander, Bertil Nygren, Ingmar Oldberg and Christer Pursiainen (eds), *Russia as a Great Power: Dimensions of Security under Putin*. London: Routledge.

Stern, Jonathan P., 2005. *The Future of Russian Gas and GAZPROM*. Oxford: Oxford University Press for the Oxford Institute for Energy Studies.

Stiglitz, Joseph, 2002. *Globalization & Its Discontents*. New York: W.W. Norton.

Strokan, Sergei, 2007. 'The price of the question', *Kommersant*, 19 March.

Sukhov, Ivan, 2005. 'Real time regime', *Vremya novostei*, 18 July.

Surkov, Vladislav, 2004. 'Putin strengthens the state not himself', interview with *Komsomolskaya pravda*, 28 September.

—— 2006a. 'Sovereignty is a political synonym of competitiveness', lecture for activists of *United Russia*, 7 February (www.test.edinros.ru/news.html?id=111148).

—— 2006b. 'Nationalization of the future', *Expert*, 20 November.

Sutela, Pekka, 2005. 'How much Russian energy is good for Europe?' presentation at the Carnegie Endowment for International Peace, 10 November (www.carnegie endowment.org/events/index.cfm?fa=eventDetail&id=829&&prog=zru).

Svechin, Aleksandr, 2002/1937. *Evolytsiya Voennogo Iskusstva* (Evolution of the Military Art). Moscow: Akademicheskii proekt.

Talyshli, Almman, 2005. 'Rumsfeld's Baku trip stirs controversy', *Eurasia Insight*, 13 April (www.eurasianet.org/departments/insight/articles/eav041305.shtml).

Tatarinov, Dmitri, 2005. 'Energy power will replace military might', *Kommersant*, 23 December.

Tavernise, Sabrina, 2002. 'In Russia, executive returns and a company disappears', *New York Times*, 26 September.

Taylor, Brian, 2001. 'Russia's passive army: Rethinking military coups', *Comparative Political Studies*, vol. 34, no. 8, pp. 924–952.

—— 2003. 'The Soviet military and the disintegration of the USSR', *Journal of Cold War Studies*, vol. 5, no. 1, pp. 17–66.

References 225

Tendler, Steward and Daniel McGrory, 2006. 'Spy's murder prompts fears over plans for dealing with "dirty bombs" attacks', *The Times*, 11 December.

Tenet, George J., 2001. Remarks of the Director of Central Intelligence at the Conference on CIA's Analysis of the Soviet Union, 1947–1991, Princeton, NJ: Princeton University, 8 March (www.fas.org/irp/cia/product/dci_speech_03082001.html).

'The head of Ukrainian MFA called the agreement with GAZPROM the "fiasco of Russian policy"', 2006. *Lenta.ru*, 4 January (www.lenta.ru/news/2006/01/04/fiasco/).

'The nationalist resurgence', 2006. *The Economist*, 2 March.

'The state and the oligarchy', 2003. The Report of the Council on National Strategy, *Komsomolskaya pravda*, 3 June.

'The supplier of energy security', 2005. *Expert*, 26 December.

'Thou shalt not steal', 2006. *The Economist*, 27 May.

Timchenko, Svyatoslav, 2006. 'Large caliber for the Caspian', *NVO*, 3 April.

Timmermann, Heinz, 2006. 'The special case of Belarus', *Russia in Global Affairs*, March–April, pp. 96–105.

Timofeeva, Olga, 2006. 'Two states, one army', *Izvestia*, 27 June.

Todres, Vladimir, 2006. 'Jupiter, you are angry', *Vedomosti*, 28 April.

Tomberg, Igor, 2007. 'Economic pluses and political minuses of a "gas OPEC"', *RIA-Novosti*, 30 January (www.rian.ru/analytics/20070130/59913519.html).

Topalov, Aleksei, 2007. 'Rosneft takes a loan to bury Yukos', *Gazeta.ru*, 20 March (www.gazeta.ru/2007/03/20/oa_234340.shtml).

Torbakov, Igor, 2002. 'Eurasian idea could bring together erstwhile enemies Turkey and Russia', *Eurasia Insight*, 18 March (www.eurasianet.org/departments/insight/articles/eav031802.shtml).

—— 2004. 'Russian policy-makers struggle to respond to political changes in Georgia', *Eurasia Insight*, 8 January (www.eurasianet.org/departments/insight/articles/eav010804.shtml).

—— 2006. 'Russia watches wearily as Chinese-Turkmen economic cooperation expands', *Eurasia Insight*, 29 August (www.eurasianet.org/departments/insight/articles/eav082906.shtml).

Trenin, Dmitri, 2003. 'Southern watch: Russia's policy in Central Asia', *Journal of International Affairs*, vol. 56, no. 2, pp. 119–131.

—— 2004a. 'Moscow's *Realpolitik*: Russia locks itself in the post-Soviet space', *Nezavisimaya gazeta*, 9 February.

—— 2004b. 'Gold eagle, red star', pp. 217–232 in Steven E. Miller and Dmitri Trenin (eds), *The Russian Military: Power and Policy*. Cambridge, MA, and London: The MIT Press.

—— 2004c. 'Somebody wants a third world war', *Novaya gazeta*, 29 November.

—— 2005. 'Moscow's relations with Belarus: An awkward ally', pp. 67–78 in Dov Lynch (ed.), *Changing Belarus*, Chaillot Paper No. 85, Paris: ISS, November.

—— 2006a. 'Former potential partner', *Gazeta.ru*, 18 May (www.gazeta.ru/comments/2006/05/16_x_640342.shtml).

—— 2006b. 'Putin's deal with the US has failed', interview with *Polit.ru*, 6 July (www.polit.ru/analytics/2006/07/06/trenin.html).

—— 2006c. 'Developments in Russia and their potential impact on the future of US-Russian relationship', testimony for the US Senate Foreign Relation Committee, 29 June (www.carnegie.ru/en/pubs/media/74442.htm).

226   References

Trenin, Dmitri V. and Alexei V. Malashenko, 2004. *Russia's Restless Frontier: The Chechnya Factor in Post-Soviet Russia*. Washington, DC: CEIP.

Tretyakov, Vitaly, 2003. 'It is America's funeral', *Rossiiskaya gazeta*, 21 March.

—— 2004a. 'Putin's choice as Russia's choice', *Rossiiskaya gazeta*, 17 September.

—— 2004b. 'Bendukidze's mission: Smart move of Georgian leadership', *Rossiiskaya gazeta*, 3 June.

Tsimbal, Vitaly, 2004a. 'Reform is a slip of tongue', *Polit.ru*, 12 February (www.polit.ru/country/2004/02/12/tzimbl.html).

—— 2004b. 'The military secret of inefficiency', *Gazeta.ru*, 30 September (www.gazeta.ru/comments/2004/09/29_x_178807.shtml).

Tsyganok, Anatoly, 2004. 'Danger! Explosion! Pipeline! On Russia's energy security', *Globalrus.ru*, 15 December (www.globalrus.ru/comments/139362/).

—— 2005a. 'National features of Russia's defense industry', *Polit.ru*, 2 September (www.polit.ru/analytics/2005/09/02/wic.html).

—— 2005b. 'State defense illusion instead of state defense order', *Polit.ru*, 11 November (www.polit.ru/analytics/2005/11/11/zakaz.html).

—— 2006. 'Military *kliykva* for the Russian society', *Polit.ru*, 12 May (www.polit.ru/author/2006/05/12/poslanie_voen.html).

Tsypin, Aron, 2004. 'How the state defense order will be spent', *Polit.ru*, 21 September (www.polit.ru/economy/2004/09/21/opk.html).

'Two geopolitical shifts: Oil', 2002. *Jane's Foreign Report* 2691, 13 June.

Tymenev, Yuri, 2002. 'Russia and world oil prices', *Mirovaya energeticheskaya politika*, August.

Tyson, Ann Scott, 2005. 'Russia and China bullying Central Asia, US says', *Washington Post*, 15 July.

'Ukraine: A view through the gas pipe', 2006. *Expert*, 23 January.

'Ukraine is preparing an asymmetric response', 2005. *Grani.ru*, 12 December (www.grani.ru/Politics/World/Europe/Ukraine/m.99493.html).

'Uneasy aftermath of Putin's Azerbaijan's visit', 2001. *Eurasia Monitor*, January 16 (www.jamestown.org/publications_details.php?volume_id=24&issue_id=1939&article _id=17942).

'US-Russia Commercial Energy Summit', 2003. *Baker Institute Study* 21, February (http://bakerinstitute.org/Pubs/study_21.pdf).

'Use a long spoon', 2006. *The Economist*, 4 May.

'Uzbekistan: In for the long-haul', 2006. *Asia Briefing* 45, International Crisis Group, 16 February (www.crisisgroup.org/home/index.cfm?id=3952&l=1).

Valiev, Bakhtiyor and Cholpon Orozobekova, 2006. 'Kyrgyz-Tajik border raid stokes fears', *IWPR Reporting Central Asia*, 19 May (www.iwpr.net/?p=rca&s= f&o=262000&apc_state=henirca200605).

Van Bladel, Joris, 2003. 'Russian soldiers in the barracks: A portrait of a subculture', pp. 60–72 in Anne C. Aldis and Roger N. McDermott (eds), *Russian Military Reform, 1992–2002*. London: Frank Cass.

Vladimirov, Aleksandr, 2006. 'Strategic essay: On the military part of the President's address', *Politicheskii klass*, July (www.politklass.ru/cgi-bin/list.pl?mon=7&year= 2006).

Vlasova, Olga, Vladimir Popov and Aleksei Khazbiev, 2005. 'The great march', *Expert*, 4 July.

Volkov, Vadim, 2003. 'The Yukos affair: Terminating the implicit contract', *PONARS Memo* 307, Washington, DC: CSIS, November.

References   227

Volodin, Viktor and Petr Iskenderov, 2006. 'Bushehr is safe', *Vremya novostei*, 25 December.

Voronov, Vladimir, 2003. 'Dezertiada', *Konservator*, 17 January (www.hro.org/editions/press/0103/17/17010318.htm).

Vorobyev, Eduard and Vitaly Tsymbal, 2006. 'The failure of the contract system is pre-programmed', *NVO*, 27 October.

Vorontsov, Vadim and Aleksandr Shirokov, 2007. 'Killer coal', *Expert*, 26 March.

Walsh, Nick Paton, 2005. 'Rise of Islamic militancy casts shadow of Chechnya over Caucasus villages', *Guardian*, 23 September.

—— 2006. 'Georgian leader attacks Russia after gas blasts', *Guardian*, 23 January.

Whalen, Jeanne, 2001. 'Potanin reaps big gain on *Sidanco* sale', *Wall Street Journal*, 3 August.

'Which way now for French policy?', 2003. *The Economist*, 24 July.

Winrow, Gareth, 1995. *Turkey in Post-Soviet Central Asia*. London: RIIA.

'World Bank report on Russia's economy', 2004. *Vremya novostei*, 22 November.

World Energy Outlook 2006, 2006. Paris: OECD/International Energy Agency.

'Would the "national projects" improve life of Russians?', 2006. Levada Center poll, 5 April (www.levada.ru/press/2006040501.html).

Yakovlev, Vladimir, 1999. 'Russia's military–political trump card', interview with *NVO*, 17 December.

Yasin, Evgeny, 2003. 'Precedent at the crossroads', *Izvestiya*, 12 August.

—— 2005. *Prizhivetsya li Demokratiya v Rossii* (Will Democracy Survive in Russia), Moscow: Novoe izdatelstvo.

Yavlinsky, Grigory, 2002. 'This could prove a costly escapade', *Moscow Times*, 23 September.

Yergin, Daniel and Thane Gustafson, 1993. *Russia 2010 and What it Means for the World*, New York: Random House.

Yermukanov, Marat, 2006. 'Kazakh–Chinese pipeline: A bond of strategic partnership or source of tensions?' *CACI Analyst*, 11 January (www.cacianalyst.org/view_article. php?articleid=3932&SMSESSION=NO).

Yuriev, Mikhail, 2004. 'The Fortress Russia: A concept for the president', *Novaya gazeta*, 15 March.

Zatulin, Konstantin, 2005. 'The struggle for Ukraine: What next?' *Russia in Global Affairs*, January–February, pp. 76–86.

Zürcher, Christoph, 2005. 'Georgia's time of troubles', pp. 83–115 in Bruno Coppieters and Robert Legvold (eds), *Statehood and Security: Georgia after the Rose Revolution*. Cambridge, MA: The MIT Press.

Zürcher, Christoph, Pavel Baev and Jan Koehler, 2005. 'Civil wars in the Caucasus', pp. 259–298 in Paul Collier and Nicholas Sambanis (eds), *Understanding Civil War: Evidence and Analysis*, vol. II, Washington, DC: The World Bank.

Zygar, Mikhail, 2005. 'Third among equals: Moscow, Delhi and Peking forge a counter-revolution union', *Kommersant*, 3 June.

All electronic references were accessed on 4 June 2007.

The titles of articles in Russian print media (*Kommersant, Vedomosti*, etc.) and electronic media (*Lenta.ru, Gazeta.ru*, etc.) are translated from Russian.

Translations of President Putin's speeches are available at the English version of the presidential website that should be accessed from the mainpage (http://president.kremlin.ru/mainpage.shtml).

Index

Abashidze, Aslan 37, 101
Abdullah Crown Prince 120
Abkhazia 37, 100
Abramovich, Roman 22, 23, 168n38
Account Chamber 47
acquisitions, military 15, 16, 48
Adydeya 114
Afghanistan 12, 19, 56, 57, 59, 63, 64, 72, 75, 76, 91, 94, 97, 99, 100, 134, 160
Africa 39, 154
Ahmadinejad, Mahmoud 89
Airborne Troops, VDV 95, 96, 104
Ajaria 37, 101
Akaev, Askar 37, 61, 98, 135
Akhmetov, Danial 136
Alekperov, Vagit 21, 22, 23, 132, 188n9
Alexander III 79
Algeria 55
Aliev, Heydar 66, 131–133, 134, 188n3, 189n16
Aliev, Ilham 131, 133, 134, 189n16, 189n18, 190n41
Aliev, Mukhu 114
Alkhanov, Alu 108
Allison, Roy 75, 175n1, 181n5, 182n16
Andijan massacre 38, 61, 63, 72, 75, 98, 134, 141
Andropov, Yuri 19
Ankara 138–140
Anti-Ballistic Missile (ABM) Treaty 36, 83
Arbatov, Alexei 12, 15, 47, 55, 96, 163n7, 179n15, 179n23, 180n30
Armed Forces units: 37th Air Army 87; 76th Airborne Division 17, 94; 77th Marine brigade 58, 64; 201st Motorized Rifle Division 98; mountain brigades 96
Armenia 68, 70, 71, 73, 131, 132
arms export 16, 50, 55, 73

Ashgabat 57, 60, 61, 63
Åslund, Anders 20, 30, 166n8
Astana 60, 63, 137
Astrakhan 57, 64
Astrakhan, gunboat 58
Atasau–Alashankou pipeline 74, 137
Atatürk, Mustafa Kemal 33
August coup, 1991 7, 20, 22, 95
August crisis, 1998 9, 18, 22, 23, 34, 35, 43, 46, 68
Aushev, Ruslan 112
Austria 140
Azerbaijan 8, 57–59, 64, 67, 68, 71, 72, 98, 130–134, 136, 139, 141

Baker, James 121
Baku 18, 57, 59, 60, 131–134, 139
Baku–Novorossiisk pipeline 64
Baku–Tbilisi–Ceyhan pipeline (BTC) 72, 101, 132, 133, 137, 139, 160
Balkans 35
Baltic Pipeline System 23, 35
Baltic Sea 123
Baltic states 8, 68, 125
Baluyevsky, Yuri 10, 11, 164n13, 170n28, 180n37
Bark missile 86
Baryatinsky, Aleksandr, Prince 106, 181n1
Barysh, Katinka 122
Basaev, Shamil 64, 108, 111, 112, 114, 115, 184n9, 185n39
BASF 123, 126
Bashneft 23
Basmachi 93
Basmanny market 111
Batdyev, Mustafa 113
Batumi 37
Baturin, Yuri 9, 163n7
Beijing 73–75, 137

Index 229

Belarus 8, 36, 37, 68, 70–73, 77, 88, 91,
123, 135, 142, 146–149, 152–154, 160;
'gas-and-oil war' 70, 77, 148
Beltransgas 148
Belyaninov, Andrei 50
Bendukidze Kaha 101
Berezovsky, Boris 22, 52, 173n23
Berlin 123
Berlusconi, Silvio 123, 139
Beslan hostage crisis 36, 48, 102, 107,
110, 111, 113
Bishkek 60, 61
Black Sea 139, 160
Blake, William 161
Blank, Stephen 9, 163n4, 175n29, 176n13,
177n22, 178n4, 182n21, 189n24
Blue stream pipeline 35, 120, 139, 140
Bogdanchikov, Sergei 28
Bogdanov, Vladimir 21, 22, 23
border troops *see* Federal Border Service
Bordyuzha, Nikolai 72
Bosporus 139, 140
Botlikh distrikt 64
Bovanenkovskoe gasfield 28
BP 23, 57, 133, 139
Bratislava 88
Brest 72
Brezhnev, Leonid 3, 19
Brodsky, Joseph 79
Browne, Lord 28, 187n24
Brussels 97, 134, 140
Budapest 123
Bulava missile 1, 86–88
Bulgaria 123, 139, 140
Burgas–Alexandropolis pipeline 138, 140
Bush, George W. 35, 36, 61, 83, 88, 89,
91, 101, 121, 123, 132, 135, 151
Bushehr nuclear station 89–91

Canada 87
Caspian area 43, 56, 57, 64–67, 89, 98,
130, 135, 136, 138, 140
Caspian exercises 57–59, 66
Caspian Flotilla 57–59, 64, 66
Caspian Guard programme 59
Caspian Pipeline Consortium (CPC) 23,
135, 138, 139
Caspian sea, shelf 57, 64, 133, 136, 137
'Caucasian frontier' exercises 102
Caucasian War 106
Caucasus 59, 64, 70, 96, 104, 115, 131,
138–140, 157
Central Asia 39, 56, 60, 61, 69–76, 93, 94,
96–100, 104, 134, 138, 141, 153

Central Asian Cooperation Organization,
CACO 73
Centre for the Study of Civil War (CSCW)
ix
Ceyhan 133
Che Guevara, Ernesto 30, 92
'Chechen generals' ('warriors') 10, 11, 12,
46, 83, 95, 157
Chechnya ix, 8, 9, 10, 47, 58, 59, 64, 65,
93, 95, 105–110, 115; 'Chechenization'
107–109; the First Chechen War 9,
12, 45, 93, 94, 163n5; the Second
Chechen War 2, 9, 12, 34, 46, 54, 56,
64, 83, 94, 100, 106, 112, 113, 138,
163n8, 184n5, 190n35; stabilization
(since 2006) 14, 54, 95, 96, 103, 104,
108
Chekists 53, 54, 194n3
Chelyabinsk oblast 75
Chemezov, Sergei 50, 54
Cheney, Richard 41, 63, 85, 126, 137,
175n29, 179n13, 188n26
Cherkessk 113
Cherkizovsky market 112
Chernomyrdin, Viktor 21, 22, 24, 119,
166n9, 180n31
Chevron 135, 136
China 3, 16, 28, 55, 63, 71, 73–77, 91,
125, 137, 161, 162
Chinese National Petroleum Corporation
137
Chirac, Jacques 36, 122, 126, 132, 169n6,
178n11
Chisinau 69
Chubais, Anatoly 20, 21, 29, 130, 168n41,
188n1
'civilization', concept of 34, 38–41,
105–107, 109, 111, 112, 115, 117, 129,
142–154, 156, 162
'clash of civilizations' 34
coal production 29, 168n41
Cold War 117, 160, 179n14, 191n2
Collective Security Treaty Organization,
CSTO 66, 68, 71–73, 98; Anti-Terrorist
Centre 71; joint air defence system 71,
176n11
'coloured revolutions' 38, 60, 61, 63, 65,
66, 70, 71, 75, 85, 133, 135, 136, 141,
150, 159
Committee for State Security (KGB) 12,
134
Committee of Soldiers' Mothers 13
Committee on Defence, State Duma 47,
165n24

230 *Index*

Common Economic Space (CES) 36, 73, 135, 149
Commonwealth of Independent States (CIS) 37, 38, 41, 59, 68–71, 98, 133, 137, 150, 156, 161
Compiegne 126
conscription *see* draft system
contract service (*kontraktniki*) 12, 14, 17, 95, 96
Conventional Forces in Europe (CFE) Treaty 92, 104
Cooperative Threat Reduction Programme, Nunn–Lugar 88, 92
Cornell, Svante 56
corruption 2, 26, 37, 51, 65, 66, 100, 113–115, 134, 136, 139, 143–145, 162, 187n14, 190n27
Council of Europe 132
Council on National Strategy 25
counter-terrorism 14, 15, 34–36, 48, 54, 59–62, 66, 71, 94, 96, 100, 109–111, 113, 115, 135, 160
Crawford 121
Crimea 153
Custom Union 73
Czech Republic 92, 123, 125

Dagestan 57, 64–67, 112, 114, 131
Dedovshchina 13, 164n20
defence budget, expenditures 15, 17, 46–50, 54, 79, 165n26
Defence Ministry, Russian 8, 10, 13, 14, 50, 83, 84, 94
Delta-IV submarine 87
Delyagin, Mikhail 69, 145, 191n4
democratic reforms and democratization 8, 34, 38, 41, 61, 63, 69, 76, 84, 91, 121, 131, 133, 135, 137, 143, 151, 153, 162, 163n4, 175n29, 184n12, 189n17
Den Oprichnika (Day of the oprichnik) 162
Derbent 65
Derluguian, Georgi 9, 38, 175n32, 184n8, 185n26, 185n38
Derzhavnost, concept of 34, 40
Deutsche Bank 123
Dmitriev, Mikhail 154
Doha 128
Dostoevsky, Fedor 41
draft system 7, 12–14, 160
Dresden 123, 127
Dresdner Kleinwort Wasserstein 123
drug production, trafficking 99, 100, 104, 174n18, 182n23

Dugin, Aleksandr 33, 169n9, 170n22, 177n18, 189n23
Dushanbe 60, 97, 98
'Dutch disease' 30

E.ON 123, 126, 186n4, 187n25
East Siberia 125
Eastern Europe 85
Eastern Ukraine 37, 152, 153
Economist, The 123
Efremov, Gerbert 91
electricity production, export 29, 130, 134, 156
'empire', concept of 33, 36–38, 40, 41, 93, 104, 117, 129, 130, 134, 138, 140, 141, 160
Energy Charter 122, 125, 127
energy crisis 30, 154, 156, 161
energy dialogue, Russia–US 35, 121, 128
energy sector, state control of 29, 30, 31, 41, 45, 142, 154, 157, 161
energy security 2, 43, 68, 76, 124–127, 129, 137, 141, 157
'Energy Strategy' 2003 24, 27, 30, 167n22
'energy super-power' 32, 117, 124, 129, 157, 161
'energy weapon' 43, 117, 126, 128
ENI 123, 139
Erdogan, Recep Tayyip 139
Ergneti market 102
Erzerum 140
Eurasia Daily Monitor ix
Eurasian Economic Community 73
Europe and Russia 38, 41, 74, 93, 105, 122, 127, 143, 146, 147, 150, 153, 162
European Parliament 122
European Union (EU) 37, 41, 62, 99, 151, 160, 182n23, n28, 190n36, n41, 193n33; energy policy 41, 70, 77, 122–129, 140, 141, 186n7, 187n17, n22, 188n30
Evans, Don 135
ExxonMobil 23, 167n32, 168n39

Faberge eggs 28
Far East 95
February 1917 revolution 159
Federal Agency for Defence Order 50
Federal Agency for Government Communication and Information (FAPSI) 110
Federal Border Service, border troops 97, 99, 104, 110,
Federal Security Service (FSB) 24, 47, 53, 54, 65, 107, 110, 111, 119

Index 231

Federal Tax Service 11
Fergana valley 97, 98
Foreign Ministry, Russian 156
'Fortress Russia', concept of 34, 41
Fradkov, Mikhail 26, 62, 134, 158
France 32, 36, 84, 89–91, 123, 129
Friedman, Thomas 144
Friendship and Cooperation Treaty,
    Russia–Turkmenistan 60
'Frontier-2006, 2007' exercises 58, 99
Furman, Dmitri 40, 152, 192n14

Gabala radar station 88
Gagarin, Yuri 33
Gaidar, Yegor 20, 21, 22, 46, 165n2,
    166n5, n6, n8, n10, 188n9
Galich, Aleksandr 117
gas, energy export 2, 18, 19, 29, 30, 35,
    41, 43, 45, 52, 61, 62, 66, 68, 70, 74,
    117, 120–128, 134, 138–141, 144, 149,
    153, 154, 157–160, 162, 165n2, 175n27,
    187n16, 190n40; *see also* oil export
'Gas OPEC' 126, 128, 140, 188n31
gas price, domestic 29, 129, 152
gas production 24, 29, 74, 123, 127, 129,
    157, 159
GAZPROM 28–30, 53, 117, 122–128,
    168n37, n39; Belarus and Ukraine
    124, 140, 147–151, 193n23, n30;
    Caucasus and Central Asia 62, 102,
    138, 174n21, n27, 175n28; Europe 120,
    122, 123, 125–129, 139, 140, 147,
    186n4, 187n14, n24, n25, 190n37;
    investment 28, 29, 74, 120, 125, 129,
    168n40, n41, 187n12; management 21,
    24, 52–54, 119, 120, 122, 127, 152,
    166n9, 167n19, n20, 186n1, n3, n10,
    187n11
General Staff, Russian 8, 10, 11, 82, 95,
    97, 101, 138, 164n11, 165n24, 170n28
Georgia 36, 69, 70–72, 77, 94, 98,
    100–104, 131, 134, 160; 'Rose
    revolution' 37, 69, 85, 101, 133, 143
Germany 36, 84, 89, 91, 122, 123, 126,
    127, 129, 147, 149, 153
Gevorkyan Natalya 105, 163n2, 167n26,
    169n10
Gimry 65
Giorgadze, Igor 100
global navigation system (GLONASS) 88
Golts, Aleksandr 10, 14, 73, 82, 113,
    155, 164n10, n18, n20, n22, 169n2,
    170n31, 171n38, n7, 178n6, n7, 179n15,
    181n11

Goltz, Thomas 133
Gomart, Thomas 77
Gorbachev, Mikhail 15, 19, 20, 163n2
GOSPLAN 19, 110
Gosudarstvennost, statism concept of 34,
    40, 142
Gottemoeller, Rose 83, 84, 90, 180n28
Grachev, Pavel 94, 163n3
Grant, Charles 122
'great game' 56, 177n19
'Great Power', Russia's status of 2, 33–36,
    38, 40, 41, 79, 81, 85, 89, 91, 92, 117,
    119, 120–122, 127–130
'greatness', desire for 2, 3, 32, 33, 35, 40,
    41, 79, 88, 91, 105, 117, 124, 130, 142,
    149, 152, 155–157
Greece 140, 191n42
Gref, German 26, 186n3, n10, 187n11
Greifswald 123
gross domestic product (GDP) 18, 19, 22,
    24, 26, 32, 46, 47, 49, 54
Group of Eight (G8) 36, 43, 92, 121, 124,
    151; Strelna summit 2006 2, 41, 76, 77,
    102, 111, 126, 137, 148, 151, 191n3
Grozny 52, 64, 66, 83, 107
GUAM 98
Gulf, Persian 121, 160
'gunboat diplomacy' 57
Gusinsky, Vladimir 52, 109
Gustafson, Thane 162

Haran, Olexiy 149
Herat 60
High Command, Russian 8–11, 14, 17,
    45–47
Hill, Fiona 139, 166n16, 167n29
Houston 121
Hungary 123
Hussein, Saddam 84

Iceland 150
Illarionov, Andrei 26, 27, 30, 53, 122, 162,
    167n30, 168n43, 193n27
Ilyin, Ivan 79, 178n1
Ilyushin 51, 146
India 55, 75, 76, 165n28
inflation 15, 16, 50, 168n43, 171n2,
    179n25
Ingush–Ossetian conflict 113
Ingushetia 95, 107, 112
initial public offering (IPO) 25, 137
Interior Ministry, troops 12, 14, 110, 113
Intermediate Nuclear Forces (INF) Treaty
    85, 179n15

232 Index

International Atomic Energy Agency
(IAEA) 89, 90
International Monetary Fund (IMF) 22
International Peace Research Institute,
Oslo (PRIO) ix
Iran 55, 57–60, 63, 76, 81, 89–92, 128,
134, 141, 180n31–n35, 189n18
Iraq, war in 36, 46, 56, 57, 60, 77, 83, 84,
91, 122, 160, 170n20, 173n4, 174n16
Irkutsk oblast 28
Islam 34, 39, 64, 89, 107, 175n42, 184n7
Islamic extremism, networks 35, 61, 62,
65, 108, 113–115, 134, 175n41, 181n13
Islamic Movement of Uzbekistan (IMU)
97
Israel 89, 90, 180n32, 190n40
Istanbul 131, 139
Italy 125, 129, 139
Itera 24, 102
Ivan IV the Terrible 93
Ivanov, Igor 101
Ivanov, Sergei 1, 10–16, 32, 47, 49, 51, 52,
54, 58, 69, 86, 102, 146, 155, 158,
164n10, 165n27, 172n20, 174n24,
176n12
Izvestia newspaper 109

Jamaat 113–115
Jordan, Boris 109

Kabardino–Balkaria 1, 65, 114
Kabul 60
Kadyrov, Akhmad-Khadzhi 107, 108
Kadyrov, Ramzan 108, 112
Kadyrovtsy 108
Kaliyzhny, Viktor 57
Kalmykia 39
Kananaskis 92
Kant airbase 72, 98, 99, 104
Karachaevo–Cherkessia 113, 114
Karamakhi 65
Karimov, Islam 61–63, 72, 75, 98, 170n29,
177n24, 182n17, n19
Karshi–Khanabad (K2) airbase 98, 99
Kashagan oilfield 136
Kasparov, Garry 27
Kaspiisk 58, 64, 66
Kaspiisk, gunboat 58
Kasyanov, Mikhail 25, 26, 53, 138,
167n29, 186n3
Kazakhstan 8, 27, 36, 58–60, 62, 66,
70–77, 88, 130, 132–138, 141, 149
Kazan 69, 70, 93
KazMunaiGaz 136

KazRosGaz 138
Kemerovo oblast 29
Key West 132
Khamenei, Ali 128
Khandym–Khauzak–Shady gasfield 62
Khasavyurt, peace accord 9, 95
Khatami, Mohammad 89
Khattab 64
Khodorkovsky, Mikhail 22–26, 35, 46, 53,
120, 121, 128, 158, 166n17, n18,
167n24, n25, n32, 169n19, 186n8, n9,
190n30, 194n1
Khristenko, Viktor 125, 126, 128
Khvalynskpe oilfield 136
Khvorov, Igor 87
Kiev 38, 61, 69, 106, 135, 151, 153, 160
Kirill, Methropolitan 39
Kiriyenko, Sergei 29, 46, 171n3
Kocharyan, Robert 132
Kokoshin, Andrei 9, 163n7, 176n7
Kommersant 40
Kommerzbank 123
Kondopoga, Karelia 39, 40
Koran 66
Kosovo crisis 34, 82, 91, 178n2
Kovykta 23, 28, 125, 168n37, 187n24
Kozak, Dmitri 1, 65, 69, 113–115, 175n37,
185n30
Krasnodar kray 65, 114
Kukura, Sergei 52
Kurmangazy oilfield 62, 136
Kuroedov, Vladimir 57
Kursk submarine 1, 86
Kvashnin, Anatoly 10, 82, 83, 88, 138,
165n24, 178n5
Kyrgyzstan 37, 64, 70, 71–73, 75, 97–100;
'Tulip revolution' 38, 61, 69, 99, 135

Lahti 127
Latynina, Yulia 39, 48, 113, 165n26,
167n31, 168n38, 173n24, 175n38, n40,
179n17, 183n38, 185n31, n34
Lavrov, Sergei 126, 194n1
Lebed, Aleksandr 9, 95, 181n7
Lebedev, Platon 25, 186n9
Leontiev, Mikhail 33, 166n6, 168n9, n10
Levada Center 155, 164n16, n21, 183n4,
185n39, 192n10
'Liberal Empire' concept 130
Lieber, Keir 88
Lieven, Dominique 155, 160, 169n9,
181n1
Lithuania 71, 96, 147
Litvinenko, Aleksandr 92

Index 233

Ljubljana 35, 132
LNG 127
London Stock Exchange 25
London terrorist attack 111
Lubyanka 111
Lukashenko, Aleksandr 37, 72, 73, 91, 106, 147–149, 176n14, 192n14–n19
Lukoil 21, 23, 27, 52, 58, 62, 120, 132, 136, 167n33, 186n8, 188n9, 190n29, n31
Lukyanov, Fedor 3, 37, 70, 77, 104, 127, 147, 150, 169n4, 176n2, n8, 187n21, 191n1

Magomedov, Magometali 65, 112, 114, 185n34
Maikop 114
Main Intelligence Directorate (GRU) 95
Makhachkala 65
Makhachkala, gunboat 58
Manas airbase 72, 75, 98
Markedonov, Sergei 108, 170n23, 175n36, 183n36
Marx, Karl 123
Mashinostroenie NPO 50
Maskhadov, Aslan 108, 184n8
Masood Ahmad Shah 97
Mazar-e-Sharif 60
media 2, 13, 52, 57, 88, 101, 102, 109, 133, 144, 151, 191n6
Medvedev, Dmitri 32, 119, 120, 144, 158, 168n1, 171n37, 186n2, n3
'mercantilism' 38, 43, 70, 117, 128, 141, 161
Merkel, Angela 126, 127
Merv 93
Mi-24 helicopter 47
Middle East 18, 121, 129, 136, 144
MiG 51, 146
military budget *see* defence budget
military doctrine 16, 82, 85, 94
military reform 7, 11, 12, 14, 15, 17, 46, 47, 49, 94, 164n18, 165n24
Military-Industrial Commission 51
military-industrial complex (VPK) 7, 19, 43, 45, 49–55, 105, 156, 159, 172n11
Military-Transport Aviation 95
Miliutin, Dmitri 11
Miller, Alexei 24, 28, 119, 120, 122, 125, 167n20, 186n1–n3, 187n23
Milov, Vladimir 29, 92, 120, 171n37, 174n21, 177n28, 186n10, 188n30, 192n12, 193n31, n36
Minsk 72, 148

missiles, strategic 1, 47, 48, 50, 71, 82, 84–88, 90, 91, 96, 176n11, 179n11, n12, n19
mobile forces 94; *see also* rapid deployment
'Mobility-2004' exercises 95
MOL 123
Moldova 69, 70, 98
Moscow Treaty 83
Mozdok 64
Mujahideen 64, 112
Mukachevo radar station 88
Munich 69
Munich speech *see* Putin
Murmansk 121
Myers, Richard 75

Nabucco pipeline 140
Nagorno Karabakh 132, 188n7, n8, 189n15
Nalchik uprising 1, 38, 65, 114
National Anti-Terrorist Committee (NAC) 111
'national projects' 48, 142, 144, 145
National Security Concept 82
National Unity Day 39
Navy Russian 1, 51, 57, 79, 86, 87, 179n17
Nazarbaev, Nursultan 62, 63, 72, 134–138, 189n19, n24, 190n34, 191n42
Nazran rebel attack 95, 107, 112
Nemtsov, Boris 12
Netherlands, the 125
'new economic policy' 27
Niyazov, Sapurmurat (Turkmenbashi) 60–63, 66, 174n21
Nizhny Novgorod 49, 51
Nobel brothers (Ludwig and Robert) 18
non-governmental organizations (NGO) 39, 143
Nord-Ost hostage crisis 94, 109, 110
North Atlantic Treaty Organization (NATO) 16, 34, 35, 48, 58, 71, 72, 76, 82, 95, 97–99, 102, 103, 128, 151, 152, 160; NATO–Russia Council 97
North Caucasus 41, 64–66, 93, 96, 104, 106, 108, 111–115
North European pipeline, *Nord Stream* 123, 125, 187n16
North Korea 71, 176n11
North Ossetia 64, 107, 113, 114, 183n37
North Pole 1
Northern Alliance 97
Northern Cyprus 139
Northern Fleet 86

234 *Index*

Novoe Vremya newspaper 155
Novorossiisk 131, 132, 134, 140
NTV channel 109, 186n1
nuclear energy 18, 29, 162
nuclear forces, arsenal, weapons 7, 8, 16, 33, 54, 81–89, 91, 92, 94, 157, 161
Nuclear Posture Review 83
Nurek radar station 88, 98

October crisis, 1993 8, 46, 95
oil export 18, 19, 21, 23, 26, 35, 74, 117, 131, 134, 135, 137, 140; *see also* gas, energy export
oil prices 18–20, 22, 24, 26, 30, 32, 43, 46, 47, 55, 74, 91, 120, 122, 132, 133, 136, 143–145, 159, 161
oil production 20, 21, 23, 24, 26, 27, 120, 157
'oligarchs' 22, 25, 26, 45, 52, 53, 101, 143, 144, 147
Oman 135
'operational command group' (GROU) 111, 113, 184n18
'Orange revolution' *see* Ukraine
Organization for Security and Cooperation in Europe (OSCE) 131, 133, 174n19
Organization of Petroleum Exporting Countries (OPEC) 18, 120, 121, 128, 186n6; *see also* 'Gas OPEC'
orthodox church 34, 39, 156
Orwell, George 155
Osh region 99
Ozal, Turgut 138

Pakistan 90
Panjshir valley 97
Pankisi gorge 36, 101
Paris 36, 132
parliamentary elections, Russian (2003) 13, 25, 26, 130, 142, 143
'Partnership-for-Peace' programme 71
Pavlov, Valentin 20
Pavlovsky, Gleb 25, 38, 174n22, 179n13, 192n19, 193n35
'Peace Mission' exercises 75
peacekeeping 72, 93, 98, 104, 161
'permanent readiness' ('high-readiness') units 14, 17, 96, 157, 165n31
Peter I, the Great 16
Petrokazakhstan 137
Petropavlovsk-Kamchatsky 86
'Petro-state' 18, 142, 144–146, 162
Piontkovsky, Andrei 1, 158, 167n32, 192n21

Pipes, Richard 33
Podvig, Pavel 87, 88, 178n6, 180n28
Poe, Marshal 105
Pogrom 39
Poland 19, 92, 93, 123, 125, 127, 129, 147, 153
Politburo 19, 63, 110, 134
Politkovskaya, Anna 128
Polonium-210 isotope 92
Potanin, Vladimir 22
presidential elections, Russian (1996, 2000, 2004) 9, 12, 21, 95, 143
Press, Daryl 88
Primakov, Evgeny 82, 97
Pristina, march on 35, 82
privatization 20–22, 27, 29, 123, 143, 149, 166n10, 193n37
Priz submarine 86
production sharing agreement (PSA) 136
Prosecutor General 13, 53
Pulikovsky, Konstantin 10
Purgaz 119
Putin, Vladimir ix, 2, 3, 69, 73, 92, 103, 110, 128, 155, 156, 158–162; addresses to the parliament 13, 14, 15, 17, 22, 32, 41, 45, 47, 48, 50, 51, 79, 81, 84, 85; authoritarian tendencies 27, 40, 69, 81, 91, 111, 105, 143, 144; Azerbaijan 57, 58, 131–134; becoming president 2, 7, 9, 14, 22, 34, 52, 56, 68, 82, 93, 97, 100, 105, 106, 109, 119, 131, 147, 157; Belarus 77, 91, 147–149; Caspian intrigues, Iran 57–66, 89–91, 128; China 3, 73, 74, 76, 77, 125; collapse of the USSR 19, 40, 55, 105; Commander-in-Chief 1, 10, 11, 81, 83, 86, 98, 115; counter-terrorism 1, 35, 59, 62, 65, 73, 94, 109, 111, 115; energy business 2, 18, 22–31, 43, 51, 52, 55, 73, 74, 117, 119–128; European diplomacy 35, 36, 41, 77, 120, 122, 123, 126, 127, 129, 139, 152; GAZPROM 24, 29, 119, 122, 123, 127, 152; Georgia 36, 69, 77, 85, 100–103; ideology, 'greatness' 2, 3, 32–41, 112, 117, 120, 121, 124, 127, 142, 144, 146, 148–150, 157, 159; Kazakhstan 58, 62, 134–138; KGB background 12, 69, 123, 127; leaving office in 2008 1, 13, 14, 31, 40, 54, 127, 143, 144, 148, 153, 158; military matters 1, 2, 7–17, 45–55, 79, 81–89, 93–98, 104, 105, 107, 157; Munich speech, 2007 3, 41, 79, 85, 91, 128, 160; 'narrow circle', team 24–26, 35, 37, 38,

47, 50, 52–54, 69, 82, 85, 97, 100, 103, 111, 113, 115, 119, 122, 130, 135, 138, 139, 143, 152, 153, 158, 159; persecution of Khodorkovsky 25, 26, 52, 53, 121; populism 39, 48, 66, 143, 144; pragmatism 2, 17, 32, 68, 94, 126, 149, 158; religion 39, 66, 107; Second Chechen War 2, 10, 12, 15, 34, 46, 54, 56, 59, 83, 93, 94, 106, 107; second term 1, 16, 17, 31, 32, 40, 45, 54, 66, 76, 93, 103, 105, 130, 142, 144, 153; system of power, 'vertical' 26, 27, 32, 52, 55, 106, 109, 112, 115, 142, 144, 156, 158, 159; Turkey 138–140; Turkmenistan 60, 61, 63, 77, 140; Ukraine 37, 38, 69, 85, 124, 125, 140, 149–152; US 35, 36, 41, 59, 77, 79, 83, 85, 88, 89, 91, 93, 97, 98, 100, 101, 121, 132, 151

Rakhmonov, Emomali 37, 75, 97, 98, 188n2
RAND 56
rapid deployment forces, capabilities 7, 72, 94–96, 157
rapid response police unit (SOBR) 110
Reagan, Ronald 19
research and development, military (R&D) 15, 16, 86
'resource curse' or 'oil curse' 30, 144, 162
Reykjavik, summit (1986) 19
Rodina (Motherland) party 38, 143
Rodionov, Igor 9
Romania 139
Rosatom 29, 30
'Rose revolution' *see* Georgia
Rosneft 23, 25, 26, 28, 30, 53, 54, 122, 137, 190n30
Rosoboronexport 50, 54
Ross, Michael 144
Rostov-on-Don 64
Rosukrenergo 124
Ruhrgas 120, 126
Rushailo, Vladimir 133
Rutland, Peter 60, 166n9
Ryabov, Andrei 145, 153
Ryazanov, Aleksandr 120

Saakashvili, Mikhail 101–103, 133, 183n33, n36
St Petersburg 24, 58, 82, 119, 120, 121, 126
'Sakhalin-1, -2' 23, 27
Saudi Arabia 32, 120, 121, 166n6, 168n43

secessionism, separatism 73, 101, 103, 106–108, 153, 183n34, n4, 184n7
Sechin, Igor 26, 28
Security Council, Russian 46, 56, 82, 83, 124, 131, 133, 135, 163n7, 169n15
September 11 terrorist attack, '9/11' 35, 56, 59, 97, 100
Serdyukov, Anatoly 11, 85, 179n15
Sergeev, Igor 9, 10, 82, 83, 85–87, 97, 164n10, 171n7, 178n7
Sevastopol 88
Severneftegazprom 126
Severodvinsk 86
Shah Deniz gasfield 139
Shaimiev, Mintimer 21
Shakirov, Raf 109
Shamanov, Vladimir 10
Shanghai Cooperation Organization (SCO) 68, 73–77, 177n16, n17, n22, n23, n27
Sharia law 64, 65, 175n40
Schröder, Gerhard 35, 36, 120, 122, 123, 169n6, 193n24
Shell 27
Shevardnadze, Eduard 37, 69, 100, 101, 182n30
Shevtsova, Lilia 40, 159, 163n1, 166n14, 170n24, 172n21, n22
Shikhmuradov, Boris 61
Shlykov, Vitaly 50, 51, 164n11, 172n11
'shock therapy' 20
short-term state bonds (GKO) 22
Shpak, Georgy 10, 95
Shtokman gasfield 28, 127
Shuvalov, Igor 43
Siberian federal district 10
Sibneft 22, 23, 27, 28, 121, 168n38
Sibur 119, 167n20, 186n3
Sidanco 22, 23
Siloviki 159, 194n3
Slovenia 132
Sochi 139, 147, 172n19
Solidarity 19
Solzhenitsyn, Aleksandr 159
Sorokin, Vladimir 162
South Caucasus pipeline (SCP) 139, 140
South Ossetia 100, 102, 183n35
South, South-Eastern Europe 123, 139
Southern District 113
Southern Siberia 23, 28, 74
'sovereign democracy' 30, 32, 40, 106, 149, 153, 155, 171n35, 175n31
'sovereignty', *suverennost*, concept of 32, 34, 40, 130, 142, 143, 146, 153, 155

236 *Index*

Soviet Union (USSR) 7, 18, 29, 33, 54, 55, 87, 117, 141, 160, 161; collapse of 7, 12, 19, 20, 40, 43, 49, 88, 93, 105, 146
Sovmen, Hazret 114, 185n35
Space Forces 88
special purpose police detachment (OMON) 110
Spetsnaz 14, 94, 95, 181n8, 183n37
Sputnik 33
SS-18, SS-19 missiles 87
Stalin, Josef 27, 111
State Armaments Programme 49, 50
State Duma 13, 47, 49, 185n24; *see also* Committee on Defence
Statoil x, 133, 139
Strategic Arms Reduction Treaty (START) 83
Strategic Missile Forces 9
Su-27 fighter 15, 71, 96
submarines, nuclear 1, 16, 47, 48, 86, 87, 173n27
Sukhoi 51, 146
Surgutneftegaz 21, 23
Surkov, Vladislav 30, 32, 40, 159, 168n2, 170n31, 171n37
Sweden 16, 125
Sychev, Andrei 13
Syria 64

T-90 main battle tank 15, 165n29, 172n16
Tajikistan 37, 62, 64, 70, 71, 73, 75, 76, 96–100, 104, 130
Taliban 60, 96, 97, 99, 177n26, 181n5, n13
Tarasyuk, Boris 151
Tashkent 62, 97, 100
Tashkent Treaty 71
Tatarstan 21, 39
Tatarstan, frigate 58
Tatneft 21, 23
Tbilisi 37, 61, 100, 102, 133, 182n27
Tehran 89–91
Tengiz–Novorossiisk pipeline 23, 35, 131, 132, 135, 138, 188n10
TNK-BP 23, 28, 125, 167n32, 168n36, n37
Todres, Vladimir 145, 187n23
Tomsk 126
Tønnesson, Stein ix
Topol-M missile 82, 86–88, 179n23
Tor-M1 missile 90, 91
'train-and-equip' programme (GTEP) 101
Transcaspian pipeline 61, 63, 140, 174n19, 175n31
Transdniestria 69, 104

Transneft 23, 135, 138, 148, 186n8, 189n20
Trenin, Dmitri 16, 17, 37, 81, 143, 147, 171n4, 176n5, 177n26, 180n34, 184n5, 191n2
Troshev, Gennady 10, 164n12
Tu-160 bomber, *Blackjack* 87
'Tulip revolution' *see* Kyrgyzstan
Tupolev 146
Turkey 33, 72, 131, 138–141, 160, 162, 174n19, 190n36
Turkmenistan 57, 58, 60, 61, 63, 66, 70, 73, 74, 77, 98, 100, 137, 138, 140, 141, 161
Tymen (TNK) 23

UK, Great Britain 84, 86, 89, 90, 92, 125
Ukraine 8, 36, 37, 38, 69–71, 73, 87, 88, 98, 129, 135, 140, 142, 149–154, 160, 162; 'gas war' 62, 70, 77, 124–126, 140, 148, 150–152; 'Orange revolution' 38, 40, 68, 85, 104, 113, 124, 147, 150, 152, 170n26, 193n28
Ulyanovskaya coal mine 29
UN Security Council 36, 81, 90–92
Unified Energy System (RAO UES) 29, 102
Union of Rightist Forces (SPS) 12, 13,
Union State, Russia–Belarus 147, 148
'United Russia' party 26
USA 16, 33, 41, 79, 83–85, 87–88, 91, 107, 143; Caucasus (Azerbaijan, Georgia) 36, 58, 59, 66, 77, 100, 101, 131, 134, 143; Central Asia, Caspian area 56, 58–63, 71, 75–77, 93, 94, 97, 98, 100, 136; energy business 27, 61, 120–122, 126–128; Iran 59, 89–91, 134; Iraq 36, 46, 57, 60, 84, 160
Ustinov, Vladimir 13, 53
Ustiyrt plateau 62
Uvarov, Sergei, Count 34, 38
Uzbekistan 62, 63, 70–74, 76, 97–100, 141, 170n29, 174n25, n27, 176n9, 177n16, 182n17, n20; *see also* Andijan

Vekselberg, Arkady 23, 28
Venezuela 16, 55
Villa Petrolea 18
Vilnius 85, 137
Vladikavkaz 64
Volga–Urals Military District 99
Volgograd 64
Voloshin, Aleksandr 26, 53, 133, 167n24
Votkinsk 87

Vyakhirev, Rem 21, 22, 24, 119, 167n19, 186n1, n2, n4
Vyborg 123

Washington x, 36, 60–63, 73, 75, 76, 84, 89–91, 97, 98, 101, 132, 133, 137, 151
Washington Post 123
weapons of mass destruction (WMD) 84, 85
Western analysis, views 7, 57, 86, 91, 126
Western companies 23, 33, 62, 120, 121, 136, 161
Western Europe 19, 29, 91
Western influence and policies 3, 19, 33–36, 38–40, 63, 72, 73, 75, 76, 81, 83–85, 86, 89–92, 100–103, 105, 121, 125, 131, 133, 134, 137, 140, 141, 143, 147, 149–152, 154, 160, 162
Western Siberia 18, 126
'Westernizers' 5
White House, US 133
Wingas 126
World Council of the Russian People 39

Xingjian 74, 137

Yamal 28, 127
Yamal–Europe pipeline 120, 122, 123
Yanukovich, Viktor 70, 187n19, 193n27
Yeltsin, Boris 2, 7–9, 12, 20–22, 32, 35, 46, 50, 52, 53, 82, 95, 100, 104, 105, 146, 147, 169n15, 172n22, 180n31, 189n19
Yergin, Daniel 162
'young reformers' 20, 46
Yuganskneftegaz 25, 28, 122
Yukos 22–28, 35, 46, 52, 53, 120–123, 128, 136, 137, 143, 158, 162, 167n27, n28, 168n36, 186n8, n9, 190n30
Yuri Dolgoruky submarine 86
Yushchenko, Viktor 38, 151, 170n27, 193n29
Yuzhno–Russkoe gasfield 28, 126

Zastoi, stagnation 3, 19, 40
Zhirinovsky, Vladimir 38
Zyazikov, Murat 112

Lightning Source UK Ltd.
Milton Keynes UK
UKOW01f0606060817
306746UK00001B/31/P